MICROSOFT® OFFICE
Excel 2003

COURSECARD EDITION

Introductory
Concepts and
Techniques

Gary B. Shelly
Thomas J. Cashman
James S. Quasney

THOMSON COURSE TECHNOLOGY
25 THOMSON PLACE
BOSTON MA 02210

SHELLY
CASHMAN
SERIES®

Australia • Canada • Denmark • Japan • Mexico • New Zealand • Philippines • Puerto Rico • Singapore • South Africa
Spain • United Kingdom • United States

THOMSON

COURSE TECHNOLOGY ™

Microsoft Office Excel 2003:
Introductory Concepts and Techniques, CourseCard Edition

Gary B. Shelly

Thomas J. Cashman

James S. Quasney

Managing Editor:
Alexandra Arnold

Senior Acquisitions Editor:
Dana Merk

Product Manager:
Reed Cotter

Editorial Assistant:
Selena Coppock

Print Buyer:
Laura Burns

Series Consulting Editor:
Jim Quasney

Director of Production:
Patty Stephan

Production Editor:
Aimee Poirier

Production Assistant:
Jill Klaffky

Development Editor:
Ginny Harvey

Copy Editors/Proofreaders:
Ginny Harvey
Nancy Lamm
Lyn Markowicz
Lori Silfen
Lisa Jedlicka
Kim Kosmatka
Marilyn Martin

Interior Design:
Becky Herrington

Cover Design:
Richard Herrera

Illustrators:
Richard Herrera
Andrew Bartel
Ken Russo

Compositors:
Jeanne Black
Andrew Bartel
Kellee LaVars
Kenny Tran
Michelle French
GEX Publishing Services

Indexer:
Cristina Haley

Printer:
Banta Menasha

MICROSOFT® OFFICE

Excel 2003

Introductory Concepts and Techniques

COURSECARD EDITION

Contents

Preface	**v**

Project One

Creating a Worksheet and an Embedded Chart

Objectives	**EX 4**
What Is Microsoft Office Excel 2003?	**EX 4**
Project One — Extreme Blading Second Quarter Sales	**EX 5**
Starting and Customizing Excel	**EX 6**
The Excel Worksheet	**EX 9**
The Worksheet	EX 10
Worksheet Window	**EX 11**
Menu Bar	EX 11
Standard Toolbar and Formatting Toolbar	EX 13
Formula Bar	EX 14
Status Bar	EX 14
Speech Recognition and Speech Playback	**EX 15**
Selecting a Cell	**EX 16**
Entering Text	**EX 16**
Entering the Worksheet Titles	EX 17
Correcting a Mistake while Typing	EX 18
AutoCorrect	EX 18
Entering Column Titles	EX 19
Entering Row Titles	EX 20
Entering Numbers	**EX 21**
Calculating a Sum	**EX 23**
Using the Fill Handle to Copy a Cell to Adjacent Cells	**EX 24**
Determining Multiple Totals at the Same Time	EX 26
Formatting the Worksheet	**EX 28**
Font Type, Style, Size, and Color	EX 28
Changing the Font Type	EX 29
Bolding a Cell	EX 30
Increasing the Font Size	EX 30
Changing the Font Color of a Cell Entry	EX 31
Centering a Cell Entry across Columns by Merging Cells	EX 32
Formatting the Worksheet Subtitle	EX 33
Using AutoFormat to Format the Body of a Worksheet	EX 34
Using the Name Box to Select a Cell	**EX 36**
Adding a 3-D Clustered Column Chart to the Worksheet	**EX 38**
Saving a Workbook	**EX 42**
Printing a Worksheet	**EX 44**
Quitting Excel	**EX 46**
Starting Excel and Opening a Workbook	**EX 47**
AutoCalculate	**EX 48**
Correcting Errors	**EX 50**
Correcting Errors While You Are Typing Data into a Cell	EX 50
Correcting Errors After Entering Data into a Cell	EX 50
Undoing the Last Cell Entry	EX 51
Clearing a Cell or Range of Cells	EX 52
Clearing the Entire Worksheet	EX 52
Excel Help System	**EX 53**
Obtaining Help Using the Type a Question for Help Box on the Menu Bar	EX 53
Quitting Excel	EX 54
Project Summary	**EX 55**
What You Should Know	**EX 55**
Learn It Online	**EX 56**
Apply Your Knowledge	**EX 57**
In the Lab	**EX 58**
Cases and Places	**EX 63**

Project Two

Formulas, Functions, Formatting, and Web Queries

Objectives	**EX 66**
Introduction	**EX 66**
Project Two — Blue Chip Stock Club Investment Analysis	**EX 67**
Starting and Customizing Excel	EX 69
Entering the Titles and Numbers into the Worksheet	**EX 70**
Entering Formulas	**EX 72**
Order of Operations	EX 74
Entering Formulas Using Point Mode	EX 75
Copying Formulas Using the Fill Handle	EX 77
Smart Tags and Option Buttons	EX 78
Determining Totals Using the AutoSum Button	EX 79
Determining the Total Percent Gain/Loss	EX 80
Using the AVERAGE, MAX, and MIN Functions	**EX 80**
Determining the Average of a Range of Numbers	EX 81
Determining the Highest Number in a Range of Numbers	EX 82
Determining the Lowest Number in a Range of Numbers	EX 84
Copying the AVERAGE, MAX, and MIN Functions	EX 87
Saving a Workbook Using the Same File Name	EX 88
Verifying Formulas Using Range Finder	**EX 89**
Formatting the Worksheet	**EX 90**
Changing the Font and Centering the Worksheet Title and Subtitle	EX 91
Changing the Background and Font Colors and Applying a Box Border to the Worksheet Title and Subtitle	EX 94
Applying Formats to the Column Titles	EX 96
Centering the Stock Symbols and Formatting the Dates and Numbers in the Worksheet	EX 96
Formatting Numbers Using the Formatting Toolbar	EX 98
Applying a Thick Bottom Border to the Row above the Total Row and Bolding the Total Row Titles	EX 100
Formatting Numbers Using the Format Cells Command on the Shortcut Menu	EX 100
Formatting Numbers Using the Percent Style Button and Increase Decimal Button	EX 102
Conditional Formatting	EX 103
Changing the Widths of Columns and Heights of Rows	EX 107
Changing the Widths of Columns	EX 107
Changing the Heights of Rows	EX 110
Checking Spelling	**EX 111**
Previewing and Printing the Worksheet	**EX 113**
Printing a Section of the Worksheet	EX 116

Displaying and Printing the Formulas Version of the Worksheet	EX 118
Changing the Print Scaling Option Back to 100%	EX 120
Importing External Data from a Web Source Using a Web Query	EX 120
Changing the Worksheet Names	EX 124
E-Mailing a Workbook from within Excel	EX 125
Saving the Workbook and Quitting Excel	EX 126
Project Summary	EX 127
What You Should Know	EX 127
Learn It Online	EX 129
Apply Your Knowledge	EX 130
In the Lab	EX 132
Cases and Places	EX 140

Project Three

What-If Analysis, Charting, and Working with Large Worksheets

Objectives	EX 146
Introduction	EX 146
Project Three — Aquatics Wear Six-Month Financial Projection	EX 148
Starting and Customizing Excel	EX 149
Bolding the Font of the Entire Worksheet	EX 150
Entering the Worksheet Titles and Saving the Workbook	EX 150
Rotating Text and Using the Fill Handle to Create a Series	EX 151
Copying a Cell's Format Using the Format Painter Button	EX 154
Increasing the Column Widths and Indenting Row Titles	EX 155
Copying a Range of Cells to a Nonadjacent Destination Area	EX 157
Using Drag and Drop to Move or Copy Cells	EX 159
Using Cut and Paste to Move or Copy Cells	EX 159
Inserting and Deleting Cells in a Worksheet	EX 159
Inserting Rows	EX 159
Inserting Columns	EX 161
Inserting Single Cells or a Range of Cells	EX 161
Deleting Columns and Rows	EX 161
Deleting Individual Cells or a Range of Cells	EX 162
Entering Numbers with Format Symbols	EX 162
Freezing Worksheet Titles	EX 163
Entering the Projected Monthly Total Net Revenues	EX 164
Displaying a System Date	EX 165
Absolute versus Relative Addressing	EX 168
Entering a Formula Containing Absolute Cell References	EX 169
Making Decisions — The IF Function	EX 170
Entering the Remaining Formulas	EX 173
Copying Formulas with Absolute Cell References	EX 174
Determining Row Totals in Nonadjacent Cells	EX 175
Unfreezing Worksheet Titles and Saving the Workbook	EX 175
Nested Forms of the IF Function	EX 176
Formatting the Worksheet	EX 177
Formatting the Numbers	EX 177
Formatting the Worksheet Titles	EX 180
Showing the Drawing Toolbar	EX 181
Moving and Docking a Toolbar	EX 182
Adding a Drop Shadow	EX 183
Formatting Nonadjacent Cells	EX 184
Formatting the Assumptions Table	EX 186
Hiding the Drawing Toolbar and Saving the Workbook	EX 187
Adding a 3-D Pie Chart to the Workbook	EX 187
Drawing a 3-D Pie Chart on a Separate Chart Sheet	EX 188
Formatting the Chart Title and Data Labels	EX 192
Changing the Colors of Slices in a Pie Chart	EX 193
Exploding the 3-D Pie Chart	EX 194
Rotating and Tilting the 3-D Pie Chart	EX 194
Showing Leader Lines with the Data Labels	EX 197
Renaming and Reordering the Sheets and Coloring Their Tabs	EX 197

Checking Spelling, Saving, Previewing, and Printing the Workbook	EX 199
Checking Spelling in Multiple Sheets	EX 199
Previewing and Printing the Workbook	EX 200
Changing the View of the Worksheet	EX 201
Shrinking and Magnifying the View of a Worksheet or Chart	EX 201
Splitting the Window into Panes	EX 202
What-If Analysis	EX 204
Analyze Data in a Worksheet by Changing Values	EX 204
Goal Seeking	EX 206
Quitting Excel	EX 208
Project Summary	EX 208
What You Should Know	EX 209
Learn It Online	EX 210
Apply Your Knowledge	EX 211
In the Lab	EX 212
Cases and Places	EX 222

Web Feature

Creating Static and Dynamic Web Pages Using Excel

Objectives	EX 225
Introduction	EX 225
Using Web Page Preview and Saving an Excel Workbook as a Static Web Page	EX 228
Web Page Preview	EX 228
Saving a Workbook as a Static Web Page in a New Folder	EX 230
File Management Tools in Excel	EX 232
Viewing the Static Web Page Using a Browser	EX 233
Saving an Excel Chart as a Dynamic Web Page	EX 234
Viewing and Manipulating the Dynamic Web Page Using a Browser	EX 236
Modifying the Worksheet on a Dynamic Web Page	EX 237
Web Feature Summary	EX 238
What You Should Know	EX 239
In the Lab	EX 239

Appendix A

Microsoft Excel Help System	APP 1

Appendix B

Speech and Handwriting Recognition and Speech Playback	APP 11

Appendix C

Publishing Office Web Pages to a Web Server	APP 24

Appendix D

Changing Screen Resolution and Resetting the Excel Toolbars and Menus	APP 25

Appendix E

Microsoft Office Specialist Certification	APP 31
Index	IND 1
Quick Reference Summary	QR 1

Excel 2003 CourseCard

Preface

The Shelly Cashman Series® offers the finest textbooks in computer education. We are proud of the fact that our series of Microsoft Office 4.3, Microsoft Office 95, Microsoft Office 97, Microsoft Office 2000, and Microsoft Office XP textbooks have been the most widely used books in education. With each new edition of our Office books, we have made significant improvements based on the software and comments made by the instructors and students. The *Microsoft Office 2003* books continue with the innovation, quality, and reliability that you have come to expect from the Shelly Cashman Series.

In this *Microsoft Office Excel 2003* book, you will find an educationally sound, highly visual, and easy-to-follow pedagogy that combines a vastly improved step-by-step approach with corresponding screens. All projects and exercises in this book are designed to take full advantage of the Excel 2003 enhancements. The popular Other Ways and More About features offer in-depth knowledge of Excel 2003. The new Q&A feature offers students a way to solidify important spreadsheet concepts. The Learn It Online page presents a wealth of additional exercises to ensure your students have all the reinforcement they need. The project material is developed to ensure that students will see the importance of learning Excel for future coursework.

Objectives of This Textbook

Microsoft Office Excel 2003: Introductory Concepts and Techniques, CourseCard Edition is intended for a course that covers a brief introduction to Excel 2003. No experience with a computer is assumed, and no mathematics beyond the high school freshman level is required. The objectives of this book are:

- To teach the fundamentals of Excel 2003
- To expose students to practical examples of the computer as a useful tool
- To acquaint students with the proper procedures to create worksheets
- To develop an exercise-oriented approach that allows learning by doing
- To introduce students to new input technologies
- To encourage independent study and help those who are working alone

The Shelly Cashman Approach

Features of the Shelly Cashman Series *Microsoft Office Excel 2003* books include:

- **Project Orientation:** Each project in the book presents a practical problem and complete solution in an easy-to-understand approach.
- **Step-by-Step, Screen-by-Screen Instructions:** Each of the tasks required to complete a project is identified throughout the project. Full-color screens accompany the steps.
- **Thoroughly Tested Projects:** Unparalleled quality is ensured because every screen in the book is produced by the author only after performing a step, and then each project must pass Thomson Course Technology's award-winning Quality Assurance program.
- **Other Ways Boxes and Quick Reference Summary:** The Other Ways boxes displayed at the end of most of the step-by-step sequences specify the other ways to do the task completed in the steps. Thus, the steps and the Other Ways box make a comprehensive reference unit.
- **More About and Q&A Features:** These marginal annotations provide background information, tips, and answers to common questions that complement the topics covered, adding depth and perspective to the learning process.
- **Integration of the World Wide Web:** The World Wide Web is integrated into the Excel 2003 learning experience by (1) More About annotations that send students to Web sites for up-to-date information and alternative approaches to tasks; (2) a Microsoft Office Specialist Certification Web page so students can prepare for the certification examinations; (3) an Excel 2003 Quick Reference Summary Web page that summarizes the ways to complete tasks (mouse, menu, shortcut menu, and keyboard); and (4) the Learn It Online page at the end of each project, which has project reinforcement exercises, learning games, and other types of student activities.

Organization of This Textbook

Microsoft Office Excel 2003: Introductory Concepts and Techniques, CourseCard Edition provides basic instruction on how to use Excel 2003. The material is divided into three projects, a Web feature, five appendices, and a Quick Reference Summary.

Project 1 – Creating a Worksheet and Embedded Chart   In Project 1, students are introduced to starting Excel, quitting Excel, Excel terminology, the Excel window, speech recognition and speech playback, the basic characteristics of a worksheet and workbook, the SUM function, the fill handle, autoformatting, editing techniques, charting, saving, printing and opening a workbook, and the Excel Help system.

Project 2 – Formulas, Functions, Formatting, and Web Queries   In Project 2, students use formulas and functions to build a worksheet and learn more about formatting and printing a worksheet. Students learn to access real-time data using Web Queries.

Project 3 – What-If-Analysis, Charting, and Working with Large Worksheets   In Project 3, students learn how to work with large worksheets, how to create a worksheet based on assumptions, how to use the IF function and absolute cell references, charting techniques, and how to perform what-if analysis.

Web Feature – Creating Static and Dynamic Web Pages Using Excel   In the Web feature, students are introduced to creating static Web pages (noninteractive pages that do not change) and dynamic Web pages (interactive pages that offer Excel functionality).

Appendices   The book includes five appendices. Appendix A presents an introduction to the Microsoft Excel Help system. Appendix B describes how to use Excel's speech and handwriting recognition and speech playback capabilities. Appendix C explains how to publish Web pages to a Web server. Appendix D shows how to change the screen resolution and reset the menus and toolbars. Appendix E introduces students to Microsoft Office Specialist certification.

Quick Reference Summary   In Excel 2003, you can accomplish a task in a number of ways, such as using the mouse, menu, shortcut menu, and keyboard. The Quick Reference Summary at the back of the book provides a quick reference to each task presented.

Excel 2003 CourseCard   New! Now includes a free, tear-off Excel 2003 CourseCard that provides students with a great way to have Excel skills at their fingertips.

End-of-Project Student Activities

A notable strength of the Shelly Cashman Series *Microsoft Excel 2003* books is the extensive student activities at the end of each project. Well-structured student activities can make the difference between students merely participating in a class and students retaining the information they learn. The activities in the Shelly Cashman Series *Excel 2003* books include the following.

- **What You Should Know**   A listing of the tasks completed within a project together with the pages on which the step-by-step, screen-by-screen explanations appear.
- **Learn It Online**   Every project features a Learn It Online page that comprises twelve exercises. These exercises include True/False, Multiple Choice, Short Answer, Flash Cards, Practice Test, Learning Games, Tips and Tricks, Newsgroup usage, Expanding Your Horizons, Search Sleuth, Office Online Training, and Office Marketplace.
- **Apply Your Knowledge**   This exercise usually requires students to open and manipulate a file on the Data Disk that parallels the activities learned in the project. To obtain a copy of the Data Disk, follow the instructions on the inside back cover of this textbook.
- **In the Lab**   Three in-depth assignments per project require students to utilize the project concepts and techniques to solve problems on a computer.
- **Cases and Places**   Five unique real-world case-study situations, including one small-group activity.

Instructor Resources CD-ROM

The Shelly Cashman Series is dedicated to providing you with all of the tools you need to make your class a success. Information on all supplementary materials is available through your Thomson Course Technology representative or by calling one of the following telephone numbers: Colleges and Universities, 1-800-648-7450; High Schools, 1-800-824-5179; Private Career Colleges, 1-800-347-7707; Canada, 1-800-268-2222; Corporations with IT Training Centers, 1-800-648-7450; and Government Agencies, Health-Care Organizations, and Correctional Facilities, 1-800-477-3692.

The Instructor Resources for this textbook include both teaching and testing aids. The contents of each item on the Instructor Resources CD-ROM (ISBN 0-619-20048-0) are described below.

INSTRUCTOR'S MANUAL   The Instructor's Manual is made up of Microsoft Word files, which include detailed lesson plans with page number references, lecture notes, teaching tips, classroom activities, discussion topics, projects to assign, and transparency references. The transparencies are available through the Figure Files described below.

LECTURE SUCCESS SYSTEM   The Lecture Success System consists of intermediate files that correspond to certain figures in the book, allowing you to step through the creation of an application in a project during a lecture without entering large amounts of data.

SYLLABUS   Sample syllabi, which can be customized easily to a course, are included. The syllabi cover policies, class and lab assignments and exams, and procedural information.

FIGURE FILES   Illustrations for every figure in the textbook are available in electronic form. Use this ancillary to present a slide show in lecture or to print transparencies for use in lecture with an overhead projector. If you have a personal computer and LCD device, this ancillary can be an effective tool for presenting lectures.

POWERPOINT PRESENTATIONS   PowerPoint Presentations is a multimedia lecture presentation system that provides slides for each project. Presentations are based on project objectives. Use this presentation system to present well-organized lectures that are both interesting and knowledge based. PowerPoint Presentations provides consistent coverage at schools that use multiple lecturers.

SOLUTIONS TO EXERCISES   Solutions are included for the end-of-project exercises, as well as the Project Reinforcement exercises.

RUBRICS AND ANNOTATED SOLUTION FILES   The grading rubrics provide a customizable framework for assigning point values to the laboratory exercises. Annotated solution files that correspond to the grading rubrics make it easy for you to compare students' results with the correct solutions whether you receive their homework as hardcopy or via e-mail.

TEST BANK & TEST ENGINE   The ExamView test bank includes 110 questions for every project (25 multiple-choice, 50 true/false, and 35 completion) with page number references, and when appropriate, figure references. A version of the test bank you can print also is included. The test bank comes with a copy of the test engine, ExamView, the ultimate tool for your objective-based testing needs. ExamView is a state-of-the-art test builder that is easy to use. ExamView enables you to create paper-, LAN-, or Web-based tests from test banks designed specifically for your Thomson Course Technology textbook. Utilize the ultra-efficient QuickTest Wizard to create tests in less than five minutes by taking advantage of Thomson Course Technology's question banks, or customize your own exams from scratch.

LAB TESTS/TEST OUT   The Lab Tests/Test Out exercises parallel the In the Lab assignments and are supplied for the purpose of testing students in the laboratory on the material covered in the project or testing students out of the course.

DATA FILES FOR STUDENTS   All the files that are required by students to complete the exercises are included. You can distribute the files on the Instructor Resources CD-ROM to your students over a network, or you can have them follow the instructions on the inside back cover of this book to obtain a copy of the Data Disk.

ADDITIONAL ACTIVITIES FOR STUDENTS   These additional activities consist of Project Reinforcement Exercises, which are true/false, multiple choice, and short answer questions that help students gain confidence in the material learned.

SAM 2003

SAM 2003 helps you energize your class exams and training assignments by allowing students to learn and test important computer skills in an active, hands-on environment.

SAM 2003 ASSESSMENT   With SAM 2003 Assessment, you create powerful interactive exams on critical applications such as Excel, Word, Access, Outlook, PowerPoint, Windows, and the Internet. The exams simulate the application environment, allowing your students to demonstrate their knowledge and think through the skill by performing real-world tasks. Build hands-on exams that allow students to work in the simulated application environment.

SAM 2003 TRAINING   Invigorate your lesson plan with SAM 2003 Training. Using highly interactive text, graphics, and sound, SAM 2003 Training gives your students the flexibility to learn computer applications by choosing the training method that fits them best. Create customized training units that employ various approaches to teaching computer skills.

SAM 2003 ASSESSMENT AND TRAINING   Designed to be used with the Shelly Cashman Series, SAM 2003 Assessment and Training includes built-in page references so students can create study guides that match the Shelly Cashman Series textbooks you use in class. Powerful administrative options allow you to schedule customized exams and assignments, secure your tests, and choose from more than one dozen reports to track testing and learning progress.

Online Content

Thomson Course Technology offers textbook-based content for Blackboard, WebCT, and MyCourse 2.1

BLACKBOARD AND WEBCT   As the leading provider of IT content for the Blackboard and WebCT platforms, Thomson Course Technology delivers rich content that enhances your textbook to give your students a unique learning experience. Thomson Course Technology has partnered with WebCT and Blackboard to deliver our market-leading content through these state-of-the-art online learning platforms.

MYCOURSE 2.1   MyCourse 2.1 is Thomson Course Technology's powerful online course management and content delivery system. Completely maintained and hosted by Thomson, MyCourse 2.1 delivers an online learning environment that is completely secure and provides superior performance. MyCourse 2.1 allows nontechnical users to create, customize, and deliver World Wide Web-based courses; post content and assignments; manage student enrollment; administer exams; track results in the online gradebook; and more.

MICROSOFT OFFICE EXCEL

MICROSOFT
Office Excel 2003

xcel

=AVERAGE(C4:C10) =MIN(D4:D10) =SUM(B8,C4,D6,E8)

NORTH AMERICA

=IF(AND(1<A3, A3<100)

Creating a Worksheet and an Embedded Chart

PROJECT

1

CASE PERSPECTIVE

In the late 1970s, Extreme Blading pioneered the sport of inline skating as an off-season training tool for hockey players. The sport quickly caught on with fitness enthusiasts, aggressive skaters, and the population in general. Today, nearly 50 million inline skaters participate in the activity worldwide and the sport continues to grow.

The Extreme Blading product line includes a variety of skates, including inline, quad, and custom models for all age levels, as well as a complete line of protective gear and other accessories.

For years, the company sold their goods via direct mail, telesales, and company-owned outlets in major cities across the country. Thanks to the popularity of personal computers and the World Wide Web, the company added an e-commerce Web site last year. This new sales channel has given the company access to more than 600 million people worldwide and has resulted in a significant increase in sales.

Sales continued to grow during the first half of this year, thus driving senior management to ask their financial analyst, Maria Lopez, to develop a better sales tracking system. As a first step, Maria has asked you to prepare an easy-to-read worksheet that shows product sales for the second quarter by sales channel (Figure 1-1 on page EX 5). In addition, Maria has asked you to create a chart showing second quarter sales, because the president of the company likes to have a graphical representation of sales that allows her quickly to identify stronger and weaker product groups by sales channel.

As you read through this project, you will learn how to use Excel to create, save, and print a financial report that includes a 3-D Column chart.

Creating a Worksheet and an Embedded Chart

Objectives

You will have mastered the material in this project when you can:

- Start and Quit Excel
- Describe the Excel worksheet
- Enter text and numbers
- Use the AutoSum button to sum a range of cells
- Copy a cell to a range of cells using the fill handle
- Format a worksheet

- Create a 3-D Clustered column chart
- Save a workbook and print a worksheet
- Open a workbook
- Use the AutoCalculate area to determine statistics
- Correct errors on a worksheet
- Use the Excel Help system to answer questions

What Is Microsoft Office Excel 2003?

Microsoft Office Excel 2003 is a powerful spreadsheet program that allows users to organize data, complete calculations, make decisions, graph data, develop professional looking reports (Figure 1-1), publish organized data to the Web, and access real-time data from Web sites. The four major parts of Excel are:

- **Worksheets** Worksheets allow users to enter, calculate, manipulate, and analyze data such as numbers and text. The term worksheet means the same as spreadsheet.
- **Charts** Excel can draw a variety of charts.
- **Lists** Lists organize and store data. For example, once a user enters data into a worksheet, Excel can sort the data, search for specific data, and select data that satisfies defined criteria.
- **Web Support** Web support allows users to save Excel worksheets or parts of a worksheet in HTML format, so a user can view and manipulate the worksheet using a browser. Excel Web support also provides access to real-time data, such as stock quotes, using Web queries.

This latest version of Excel makes it much easier to create and manipulate lists of data. It also offers industry-standard XML support that simplifies the sharing of data within and outside an organization; improved statistical functions; smart documents that automatically fill with data; information rights management; allows two workbooks to be compared side by side; and includes the capability of searching a variety of reference information.

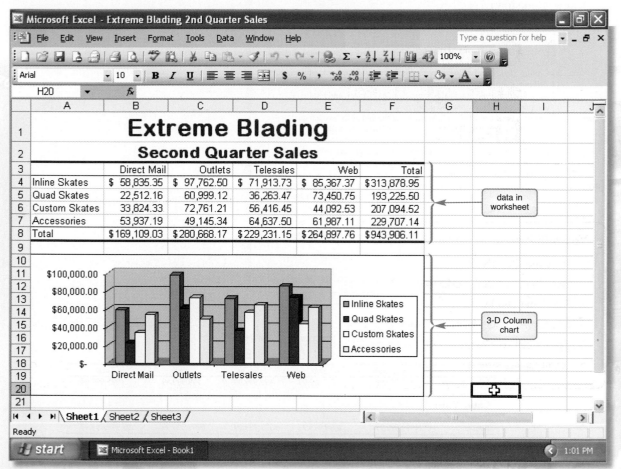

FIGURE 1-1

Project One — Extreme Blading Second Quarter Sales

The first step in creating an effective worksheet is to make sure you understand what is required. The person or persons requesting the worksheet should supply their requirements in a requirements document. A **requirements document** includes a needs statement, source of data, summary of calculations, and any other special requirements for the worksheet, such as charting and Web support. Figure 1-2 on the next page shows the requirements document for the new worksheet to be created in this project.

After carefully reviewing the requirements document, the next step is to design a solution or draw a sketch of the worksheet based on the requirements, including titles, column and row headings, location of data values, and the 3-D Column chart, as shown in Figure 1-3 on the next page. The dollar signs, 9s, and commas that you see in the sketch of the worksheet indicate formatted numeric values.

More About

Worksheet Development Cycle

Spreadsheet specialists do not sit down and start entering text, formulas, and data into a blank Excel worksheet as soon as they have a spreadsheet assignment. Instead, they follow an organized plan, or methodology, that breaks the development cycle into a series of tasks. The recommended methodology for creating worksheets includes (1) analyze requirements (supplied in a requirements document); (2) design solution; (3) validate design; (4) implement design; (5) test solution; and (6) document solution.

REQUEST FOR NEW WORKSHEET

Date Submitted:	May 2, 2005
Submitted By:	Maria Lopez
Worksheet Title:	Second Quarter Sales
Needs:	An easy-to-read worksheet that shows Extreme Blading's second quarter sales for each of the product groups (Inline Skates, Quad Skates, Custom Skates, and Accessories) by sales channel (Direct Mail, Outlets, Telesales, and Web). The worksheet also should include total sales for each product group, total sales for each sales channel, and total company sales for the second quarter.
Source of Data:	The data for the worksheet is available at the end of the second quarter from the chief financial officer (CFO) of Extreme Blading.
Calculations:	The following calculations must be made for the worksheet: (a) total second quarter sales for each of the four product groups; (b) total second quarter sales for each of the four sales channels; and (c) total second quarter sales for the company.
Chart Requirements:	Below data in the worksheet, construct a 3-D Clustered column chart that compares the total sales for each product group within each sales channel.

Approvals

Approval Status:	X	Approved
		Rejected
Approved By:	Sylvia Strong	
Date:	May 5, 2005	
Assigned To:	J. Quasney, Spreadsheet Specialist	

requirements document

FIGURE 1-2

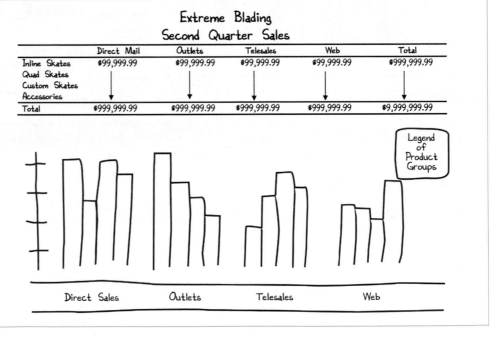

FIGURE 1-3

sketch of worksheet

With a good understanding of the requirements document and a sketch of the worksheet, the next step is to use Excel to create the worksheet and chart.

Starting and Customizing Excel

If you are stepping through this project on a computer and you want your screen to match the figures in this book, then you should change your computer's resolution to 800 × 600. For more information on how to change the resolution on your computer, see Appendix D. The following steps show how to start Excel.

To Start Excel

1

• **Click the Start button on the Windows taskbar, point to All Programs on the Start menu, point to Microsoft Office on the All Programs submenu, and then point to Microsoft Office Excel 2003 on the Microsoft Office submenu.**

Windows displays the Start menu, the All Programs submenu, and the Microsoft Office submenu (Figure 1-4).

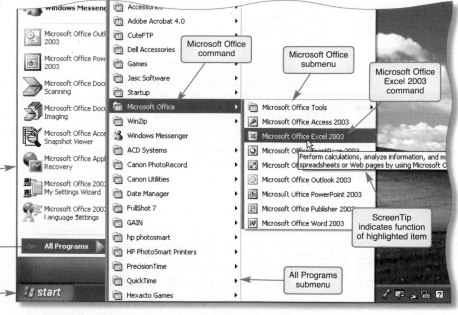

FIGURE 1-4

2

• **Click Microsoft Office Excel 2003.**

Excel starts. After several seconds, Excel displays a blank workbook titled Book1 in the Excel window (Figure 1-5).

3

• **If the Excel window is not maximized, double-click its title bar to maximize it.**

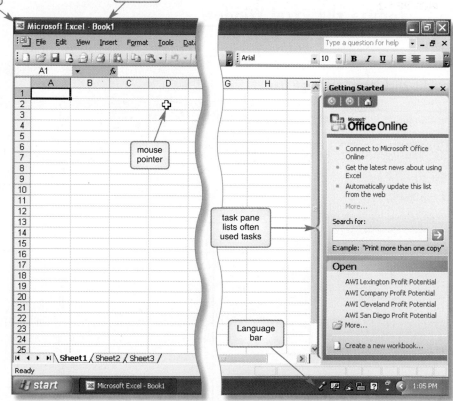

FIGURE 1-5

Other Ways

1. Double-click Excel icon on desktop
2. Click Microsoft Office Excel 2003 on Start menu
3. Click Start button, point to All Programs, click New Office Document, click General tab, double-click Blank Workbook icon

The screen shown in Figure 1-5 on the previous page illustrates how the Excel window looks the first time you start Excel after installation on most computers. If the Office Speech Recognition software is installed and active on your computer, then when you start Excel, the Language bar is displayed on the screen. The **Language bar** contains buttons that allow you to speak commands and dictate text. It usually is located on the right side of the Windows taskbar next to the notification area, and it changes to include the speech recognition functions available in Excel. In this book, the Language bar is closed because it takes up computer resources and with the Language bar active, the microphone can be turned on accidentally by clicking the Microphone button causing your computer to act in an unstable manner. For additional information about the Language bar, see page EX 15 and Appendix B.

As shown in Figure 1-5, Excel displays a task pane on the right side of the screen. A **task pane** is a separate window that enables users to carry out some Excel tasks more efficiently. When you start Excel, it displays the Getting Started task pane, which is a small window that provides commonly used links and commands that allow you to open files, create new files, or search Office-related topics on the Microsoft Web site. In this book, the Getting Started task pane is hidden to allow the maximum number of columns to appear in Excel.

At startup, Excel also displays two toolbars on a single row. A **toolbar** contains buttons, boxes, and menus that allow you to perform tasks quickly. To allow for more efficient use of the buttons, the toolbars should appear on two separate rows, instead of sharing a single row. The following steps show how to close the Language bar, close the Getting Started task pane, and instruct Excel to display the toolbars on two separate rows.

Microsoft Office
Excel 2003

More About

Task Panes

You can drag a task pane title bar to float the pane in your work area or dock it on either the left or right side of a screen, depending on your personal preference.

To Customize the Excel Window

1

• **Right-click the Language bar.**

The Language bar shortcut menu appears (Figure 1-6).

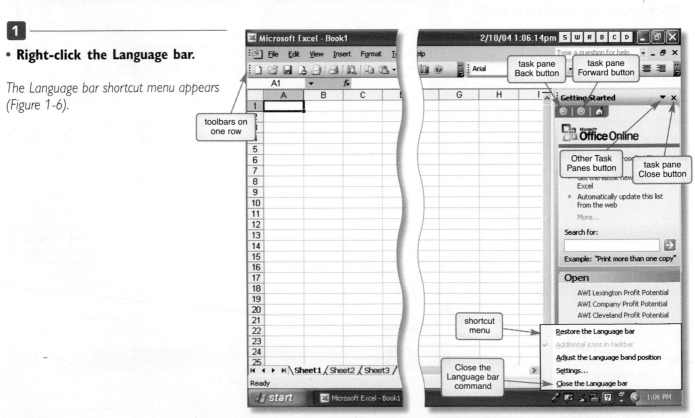

FIGURE 1-6

2

• **Click Close the Language bar.**

• **Click the Getting Started task pane Close button in the upper-right corner of the task pane.**

• **If the toolbars are positioned on the same row, click the Toolbar Options button.**

The Language bar disappears. Excel closes the Getting Started task pane and displays additional columns. Excel also displays the Toolbar Options list showing the buttons that do not fit on the toolbars when toolbars appear on one row (Figure 1-7).

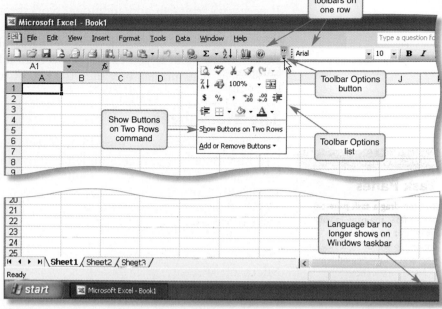

FIGURE 1-7

3

• **Click Show Buttons on Two Rows.**

Excel displays the toolbars on two separate rows (Figure 1-8). With the toolbars on two separate rows, all of the buttons fit on the two toolbars.

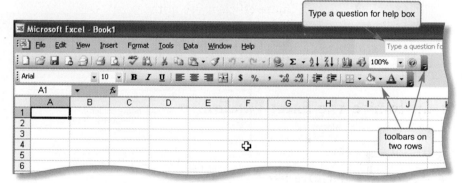

FIGURE 1-8

As you work through creating a worksheet, you will find that certain Excel operations cause Excel to display a task pane. Excel provides eleven task panes, in addition to the Getting Started task pane shown in Figure 1-6. Some of the more important ones are the Clipboard task pane, the Excel Help task pane, and the Clip Art task pane. Throughout the book, these task panes are discussed when they are used.

At any point while working with an Excel worksheet, you can open or close a task pane by clicking the Task Pane command on the View menu. You can activate additional task panes by clicking the Other Task Panes button to the left of the Close button on the task pane title bar (Figure 1-6) and then selecting a task pane in the Other Task Panes list. The Back and Forward buttons below the task pane title bar allow you to switch between task panes that you opened during a session.

The Excel Worksheet

When Excel starts, it creates a new blank workbook, called Book1. The **workbook** (Figure 1-9 on the next page) is like a notebook. Inside the workbook are sheets, each of which is called a **worksheet**. Excel opens a new workbook with three worksheets.

More About

The Excel Help System

Need Help? It is no further away than the Type a question for help box on the menu bar in the upper-right corner of the window. Click the box that contains the text, Type a question for help (Figure 1-8), type help, and then press the ENTER key. Excel responds with a list of topics you can click to learn about obtaining help on any Excel-related topic. To find out what is new in Excel 2003, type what is new in Excel in the Type a question for help box.

If necessary, you can add additional worksheets to a maximum of 255. Each worksheet has a sheet name that appears on a **sheet tab** at the bottom of the workbook. For example, Sheet1 is the name of the active worksheet displayed in the Book1 workbook. If you click the sheet tab labeled Sheet2, Excel displays the Sheet2 worksheet. This project uses only the Sheet1 worksheet.

The Worksheet

The worksheet is organized into a rectangular grid containing vertical columns and horizontal rows. A column letter above the grid, also called the **column heading**, identifies each column. A row number on the left side of the grid, also called the **row heading**, identifies each row. With the screen resolution set to 800 × 600 and the Excel window maximized, Excel displays 12 columns (A through L) and 23 rows (1 through 23) of the worksheet on the screen, as shown in Figure 1-9.

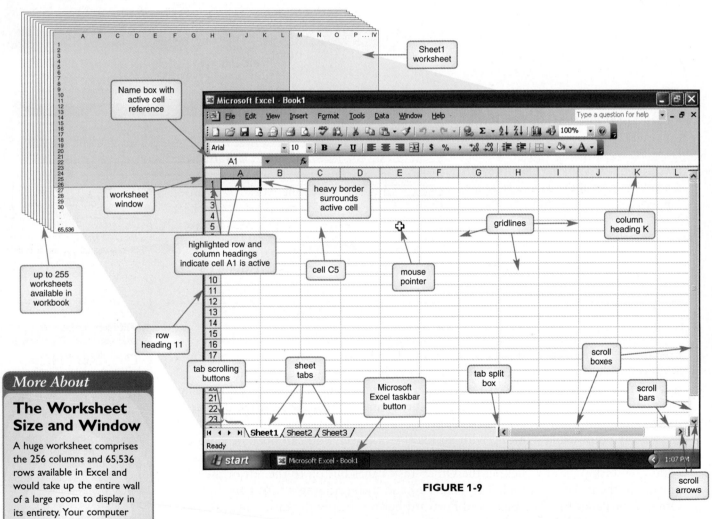

FIGURE 1-9

More About

The Worksheet Size and Window

A huge worksheet comprises the 256 columns and 65,536 rows available in Excel and would take up the entire wall of a large room to display in its entirety. Your computer screen, by comparison, is a small window that allows you to view only a minute area of the worksheet at one time. While you cannot see the entire worksheet, you can move the window over the worksheet to view any part of it.

The intersection of each column and row is a cell. A **cell** is the basic unit of a worksheet into which you enter data. Each worksheet in a workbook has 256 columns and 65,536 rows for a total of 16,777,216 cells. The column headings begin with A and end with IV. The row headings begin with 1 and end with 65,536. Only a small fraction of the active worksheet appears on the screen at one time.

A cell is referred to by its unique address, or **cell reference**, which is the coordinates of the intersection of a column and a row. To identify a cell, specify the column letter first, followed by the row number. For example, cell reference C5 refers to the cell located at the intersection of column C and row 5 (Figure 1-9).

One cell on the worksheet, designated the **active cell**, is the one into which you can enter data. The active cell in Figure 1-9 is A1. The active cell is identified in three ways. First, a heavy border surrounds the cell; second, the active cell reference shows immediately above column A in the Name box; and third, the column heading A and row heading 1 are highlighted so it is easy to see which cell is active (Figure 1-9).

The horizontal and vertical lines on the worksheet itself are called **gridlines**. Gridlines make it easier to see and identify each cell in the worksheet. If desired, you can turn the gridlines off so they do not show on the worksheet, but it is recommended that you leave them on for now.

The mouse pointer in Figure 1-9 has the shape of a block plus sign. The mouse pointer appears as a block plus sign whenever it is located in a cell on the worksheet. Another common shape of the mouse pointer is the block arrow. The mouse pointer turns into the block arrow whenever you move it outside the worksheet or when you drag cell contents between rows or columns. The other mouse pointer shapes are described when they appear on the screen.

Worksheet Window

You view the portion of the worksheet displayed on the screen through a **worksheet window** (Figure 1-9). Below and to the right of the worksheet window are **scroll bars**, **scroll arrows**, and **scroll boxes** that you can use to move the worksheet window around to view different parts of the active worksheet. To the right of the sheet tabs at the bottom of the screen is the tab split box. You can drag the **tab split box** to increase or decrease the view of the sheet tabs (Figure 1-9). When you decrease the view of the sheet tabs, you increase the length of the horizontal scroll bar, and vice versa.

The menu bar, Standard toolbar, Formatting toolbar, and formula bar appear at the top of the screen, above the worksheet window and below the title bar.

Menu Bar

The **menu bar** is a special toolbar that includes the menu names as shown in Figure 1-10a on the next page. Each **menu name** represents a menu. A **menu** is a list of commands that you can use to retrieve, store, print, and manipulate data on the worksheet. When you point to a menu name on the menu bar, the area of the menu bar containing the name changes to a button. To display a menu, such as the Edit menu, click the Edit menu name on the menu bar (Figures 1-10b and 1-10c on the next page). If you point to a menu command with an arrow to its right, Excel displays a **submenu** from which you can choose a command.

More About

The Mouse Pointer

The mouse pointer can change to one of more than 15 different shapes, such as a block arrow, cross hair, or chart symbol, depending on the task you are performing in Excel and the mouse pointer's location on the screen.

Q & A

Q: Can the Excel window or viewing area be increased to show more of the worksheet?

A: Yes. Two ways exist to increase what you can see in the viewing area: (1) on the View menu, click Full Screen; and (2) change to a higher resolution. See Appendix D for information about how to change to a higher resolution.

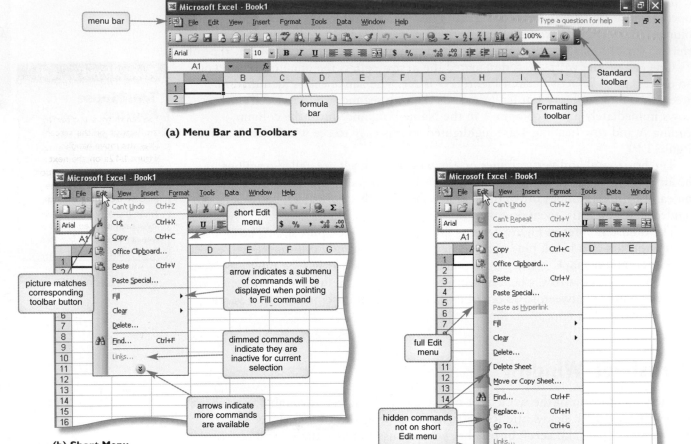

FIGURE 1-10

When you click a menu name on the menu bar, Excel displays a **short menu** listing the most recently used commands (Figure 1-10b). If you wait a few seconds or click the arrows at the bottom of the short menu, Excel displays the full menu. The **full menu** lists all of the commands associated with a menu (Figure 1-10c). You also can display a full menu immediately by double-clicking the menu name on the menu bar. In this book, use one of the following techniques to ensure that Excel always displays the full menu.

1. Click the menu name on the menu bar and then wait a few seconds.
2. Click the menu name on the menu bar and then click the arrows at the bottom of the short menu.
3. Click the menu name on the menu bar and then point to the arrows at the bottom of the short menu.
4. Double-click the menu name on the menu bar.

Both short and full menus display some dimmed commands. A **dimmed command** appears gray, or dimmed, instead of black, which indicates it is not available for the current selection. A command with medium blue shading to the left of it on a full menu is called a **hidden command** because it does not appear on a short menu. As you use Excel, it automatically personalizes the short menus for you based on how often you use commands. That is, as you use hidden commands, Excel *unhides* them and places them on the short menu.

The menu bar can change to include other menu names depending on the type of work you are doing in Excel. For example, if you are working with a chart sheet rather than a worksheet, Excel displays the Chart menu bar with menu names that reflect charting commands.

Standard Toolbar and Formatting Toolbar

The Standard toolbar and the Formatting toolbar (Figure 1-11) contain buttons and boxes that allow you to perform frequent tasks more quickly than when using the menu bar. For example, to print a worksheet, you click the Print button on the Standard toolbar. Each button has a picture on the button face to help you remember the button's function. Also, when you move the mouse pointer over a button or box, Excel displays the name of the button or box below it in a **ScreenTip**.

Figures 1-11a and 1-11b illustrate the Standard and Formatting toolbars and describe the functions of the buttons. Each of the buttons and boxes will be explained in detail when they are used.

More About

Toolbars

You can move a toolbar to any location on the screen. Drag the move handle (Figure 1-12a on the next page) to the desired location. Once the toolbar is in the window area, drag the title bar to move it. Each side of the screen is called a dock. You can drag a toolbar to a dock so it does not clutter the window.

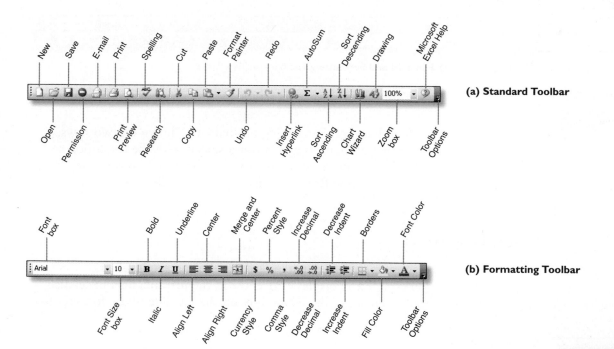

(a) Standard Toolbar

(b) Formatting Toolbar

FIGURE 1-11

When you first install Excel, both the Standard and Formatting toolbars are preset to display on the same row (Figure 1-12a on the next page), immediately below the menu bar. Unless the resolution of your display device is greater than 800 × 600, many of the buttons that belong on these toolbars are hidden. Hidden buttons appear in the Toolbar Options list (Figure 1-12b on the next page). In this mode, you also can display all the buttons on either toolbar by double-clicking the **move handle** on the left of each toolbar (Figure 1-12a).

More About

Resetting Toolbars

If your toolbars have a different set of buttons than shown in Figure 1-11, it probably means that a previous user added or deleted buttons. To reset the toolbars to their default, see Appendix D.

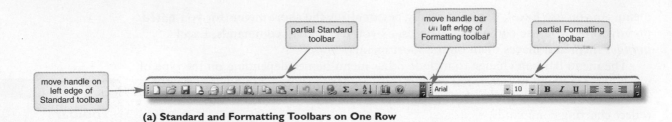

(a) Standard and Formatting Toolbars on One Row

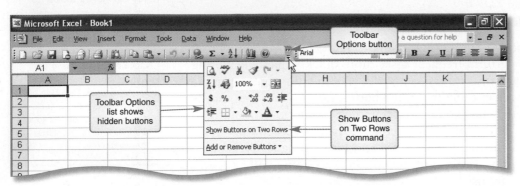

(b) Toolbar Options List

(c) Standard and Formatting Toolbars on Two Rows

FIGURE 1-12

In this book, the Standard and Formatting toolbars are shown on two rows, one below the other, so that all buttons appear on a screen with the resolution set to 800 × 600 (Figure 1-12c). You can show the two toolbars on two rows by clicking the Show Buttons on Two Rows command in the Toolbar Options list (Figure 1-12b).

Formula Bar

The formula bar appears below the Standard and Formatting toolbars (Figure 1-13). As you type, Excel displays the entry in the **formula bar**. Excel also displays the active cell reference in the Name box on the left side of the formula bar.

Status Bar

The status bar is located immediately above the Windows taskbar at the bottom of the screen (Figure 1-13). The **status bar** displays a brief description of the command selected (highlighted) on a menu, the function of the button the mouse pointer is pointing to, or the mode of Excel. **Mode indicators**, such as Enter and Ready, appear on the status bar and specify the current mode of Excel. When the mode is **Ready**, Excel is ready to accept the next command or data entry. When the mode indicator reads **Enter**, Excel is in the process of accepting data through the keyboard into the active cell.

In the middle of the status bar is the AutoCalculate area. The **AutoCalculate area** can be used in place of a calculator or formula to view the sum, average, or other types of totals of a group of numbers on the worksheet. The AutoCalculate area is discussed in detail later in this project.

Keyboard indicators, such as CAPS (Caps Lock), NUM (Num Lock), and SCRL (Scroll), show which keys are engaged. Keyboard indicators appear in the small rectangular boxes on the right side of the status bar (Figure 1-13).

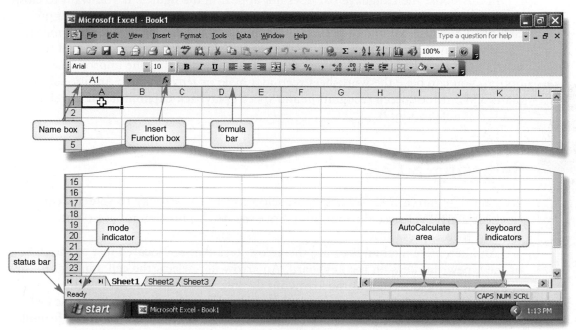

FIGURE 1-13

Speech Recognition and Speech Playback

With the **Office Speech Recognition software** installed and a microphone, you can speak the names of toolbar buttons, menus, menu commands, list items, alerts, and dialog box controls, such as OK and Cancel. You also can dictate cell entries, such as text and numbers. To indicate whether you want to speak commands or dictate cell entries, you use the Language bar. The Language bar can be in one of four states: (1) **restored**, which means it is displayed somewhere in the Excel window (Figure 1-14a); (2) **minimized**, which means it is displayed on the Windows taskbar (Figure 1-14b); (3) **hidden**, which means you do not see it on the screen but it will be displayed the next time you start your computer; (4) **closed**, which means it is hidden permanently until you enable it. If the Language bar is hidden or closed and you want it to display, then do the following:

1. Right-click an open area on the Windows taskbar at the bottom of the screen.
2. Point to Toolbars on the shortcut menu and then click Language bar on the Toolbars submenu.

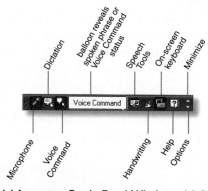

(a) Language Bar in Excel Window with Microphone Enabled

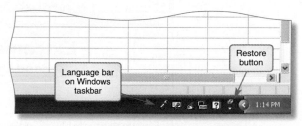

(b) Language Bar Minimized on Windows Taskbar

FIGURE 1-14

If the Language bar command is dimmed on the Toolbars submenu or if the Speech command is dimmed on the Tools menu, the Office Speech Recognition software is not installed.

In this book, the Language bar does not appear in the figures. If you want to close the Language bar so that your screen is identical to what you see in the book, right-click the Language bar and then click Close the Language bar on the shortcut menu.

If you have speakers, you can use the **speech playback** functions of Excel to instruct the computer to read a worksheet to you. By selecting the appropriate option, you can have the worksheet read in a male or female voice. Additional information about the speech recognition and speech playback capabilities of Excel is available in Appendix B.

Selecting a Cell

More About

Selecting a Cell

You can select any cell by entering its cell reference, such as b4, in the Name box on the left side of the formula bar.

To enter data into a cell, you first must select it. The easiest way **to select a cell** (make it active) is to use the mouse to move the block plus sign mouse pointer to the cell and then click.

An alternative method is to use the arrow keys that are located just to the right of the typewriter keys on the keyboard. An arrow key selects the cell adjacent to the active cell in the direction of the arrow on the key.

You know a cell is selected, or active, when a heavy border surrounds the cell and the active cell reference appears in the Name box on the left side of the formula bar. Excel also changes the active cell's column heading and row heading to a gold color.

Entering Text

Q&A

Q: What is the maximum allowable length of a text entry?

A: A text entry in a cell can contain from 1 to **32,767** characters. Although text entries primarily are used to identify parts of a worksheet, some worksheet applications use text entries as data that you dissect, string together, and manipulate using text functions.

In Excel, any set of characters containing a letter, hyphen (as in a telephone number), or space is considered text. **Text** is used to place titles, such as worksheet titles, column titles, and row titles, on the worksheet. For example, as shown in Figure 1-15, the worksheet title, Extreme Blading, identifies the worksheet created in Project 1. The worksheet subtitle, Second Quarter Sales, identifies the type of report. The column titles in row 3 (Direct Mail, Outlets, Telesales, Web, and Total) identify the numbers in each column. The row titles in column A (Inline Skates, Quad Skates, Custom Skates, Accessories, and Total) identify the numbers in each row.

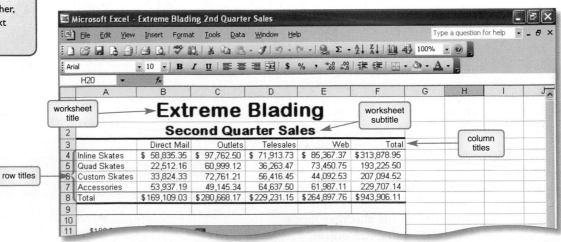

FIGURE 1-15

Entering the Worksheet Titles

The following steps show how to enter the worksheet titles in cells A1 and A2. Later in this project, the worksheet titles will be formatted so they appear as shown in Figure 1-15.

To Enter the Worksheet Titles

• **Click cell A1.**

Cell A1 becomes the active cell and a heavy border surrounds it (Figure 1-16).

cell A1 selected

FIGURE 1-16

Cancel box   Enter box

2

• **Type** Extreme Blading **in cell A1 and then point to the Enter box in the formula bar.**

Excel displays the title in the formula bar and in cell A1 (Figure 1-17). When you begin typing a cell entry, Excel displays two additional boxes in the formula bar: the Cancel box and the Enter box.

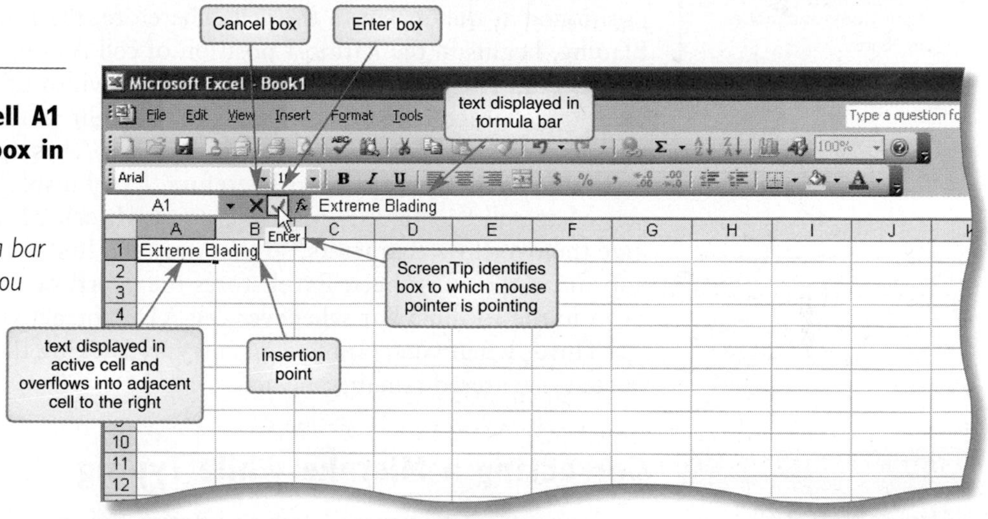

text displayed in formula bar

ScreenTip identifies box to which mouse pointer is pointing

text displayed in active cell and overflows into adjacent cell to the right

insertion point

FIGURE 1-17

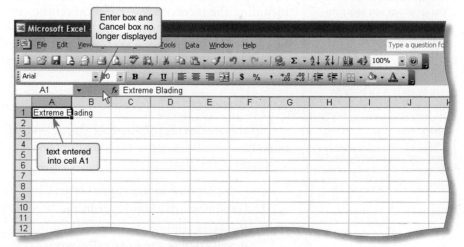

3

• **Click the Enter box to complete the entry.**

Excel enters the worksheet title in cell A1 (Figure 1-18).

Enter box and Cancel box no longer displayed

text entered into cell A1

FIGURE 1-18

4

• **Click cell A2 to select it. Type** Second Quarter Sales **as the cell entry. Click the Enter box to complete the entry.**

Excel enters the worksheet subtitle in cell A2 (Figure 1-19).

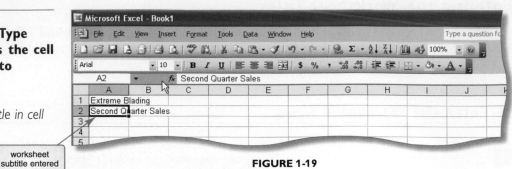

worksheet subtitle entered into cell A2

FIGURE 1-19

In Figure 1-17 on the previous page, the text in cell A1 is followed by the insertion point. The **insertion point** is a blinking vertical line that indicates where the next typed character will appear. In Steps 3 and 4, clicking the **Enter box** completes the entry. Clicking the **Cancel box** cancels the entry.

When you complete a text entry into a cell, a series of events occurs. First, Excel positions the text left-aligned in the cell. **Left-aligned** means the cell entry is positioned at the far left in the cell. Therefore, the E in the worksheet title, Extreme Blading, begins in the leftmost position of cell A1.

Second, when the text is longer than the width of a column, Excel displays the overflow characters in adjacent cells to the right as long as these adjacent cells contain no data. In Figure 1-19, the width of cell A1 is approximately 9 characters. The text consists of 15 characters. Therefore, Excel displays the overflow characters from cell A1 in cell B1, because cell B1 is empty. If cell B1 contained data, Excel would hide the overflow characters, so that only the first 9 characters in cell A1 would appear on the worksheet. Excel stores the overflow characters in cell A1 and displays them in the formula bar whenever cell A1 is the active cell.

Third, when you complete an entry by clicking the Enter box, the cell in which the text is entered remains the active cell.

Correcting a Mistake while Typing

If you type the wrong letter and notice the error before clicking the Enter box or pressing the ENTER key, use the BACKSPACE key to delete all the characters back to and including the incorrect letter. To cancel the entire entry before entering it into the cell, click the Cancel box in the formula bar or press the ESC key. If you see an error in a cell after entering the text, select the cell and retype the entry. Later in this project, additional error-correction techniques are discussed.

AutoCorrect

The **AutoCorrect feature** of Excel works behind the scenes, correcting common mistakes when you complete a text entry in a cell. AutoCorrect makes three types of corrections for you:

1. Corrects two initial capital letters by changing the second letter to lowercase.
2. Capitalizes the first letter in the names of days.
3. Replaces commonly misspelled words with their correct spelling. For example, it will change the misspelled word *recieve* to *receive* when you complete the entry. AutoCorrect will correct the spelling of hundreds of commonly misspelled words automatically.

Entering Column Titles

To enter the column titles in row 3, select the appropriate cell and then enter the text, as described in the following steps.

To Enter Column Titles

1

• **Click cell B3.**

Cell B3 becomes the active cell. The active cell reference in the Name box changes from A2 to B3 (Figure 1-20).

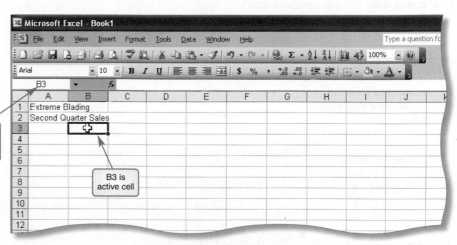

active cell reference in Name box changes to B3

B3 is active cell

FIGURE 1-20

2

• **Type** Direct Mail **in cell B3.**

Excel displays Direct Mail in the formula bar and in cell B3 (Figure 1-21).

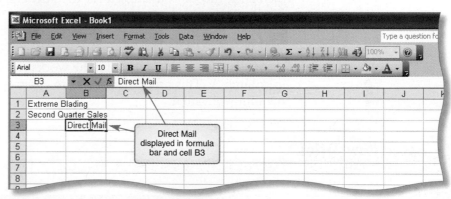

Direct Mail displayed in formula bar and cell B3

FIGURE 1-21

3

• **Press the RIGHT ARROW key.**

Excel enters the column title, Direct Mail, in cell B3 and makes cell C3 the active cell (Figure 1-22).

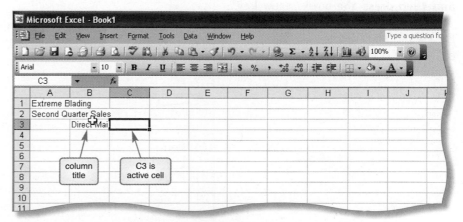

column title

C3 is active cell

FIGURE 1-22

4

• **Repeat Steps 2 and 3 for the remaining column titles in row 3; that is, enter** Outlets **in cell C3,** Telesales **in cell D3,** Web **in cell E3, and** Total **in cell F3 (complete the last entry in cell F3 by clicking the Enter box in the formula bar).**

Excel displays the column titles left-aligned as shown in Figure 1-23.

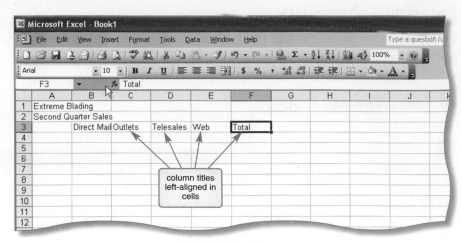

FIGURE 1-23

If the next entry is in an adjacent cell, use the arrow keys to complete the entry in a cell. When you press an arrow key to complete an entry, the adjacent cell in the direction of the arrow (up, down, left, or right) becomes the active cell. If the next entry is in a nonadjacent cell, complete an entry by clicking the next cell in which you plan to enter data. You also can click the Enter box or press the ENTER key and then click the appropriate cell for the next entry.

Entering Row Titles

The next step in developing the worksheet in Project 1 is to enter the row titles in column A. This process is similar to entering the column titles and is described in the following steps.

To Enter Row Titles

1

• **Click cell A4. Type** Inline Skates **and then press the DOWN ARROW key.**

Excel enters the row title, Inline Skates, in cell A4, and cell A5 becomes the active cell (Figure 1-24).

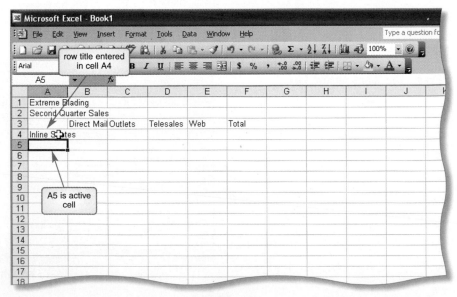

FIGURE 1-24

2

- **Repeat Step 1 for the remaining row titles in column A; that is, enter** Quad Skates **in cell A5,** Custom Skates **in cell A6,** Accessories **in cell A7, and** Total **in cell A8.**

Excel displays the row titles as shown in Figure 1-25.

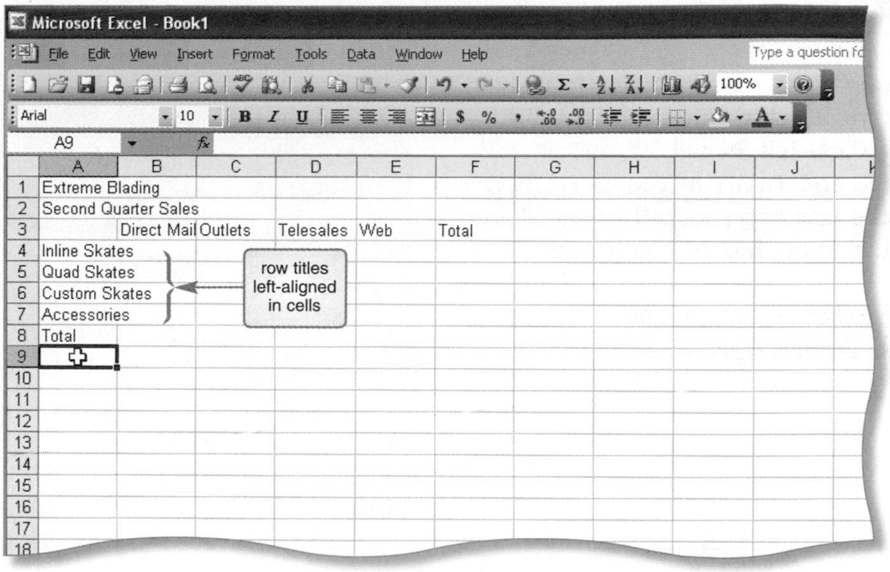

FIGURE 1-25

When you enter text, Excel automatically left-aligns the text in the cell. Excel treats any combination of numbers, spaces, and nonnumeric characters as text. For example, the following entries are text:

401AX21, 921-231, 619 321, 883XTY

You can change the text alignment in a cell by realigning it. Several alignment techniques are discussed later in the project.

Entering Numbers

In Excel, you can enter numbers into cells to represent amounts. A **number** can contain only the following characters:

0 1 2 3 4 5 6 7 8 9 + - ( ) , / . $ % E e

If a cell entry contains any other keyboard character (including spaces), Excel interprets the entry as text and treats it accordingly. The use of the special characters is explained when they are used in the project.

The Extreme Blading Second Quarter numbers used in Project 1 are summarized in Table 1-1. These numbers, which represent second quarter sales for each of the sales channels and product groups, must be entered in rows 4, 5, 6, and 7. The steps on the next page enter the numbers in Table 1-1 one row at a time.

> ### More About
>
> **Entering Numbers as Text**
>
> Sometimes, you will want Excel to treat numbers, such as Zip codes and telephone numbers, as text. To enter a number as text, start the entry with an apostrophe (').

Table 1-1 Extreme Blading Second Quarter Data				
	Direct Mail	**Outlets**	**Telesales**	**Web**
Inline Skates	58835.35	97762.50	71913.73	85367.37
Quad Skates	22512.16	60999.12	36263.47	73450.75
Custom Skates	33824.33	72761.21	56416.45	44092.53
Accessories	53937.19	49145.34	64637.50	61987.11

To Enter Numbers

1

• **Click cell B4.**

• **Type** 58835.35 **and then press the** RIGHT ARROW **key.**

Excel enters the number 58835.35 in cell B4 and changes the active cell to cell C4 (Figure 1-26).

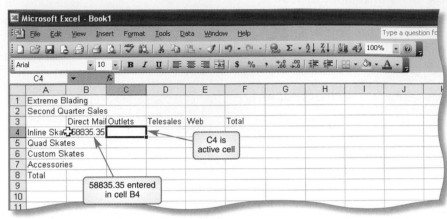

FIGURE 1-26

2

• **Enter** 97762.50 **in cell C4,** 71913.73 **in cell D4, and** 85367.37 **in cell E4.**

Row 4 now contains the second quarter sales by sales channel for the Inline Skates product group (Figure 1-27). The numbers in row 4 are right-aligned, which means Excel displays the cell entry to the far right in the cell.

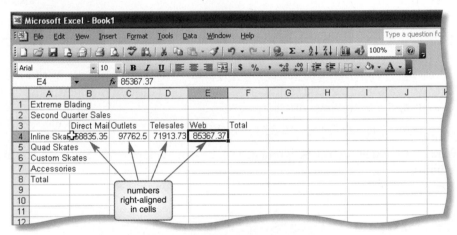

FIGURE 1-27

3

• **Click cell B5.**

• **Enter the remaining second quarter sales provided in Table 1-1 on the previous page for each of the three remaining product groups in rows 5, 6, and 7.**

Excel displays the second quarter sales as shown in Figure 1-28.

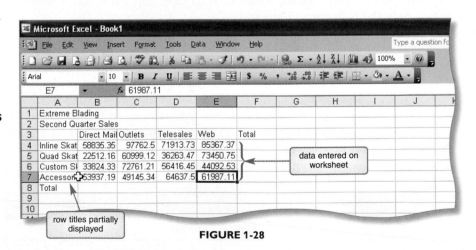

FIGURE 1-28

When the numbers are entered into the cells in column B, Excel only partially displays the row titles in column A. When the worksheet is formatted later in the project, the row titles will appear in their entirety.

Steps 1 through 3 complete the numeric entries. As shown in Figure 1-28, Excel does not display trailing zeros in cells C4 and D7. You are not required to type dollar signs, commas, or trailing zeros. When you enter a dollar value that has cents, however, you must add the decimal point and the numbers representing the cents. Later in this project, the numbers will be formatted to use dollar signs, commas, and trailing zeros to improve the appearance and readability of the numbers.

Calculating a Sum

The next step in creating the worksheet is to determine the total second quarter sales for the Direct Mail sales channel in column B. To calculate this value in cell B8, Excel must add, or sum, the numbers in cells B4, B5, B6, and B7. Excel's **SUM function**, which adds all of the numbers in a range of cells, provides a convenient means to accomplish this task.

A **range** is a series of two or more adjacent cells in a column or row or a rectangular group of cells. For example, the group of adjacent cells B4, B5, B6, and B7 is called a range. Many Excel operations, such as summing numbers, take place on a range of cells.

The following steps show how to sum the numbers in column B.

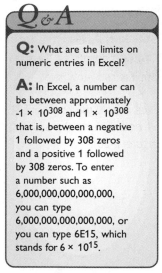

To Sum a Column of Numbers

1

• **Click cell B8.**

Cell B8 becomes the active cell (Figure 1-29).

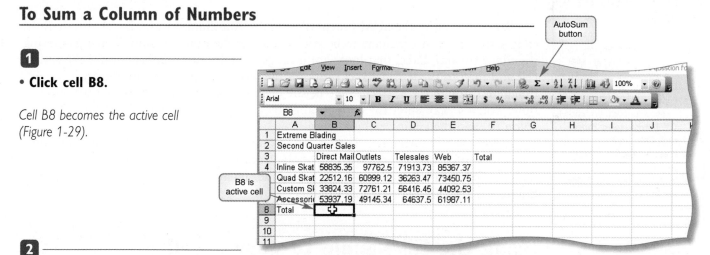

FIGURE 1-29

2

• **Click the AutoSum button on the Standard toolbar.**

Excel responds by displaying =SUM(B4:B7) in the formula bar and in the active cell B8 (Figure 1-30). Excel displays a ScreenTip below the active cell. The B4:B7 within parentheses following the function name SUM is Excel's way of identifying that the SUM function will add the numbers in the range B4 through B7. Excel also surrounds the proposed cells to sum with a moving border, called a **marquee***.*

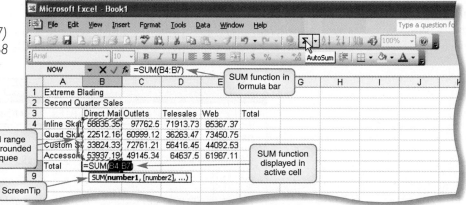

FIGURE 1-30

3

• **Click the AutoSum button a second time.**

Excel enters the sum of the second quarter sales for the Direct Mail sales channel in cell B8 (Figure 1-31). The SUM function assigned to cell B8 appears in the formula bar when cell B8 is the active cell.

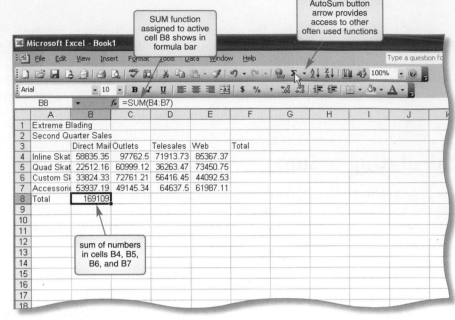

FIGURE 1-31

When you enter the SUM function using the AutoSum button, Excel automatically selects what it considers to be your choice of the range to sum. When proposing the range to sum, Excel first looks for a range of cells with numbers above the active cell and then to the left. If Excel proposes the wrong range, you can correct it by dragging through the correct range before clicking the AutoSum button a second time. You also can enter the correct range by typing the beginning cell reference, a colon (:), and the ending cell reference.

If you click the AutoSum button arrow on the right side of the AutoSum button, Excel displays a list of often used functions from which you can choose. The list includes functions that allow you to determine the average, the minimum value, or the maximum value of a range of numbers.

Using the Fill Handle to Copy a Cell to Adjacent Cells

Excel also must calculate the totals for Outlets in cell C8, Telesales in cell D8, and for Web in cell E8. Table 1-2 illustrates the similarities between the entry in cell B8 and the entries required to sum the totals in cells C8, D8, and E8.

Table 1-2 Sum Function Entries in Row 8		
CELL	**SUM FUNCTION ENTRIES**	**REMARK**
B8	=SUM(B4:B7)	Sums cells B4, B5, B6, and B7
C8	=SUM(C4:C7)	Sums cells C4, C5, C6, and C7
D8	=SUM(D4:D7)	Sums cells D4, D5, D6, and D7
E8	=SUM(E4:E7)	Sums cells E4, E5, E6, and E7

To place the SUM functions in cells C8, D8, and E8, follow the same steps shown previously in Figures 1-29 through 1-31. A second, more efficient method is to copy the SUM function from cell B8 to the range C8:E8. The cell being copied is called the **source area** or **copy area**. The range of cells receiving the copy is called the **destination area** or **paste area**.

Although the SUM function entries in Table 1-2 are similar, they are not exact copies. The range in each SUM function entry uses cell references that are one column to the right of the previous column. When you copy cell references, Excel automatically adjusts them for each new position, resulting in the SUM function entries illustrated in Table 1-2. Each adjusted cell reference is called a **relative reference**.

The easiest way to copy the SUM formula from cell B8 to cells C8, D8, and E8 is to use the fill handle. The **fill handle** is the small black square located in the lower-right corner of the heavy border around the active cell. The following steps show how to use the fill handle to copy cell B8 to the adjacent cells C8:E8.

To Copy a Cell to Adjacent Cells in a Row

1

• **With cell B8 active, point to the fill handle.**

The mouse pointer changes to a cross hair (Figure 1-32).

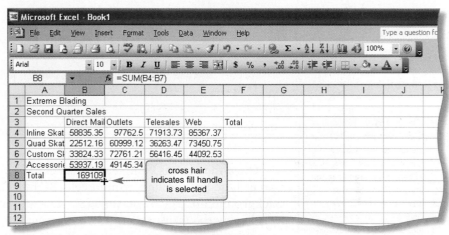

FIGURE 1-32

2

• **Drag the fill handle to select the destination area, range C8:E8. Do not release the mouse button.**

Excel displays a shaded border around the destination area, range C8:E8, and the source area, cell B8 (Figure 1-33).

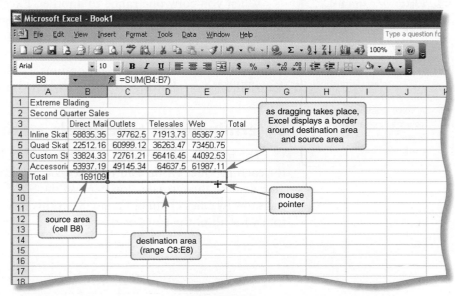

FIGURE 1-33

3

• **Release the mouse button.**

Excel copies the SUM function in cell B8 to the range C8:E8 (Figure 1-34). In addition, Excel calculates the sums and enters the results in cells C8, D8, and E8. The Auto Fill Options button appears to the right and below the destination area.

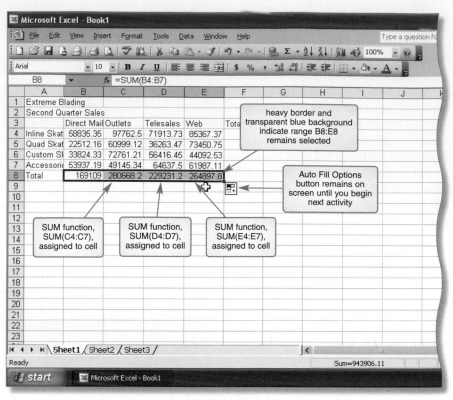

FIGURE 1-34

Once the copy is complete, Excel continues to display a heavy border and transparent blue background around cells B8:E8. The heavy border and transparent blue background are called **see-through view** and indicates a selected range. Excel does not display the transparent blue background around cell B8, the first cell in the range, because it is the active cell. If you click any cell, Excel will remove the heavy border and transparent blue background of the see-through view.

When you copy one range to another, Excel displays an Auto Fill Options button to the right and below the destination area (Figure 1-34). The Auto Fill Options button allows you to choose whether you want to copy the values from the source area to the destination area with formatting, without formatting, or only copy the format. To view the available fill options, click the Auto Fill Options button. The Auto Fill Options button disappears when you begin another activity.

Determining Multiple Totals at the Same Time

The next step in building the worksheet is to determine total second quarter sales for each product group and total second quarter sales for the company in column F. To calculate these totals, you can use the SUM function much as you used it to total the sales by sales channel in row 8. In this example, however, Excel will determine totals for all of the rows at the same time. The following steps illustrate this process.

To Determine Multiple Totals at the Same Time

1

• **Click cell F4.**

Cell F4 becomes the active cell (Figure 1-35).

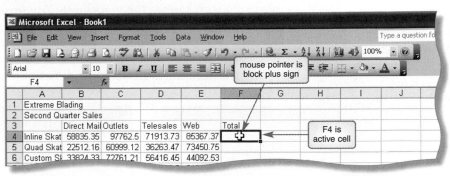

FIGURE 1-35

2

• **With the mouse pointer in cell F4 and in the shape of a block plus sign, drag the mouse pointer down to cell F8.**

Excel highlights the range F4:F8 with a see-through view (Figure 1-36).

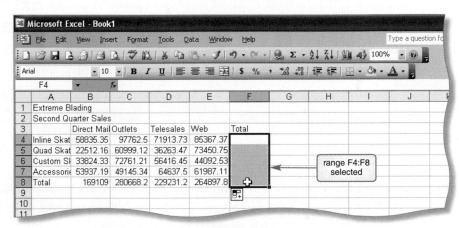

FIGURE 1-36

3

• **Click the AutoSum button on the Standard toolbar.**

Excel assigns the appropriate SUM functions to cells F4, F5, F6, F7, and F8, and then calculates and displays the sums in the respective cells (Figure 1-37).

4

• **Select cell A9 to deselect the range F4:F8.**

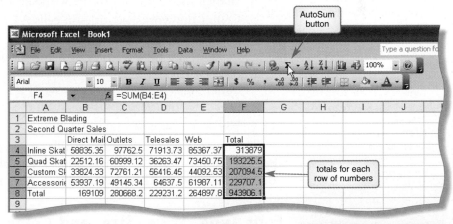

FIGURE 1-37

If each cell in a selected range is next to a row of numbers, Excel assigns the SUM function to each cell when you click the AutoSum button. Thus, as shown in the previous steps, each of the five cells in the selected range is assigned a SUM function with a different range, based on its row. This same procedure could have been used earlier to sum the columns. That is, instead of clicking cell B8, clicking the AutoSum button twice, and then copying the SUM function to the range C8:E8, the range B8:E8 could have been selected and then the AutoSum button clicked once, which would have assigned the SUM function to the entire range.

Formatting the Worksheet

The text, numeric entries, and functions for the worksheet now are complete. The next step is to format the worksheet. You **format** a worksheet to emphasize certain entries and make the worksheet easier to read and understand.

Figure 1-38a shows the worksheet before formatting. Figure 1-38b shows the worksheet after formatting. As you can see from the two figures, a worksheet that is formatted not only is easier to read, but also looks more professional.

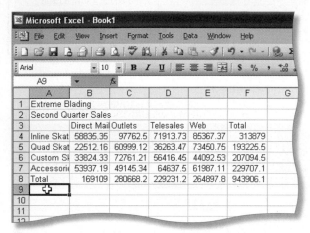

(a) Before Formatting   **(b) After Formatting**

FIGURE 1-38

To change the unformatted worksheet in Figure 1-38a to the formatted worksheet in Figure 1-38b, the following tasks must be completed:

1. Change the font type, change the font style to bold, increase the font size, and change the font color of the worksheet titles in cells A1 and A2.
2. Center the worksheet titles in cells A1 and A2 across columns A through F.
3. Format the body of the worksheet. The body of the worksheet, range A3:F8, includes the column titles, row titles, and numbers. Formatting the body of the worksheet changes the numbers to use a dollars-and-cents format, with dollar signs in the first row (row 4) and the total row (row 8); adds underlining that emphasizes portions of the worksheet; and modifies the column widths to make the text and numbers readable.

The remainder of this section explains the process required to format the worksheet. Although the format procedures are explained in the order described above, you should be aware that you can make these format changes in any order.

Font Type, Style, Size, and Color

The characters that Excel displays on the screen are a specific font type, style, size, and color. The **font type**, or font face, defines the appearance and shape of the letters, numbers, and special characters. Examples of font types include Times New Roman, Arial, and Courier. **Font style** indicates how the characters are formatted. Common font styles include regular, bold, underline, or italic. The **font size** specifies the size of the characters on the screen. Font size is gauged by a measurement system called points. A single point is about 1/72 of one inch in height. Thus, a character with a **point size** of 10 is about 10/72 of one inch in height. The **font color** defines the color of the characters. Excel can display characters in a wide variety of colors, including black, red, orange, and blue.

When Excel begins, the preset font type for the entire workbook is Arial, with a font size and font style of 10-point regular black. Excel allows you to change the font characteristics in a single cell, a range of cells, the entire worksheet, or the entire workbook.

Changing the Font Type

Different font types often are used in a worksheet to make it more appealing to the reader. The following steps show how to change the worksheet title font type from Arial to Arial Rounded MT Bold.

To Change the Font Type

1

• **Click cell A1 and then point to the Font box arrow on the Formatting toolbar.**

Cell A1 is the active cell (Figure 1-39).

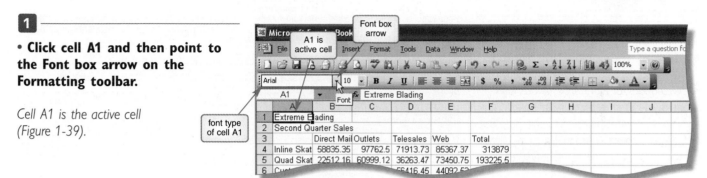

FIGURE 1-39

2

• **Click the Font box arrow and then point to Arial Rounded MT Bold.**

Excel displays the Font list with Arial Rounded MT Bold highlighted (Figure 1-40).

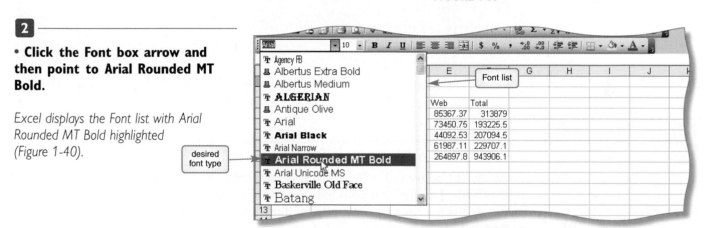

FIGURE 1-40

3

• **Click Arial Rounded MT Bold.**

Excel changes the font type of cell A1 from Arial to Arial Rounded MT Bold (Figure 1-41).

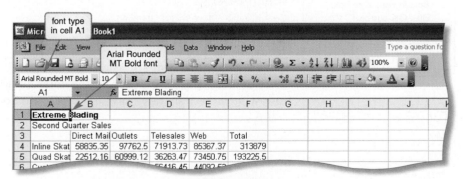

FIGURE 1-41

Because many applications supply additional font types beyond what comes with the Windows operating system, the number of font types available on your computer will depend on the applications installed. This book only uses font types that come with the Windows operating system.

Bolding a Cell

You **bold** an entry in a cell to emphasize it or make it stand out from the rest of the worksheet. The following step shows how to bold the worksheet title in cell A1.

To Bold a Cell

1

• **With cell A1 active, click the Bold button on the Formatting toolbar.**

Excel changes the font style of the worksheet title, Extreme Blading, to bold. With the mouse pointer pointing to the Bold button, Excel displays a ScreenTip immediately below the Bold button to identify the function of the button (Figure 1-42).

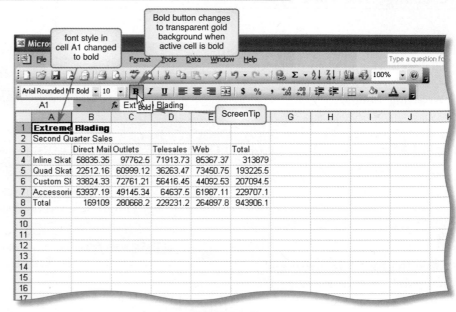

FIGURE 1-42

When the active cell is bold, Excel displays the Bold button on the Formatting toolbar with a transparent gold background (Figure 1-42). If you point to the Bold button and the active cell is already bold, then Excel displays the button with a transparent red background. Clicking the Bold button a second time removes the bold font style.

Increasing the Font Size

Increasing the font size is the next step in formatting the worksheet title. You increase the font size of a cell so the entry stands out and is easier to read. The following steps illustrate how to increase the font size of the worksheet title in cell A1.

To Increase the Font Size of a Cell Entry

1

• **With cell A1 selected, click the Font Size box arrow on the Formatting toolbar.**

Excel displays the Font Size list as shown in Figure 1-43.

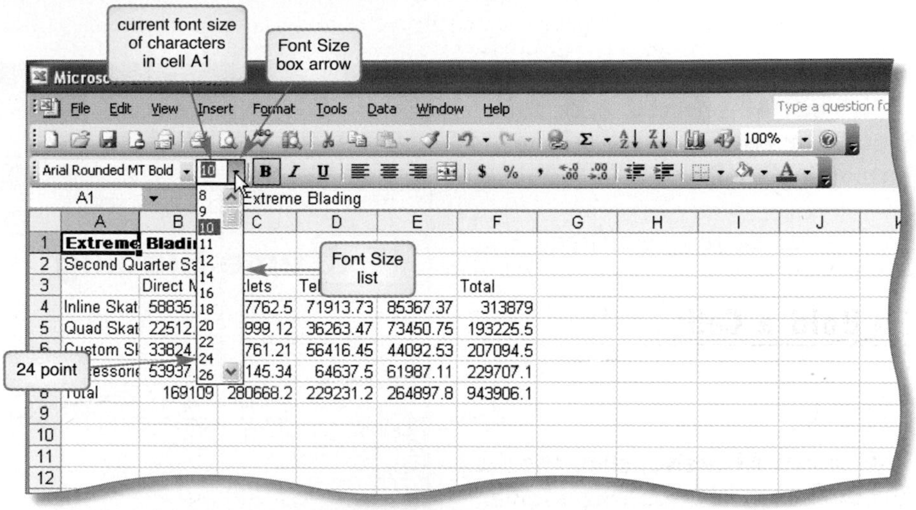

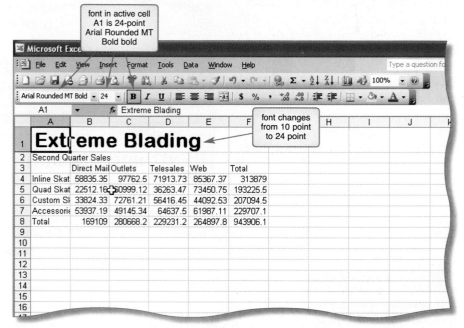

FIGURE 1-43

2

• **Click 24 in the Font Size list.**

The font size of the characters in cell A1 increase from 10 point to 24 point (Figure 1-44). The increased font size makes the worksheet title easier to read.

FIGURE 1-44

An alternative to clicking a font size in the Font Size list is to click the Font Size box, type the font size, and then press the ENTER key. This procedure allows you to assign a font size not available in the Font Size list to a selected cell entry. With cell A1 selected (Figure 1-44), the Font Size box shows that the new font size is 24 and the transparent gold Bold button shows that the font style is bold.

Changing the Font Color of a Cell Entry

The next step is to change the color of the font in cell A1 from black to violet. The steps on the next page show how to change the font color of a cell entry.

Other Ways

1. On Format menu click Cells, click Font tab, select font size in Size box, click OK button
2. Right-click cell, click Format Cells on shortcut menu, click Font tab, select font size in Size box, click OK button
3. In Voice Command mode, say "Font Size, [desired font size]"

To Change the Font Color of a Cell Entry

1

• **With cell A1 selected, click the Font Color button arrow on the Formatting toolbar.**

Excel displays the Font Color palette (Figure 1-45).

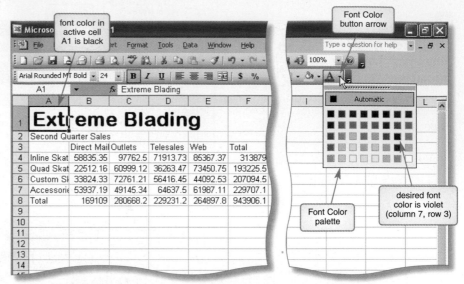

FIGURE 1-45

2

• **Click Violet (column 7, row 3) on the Font Color palette.**

The font in the worksheet title in cell A1 changes from black to violet (Figure 1-46).

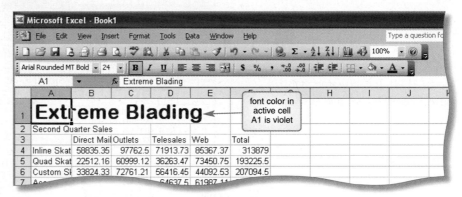

FIGURE 1-46

Other Ways

1. On Format menu click Cells, click Font tab, click Color box arrow, select color on Color palette, click OK button
2. Right-click cell, click Format Cells on shortcut menu, click Font tab, click Color box arrow, select color on Color palette, click OK button
3. In Voice Command mode, say "Font Color, [desired color]"

As shown in Figure 1-45, you can choose from 40 different font colors on the Font Color palette. Your Font Color palette may have more or fewer colors, depending on color settings of your operating system. When you choose a color on the Font Color palette, Excel changes the Font Color button on the Formatting toolbar to the chosen color. Thus, to change the font color of the cell entry in another cell to the same color, you only need to select the cell and then click the Font Color button.

Centering a Cell Entry across Columns by Merging Cells

The final step in formatting the worksheet title is to center it across columns A through F. Centering a worksheet title across the columns used in the body of the worksheet improves the worksheet's appearance. To do this, the six cells in the range A1:F1 are combined, or merged, into a single cell that is the width of the columns in the body of the worksheet. **Merging cells** involves creating a single cell by combining two or more selected cells. The following steps illustrate how to center the worksheet title across columns by merging cells.

To Center a Cell Entry across Columns by Merging Cells

1

• **With cell A1 selected, drag to cell F1.**

Excel highlights the selected cells (Figure 1-47).

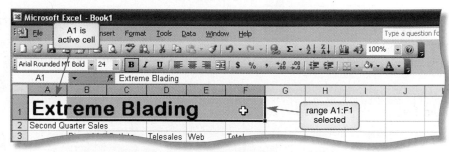

FIGURE 1-47

2

• **Click the Merge and Center button on the Formatting toolbar.**

Excel merges the cells A1 through F1 to create a new cell A1 and centers the contents of cell A1 across columns A through F (Figure 1-48). After the merge, cells B1 through F1 no longer exist on the worksheet.

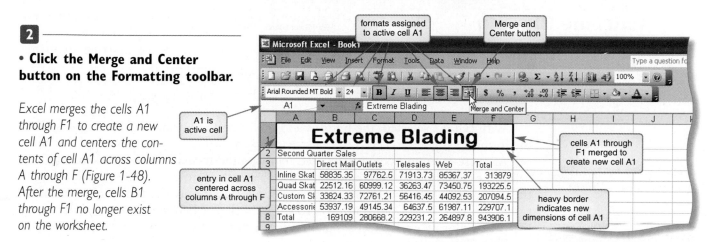

FIGURE 1-48

Other Ways

1. On Format menu click Cells, click Alignment tab, select Center in Horizontal list, click Merge cells check box, click OK button
2. Right-click cell, click Format Cells on shortcut menu, click Alignment tab, select Center in Horizontal list, click Merge cells check box, click OK button
3. In Voice Command mode, say "Merge and Center"

Excel not only centers the worksheet title across the range A1:F1, but it also merges cells A1 through F1 into one merged cell, cell A1. For the Merge and Center button to work properly, all the cells except the leftmost cell in the selected range must be empty.

The opposite of merging cells is **splitting a merged cell**. After you have merged multiple cells to create one merged cell, you can unmerge, or split, the merged cell to display the original cells on the worksheet. You split a merged cell by selecting it and clicking the Merge and Center button. For example, if you click the Merge and Center button a second time in Step 2, it will split the merged cell A1 to cells A1, B1, C1, D1, E1, and F1.

Most formats assigned to a cell will appear on the Formatting toolbar when the cell is selected. For example, with cell A1 selected in Figure 1-48, Excel displays the font type and font size of the active cell in their appropriate boxes. Transparent gold buttons on the Formatting toolbar indicate other assigned formatting. To determine if less frequently used formats are assigned to a cell, right-click the cell, click Format Cells on the shortcut menu, and then click each of the tabs in the Format Cells dialog box.

Formatting the Worksheet Subtitle

The worksheet subtitle in cell A2 is to be formatted the same as the worksheet title in cell A1, except that the font size should be 16 rather than 24. The steps on the next page show how to format the worksheet subtitle in cell A2.

To Format the Worksheet Subtitle

1 Select cell A2.

2 Click the Font box arrow on the Formatting toolbar and then click Arial Rounded MT Bold.

3 Click the Bold button on the Formatting toolbar.

4 Click the Font Size box arrow on the Formatting toolbar and then click 16.

5 Click the Font Color button on the Formatting toolbar.

6 Select the range A2:F2 and then click the Merge and Center button on the Formatting toolbar.

Excel displays the worksheet subtitle in cell A2 as shown in Figure 1-49.

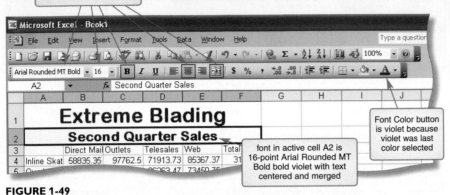

buttons and boxes on Formatting toolbar identify formats assigned to active cell A2

font in active cell A2 is 16-point Arial Rounded MT Bold bold violet with text centered and merged

Font Color button is violet because violet was last color selected

FIGURE 1-49

With cell A2 selected, the buttons and boxes on the Formatting toolbar describe the formats assigned to cell A2. The steps used to format the worksheet subtitle in cell A2 were the same as the steps used to assign the formats to the worksheet title in cell A1, except for the step that assigned violet as the font color. The step to change the font color of the worksheet subtitle in cell A2 used only the Font Color button, rather than the Font Color button arrow. Recall that, when you choose a color on the Font Color palette, Excel assigns the last font color used (in this case, violet) to the Font Color button.

Using AutoFormat to Format the Body of a Worksheet

Excel has customized autoformats that allow you to format the body of the worksheet to give it a professional look. An **autoformat** is a built-in collection of formats such as font style, font color, borders, and alignment, which you can apply to a range of cells. The following steps format the range A3:F8 using the AutoFormat command on the Format menu.

To Use AutoFormat to Format the Body of a Worksheet

1

• **Select cell A3, the upper-left corner cell of the rectangular range to format.**

• **Drag the mouse pointer to cell F8, the lower-right corner cell of the range to format.**

Excel highlights the range to format with a heavy border and transparent blue background (Figure 1-50).

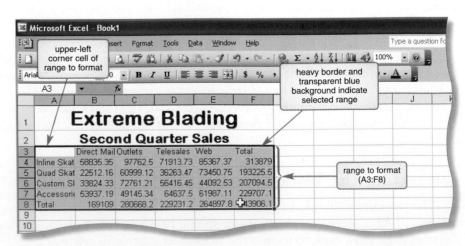

upper-left corner cell of range to format

heavy border and transparent blue background indicate selected range

range to format (A3:F8)

FIGURE 1-50

2

• **Click Format on the menu bar.**

Excel displays the Format menu (Figure 1-51).

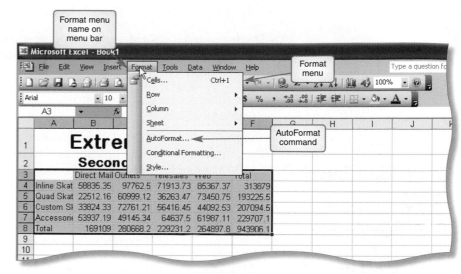

FIGURE 1-51

3

• **Click AutoFormat on the Format menu.**

• **When Excel displays the AutoFormat dialog box, click the Accounting 2 format.**

Excel displays the AutoFormat dialog box with a list of available autoformats (Figure 1-52). For each autoformat, Excel provides a sample to illustrate how the body of the worksheet will appear if that autoformat is chosen.

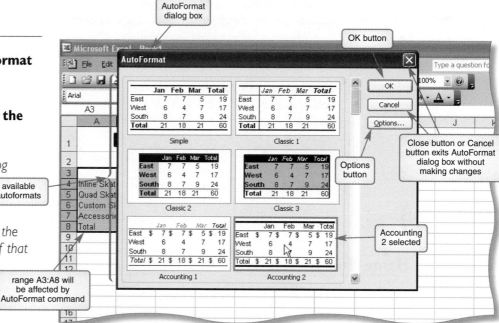

FIGURE 1-52

4

• **Click the OK button.**

• **Select cell A10 to deselect the range A3:F8.**

Excel displays the worksheet with the range A3:F8 formatted using the autoformat, Accounting 2 (Figure 1-53).

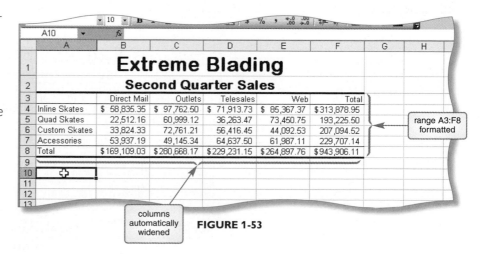

FIGURE 1-53

More About

Merging Table Formats

It is not uncommon to apply two or more of the table formats (Figure 1-52 on the previous page) to the same range. If you assign two table formats to a range, Excel does not remove the original format from the range; it simply adds the second table format to the first. Thus, if you decide to change a table format to another, select the table format None from the bottom of the list to clear the first table format.

More About

Navigation

For more information about selecting cells that contain certain entries, such as constants or formulas, visit the Excel 2003 More About Web page (scsite.com/ex2003/more) and click Using Go To Special.

The formats associated with the autoformat Accounting 2 include right-aligned column titles; numbers displayed as dollars and cents with comma separators; numbers aligned on the decimal point; the first row and total row of numbers displayed with dollar signs; and top and bottom rows displayed with borders. The width of column A has been increased so the longest row title in cell A6, Custom Skates, just fits in the column. The widths of columns B through F also have been increased so that the formatted numbers will fit in the cells.

The AutoFormat dialog box shown in Figure 1-52 on the previous page includes 17 autoformats and four buttons. Use the vertical scroll bar in the dialog box to view the autoformats that are not displayed when the dialog box first opens. Each one of these autoformats offers a different look. The one you choose depends on the worksheet you are creating. The last autoformat in the list, called None, removes all formats.

The four buttons in the AutoFormat dialog box allow you to complete the entries, modify an autoformat, or cancel changes and close the dialog box. The Close button on the title bar and the Cancel button both terminate the current activity and close the AutoFormat dialog box without making changes. The Options button allows you to deselect formats, such as fonts or borders, within an autoformat.

The worksheet now is complete. The next step is to chart the second quarter sales for the four product groups by sales channel. To create the chart, you must select the cell in the upper-left corner of the range to chart (cell A3). Rather than clicking cell A3 to select it, the next section describes how to use the Name box to select the cell.

Using the Name Box to Select a Cell

As previously noted, the Name box is located on the left side of the formula bar. To select any cell, click the Name box and enter the cell reference of the cell you want to select. The following steps show how to select cell A3.

To Use the Name Box to Select a Cell

1

• **Click the Name box in the formula bar and then type** a3 **as the cell to select.**

Even though cell A10 is the active cell, Excel displays the typed cell reference a3 in the Name box (Figure 1-54).

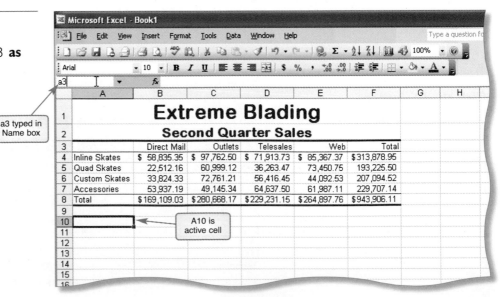

FIGURE 1-54

2

• **Press the ENTER key.**

Excel changes the active cell from cell A10 to cell A3 (Figure 1-55).

A3 is active cell

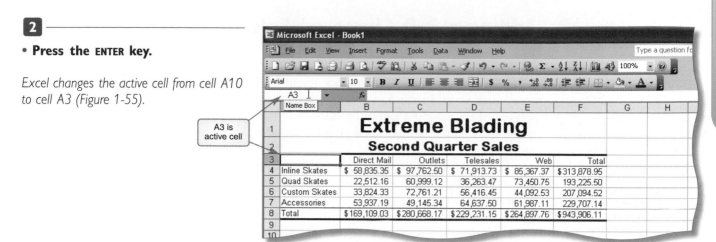

FIGURE 1-55

As you will see in later projects, in addition to using the Name box to select any cell in a worksheet, you also can use it to assign names to a cell or range of cells. Excel supports several additional ways to select a cell, as summarized in Table 1-3.

Table 1-3 Selecting Cells in Excel	
KEY, BOX, OR COMMAND	**FUNCTION**
ALT+PAGE DOWN	Selects the cell one worksheet window to the right and moves the worksheet window accordingly.
ALT+PAGE UP	Selects the cell one worksheet window to the left and moves the worksheet window accordingly.
ARROW	Selects the adjacent cell in the direction of the arrow on the key.
CTRL+ARROW	Selects the border cell of the worksheet in combination with the arrow keys and moves the worksheet window accordingly. For example, to select the rightmost cell in the row that contains the active cell, press CTRL+RIGHT ARROW. You also can press the END key, release it, and then press the appropriate arrow key to accomplish the same task.
CTRL+HOME	Selects cell A1 or the cell one column and one row below and to the right of frozen titles and moves the worksheet window accordingly.
Find command on Edit menu or SHIFT+F5	Finds and selects a cell that contains specific contents that you enter in the Find dialog box. If necessary, Excel moves the worksheet window to display the cell. You also can press CTRL+F to display the Find dialog box.
Go To command on Edit menu or F5	Selects the cell that corresponds to the cell reference you enter in the Go To dialog box and moves the worksheet window accordingly. You also can press CTRL+G to display the Go To dialog box.
HOME	Selects the cell at the beginning of the row that contains the active cell and moves the worksheet window accordingly.
Name box	Selects the cell in the workbook that corresponds to the cell reference you enter in the Name box.
PAGE DOWN	Selects the cell down one worksheet window from the active cell and moves the worksheet window accordingly.
PAGE UP	Selects the cell up one worksheet window from the active cell and moves the worksheet window accordingly.

Adding a 3-D Clustered Column Chart to the Worksheet

As outlined in the requirements document in Figure 1-2 on page EX 6, the worksheet should include a 3-D Clustered column chart to graphically represent sales for each product group by sales channel. The 3-D Clustered column chart shown in Figure 1-56 is called an **embedded chart** because it is drawn on the same worksheet as the data.

The chart uses different colored columns to represent sales for different product groups. For the Direct Mail sales channel, for example, the light blue column represents the second quarter sales for the Inline Skates product group ($58,835.35); for the Outlets sales channel, the purple column represents the second quarter sales for Quad Skates ($60,999.12); for the Telesales sales channel, the light yellow column represents the second quarter sales for Custom Skates ($56,416.45); and for the Web sales channel, the turquoise column represents the second quarter sales for Accessories ($61,987.11). For the Outlets, Telesales, and Web sales channels, the columns follow the same color scheme to represent the comparable second quarter sales. The totals from the worksheet are not represented because the totals are not in the range specified for charting.

Excel derives the chart scale based the values in the worksheet and then displays the scale along the vertical axis (also called the **y-axis** or **value axis**) of the chart. For example, no value in the range B4:E7 is less than 0 or greater than $100,000.00, so the scale ranges from 0 to $100,000.00. Excel also determines the $20,000.00 increments of the scale automatically. For the numbers along the y-axis, Excel uses a format that includes representing the 0 value with a dash (Figure 1-56).

Q&A

Q: If I change a cell value on which the chart is dependent, will Excel redraw the chart?

A: Yes. Excel redraws the chart instantaneously, unless automatic recalculation is disabled. If automatic recalculation is disabled, then you must press function key F9 to redraw the chart. To enable or disable automatic recalculation, invoke the Options command on the Tools menu and click the Calculation tab.

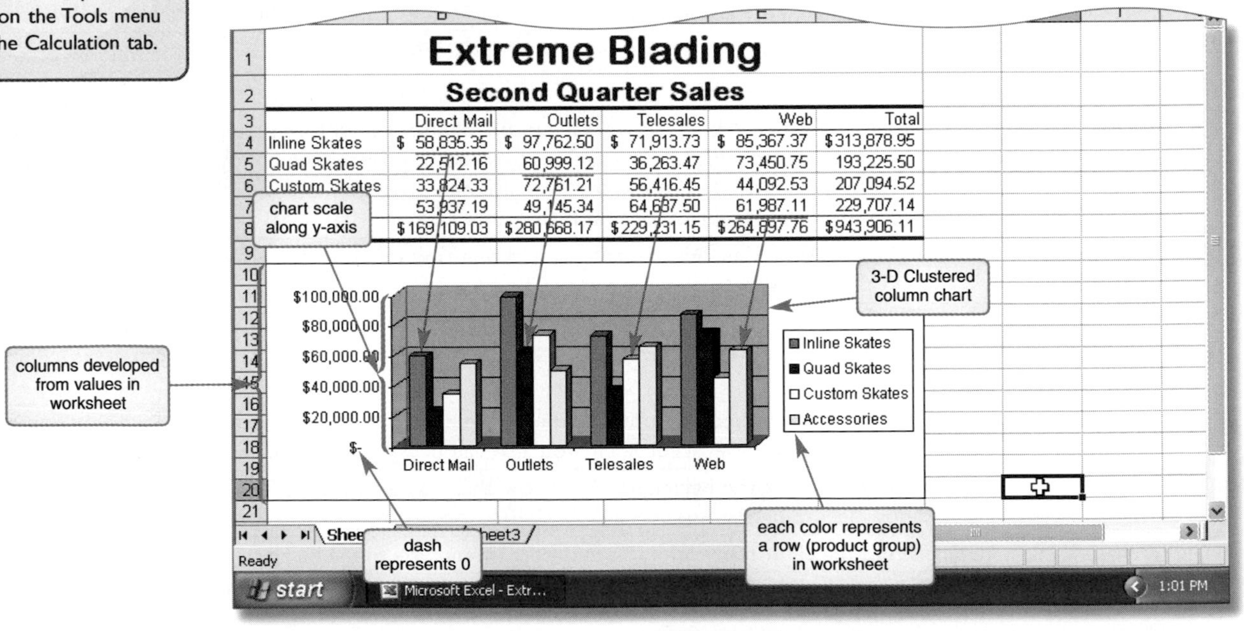

FIGURE 1-56

With the range to chart selected, you click the Chart Wizard button on the Standard toolbar to initiate drawing the chart. The area on the worksheet where the chart appears is called the **chart location**. As shown in Figure 1-56, the chart location in this worksheet is the range A10:F20, immediately below the worksheet data.

The following steps show how to draw a 3-D Clustered column chart that compares the second quarter sales by product group for the four sales channels.

To Add a 3-D Clustered Column Chart to the Worksheet

1

• **With cell A3 selected, position the block plus sign mouse pointer within the cell's border and drag the mouse pointer to the lower-right corner cell (cell E7) of the range to chart (A3:E7).**

Excel highlights the range to chart (Figure 1-57).

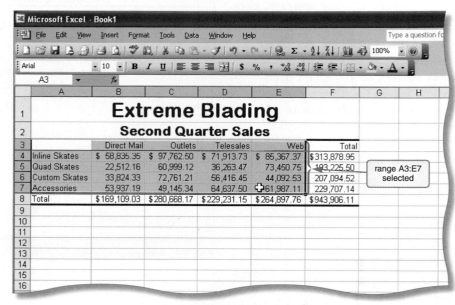

FIGURE 1-57

2

• **Click the Chart Wizard button on the Standard toolbar.**

• **When Excel displays the Chart Wizard - Step 1 of 4 - Chart Type dialog box, and with Column selected in the Chart type list, click Clustered column with a 3-D visual effect (column 1, row 2) in the Chart sub-type area.**

Excel displays the Chart Wizard - Step 1 of 4 - Chart Type dialog box as shown in Figure 1-58.

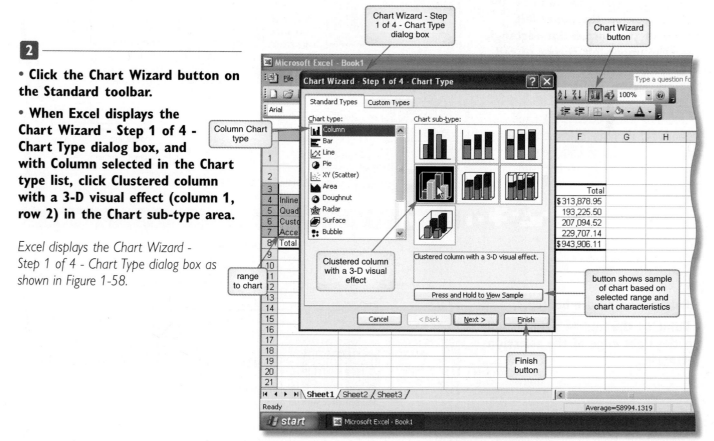

FIGURE 1-58

3

- **Click the Finish button.**

- **If the Chart toolbar appears, click its Close button.**

- **When Excel displays the chart, point to an open area in the lower-right section of the chart area so the ScreenTip, Chart Area, appears next to the mouse pointer.**

Excel draws the 3-D Clustered column chart (Figure 1-59). The chart appears in the middle of the worksheet window in a selection rectangle. The small sizing handles at the corners and along the sides of the selection rectangle indicate the chart is selected.

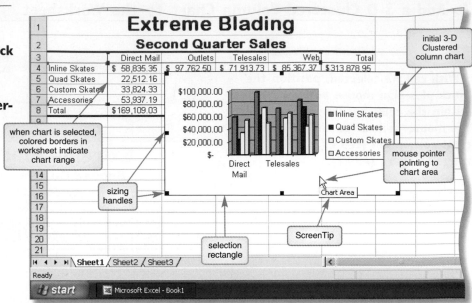

FIGURE 1-59

4

- **Drag the chart down and to the left to position the upper-left corner of the dotted line rectangle over the upper-left corner of cell A10. Do not release the mouse button (Figure 1-60).**

As you drag the selected chart, Excel displays a dotted line rectangle showing the new chart location and the mouse pointer changes to a cross hair with four arrowheads.

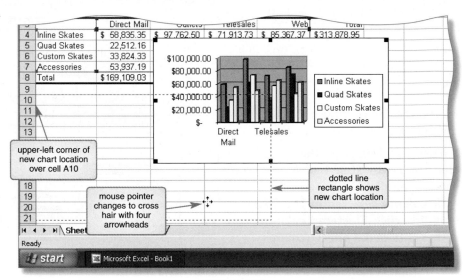

FIGURE 1-60

5

- **Release the mouse button.**

- **Point to the middle sizing handle on the right edge of the selection rectangle.**

The chart appears in a new location (Figure 1-61). The mouse pointer changes to a horizontal line with two arrowheads when it points to a sizing handle.

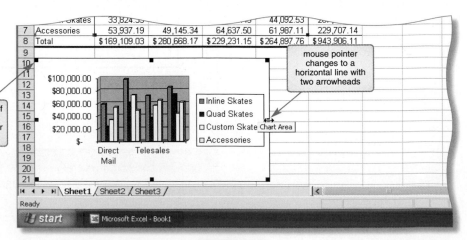

FIGURE 1-61

6

• **While holding down the ALT key, drag the sizing handle to the right edge of column F.**

While you drag, the dotted line rectangle shows the new chart location (Figure 1-62). Holding down the ALT key while you drag a chart **snaps** *(aligns) the edge of the chart area to the worksheet gridlines.*

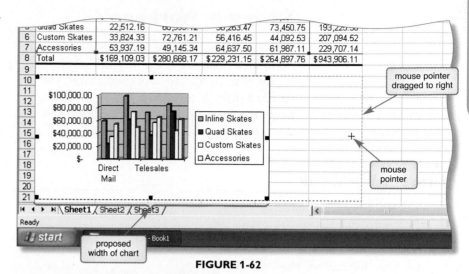

FIGURE 1-62

7

• **If necessary, hold down the ALT key and drag the lower-middle sizing handle up to the bottom border of row 20.**

• **Click cell H20 to deselect the chart.**

The new chart location extends from the top of cell A10 to the bottom of cell F20 (Figure 1-63).

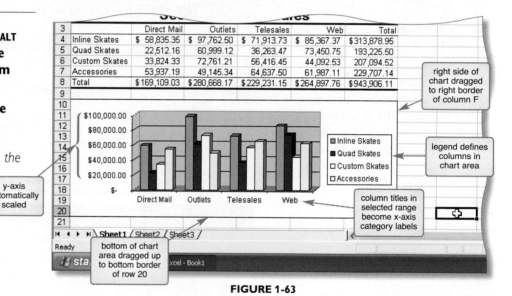

FIGURE 1-63

The embedded 3-D Clustered column chart in Figure 1-63 compares the second quarter sales for the four product groups by each sales channel. It also allows you to compare second quarter sales for the four product groups among the sales channels.

Excel automatically selects the entries in the topmost row of the chart range (row 3) as the titles for the horizontal axis (also called the **x-axis** or **category axis**) and draws a column for each of the 16 cells in the range containing numbers. The small box to the right of the column chart in Figure 1-63 contains the **legend**, which identifies the colors assigned to each bar in the chart. Excel automatically selects the entries in the leftmost column of the chart range (column A) as titles within the legend. As indicated earlier, Excel also automatically derives the chart scale on the y-axis based on the highest and lowest numbers in the chart range.

Excel offers 14 different chart types (Figure 1-58 on page EX 39). The **default chart type** is the chart Excel draws if you click the Finish button in the first Chart Wizard dialog box. When you install Excel on a computer, the default chart type is the 2-D (two-dimensional) Column chart.

Other Ways

1. On Insert menu click Chart
2. Press F11
3. In Voice Command mode, say "Chart Wizard"

More About

Printing Only the Chart

To print the embedded chart without printing the worksheet, select the chart, click File on the menu bar, click Page Setup, click the Chart tab, click the Scale to fit page in the Printed chart size area, click the Print button, and then click the OK button.

Saving a Workbook

While you are building a workbook, the computer stores it in memory. If the computer is turned off or if you lose electrical power, the workbook is lost. Hence, if you plan to use the workbook later, you must save the workbook on a floppy disk or hard disk. A saved workbook is referred to as a **file**. The following steps illustrate how to save a workbook on a floppy disk in drive A using the Save button on the Standard toolbar.

To Save a Workbook

 1

• **With a floppy disk in drive A, click the Save button on the Standard toolbar.**

Excel displays the Save As dialog box (Figure 1-64). The default Save in folder is Documents (your Save in folder may be different), the default file name is Book1, and the default file type is Microsoft Office Excel Workbook.

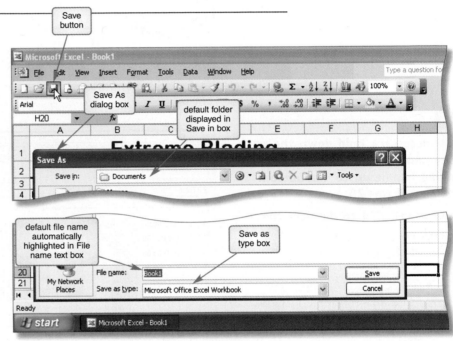

FIGURE 1-64

2

• **Type** Extreme Blading 2nd Quarter Sales **in the File name text box.**

• **Click the Save in box arrow.**

The new file name replaces Book1 in the File name text box (Figure 1-65). A file name can be up to 255 characters and can include spaces. Excel displays a list of available drives and folders.

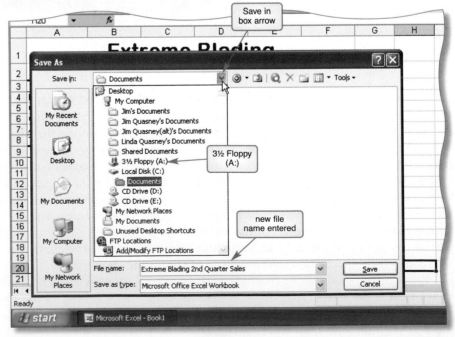

FIGURE 1-65

3

• **Click 3½ Floppy (A:) in the Save in list.**

Drive A becomes the selected drive (Figure 1-66). The buttons on the top and on the side of the dialog box are used to select folders, change the appearance of file names, and complete other tasks.

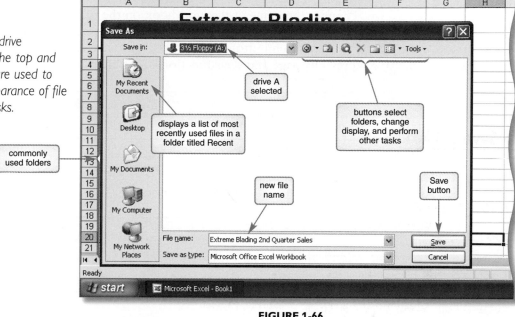

FIGURE 1-66

4

• **Click the Save button in the Save As dialog box.**

Excel saves the workbook on the floppy disk in drive A using the file name, Extreme Blading 2nd Quarter Sales. Excel automatically appends the extension .xls to the file name you entered in Step 2, which stands for Excel workbook. Although the workbook is saved on a floppy disk, it also remains in memory and is displayed on the screen (Figure 1-67). Excel displays the new file name on the title bar.

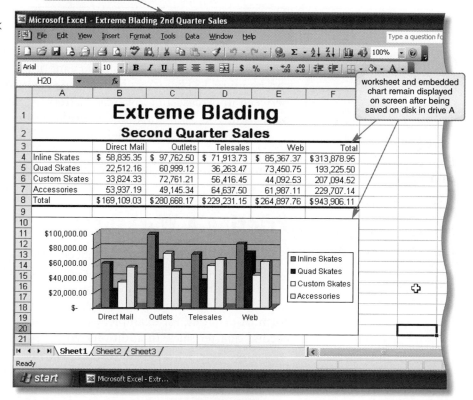

FIGURE 1-67

Other Ways

1. On File menu click Save As, type file name, select drive or folder, click Save button
2. Right-click workbook Control-menu icon on menu bar, click Save As on shortcut menu, type file name, select drive or folder, click Save button
3. Press CTRL+S, type file name, select drive or folder, click Save button
4. In Voice Command mode, say "File, Save As", [type desired file name], say "Save"

While Excel is saving the workbook, it momentarily changes the word Ready on the status bar to Saving. It also displays a horizontal bar on the status bar indicating the amount of the workbook saved. After the save operation is complete, Excel changes the name of the workbook on the title bar from Book1 to Extreme Blading 2nd Quarter Sales (Figure 1-67 on the previous page).

The seven buttons at the top of the Save As dialog box in Figure 1-66 on the previous page and their functions are summarized in Table 1-4.

Table 1-4 Save As Dialog Box Toolbar Buttons		
BUTTON	**BUTTON NAME**	**FUNCTION**
	Default File Location	Displays contents of default file location
	Up One Level	Displays contents of folder one level up from current folder
	Search the Web	Starts browser and displays search engine
	Delete	Deletes selected file or folder
	Create New Folder	Creates new folder
	Views	Changes view of files and folders
Tools ▾	Tools	Lists commands to print or modify file names and folders

When you click the Tools button in the Save As dialog box, Excel displays the Tools menu. The General Options command on the menu allows you to save a backup copy of the workbook, create a password to limit access to the workbook, and carry out other functions that are discussed later. Saving a **backup copy** of the workbook means that each time you save a workbook, Excel copies the current version of the workbook on disk to a file with the same name, but with the words, Backup of, appended to the front of the file name. In the case of a power failure or some other problem, you can use the backup copy to restore your work.

You also can use the General Options command on the Tools menu to assign a password to a workbook so others cannot open it. A password is case-sensitive and can be up to 15 characters long. **Case-sensitive** means Excel can differentiate between uppercase and lowercase letters. If you assign a password and forget the password, you cannot access the workbook.

The five buttons on the left of the Save As dialog box in Figure 1-66 allow you to select frequently used folders. The My Recent Documents button displays a list of shortcuts (pointers) to the most recently used files in a folder titled Recent.

Printing a Worksheet

Once you have created the worksheet, you might want to print it. A printed version of the worksheet is called a **hard copy** or **printout**.

You might want a printout for several reasons. First, to present the worksheet and chart to someone who does not have access to a computer, it must be in printed form. A printout, for example, can be handed out in a management meeting about second quarter sales. In addition, worksheets and charts often are kept for reference by people other than those who prepare them. In many cases, worksheets and charts are printed and kept in binders for use by others. The following steps illustrate how to print the worksheet.

More About

Saving

Excel allows you to save a workbook in more than 30 different file formats. Choose the file format by clicking the Save as type box arrow at the bottom of the Save As dialog box (Figure 1-66). Microsoft Office Excel Workbook is the default file format.

To Print a Worksheet

1

• **Ready the printer according to the printer instructions and then click the Print button on the Standard toolbar (Figure 1-68).**

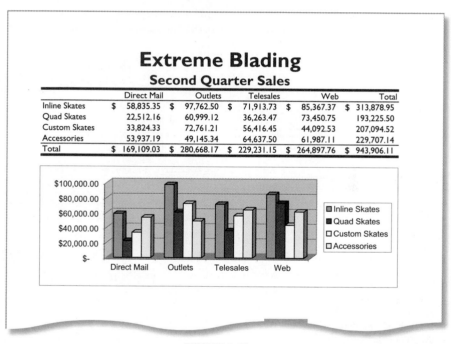

FIGURE 1-68

2

• **When the printer stops printing the worksheet and the chart, retrieve the printout.**

Excel sends the worksheet to the printer, which prints it (Figure 1-69).

Extreme Blading
Second Quarter Sales

	Direct Mail	Outlets	Telesales	Web	Total
Inline Skates	$ 58,835.35	$ 97,762.50	$ 71,913.73	$ 85,367.37	$ 313,878.95
Quad Skates	22,512.16	60,999.12	36,263.47	73,450.75	193,225.50
Custom Skates	33,824.33	72,761.21	56,416.45	44,092.53	207,094.52
Accessories	53,937.19	49,145.34	64,637.50	61,987.11	229,707.14
Total	$ 169,109.03	$ 280,668.17	$ 229,231.15	$ 264,897.76	$ 943,906.11

FIGURE 1-69

Prior to clicking the Print button, you can select which columns and rows in the worksheet to print. The range of cells you choose to print is called the **print area**. If you do not select a print area, as was the case in the previous set of steps, Excel automatically selects a print area on the basis of used cells. As you will see in future projects, Excel has many different print options, such as allowing you to preview the printout on the screen to see if the printout is satisfactory before sending it to the printer.

Other Ways

1. On File menu click Print, click OK button
2. Right-click workbook Control-menu icon on menu bar, click Print on shortcut menu, click OK button
3. Press CTRL+P, click OK button
4. In Voice Command mode, say "Print"

Quitting Excel

The Project 1 worksheet and embedded chart are complete. The following steps show how to quit Excel.

To Quit Excel

1

• **Point to the Close button on the right side of the title bar (Figure 1-70).**

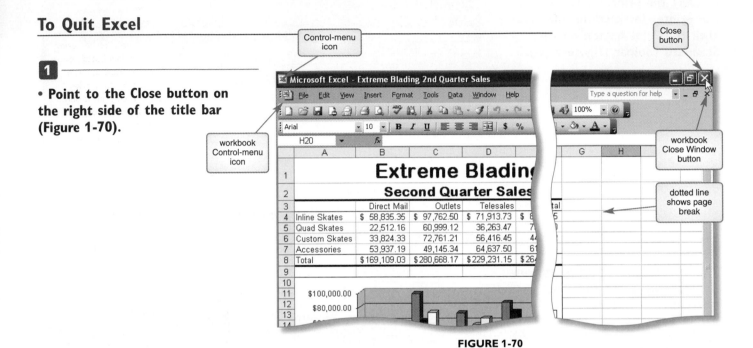

FIGURE 1-70

2

• **Click the Close button.**

If the worksheet was changed or printed, the Microsoft Excel dialog box displays the question, Do you want to save the changes you made to 'Extreme Blading 2nd Quarter Sales.xls'? (Figure 1-71). Clicking the Yes button saves the changes before quitting Excel. Clicking the No button quits Excel without saving the changes. Clicking the Cancel button closes the dialog box and returns control to the worksheet without saving the changes.

3

• **Click the No button.**

Other Ways

1. On File menu click Exit
2. Right-click Microsoft Excel button on taskbar, click Close on shortcut menu
3. Double-click Control-menu icon
4. In Voice Command mode, say "File, Exit"

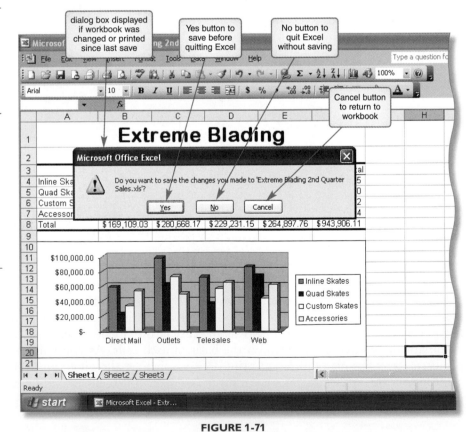

FIGURE 1-71

In Figure 1-70, you can see that the Excel window includes two Close buttons and two Control-menu icons. The Close button and Control-menu icon on the title bar can be used to quit Excel. The Close Window button and Control-menu icon on the menu bar can be used to close the workbook, but not to quit Excel.

Starting Excel and Opening a Workbook

After creating and saving a workbook, you often will have reason to retrieve it from a floppy disk. For example, you might want to review the calculations on the worksheet and enter additional or revised data. The following steps assume Excel is not running.

To Start Excel and Open a Workbook

1

- **With your floppy disk in drive A, click the Start button on the Windows taskbar, point to All Programs on the Start menu, point to Microsoft Office on the All Programs submenu, and then click Microsoft Office Excel 2003 on the Microsoft Office submenu.**

Excel starts. The Getting Started task pane lists the four most recently used files in the Open area (Figure 1-72).

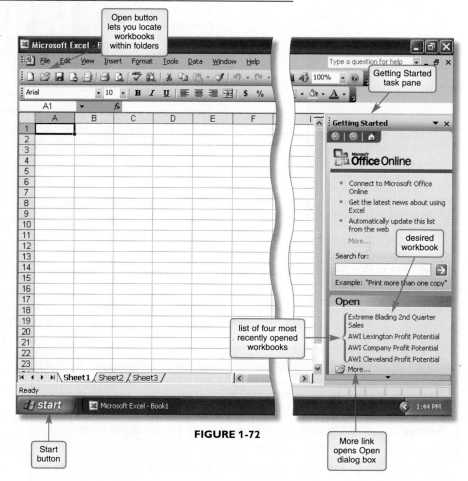

FIGURE 1-72

2

• **Click Extreme Blading 2nd Quarter Sales in the Open area in the Getting Started task pane.**

Excel opens the workbook Extreme Blading 2nd Quarter Sales (Figure 1-73). The Getting Started task pane closes.

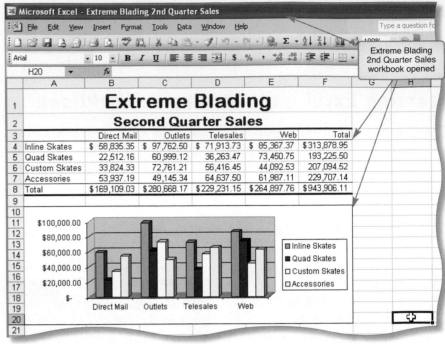

FIGURE 1-73

Other Ways

1. Click Start button, point to All Programs on Start menu, click Open Office Document on All Programs submenu, select drive A, double-click file name
2. Right-click Start button, click Explore on shortcut menu, display contents of drive A, double-click file name
3. With Excel active, in Voice Command mode, say "Open", [select file name], say "Open"

If you want to open a workbook other than one of the four most recently opened ones, click the Open button on the Standard toolbar or the More link in the Getting Started task pane. Clicking the Open button or the More link displays the Open dialog box, which allows you to navigate to a workbook stored on disk.

AutoCalculate

You easily can obtain a total, an average, or other information about the numbers in a range by using the **AutoCalculate area** on the status bar. First, select the range of cells containing the numbers you want to check. Next, right-click the AutoCalculate area to display the shortcut menu (Figure 1-74). The check mark to the left of the active function (Sum) indicates that the sum of the selected range is displayed in the AutoCalculate area on the status bar. The function of the commands on the AutoCalculate shortcut menu are described in Table 1-5.

The following steps show how to display the average second quarter sales for the Custom Skates product group.

Table 1-5 AutoCalculate Shortcut Menu Commands

COMMAND	FUNCTION
None	No value is displayed in the AutoCalculate area
Average	AutoCalculate area displays the average of the numbers in the selected range
Count	AutoCalculate area displays the number of nonblank cells in the selected range
Count Nums	AutoCalculate area displays the number of cells containing numbers in the selected range
Max	AutoCalculate area displays the highest value in the selected range
Min	AutoCalculate area displays the lowest value in the selected range
Sum	AutoCalculate area displays the sum of the numbers in the selected range

To Use the AutoCalculate Area to Determine an Average

1

• **Select the range B6:E6 and then right-click the AutoCalculate area on the status bar.**

The sum of the numbers in the range B6:E6 is displayed (207,094.52) in the AutoCalculate area, because Sum is the active function (Figure 1-74). Excel displays a shortcut menu listing the other available functions above the AutoCalculate area. If another function is active on your shortcut menu, you may see a different value in the AutoCalculate area.

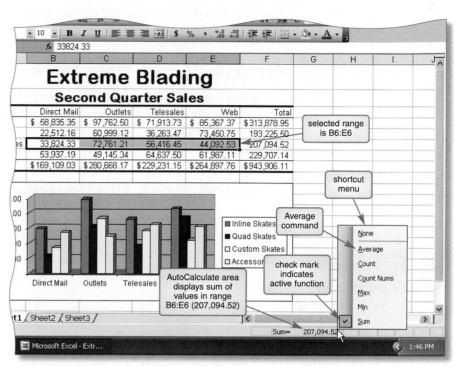

FIGURE 1-74

2

• **Click Average on the shortcut menu.**

Excel displays the average of the numbers in the range B6:E6 (51,773.63) in the AutoCalculate area (Figure 1-75).

3

• **Right-click the AutoCalculate area and then click Sum on the shortcut menu.**

The AutoCalculate area displays the sum as shown earlier in Figure 1-74.

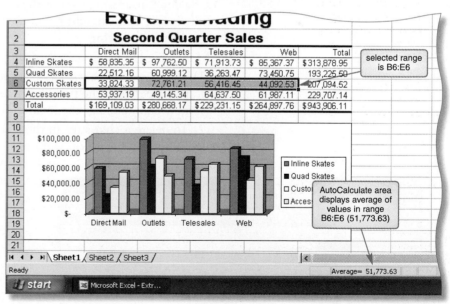

FIGURE 1-75

To change to any one of the other five functions for the range B6:E6, right-click the AutoCalculate area and then click the desired function. Clicking None at the top of the AutoCalculate shortcut menu in Figure 1-74 turns off the AutoCalculate area. Thus, if you select None, then no value will be displayed in the AutoCalculate area when you select a range.

More About

Shortcut Menus

Shortcut menus contain the most frequently used commands that relate to the object to which the mouse pointer is pointing.

Correcting Errors

You can correct errors on a worksheet using one of several methods. The method you choose will depend on the extent of the error and whether you notice it while typing the data or after you have entered the incorrect data into the cell.

Correcting Errors While You Are Typing Data into a Cell

If you notice an error while you are typing data into a cell, press the BACKSPACE key to erase the incorrect characters and then type the correct characters. If the error is a major one, click the Cancel box in the formula bar or press the ESC key to erase the entire entry and then reenter the data from the beginning.

Correcting Errors After Entering Data into a Cell

If you find an error in the worksheet after entering the data, you can correct the error in one of two ways:

1. If the entry is short, select the cell, retype the entry correctly, and then click the Enter box or press the ENTER key. The new entry will replace the old entry.

2. If the entry in the cell is long and the errors are minor, using Edit mode may be a better choice than retyping the cell entry. Use the Edit mode as described below.

   a. Double-click the cell containing the error to switch Excel to Edit mode. In **Edit mode**, Excel displays the active cell entry in the formula bar and a flashing insertion point in the active cell (Figure 1-76). With Excel in Edit mode, you can edit the contents directly in the cell — a procedure called **in-cell editing**.

   b. Make changes using in-cell editing, as indicated below.

      (1) To insert new characters between two characters, place the insertion point between the two characters and begin typing. Excel inserts the new characters at the location of the insertion point.

      (2) To delete a character in the cell, move the insertion point to the left of the character you want to delete and then press the DELETE key or place the insertion point to the right of the character you want to delete and then press the BACKSPACE key. You also can use the mouse to drag through the character or adjacent characters you want to delete and then press the DELETE key or click the Cut button on the Standard toolbar.

      (3) When you are finished editing an entry, click the Enter box or press the ENTER key.

More About

In-Cell Editing

An alternative to double-clicking the cell to edit is to select the cell and then press F2.

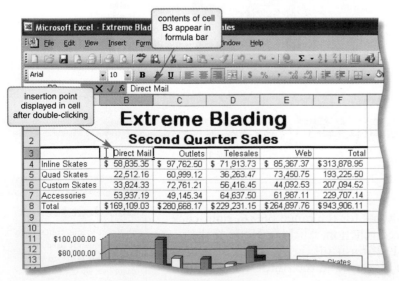

FIGURE 1-76

When Excel enters the Edit mode, the keyboard usually is in Insert mode. In **Insert mode**, as you type a character, Excel inserts the character and moves all characters to the right of the typed character one position to the right. You can change to Overtype mode by pressing the INSERT key. In **Overtype mode**, Excel overtypes, or replaces, the character to the right of the insertion point. The INSERT key toggles the keyboard between Insert mode and Overtype mode.

While in Edit mode, you may have reason to move the insertion point to various points in the cell, select portions of the data in the cell, or switch from inserting characters to overtyping characters. Table 1-6 summarizes the more common tasks used during in-cell editing.

More About

Editing the Contents of a Cell

Rather than using in-cell editing, you can select the cell and then click the formula bar to edit the contents.

Table 1-6   Summary of In-Cell Editing Tasks

	TASK	MOUSE	KEYBOARD
1	Move the insertion point to the beginning of data in a cell.	Point to the left of the first character and click.	Press HOME
2	Move the insertion point to the end of data in a cell.	Point to the right of the last character and click.	Press END
3	Move the insertion point anywhere in a cell.	Point to the appropriate position and click the character.	Press RIGHT ARROW or LEFT ARROW
4	Highlight one or more adjacent characters.	Drag the mouse pointer through adjacent characters.	Press SHIFT+RIGHT ARROW or SHIFT+LEFT ARROW
5	Select all data in a cell.	Double-click the cell with the insertion point in the cell.	
6	Delete selected characters.	Click the Cut button on the Standard toolbar.	Press DELETE
7	Delete characters to the left of the insertion point.		Press BACKSPACE
8	Toggle between Insert and Overtype modes.		Press INSERT

Undoing the Last Cell Entry

Excel provides the Undo command on the Edit menu and the Undo button on the Standard toolbar (Figure 1-77), both of which allow you to erase recent cell entries. Thus, if you enter incorrect data in a cell and notice it immediately, click the Undo command or Undo button and Excel changes the cell entry to what it was prior to the incorrect data entry.

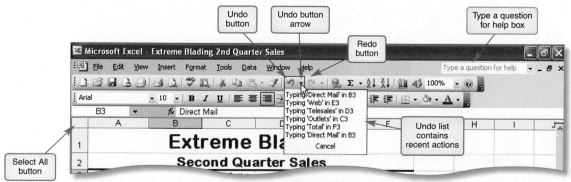

FIGURE 1-77

More About

The Undo Button

The Undo button can undo far more complicated worksheet activities than just removing the latest entry from a cell. In fact, most commands can be undone if you click the Undo button before you make another entry or issue another command. You cannot undo a save or print, but, as a rule, the Undo button can restore the worksheet data and settings to what they were the last time Excel was in Ready mode. With Excel, you have multiple-level undo and redo capabilities.

Excel remembers the last 16 actions you have completed. Thus, you can undo up to 16 previous actions by clicking the Undo button arrow to display the Undo list and then clicking the action to be undone (Figure 1-77 on the previous page). You can drag through several actions in the Undo list to undo all of them at once. If no actions are available for Excel to undo, then the Undo button is dimmed and inoperative.

The Redo button, next to the Undo button on the Standard toolbar, allows you to repeat previous actions. You also can click Redo on the Edit menu, instead of using the Redo button.

Clearing a Cell or Range of Cells

If you enter data into the wrong cell or range of cells, you can erase, or clear, the data using one of the first four methods listed below. The fifth method clears the formatting from the selected cells.

To Clear Cell Entries Using the Fill Handle

1. Select the cell or range of cells and then point to the fill handle so the mouse pointer changes to a cross hair.
2. Drag the fill handle back into the selected cell or range until a shadow covers the cell or cells you want to erase. Release the mouse button.

To Clear Cell Entries Using the Shortcut Menu

1. Select the cell or range of cells to be cleared.
2. Right-click the selection.
3. Click Clear Contents on the shortcut menu.

To Clear Cell Entries Using the DELETE Key

1. Select the cell or range of cells to be cleared.
2. Press the DELETE key.

More About

Getting Back to Normal

If you accidentally assign unwanted formats to a range of cells, you can use the Clear command on the Edit menu to delete the formats of a selected range. Doing so changes the format to Normal style. To view the characteristics of the Normal style, click Style on the Format menu or press ALT+APOSTROPHE (').

To Clear Cell Entries Using the Clear Command

1. Select the cell or range of cells to be cleared.
2. Click Edit on the menu bar and then point to Clear.
3. Click All on the Clear submenu.

To Clear Formatting Using the Clear Command

1. Select the cell or range of cells that you want to remove the formatting from.
2. Click Edit on the menu bar and then point to Clear.
3. Click Formats on the Clear submenu.

More About

The Quick Reference

For a table that lists how to complete the tasks covered in this book using the mouse, menu, shortcut menu, and keyboard, see the Quick Reference Summary at the back of this book, or visit the Excel 2003 Quick Reference Web page (scsite.com/ex2003/qr).

The All command on the Clear submenu is the only command that clears both the cell entry and the cell formatting. As you are clearing cell entries, always remember that you should *never press the SPACEBAR to clear a cell*. Pressing the SPACEBAR enters a blank character. A blank character is text and is different from an empty cell, even though the cell may appear empty.

Clearing the Entire Worksheet

If required worksheet edits are extremely extensive, you may want to clear the entire worksheet and start over. To clear the worksheet or delete an embedded chart, use the following steps.

To Clear the Entire Worksheet

1. Click the Select All button on the worksheet (Figure 1-77 on page EX 51).
2. Press the DELETE key to delete all the entries. Click Edit on the menu bar, point to Clear, and then click All on the Clear submenu to delete both the entries and formats.

The Select All button selects the entire worksheet. Instead of clicking the Select All button, you also can press CTRL+A. To clear an unsaved workbook, click the workbook's Close Window button or click the Close command on the File menu. Click the No button if the Microsoft Excel dialog box asks if you want to save changes. To start a new, blank workbook, click the New button on the Standard toolbar or click the New command on the File menu and begin working on a new workbook.

To delete an embedded chart, complete the following steps.

To Delete an Embedded Chart

1. Click the chart to select it.
2. Press the DELETE key.

Excel Help System

At any time while you are using Excel, you can get answers to questions using the **Excel Help** system. You can activate the Excel Help system by using the Type a question for help box on the menu bar, the Microsoft Excel Help button on the Standard toolbar, or by clicking Help on the menu bar (Figure 1-78). Used properly, this form of online assistance can increase your productivity and reduce your frustrations by minimizing the time you spend learning how to use Excel.

The following section shows how to get answers to your questions using the Type a question for help box. Additional information on using the Excel Help system is available in Appendix A.

Obtaining Help Using the Type a Question for Help Box on the Menu Bar

The Type a question for help box on the right side of the menu bar (see Figure 1-77 on page EX 51) lets you type free-form questions such as, how do I save or how do I create a Web page, phrases such as save a workbook or print a worksheet, or key terms such as, copy, save, or formatting. Excel responds by displaying a list of topics related to the question or terms you entered in the Search Results task pane. The following steps show how to use the Type a question for help box to obtain information on saving a workbook.

To Obtain Help Using the Type a Question for Help Box

1

• **Type** save a workbook **in the Type a question for help box on the right side of the menu bar (Figure 1-78).**

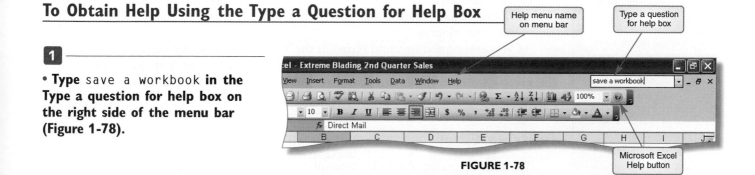

FIGURE 1-78

- **Press the ENTER key.**
- **When Excel displays the Search Results task pane, scroll down and then click the link Save a file.**
- **If necessary, click the AutoTile button (see Figure 1-80) to tile the windows.**

Excel displays the Search Results task pane with a list of topics related to the term, save. Excel found 30 search results (Figure 1-79). When the Save a file link is clicked, Excel opens the Microsoft Excel Help window on the left side of the screen.

3

- **Click the Show All link on the right side of the Microsoft Excel Help window to expand the links in the window.**
- **Double-click the Microsoft Excel Help title bar to maximize it.**

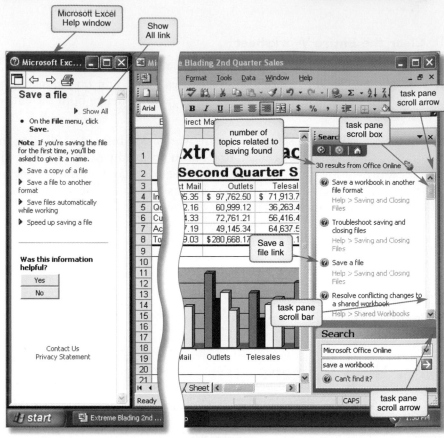

FIGURE 1-79

The links in the Microsoft Excel Help window are expanded. Excel maximizes the window that provides Help information about saving a file (Figure 1-80).

4

- **Click the Close button on the Microsoft Excel Help window title bar.**

The Microsoft Excel Help window closes and the worksheet is active.

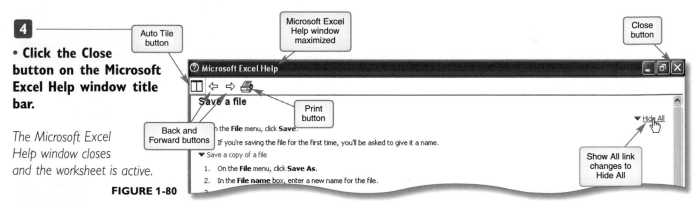

FIGURE 1-80

More About

Quitting Excel

Do not forget to remove your floppy disk from drive A after quitting Excel, especially if you are working in a laboratory environment. Nothing can be more frustrating than leaving all of your hard work behind on a floppy disk for the next user.

Use the buttons in the upper-left corner of the Microsoft Excel Help window (Figure 1-80) to navigate through the Help system, change the display, and print the contents of the window.

As you enter questions and terms in the Type a question for help box, Excel adds them to its list. Thus, if you click the Type a question for help box arrow (Figure 1-78 on the previous page), Excel will display a list of previously entered questions and terms.

Quitting Excel

The following step shows how to quit Excel.

To Quit Excel

1 Click the Close button on the right side of the title bar, and if necessary, click the No button in the Microsoft Excel dialog box.

Project Summary

This project presented Excel basics. First, you were introduced to starting Excel. You learned about the Excel window and how to enter text and numbers to create a worksheet. You learned how to select a range and how to use the AutoSum button to sum numbers in a column or row. Using the fill handle, you learned how to copy a cell to adjacent cells. Once the worksheet was built, you learned how to format cells one at a time using buttons on the Formatting toolbar and how to format a range using the AutoFormat command. You then learned how to use the Chart Wizard to add a 3-D Clustered column chart to the worksheet. After completing the worksheet, you learned how to save the workbook on a floppy disk, print the worksheet and chart, and then quit Excel. You also learned how to start Excel by opening an Excel document, use the AutoCalculate area, and edit data in cells. Finally, you learned how to use the Excel Help system to answer your questions.

 If you have a SAM user profile, you may have access to hands-on instruction, practice, and assessment of the skills covered in this project. Log in to your SAM account and go to your assignments page to see what your instructor has assigned.

What You Should Know

Having completed this project, you should be able to perform the tasks below. The tasks are listed in the same order they were presented in this project. For a list of the buttons, menus, toolbars, and commands introduced in this project, see the Quick Reference Summary at the back of this book and refer to the Page Number column.

1. Start Excel   (EX 7)
2. Customize the Excel Window   (EX 8)
3. Enter the Worksheet Titles   (EX 17)
4. Enter Column Titles   (EX 19)
5. Enter Row Titles   (EX 20)
6. Enter Numbers   (EX 22)
7. Sum a Column of Numbers   (EX 23)
8. Copy a Cell to Adjacent Cells in a Row   (EX 25)
9. Determine Multiple Totals at the Same Time (EX 27)
10. Change the Font Type   (EX 29)
11. Bold a Cell   (EX 30)
12. Increase the Font Size of a Cell Entry   (EX 31)
13. Change the Font Color of a Cell Entry   (EX 32)
14. Center a Cell Entry across Columns by Merging Cells   (EX 33)
15. Format the Worksheet Subtitle   (EX 34)
16. Use AutoFormat to Format the Body of a Worksheet   (EX 34)
17. Use the Name Box to Select a Cell   (EX 36)
18. Add a 3-D Clustered Column Chart to the Worksheet   (EX 39)
19. Save a Workbook   (EX 42)
20. Print a Worksheet   (EX 45)
21. Quit Excel   (EX 46)
22. Start Excel and Open a Workbook   (EX 47)
23. Use the AutoCalculate Area to Determine an Average   (EX 49)
24. Clear Cell Entries Using the Fill Handle   (EX 52)
25. Clear Cell Entries Using the Shortcut Menu   (EX 52)
26. Clear Cell Entries Using the DELETE Key   (EX 52)
27. Clear Cell Entries Using the Clear Command (EX 52)
28. Clear the Entire Worksheet   (EX 53)
29. Delete an Embedded Chart   (EX 53)
30. Obtain Help Using the Type a Question for Help Box   (EX 53)
31. Quit Excel   (EX 55)

Learn It Online

Instructions: To complete the Learn It Online exercises, start your browser, click the Address bar, and then enter the Web address scsite.com/ex2003/learn. When the Excel 2003 Learn It Online page is displayed, follow the instructions in the exercises below. Each exercise has instructions for printing your results, either for your own records or for submission to your instructor.

1 Project Reinforcement TF, MC, and SA

Below Excel Project 1, click the Project Reinforcement link. Print the quiz by clicking Print on the File menu for each page. Answer each question.

2 Flash Cards

Below Excel Project 1, click the Flash Cards link and read the instructions. Type 20 (or a number specified by your instructor) in the Number of playing cards text box, type your name in the Enter your Name text box, and then click the Flip Card button. When the flash card is displayed, read the question and then click the ANSWER box arrow to select an answer. Flip through Flash Cards. If your score is 15 (75%) correct or greater, click Print on the File menu to print your results. If your score is less than 15 (75%) correct, then redo this exercise by clicking the Replay button.

3 Practice Test

Below Excel Project 1, click the Practice Test link. Answer each question, enter your first and last name at the bottom of the page, and then click the Grade Test button. When the graded practice test is displayed on your screen, click Print on the File menu to print a hard copy. Continue to take practice tests until you score 80% or better.

4 Who Wants To Be a Computer Genius?

Below Excel Project 1, click the Computer Genius link. Read the instructions, enter your first and last name at the bottom of the page, and then click the PLAY button. When your score is displayed, click the PRINT RESULTS link to print a hard copy.

5 Wheel of Terms

Below Excel Project 1, click the Wheel of Terms link. Read the instructions, and then enter your first and last name and your school name. Click the PLAY button. When your score is displayed, right-click the score and then click Print on the shortcut menu to print a hard copy.

6 Crossword Puzzle Challenge

Below Excel Project 1, click the Crossword Puzzle Challenge link. Read the instructions, and then enter your first and last name. Click the SUBMIT button. Work the crossword puzzle. When you are finished, click the Submit button. When the crossword puzzle is redisplayed, click the Print Puzzle button to print a hard copy.

7 Tips and Tricks

Below Excel Project 1, click the Tips and Tricks link. Click a topic that pertains to Project 1. Right-click the information and then click Print on the shortcut menu. Construct a brief example of what the information relates to in Excel to confirm you understand how to use the tip or trick.

8 Newsgroups

Below Excel Project 1, click the Newsgroups link. Click a topic that pertains to Project 1. Print three comments.

9 Expanding Your Horizons

Below Excel Project 1, click the Expanding Your Horizons link. Click a topic that pertains to Project 1. Print the information. Construct a brief example of what the information relates to in Excel to confirm you understand the contents of the article.

10 Search Sleuth

Below Excel Project 1, click the Search Sleuth link. To search for a term that pertains to this project, select a term below the Project 1 title and then use the Google search engine at google.com (or any major search engine) to display and print two Web pages that present information on the term.

11 Excel Online Training

Below Excel Project 1, click the Excel Online Training link. When your browser displays the Microsoft Office Online Web page, click the Excel link. Click one of the Excel courses that covers one or more of the objectives listed at the beginning of the project on page EX 4. Print the first page of the course before stepping through it.

12 Office Marketplace

Below Excel Project 1, click the Office Marketplace link. When your browser displays the Microsoft Office Online Web page, click the Office Marketplace link. Click a topic that relates to Excel. Print the first page.

Apply Your Knowledge

1 Changing the Values in a Worksheet

Instructions: Start Excel. Open the workbook Apply 1-1 Watson's Computer Discount Annual Sales from the Data Disk. See the inside back cover of this book for instructions for downloading the Data Disk or see your instructor for information on accessing the files required in this book.

Make the changes to the worksheet described in Table 1-7 so that the worksheet appears as shown in Figure 1-81. As you edit the values in the cells containing numeric data, watch the totals in row 7, the totals in column F, and the chart change.

Change the worksheet title in cell A1 to 20-point Arial Black brown, bold font and then center it across columns A through F. Change the worksheet subtitle in cell A2 to 14-point Arial Black brown, bold font and then center it across columns A through F.

Enter your name, course, laboratory assignment number, date, and instructor name in cells A21 through A25. Save the workbook using the file name, Apply 1-1 Babbage's Computer Discount Annual Sales. Print the revised worksheet and hand in the printout to your instructor.

Table 1-7 New Worksheet Data	
CELL	**CHANGE CELL CONTENTS TO**
A1	Babbage's Computer Discount
B4	43200.75
C4	17563.52
D5	38152.43
E5	28968.78
E6	38751.49

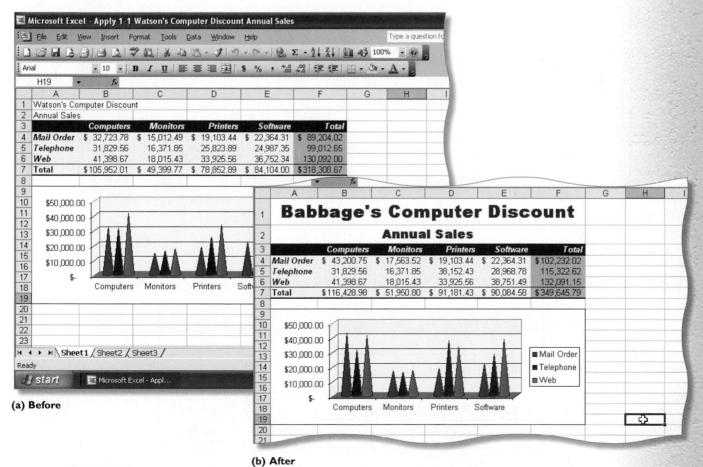

(a) Before

(b) After

FIGURE 1-81

In the Lab

1 Monthly Sales Analysis Worksheet

Problem: You work part-time as a spreadsheet specialist for Knotting Hill Bookstore, one of the larger bookstores in the world. Your manager has asked you to develop a monthly sales analysis worksheet similar to the one shown in Figure 1-82.

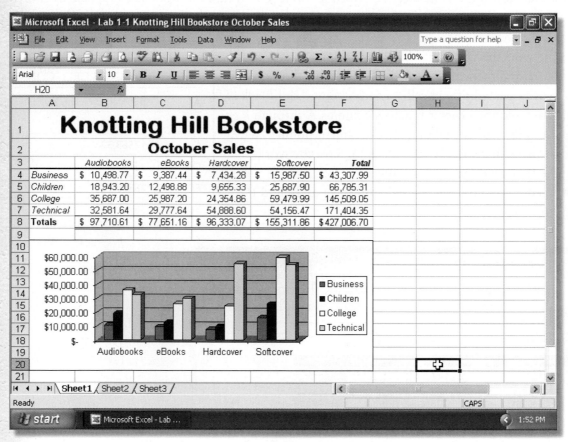

FIGURE 1-82

Instructions: Perform the following tasks.

1. Create the worksheet shown in Figure 1-82 using the sales amounts and categories in Table 1-8.

Table 1-8 Knotting Hill Bookstore October Sales				
	Audiobooks	**eBooks**	**Hardcover**	**Softcover**
Business	10498.77	9387.44	7434.28	15987.50
Children	18943.20	12498.88	9655.33	25687.90
College	35687.00	25987.20	24354.86	59479.99
Technical	32581.64	29777.64	54888.60	54156.47

In the Lab

2. Use the SUM function to determine the totals for the types of books, subject area, and company totals.
3. Format the worksheet title to 26-point Arial Rounded MT Bold dark blue, bold font and center it across columns A through F. Do not be concerned if the edges of the worksheet title are not displayed.
4. Format the worksheet subtitle to 16-point Arial Rounded MT Bold dark blue, bold font and center it across columns A through F.
5. Format the range A3:F8 using the AutoFormat command. Select the Accounting 3 autoformat.
6. Select the range A3:E7 and then use the Chart Wizard button on the Standard toolbar to draw a Clustered column with a 3-D visual effect chart (column 1, row 2 in the Chart sub-type list). Move and resize the chart so that it appears in the range A10:F20. If the labels along the horizontal axis (x-axis) do not appear as shown in Figure 1-82, then drag the right side of the chart so that it is displayed in the range A10:H20.
7. Enter your name, course, laboratory assignment number, date, and instructor name in cells A22 through A26.
8. Save the workbook using the file name Lab 1-1 Knotting Hill Bookstore October Sales.
9. Print the worksheet.
10. Make the following two corrections to the sales amounts: $14,785.21 for Children eBooks (cell C5), $57,752.54 for Technical Softcover books (cell E7). After you enter the corrections, the company totals in cell F8 should equal $432,889.10.
11. Print the revised worksheet. Close the workbook without saving the changes.

2 Quarterly Expense Analysis Worksheet

Problem: As the chief accountant for College Travel, Inc., you have been asked by the vice president to create a worksheet to analyze the 4th quarter expenses for the company by office and expense category (Figure 1-83 on the next page). The office locations and corresponding expenses for the 4th quarter are shown in Table 1-9.

Table 1-9	College Travel 4th Quarter Expenses			
	Atlanta	Nashville	New Orleans	Orlando
Marketing	42502.23	19231.56	32012.40	14012.00
Rent	43970.50	57510.00	29089.32	31765.23
Supplies	31892.70	18429.34	26723.15	22914.50
Travel	9512.45	12323.21	9012.56	8910.32
Wages	83463.30	72135.45	63908.55	92364.50

Instructions: Perform the following tasks.

1. Create the worksheet shown in Figure 1-83 using the data in Table 1-9.
2. Use the SUM function to determine totals expenses for the four offices, the totals for each expense category, and the company total. Add column and row headings for the totals, as appropriate.

(continued)

In the Lab

Quarterly Expense Analysis Worksheet *(continued)*

3. Change the worksheet title to 26-point Arial Black dark red, bold font, and center it across columns A through F. Format the worksheet subtitle to 16-point Arial Black dark red, bold font, and center it across columns A through F.

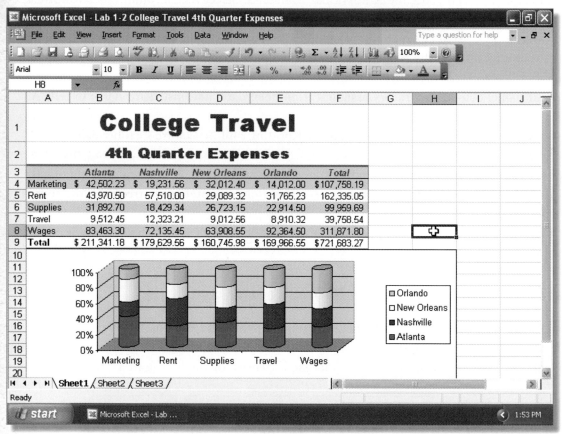

FIGURE 1-83

4. Format the range A3:F9 using the AutoFormat command on the Format menu as follows: (a) apply the autoformat Accounting 1; and (b) with the range A3:F9 still selected, apply the autoformat List 1. If you make a mistake, apply the autoformat None and then apply the autoformats again.
5. Chart the range A3:E8. Draw the 100% Stacked column with a cylindrical shape chart, as shown in Figure 1-83, by clicking the Chart Wizard button on the Standard toolbar. When Excel displays the Chart Wizard dialog box, select Cylinder in the Chart type list, and then select column 3, row 1 in the Chart sub-type list. Use the chart location A10:H20.
6. Enter your name, course, laboratory assignment number, date, and instructor name in cells A23 through A27.
7. Save the workbook using the file name, Lab 1-2 College Travel 4th Quarter Expenses. Print the worksheet.
8. Two corrections to the expenses were sent in from the accounting department. The correct expenses are $62,345.12 for the Nashville's quarterly rent (cell C5) and $18,615.42 for Orlando's quarterly travel expenses (cell E7). After you enter the two corrections, the company total in cell F9 should equal $736,223.49. Print the revised worksheet.

In the Lab

9. Use the Undo button to change the worksheet back to the original numbers in Table 1-9. Use the Redo button to change the worksheet back to the revised state.

10. Close Excel without saving the latest changes. Start Excel and open the workbook saved in step 7. Double-click cell D6 and use in-cell editing to change the New Orleans quarterly supplies expense to $29,098.32. Write the company total in cell F9 at the top of the first printout. Click the Undo button.

11. Click cell A1 and then click the Merge and Center button to split cell A1 into cells A1, B1, C1, D1, E1, and F1. To re-merge the cells into one, select the range A1:F1 and then click the Merge and Center button.

12. Hand in the two printouts to your instructor. Close the workbook without saving the changes.

3 College Expenses and Resources Worksheet

Problem: Attending college is an expensive proposition and your resources are limited. To plan for your four-year college career, you have decided to organize your anticipated resources and expenses in a worksheet. The data required to prepare your worksheet is shown in Table 1-10.

Table 1-10 College Expenses and Resources				
Expenses	Freshman	Sophomore	Junior	Senior
Room & Board	3390.00	3627.30	3881.21	4152.90
Tuition & Books	4850.00	5189.50	5552.77	5941.46
Clothes	540.00	577.80	618.25	661.52
Entertainment	635.00	679.45	727.01	777.90
Miscellaneous	325.00	347.75	372.09	398.14
Resources	Freshman	Sophomore	Junior	Senior
Savings	1700.00	1819.00	1946.33	2082.57
Parents	2390.00	2557.30	2736.31	2927.85
Job	1450.00	1551.50	1660.11	1776.32
Financial Aid	4200.00	4494.00	4808.58	5145.18

Instructions Part 1: Using the numbers in Table 1-10, create the worksheet shown in columns A through F in Figure 1-84 on the next page. Format the range A3:F9 using the AutoFormat command on the Format menu as follows: (a) select the range A3:F9 and then apply the autoformat Accounting 1; and (b) with the range A3:F9 still selected, apply the autoformat Colorful 2. Use the same autoformats for the range A11:F16.

Enter your identification on the worksheet and save the workbook using the file name Lab 1-3 Part 1 College Expenses and Resources. Print the worksheet in landscape orientation. You print in landscape orientation by invoking the Page Setup command on the File menu and then clicking Landscape in the Page sheet in the Page Setup dialog box. Click the Save button on the Standard toolbar to save the workbook with the new print settings.

(continued)

College Expenses and Resources Worksheet *(continued)*

After reviewing the numbers, you realize you need to increase manually each of the Junior-year expenses in column D by $400. Change the Junior-year expenses to reflect this change. Manually change the financial aid for the Junior year by the amount required to cover the increase in expenses. The totals in cells F9 and F16 should equal $45,245.05. Print the worksheet. Close the workbook without saving changes. Hand in the two printouts to your instructor.

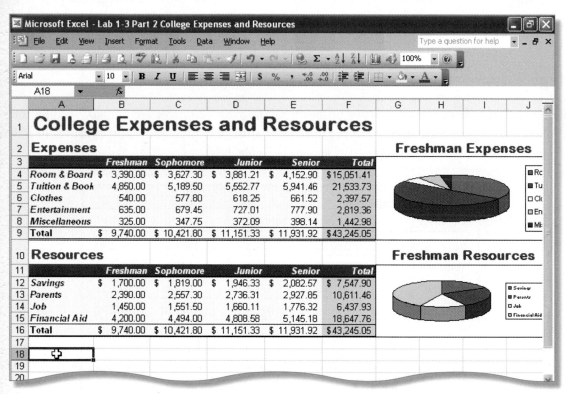

FIGURE 1-84

Instructions Part 2: Open the workbook Lab 1-3 Part 1 College Expenses and Resources. Draw a 3-D Pie chart in the range G3:J9 to show the contribution of each category of expenses for the Freshman year. Chart the range A4:B8. Add the Pie chart title as shown in cell G2 in Figure 1-84. Draw a 3-D Pie chart in the range G11:J16 to show the contribution of each category of resources for the Freshman year. Chart the range A12:B15. Add the Pie chart title shown in cell G10 in Figure 1-84. Save the workbook using the file name, Lab 1-3 Part 2 College Expenses and Resources. Print the worksheet. Hand in the printout to your instructor.

Instructions Part 3: Open the workbook Lab 1-3 Part 2 College Expenses and Resources. A close inspection of Table 1-10 shows that both expenses and resources increase 7% each year. Use the Type a question for help box on the menu bar to learn how to enter the data for the last three years using a formula and the Copy command. For example, the formula to enter in cell C4 is =B4 * 1.07. Enter formulas to replace all the numbers in the range C4:E8 and C12:E15. If necessary, reformat the tables using the autoformats, as described in Part 1. The worksheet should appear as shown in Figure 1-84, except that some of the totals will be off by 0.01 due to rounding errors. Save the worksheet using the file name, Lab 1-3 Part 3 College Expenses and Resources. Print the worksheet. Press CTRL+ACCENT MARK(`) to display the formulas. Print the formulas version. Close the workbook without saving changes. Hand in both printouts to your instructor.

Cases and Places

The difficulty of these case studies varies:
■ are the least difficult and ■■ are more difficult. The last exercise is a group exercise.

1 ■ You are employed by the Reggae Music Company. Your manager has asked you to prepare a worksheet to help her analyze monthly sales by store and by type of reggae music (Table 1-11). Use the concepts and techniques presented in this project to create the worksheet and an embedded Clustered bar chart with a 3-D visual effect.

Table 1-11	Reggae Music Company Monthly Sales			
	Boston	Kansas City	Portland	San Diego
Dancehall	6734	7821	4123	7989
Dub	5423	2134	6574	3401
Dub Poetry	3495	6291	7345	7098
Lovers Rock	6789	4523	9102	7812
Ragga	8920	9812	5637	3456
Rocksteady	2134	2190	3401	2347
Ska	5462	2923	8034	5135

2 ■ To estimate the funds you need to make it through the upcoming year, you decide to create a personal budget itemizing your expected quarterly expenses. The anticipated expenses are listed in Table 1-12. Use the concepts and techniques presented in this project to create the worksheet and an embedded 100% Stacked column chart with a conical shape that compares the quarterly cost of each expense. If necessary, reduce the size of the font in the chart so that each expense category name appears on the horizontal axis (x-axis). Use the AutoCalculate area to determine the average amount spent per quarter on each expense. Manually insert the averages with appropriate titles in an empty area on the worksheet.

Table 1-12	Quarterly Personal Budget			
	Jan - Mar	April - June	July - Sept	Oct - Dec
Mortgage	1500	1500	1500	1500
Food	900	950	950	1000
Car & Ins.	600	600	600	600
Clothes	567	433	200	459
Utilities	600	400	400	550
Miscellaneous	149	121	159	349

Cases and Places

3 ■■ The Magic Theater is a movie house that shows movies at weekday evening, weekend matinee, and weekend evening screenings. Three types of tickets are sold at each presentation: general admission, senior citizen, and children. The theater management has asked you to prepare a worksheet, based on the revenue from a typical week, that can be used to reevaluate its ticket structure. During an average week, weekday evening shows generate $7,250 from general admission ticket sales, $6,715 from senior citizen ticket sales, and $1,575 from children ticket sales. Weekend matinee shows make $6,723 from general admission ticket sales, $2,050 from senior citizen ticket sales, and $2,875 from children ticket sales. Weekend evening shows earn $9,415 from general admission ticket sales, $9,815 from senior citizen ticket sales, and $1,235 from children ticket sales. Use the concepts and techniques presented in this project to prepare a worksheet that includes total revenues for each type of ticket and for each presentation time, and a Clustered Bar chart illustrating ticket revenues.

4 ■■ Jasmine's Floral Shop on Michigan Avenue in Chicago sells floral arrangments to an exclusive clientele. The company is trying to decide whether it is feasible to open another boutique in the Chicago area. You have been asked to develop a worksheet totaling all the revenue received last year from customers living in the Chicago area. The revenue from customers living in the Chicago area by quarter is: Quarter 1, $221,565.56; Quarter 2, $182,704.34; Quarter 3, $334,116.31; and Quarter 4, $421,333.50. Create a Pie chart with a 3-D visual effect to illustrate Chicago-area revenue contribution by quarter. Use the AutoCalculate area to find the average, maximum, and minimum quarterly revenue and manually enter them and their corresponding identifiers in an empty area on the worksheet.

5 ■■ **Working Together** Visit the Registrar's office at your school and obtain data, such as age, gender, and resident status, for the students majoring in at least five different academic departments this semester. Have each member of your team divide the data into different categories. For example, separate the data by:

1. Age, divided into four different age groups
2. Gender, divided into male and female
3. Resident status, divided into resident and nonresident

After coordinating the data as a group, have each member independently use the concepts and techniques presented in this project to create a worksheet and appropriate chart to show the total students by characteristics by academic department. As a group, critique each worksheet and have each member re-do his or her worksheet based on the group recommendations. Hand in printouts of your original worksheet and final worksheet.

Formulas, Functions, Formatting, and Web Queries

PROJECT

2

CASE PERSPECTIVE

Several years ago, while Alisha Wright was taking an Investment course as a sophomore in college, she persuaded six of her classmates to start a stock club geared towards researching and investing in stocks of large, well-established, and consistently profitable companies, which are referred to as blue chip stocks. They decided to call themselves the Blue Chip Stock Club. While in college, each member of the club contributed $20 per month.

Now, the club members are out of college, married, and have taken jobs around the country. They continue to invest in the stock market as a group, however, using e-mail, chat rooms, and Web cams to communicate and conduct their monthly meetings via the Internet. A few years ago, they increased their monthly contribution to $100.

At the end of each month, Alisha, the Blue Chip Stock Club's permanent treasurer, summarizes the club's financial status. Alisha plans to use Excel to create a worksheet summarizing the club's stock activities, which she can use to track and analyze the investment portfolio, answer questions posed by club members in their e-mails, and e-mail a monthly closing report to the club members. She also plans to use its Web query capabilities to access real-time stock quotes.

Alisha knows little about Excel 2003 and has asked you to show her how to create the worksheet (Figure 2-1a) and access real-time stock quotes over the Internet (Figure 2-1b).

As you read through this project, you will learn how to enter formulas and functions, how to improve the appearance of a worksheet, how to perform Web queries, and how to e-mail from within Excel.

MICROSOFT
Office Excel 2003

Formulas, Functions, Formatting, and Web Queries

PROJECT

2

Objectives

You will have mastered the material in this project when you can:

- Enter formulas using the keyboard and Point mode
- Recognize smart tags and option buttons
- Apply the AVERAGE, MAX, and MIN functions
- Verify a formula using Range Finder
- Format a worksheet using buttons and commands
- Add conditional formatting to a range of cells
- Change the width of a column and height of a row
- Check the spelling of a worksheet

- Preview how a printed copy of the worksheet will look
- Print a partial or complete worksheet
- Display and print the formulas version of a worksheet
- Use a Web query to get real-time data from a Web site
- Rename sheets in a workbook
- E-mail the active workbook from within Excel

Introduction

In Project 1, you learned how to enter data, sum values, format the worksheet to make it easier to read, and draw a chart. You also learned about online Help and saving, printing, and opening a workbook. This project continues to emphasize these topics and presents some new ones.

The new topics covered in this project include using formulas and functions to create the worksheet shown in Figure 2-1a. Other new topics include smart tags and option buttons, verifying formulas, adding borders, formatting numbers and text, using conditional formatting, changing the widths of columns and heights of rows, spell checking, e-mailing from within an application, renaming worksheets, and using alternative types of worksheet displays and printouts. One alternative worksheet display and printout shows the formulas in the worksheet, instead of the values. When you display the formulas in the worksheet, you see exactly what text, data, formulas, and functions you have entered into it. Finally, this project covers Web queries to obtain real-time data from a Web site (Figure 2-1b).

(a) Worksheet

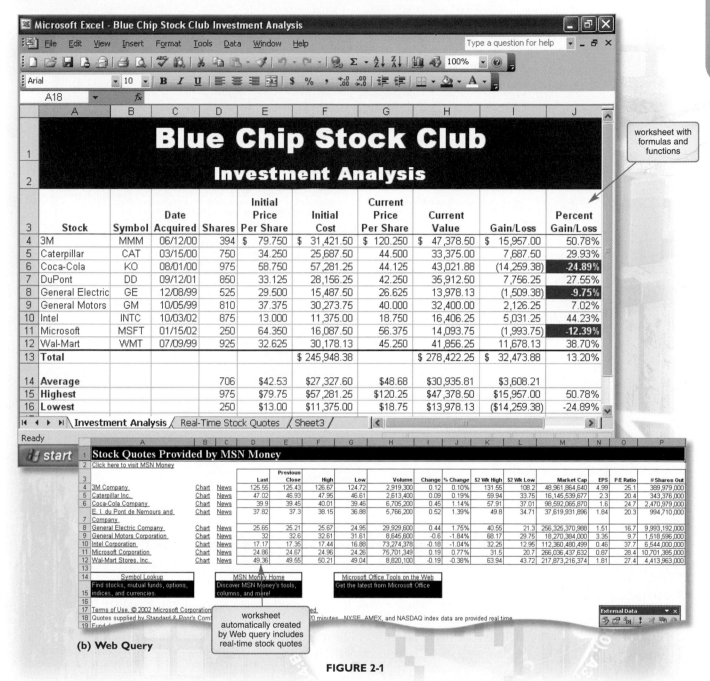

FIGURE 2-1

Project Two — Blue Chip Stock Club Investment Analysis

Recall that the first step in creating an effective worksheet is to make sure you understand what is required. Requirements usually are provided by the people who will use the worksheet. The requirements document for the Blue Chip Stock Club Investment Analysis worksheet includes the following: needs, source of data, summary of calculations, Web requirements, and other facts about its development (Figure 2-2 on the next page).

REQUEST FOR NEW WORKBOOK

Date Submitted:	July 1, 2005
Submitted By:	Alisha Wright
Worksheet Title:	Blue Chip Stock Club Investment Analysis
Needs:	An easy-to-read workbook with two worksheets to provide information on the current investment portfolio and updated stock quote data. The first worksheet will summarize the club's investment portfolio (Figure 2-3). For each stock, the worksheet will include the stock name, stock symbol, date acquired, shares, initial price per share, initial cost, current price per share, current value, gain/loss, and percent gain/loss. The worksheet also will include (1) totals for initial cost, current value, and gain loss and (2) the average, highest value, and lowest value for each column of numbers. The second worksheet will use the import data capabilities of Excel to access real-time stock quotes using Web queries.
Source of Data:	The data supplied by Alisha includes the stock names, stock symbols, dates acquired, number of shares, initial price per share, and current price per share. This data is shown in Table 2-1, Blue Chip Stock Club Portfolio.
Calculations:	1. Complete the following calculations for each of the stocks: a. Initial Cost = Shares _ Initial Price Per Share b. Current Value = Shares _ Current Price Per Share c. Gain/Loss = Current Value – Initial Cost d. Percent Gain/Loss = Gain/Loss / Initial Cost 2. Compute the totals for initial cost, current value, and gain/loss. 3. Use the AVERAGE function to determine the average for the number of shares, initial price per share, initial cost per share, current price per share, current value, and gain/loss. 4. Use the MAX and MIN functions to determine the highest and lowest values for the number of shares, initial price per share, initial cost per share, current price per share, current value, gain/loss, and percent gain/loss.
Web Requirements:	Use the Web query feature of Excel to get real-time stock quotes for the stocks owned by the Blue Chip Stock Club.

Approvals

Approval Status:	X	Approved
		Rejected
Approved By:		Members of the Blue Chip Stock Club
Date:		July 6, 2005
Assigned To:		J. Quasney, Spreadsheet Specialist

FIGURE 2-2

In addition, using a sketch of the worksheet can help you visualize its design. The sketch for the Blue Chip Stock Club Investment Analysis worksheet (Figure 2-3) includes a title, a subtitle, column and row headings, and the location of data values. It also uses specific characters to define the desired formatting for the worksheet as follows:

1. The row of Xs below the two leftmost columns defines the cell entries as text, such as stock names and stock symbols.
2. The rows of Zs and 9s with slashes, dollar signs, decimal points, commas, and percent signs in the remaining columns define the cell entries as numbers. The Zs indicate that the selected format should instruct Excel to suppress leading 0s. The 9s indicate that the selected format should instruct Excel to display any digits, including 0s.

3. The decimal point means that a decimal point should appear in the cell entry and indicates the number of decimal places to use.

4. The commas indicate that the selected format should instruct Excel to display a comma separator only if the number has enough digits to the left of the decimal point.

5. The slashes in the third column identify the cell entry as a date.

6. The dollar signs that are not adjacent to the Zs in the first row below the column headings and in the total row signify a fixed dollar sign. The dollar signs that are adjacent to the Zs below the total row signify a floating dollar sign, or one that appears next to the first significant digit.

7. The percent sign (%) in the far right column indicates a percent sign should appear after the number.

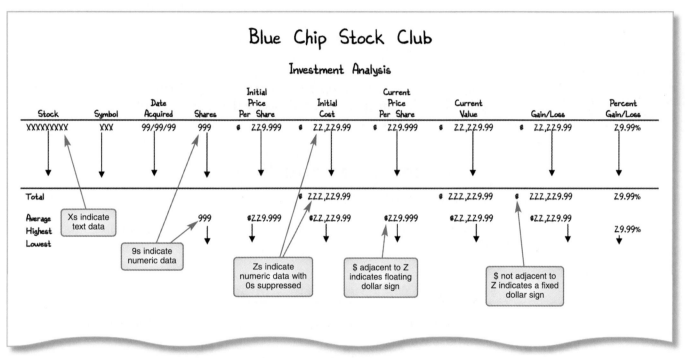

FIGURE 2-3

The real-time stock quotes (shown in Figure 2-1b on page EX 67) will be accessed via a Web query. The stock quotes will be returned to the active workbook on a separate worksheet. Microsoft determines the content and format of the Real-Time Stock Quotes worksheet.

Starting and Customizing Excel

With the requirements document and sketch of the worksheet complete, the next step is to use Excel to create the worksheet. To start and customize Excel, Windows must be running. If you are stepping through this project on a computer and you want your screen to match the figures in this book, then you should change your computer's resolution to 800 × 600. For more information on how to change the resolution on your computer, see Appendix B. The steps on the next page start Excel and customize the Excel window.

More About

Starting Excel

You can use a command-line switch to start Excel and control how it starts. First, click the Start button on the Windows taskbar and then click Run. Next, enter the complete path to Excel's application file including the switch (for example, "C:\ Program Files\Microsoft Office\Office\Excel.exe" /e). The switch /e opens Excel without opening a new work-book; /i starts Excel with a maximized window; /p "folder" sets the active path to folder and ignores the default folder; /r "filename" opens filename in read-only mode; and /s starts Excel in safe mode.

To Start and Customize Excel

1 Click the Start button on the Windows taskbar, point to All Programs on the Start menu, point to Microsoft Office on the All Programs submenu, and then click Microsoft Office Excel 2003 on the Microsoft Office submenu.

2 If the Excel window is not maximized, double-click its title bar to maximize it.

3 If the Language bar appears, right-click it and then click Close the Language bar on the shortcut menu.

4 If the Getting Started task pane appears in the Excel window, click its Close button in the upper-right corner.

5 If the Standard and Formatting toolbars are positioned on the same row, click the Toolbar Options button and then click Show Buttons on Two Rows.

The Excel window with the Standard and Formatting toolbars on two rows appears as shown in Figure 2-1a on page EX 67.

After the Excel window is opened, Steps 3 through 5 close the Getting Started task pane, close the Language bar, and ensure that the Standard and Formatting toolbars appear on two rows.

Entering the Titles and Numbers into the Worksheet

The following steps show how to enter the worksheet title and subtitle into cells A1 and A2.

To Enter the Worksheet Title and Subtitle

1 Select cell **A1**. Type Blue Chip Stock Club **in the cell and then press the DOWN ARROW key.**

2 Type Investment Analysis **in cell A2 and then press the DOWN ARROW key.**

Excel displays the worksheet title in cell A1 and the worksheet subtitle in cell A2, as shown in Figure 2-4 on page EX 73.

The column titles in row 3 begin in cell A3 and extend through cell J3. The column titles in Figure 2-3 include multiple lines of text. To start a new line in a cell, press ALT+ENTER after each line, except for the last line, which is completed by clicking the Enter box, pressing the ENTER key, or pressing one of the arrow keys. When you see ALT+ENTER in a step, press the ENTER key while holding down the ALT key and then release both keys.

The stock names and the row titles Total, Average, Highest, and Lowest in the leftmost column begin in cell A4 and continue down to cell A16.

The stock club's investments are summarized in Table 2-1. This data is entered into rows 4 through 12 of the worksheet. The remainder of this section explains the steps required to enter the column titles, stock data, and row titles as shown in Figure 2-4 and then save the workbook.

Table 2-1	Blue Chip Stock Club Portfolio				
Stock	Symbol	Date Acquired	Shares	Initial Price Per Share	Current Price Per Share
3M	MMM	6/12/00	394	79.75	120.25
Caterpillar	CAT	3/15/00	750	34.25	44.50
Coca-Cola	KO	8/01/00	975	58.75	44.125
DuPont	DD	9/12/01	850	33.125	42.25
General Electric	GE	12/08/99	525	29.50	26.625
General Motors	GM	10/05/99	810	37.375	40.00
Intel	INTC	10/03/02	875	13.00	18.75
Microsoft	MSFT	1/15/02	250	64.35	56.375
Wal-Mart	WMT	7/09/99	925	32.625	45.25

To Enter the Column Titles

1 With cell **A3** selected, type `Stock` and then press the RIGHT ARROW key.

2 Type `Symbol` in cell **B3** and then press the RIGHT ARROW key.

3 In cell **C3**, type `Date` and then press ALT+ENTER. Type `Acquired` and then press the RIGHT ARROW key.

4 Type `Shares` in cell **D3** and then press the RIGHT ARROW key.

5 In cell **E3**, type `Initial` and then press ALT+ENTER. Type `Price` and then press ALT+ENTER. Type `Per Share` and then press the RIGHT ARROW key.

6 In cell **F3**, type `Initial` and then press ALT+ENTER. Type `Cost` and then press the RIGHT ARROW key.

7 In cell **G3**, type `Current` and then press ALT+ENTER. Type `Price` and then press ALT+ENTER. Type `Per Share` and then press the RIGHT ARROW key.

8 In cell **H3**, type `Current` and then press ALT+ENTER. Type `Value` and then press the RIGHT ARROW key.

9 Type `Gain/Loss` in cell **I3** and then press the RIGHT ARROW key.

10 In cell **J3**, type `Percent` and then press ALT+ENTER. Type `Gain/Loss` and then click cell **A4**.

The column titles appear as shown in row 3 of Figure 2-4 on page EX 73. When you press ALT+ENTER to add more lines to a cell, Excel automatically increases the height of the entire row.

The stock data in Table 2-1 includes a date on which each stock was acquired. Excel considers a date to be a number and, therefore, it displays the date right-aligned in the cell. The steps on the next page describe how to enter the stock data shown in Table 2-1.

> ### More About
>
> ### Wrapping Text
>
> If you have a long text entry, such as a paragraph, you can instruct Excel to wrap the text in a cell, rather than pressing ALT+ENTER to end a line. To wrap text, right-click in the cell, click Format Cells on the shortcut menu, click the Alignment tab, and then click Wrap text. Excel will increase the height of the cell automatically so the additional lines will fit. If you want to control where each line ends in the cell, rather than letting Excel wrap based on the cell width, however, then you must end each line with ALT+ENTER.

More About

Two-Digit Years

When you enter a two-digit year value, Excel changes a two-digit year less than 30 to 20xx and a two-digit year of 30 and greater to 19xx. Use four-digit years to ensure that Excel interprets year values the way you intend, if necessary.

To Enter the Stock Data

1 **With cell A4 selected, type** 3M **and then press the RIGHT ARROW key. Type** MMM **in cell B4 and then press the RIGHT ARROW key.**

2 **Type** 6/12/00 **in cell C4 and then press the RIGHT ARROW key. Type** 394 **in cell D4 and then press the RIGHT ARROW key.**

3 **Type** 79.75 **in cell E4 and then press the RIGHT ARROW key twice. Type** 120.25 **in cell G4 and then press the ENTER key.**

4 **Click cell A5. Enter the data in Table 2-1 for the eight remaining stocks in rows 5 through 12.**

The stock data appears in rows 4 through 12 as shown in Figure 2-4.

To Enter the Row Titles

More About

Formatting a Worksheet

With early worksheet packages, users often skipped rows to improve the appearance of the worksheet. With Excel it is not necessary to skip rows because you can increase row heights to add white space between information.

1 **Click cell A13. Type** Total **and then press the DOWN ARROW key. Type** Average **in cell A14 and then press the DOWN ARROW key.**

2 **Type** Highest **in cell A15 and then press the DOWN ARROW key. Type** Lowest **in cell A16 and then press the ENTER key. Click cell F4.**

The row titles appear in rows 13 through 16 as shown in Figure 2-4.

With the data entered into the worksheet, the next step is to save the workbook using the file name Blue Chip Stock Club Investment Analysis. As you are building a workbook, it is a good idea to save it often so that you do not lose your work if the computer is turned off or if you lose electrical power.

To Save the Workbook

More About

Entering Numbers into a Range

An efficient way to enter data into a range of cells is to select a range and then enter the first number in the upper-left cell of the range. Excel responds by entering the value and moving the active cell selection down one cell. When you enter the last value in the first column, Excel moves the active cell selection to the top of the next column.

1 **With a floppy disk in drive A, click the Save button on the Standard toolbar.**

2 **When Excel displays the Save As dialog box, type** Blue Chip Stock Club Investment Analysis **in the File name text box.**

3 **If necessary, click 3½ Floppy (A:) in the Save in list. Click the Save button in the Save As dialog box.**

Excel saves the workbook on the floppy disk in drive A using the file name, Blue Chip Stock Club Investment Analysis.

This concludes entering the data into the worksheet. After saving the file, the worksheet remains on the screen with the file name, Blue Chip Stock Club Investment Analysis, on the title bar.

Entering Formulas

The initial cost for each stock, which appears in column F, is equal to the number of shares in column D times the initial price per share in column E. Thus, the initial cost for 3M in cell F4 is obtained by multiplying 394 (cell D4) by 79.75 (cell E4).

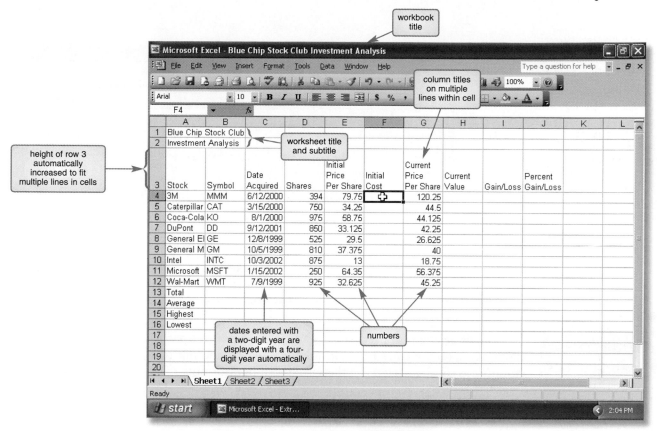

FIGURE 2-4

One of the reasons Excel is such a valuable tool is that you can assign a **formula** to a cell and Excel will calculate the result. Consider, for example, what would happen if you had to multiply 394 × 79.75 and then manually enter the product, 31421.5, in cell F4. Every time the values in cells D4 or E4 changed, you would have to recalculate the product and enter the new value in cell F4. By contrast, if you enter a formula in cell F4 to multiply the values in cells D4 and E4, Excel recalculates the product whenever new values are entered into those cells and displays the result in cell F4. The following steps enter the initial cost formula in cell F4 using the keyboard.

To Enter a Formula Using the Keyboard

1

• With cell F4 selected, type =d4*e4 in the cell.

Excel displays the formula in the formula bar and in cell F4 (Figure 2-5). Excel also displays colored borders around the cells referenced in the formula.

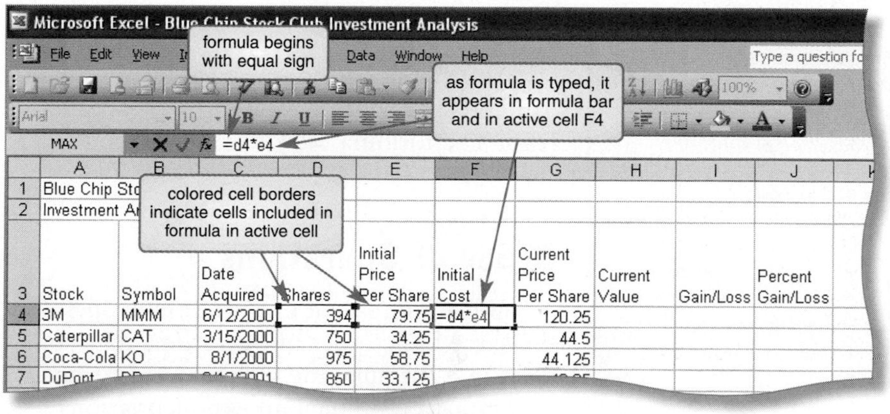

FIGURE 2-5

2

• **Press the RIGHT ARROW key twice to select cell H4.**

Instead of displaying the formula in cell F4, Excel completes the arithmetic operation indicated by the formula and displays the result, 31421.5 (Figure 2-6).

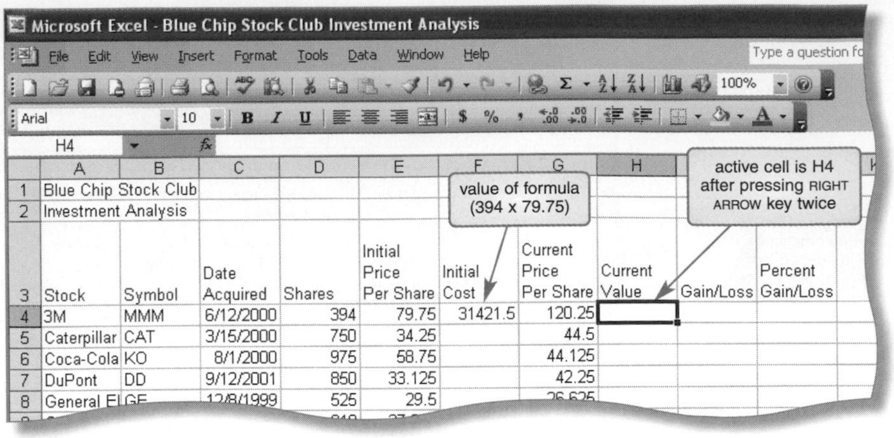

FIGURE 2-6

More About

Automatic Recalculation

Every time you enter a value into a cell in the worksheet, Excel automatically recalculates all formulas. You can change to manual recalculation by clicking Options on the Tools menu and then clicking Manual on the Calculation sheet. In manual calculation mode, press F9 to instruct Excel to recalculate all formulas.

The **equal sign** (=) preceding d4*e4 is an important part of the formula: it alerts Excel that you are entering a formula or function and not text. Because the most common error is to reference the wrong cell in a formula mistakenly, Excel colors the borders of the cells referenced in the formula (Figure 2-5 on the previous page). The coloring helps in the reviewing process to ensure the cell references are correct. The **asterisk** (*) following d4 is the arithmetic operator that directs Excel to perform the multiplication operation. Table 2-2 describes multiplication and other valid Excel arithmetic operators.

Table 2-2   Summary of Arithmetic Operators

ARITHMETIC OPERATOR	MEANING	EXAMPLE OF USAGE	MEANING
–	Negation	–63	Negative 63
%	Percentage	=13%	Multiplies 13 by 0.01
^	Exponentiation	=5 ^ 2	Raises 5 to the second power
*	Multiplication	=17.5 * E4	Multiplies the contents of cell E4 by 17.5
/	Division	=A2 / A4	Divides the contents of cell A2 by the contents of cell A4
+	Addition	=4 + 8	Adds 4 and 8
–	Subtraction	=K15 – 13	Subtracts 13 from the contents of cell K15

You can enter the cell references in formulas in uppercase or lowercase, and you can add spaces before and after arithmetic operators to make the formulas easier to read. The formula, =d4*e4, is the same as the formulas, =d4 * e4, =D4 * e4, or =D4 * E4.

Order of Operations

When more than one arithmetic operator is involved in a formula, Excel follows the same basic order of operations that you use in algebra. Moving from left to right in a formula, the **order of operations** is as follows: first negation (–), then all percentages (%), then all exponentiations (^), then all multiplications (*) and divisions (/), and finally, all additions (+) and subtractions (–).

Q&A

Q: Must all formulas begin with an equal sign?

A: No. Besides the equal sign (=), you can start a formula with a plus sign (+) or a minus sign (-). If you do not begin a formula with one of these three characters, Excel interprets the formula as text.

You can use parentheses to override the order of operations. For example, if Excel follows the order of operations, 8 * 3 + 2 equals 26. If you use parentheses, however, to change the formula to 8 * (3 + 2), the result is 40, because the parentheses instruct Excel to add 3 and 2 before multiplying by 8. Table 2-3 illustrates several examples of valid Excel formulas and explains the order of operations.

Table 2-3   Examples of Excel Formulas

FORMULA	MEANING
=M5	Assigns the value in cell M5 to the active cell.
=12 + – 3^2	Assigns the sum of 12 + 9 (or 21) to the active cell.
=6 * E22 or =E22 * 6 or =(6 * E22)	Assigns six times the contents of cell E22 to the active cell.
=70% * 6	Assigns the product of 0.70 times 6 (or 4.2) to the active cell.
= – (G7 * V67)	Assigns the negative value of the product of the values contained in cells G7 and V67 to the active cell.
=5 * (P4 – G4)	Assigns the product of five times the difference between the values contained in cells P4 and G4 to the active cell.
=K5 / Y7 – D6 * L9 + W4 ^ V10	Instructs Excel to complete the following arithmetic operations, from left to right: first exponentiation (W4 ^ V10), then division (K5 / Y7), then multiplication (D6 * L9), then subtraction (K5 / Y7) – (D6 * L9), and finally addition (K5 / Y7 – D6 * L9) + (W4 ^ V10). If cells K5 = 10, D6 = 6, L9 = 2, W4 = 5, V10 = 2, and Y7 = 2, then Excel assigns the active cell the value 18; that is, 10 / 2 – 6 * 2 + 5 ^ 2 = 18.

Entering Formulas Using Point Mode

The sketch of the worksheet in Figure 2-3 on page EX 69 calls for the current value, gain/loss, and percent gain/loss of each stock to appear in columns H, I, and J, respectively. All three of these values are calculated using formulas. The formula used to calculate the current value for 3M in cell H4 multiples the number of shares in cell D4 by the current price per share in cell G4 (=D4*G4). The formula used to calculate the gain/loss for 3M in cell I4 is equal to the current value in cell H4 minus the initial cost in cell F4 (=H4 – F4). The formula used to calculate the percent gain/loss for 3M in cell J4 is equal to the gain/loss in cell I4 divided by the initial cost in cell F4 (=I4/F4).

An alternative to entering the formulas in cell H4, I4, and J4 using the keyboard is to enter the formulas using the mouse and Point mode. **Point mode** allows you to select cells for use in a formula by using the mouse. The following steps illustrate how to enter formulas using Point mode.

More About

Using Point Mode

Point mode allows you to create formulas using the mouse. You can enter arithmetic operators using the mouse and on-screen keyboard that is available through the Language bar (see Appendix B). Thus, with Excel, you can enter entire formulas without ever touching the keyboard.

To Enter Formulas Using Point Mode

1

• **With cell H4 selected, type = (equal sign) to begin the formula and then click cell D4.**

Excel surrounds cell D4 with a marquee and appends D4 to the equal sign (=) in cell H4 (Figure 2-7).

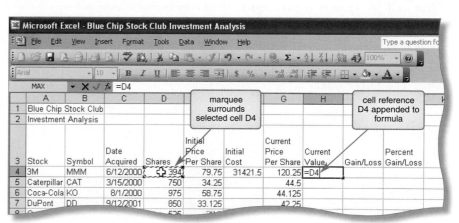

FIGURE 2-7

2

• **Type * (asterisk) and then click cell G4.**

Excel surrounds cell G4 with a marquee and appends G4 to the asterisk (*) in cell H4. The formula =D4*G4 appears in cell H4 and in the formula bar (Figure 2-8).

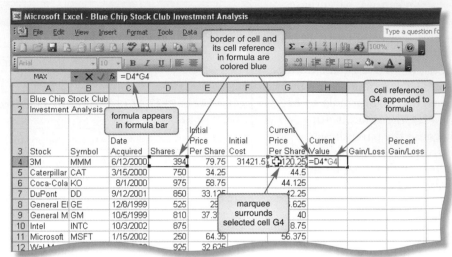

FIGURE 2-8

3

• **Click the Enter box and then click cell I4.**

• **Type = (equal sign) and then click cell H4.**

• **Type – (minus sign) and then click cell F4.**

Excel determines the result of the formula =D4*G4 and displays the result, 47378.5, in cell H4. The formula =H4–F4 appears in cell I4 and in the formula bar (Figure 2-9).

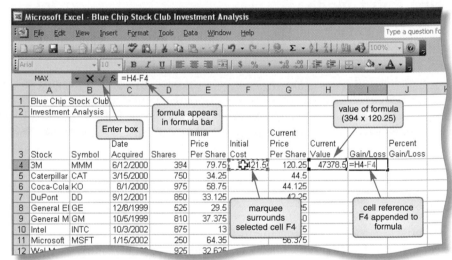

FIGURE 2-9

4

• **Click the Enter box.**

• **Click cell J4. Type = (equal sign) and then click cell I4.**

• **Type / (division sign) and then click cell F4.**

• **Click the Enter box.**

Excel calculates and then displays the gain/loss for 3M (15957) in cell I4 and the Percent gain/loss for 3M (0.507837) in cell J4 (Figure 2-10). The 0.507837 represents approximately 50.78%.

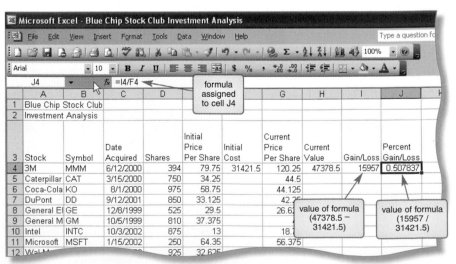

FIGURE 2-10

Depending on the length and complexity of the formula, using Point mode to enter formulas often is faster and more accurate than using the keyboard to type the entire formula. In many instances, as in the previous steps, you may want to use both the keyboard and mouse when entering a formula in a cell. You can use the keyboard to begin the formula, for example, and then use the mouse to select a range of cells.

The actual value assigned by Excel to cell J4 from the division operation in Step 4 is 0.507836990595611. While all the decimal places do not appear in Figure 2-10, Excel maintains all of them for computational purposes. Thus, if cell J4 is referenced in a formula, the value used for computational purposes is 0.507836990595611, not 0.507837. Excel displays the value in cell J4 as 0.507837 because the cell formatting is set to display only 6 digits after the decimal point. If you change the cell formatting of column J to display 15 digits after the decimal point, then Excel displays the true value 0.507836990595611. It is important to recognize this difference between the value Excel displays in a cell and the actual value to understand why the sum of data in a column sometimes is a tenth or hundredth off from the expected value.

More About

Troubling Formulas

If Excel does not accept a formula, remove the equal sign from the left side and complete the entry as text. Later, after you have entered additional data or determined the error, reinsert the equal sign to change the text back to a formula and edit the formula, as needed.

Copying Formulas Using the Fill Handle

The four formulas for 3M in cells F4, H4, I4, and J4 now are complete. You could enter the same four formulas one at a time for the eight remaining stocks, Caterpillar, Coca-Cola, DuPont, General Electric, General Motors, Intel, Microsoft, and Wal-Mart. A much easier method of entering the formulas, however, is to select the formulas in row 4 and then use the fill handle to copy them through row 12. Recall from Project 1 that the fill handle is a small rectangle in the lower-right corner of the active cell. The following steps show how to copy the formulas using the fill handle.

To Copy Formulas Using the Fill Handle

1

• **Click cell F4 and then point to the fill handle.**

• **Drag the fill handle down through cell F12 and continue to hold down the mouse button.**

A border surrounds the source and destination areas (range F4:F12) and the mouse pointer changes to a cross hair (Figure 2-11).

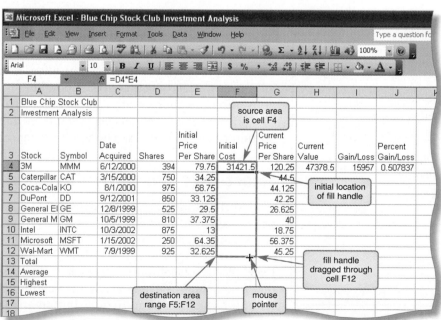

FIGURE 2-11

2

• **Release the mouse button.**

• **Select the range H4:J4 and then point to the fill handle.**

Excel copies the formula =D4*E4 to the range F5:F12 and displays the initial costs for the remaining eight stocks. Excel highlights the selected range H4:J4 (Figure 2-12). The Auto Fill Options button, which allows you to refine the copy, appears at the lower right of the destination range.

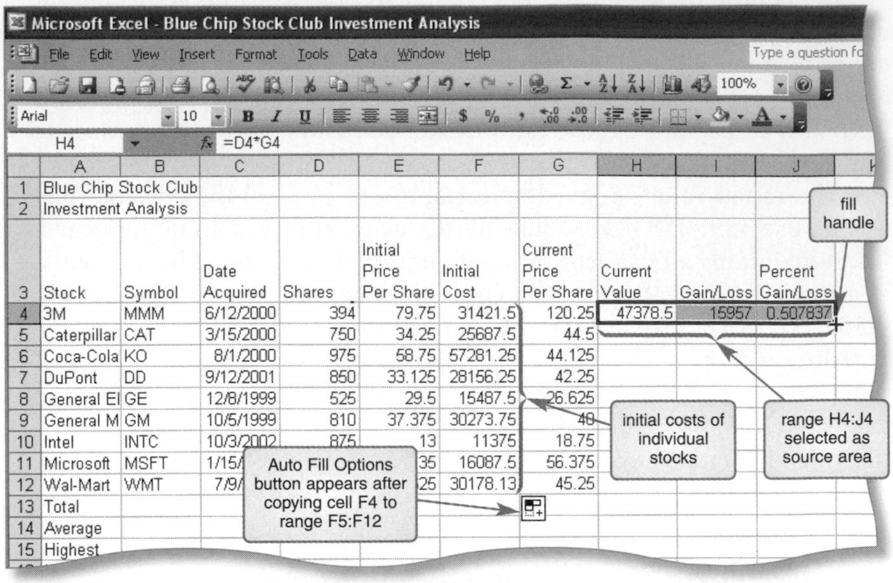

FIGURE 2-12

3

• **Drag the fill handle down through the range H5:J12.**

Excel copies the three formulas =D4*G4 in cell H4, =H4-F4 in cell I4, and =I4/F4 in cell J4 to the range H5:J12. The worksheet now displays the current value, gain/loss, and percent gain/loss for the remaining eight stocks (Figure 2-13).

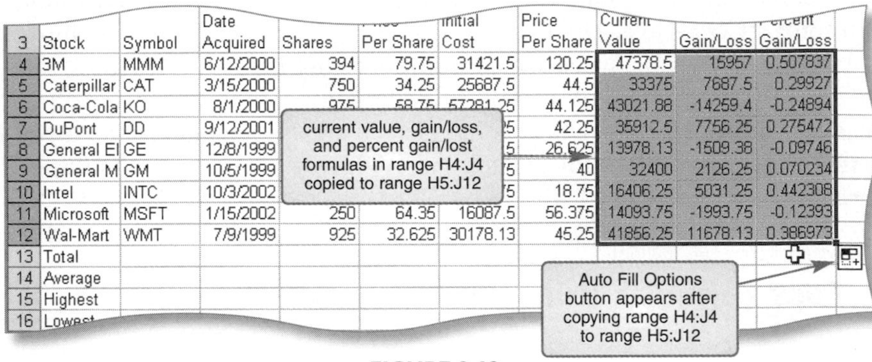

FIGURE 2-13

Other Ways

1. Select source area, click Copy button on Standard toolbar, select destination area, click Paste button on Standard toolbar
2. Select source area, on Edit menu click Copy, select destination area, on Edit menu click Paste
3. Select source area, right-click copy area, click Copy on shortcut menu, select destination area, right-click paste area, click Paste on shortcut menu
4. In Voice Command mode, [select source area], say "Copy", [select destination area], say "Paste"

Recall that when you copy a formula, Excel adjusts the cell references so the new formulas contain references corresponding to the new location and performs calculations using the appropriate values. Thus, if you copy downward, Excel adjusts the row portion of cell references. If you copy across, then Excel adjusts the column portion of cell references. These cell references are called **relative references**.

Smart Tags and Option Buttons

Excel can identify certain actions to take on specific data in workbooks using **smart tags**. Data labeled with smart tags includes dates, financial symbols, people's names, and more. To use smart tags, you must turn on smart tags using the AutoCorrect Options command on the Tools menu. Once smart tags are turned on, Excel places a small purple triangle, called a **smart tag indicator**, in a cell to indicate that a smart tag is available. When you move the insertion point over the smart tag indicator, the Smart Tag Actions button appears. Clicking the Smart Tag Actions button arrow produces a list of actions you can perform on the data in that specific cell.

In addition to smart tags, Excel also displays Options buttons in a workbook while you are working on it to indicate that you can complete an operation using automatic features such as AutoCorrect, Auto Fill, error checking, and others. For example, the Auto Fill Options button shown in Figures 2-12 and 2-13 appears after a fill operation, such as dragging the fill handle. When an error occurs in a formula in a cell, Excel displays the Trace Error button next to the cell and identifies the cell with the error by placing a green triangle in the upper left of the cell.

Table 2-4 summarizes the smart tag and Options buttons available in Excel. When one of these buttons appears on your worksheet, click the button arrow to produce the list of options for modifying the operation or to obtain additional information.

Table 2-4 Smart Tag and Options Buttons in Excel

BUTTON	NAME	MENU FUNCTION
	Auto Fill Options	Gives options for how to fill cells following a fill operation, such as dragging the fill handle
	AutoCorrect Options	Undoes an automatic correction, stops future automatic corrections of this type, or causes Excel to display the AutoCorrect Options dialog box
	Insert Options	Lists formatting options following an insert of cells, rows, or columns
	Paste Options	Specifies how moved or pasted items should appear (for example, with original formatting, without formatting, or with different formatting)
	Smart Tag Actions	Lists information options for a cell containing data recognized by Excel, such as a stock symbol (see In the Lab 3, Part 4 on Page EX 139)
	Trace Error	Lists error checking options following the assignment of an invalid formula to a cell

Determining Totals Using the AutoSum Button

The next step is to determine the totals in row 13 for the initial cost in column F, current value in column H, and gain/loss in column I. To determine the total initial cost in column F, the values in the range F4 through F12 must be summed. To do so, enter the function =sum(f4:f12) in cell F13 or select cell F13 and then click the AutoSum button on the Standard toolbar twice. Similar SUM functions or the AutoSum button can be used in cells H13 and I13 to determine total current value and total gain/loss, respectively. Recall from Project 1 that when you select one cell and use the AutoSum button, you must click the AutoSum button twice. If you select a range, then you need only click the AutoSum button once.

To Determine Totals Using the AutoSum Button

1 Select cell F13. Click the AutoSum button on the Standard toolbar twice.

2 Select the range H13:I13. Click the AutoSum button.

Excel displays the three totals in row 13 as shown in Figure 2-14.

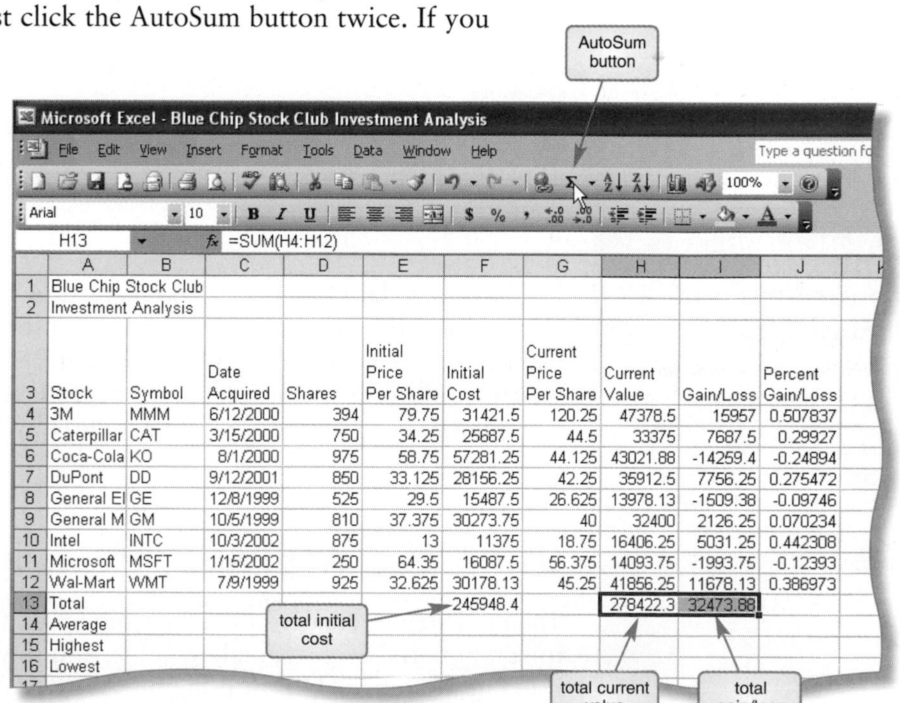

FIGURE 2-14

Microsoft Office
Excel 2003

Rather than using the AutoSum button to calculate column totals individually, you can select all three cells before clicking the AutoSum button to calculate all three column totals at one time. To select the nonadjacent range F13, H13, and I13, select cell F13, and then, while holding down the CTRL key, drag through the range H13:I13. Next, click the AutoSum button on the Standard toolbar.

Determining the Total Percent Gain/Loss

With the totals in row 13 determined, the next step is to copy the percent gain/loss formula in cell J12 to cell J13 as shown in the following steps.

To Determine the Total Percent Gain/Loss

1 Select cell J12 and then point to the fill handle.

2 Drag the fill handle down through cell J13.

Excel copies the formula, =I12/F12, in cell J12 to cell J13 and then adjusts the row references. The resulting formula in cell J13 is =I13/F13, which shows the club's holdings had a total gain of 0.132035 or 13.2035% (Figure 2-15).

	A	B	C	D	E	F	G	H	I	J	K	L
1	Blue Chip Stock Club											
2	Investment Analysis											
3	Stock	Symbol	Date Acquired	Shares	Initial Price Per Share	Initial Cost	Current Price Per Share	Current Value	Gain/Loss	Percent Gain/Loss		
4	3M	MMM	6/12/2000	394	79.75	31421.5	120.25	47378.5	15957	0.507837		
5	Caterpillar	CAT	3/15/2000	750	34.25	25687.5	44.5	33375	7687.5	0.29927		
6	Coca-Cola	KO	8/1/2000	975	58.75	57281.25	44.125	43021.88	-14259.4	-0.24894		
7	DuPont	DD	9/12/2001	850	33.125	28156.25	42.25	35912.5	7756.25	0.275472		
8	General El	GE	12/8/1999	525	29.5	15487.5	26.625	13978.13	-1509.38	-0.09746		
9	General M	GM	10/5/1999	810	37.375	30273.75	40	32400	2126.25	0.070234		
10	Intel	INTC	10/3/2002	875	13	11375	18.75	16406.25	5031.25	0.442308		
11	Microsoft	MSFT	1/15/2002	250	64.35	16087.5	56.375	14093.75	-1993.75	-0.12393		
12	Wal-Mart	WMT	7/9/1999	925	32.625	30178.13	45.25	41856.25	11678.13	0.386973		
13	Total					245948.4		278422.3	32473.88	0.132035		
14	Average											
15	Highest											
16	Lowest											

formula is =I12/F12

formula is =I13/F13

Auto Fill Options button appears after copying cell J12 to cell J13

FIGURE 2-15

The formula, I13/F13, was not copied to cell J13 when cell J4 was copied to the range J5:J12 because both cells involved in the computation (I13 and F13) were blank, or zero, at the time. A **blank cell** in Excel has a numerical value of zero, which would have resulted in an error message in cell J13. Once the totals were determined, both cells I13 and F13 (especially F13, because it is the divisor) had non-zero numerical values.

Using the AVERAGE, MAX, and MIN Functions

The next step in creating the Blue Chip Stock Club Investment Analysis worksheet is to compute the average, highest value, and lowest value for the number of shares listed in the range D4:D12 using the AVERAGE, MAX, and MIN functions in the range D14:D16. Once the values are determined for column D, the entries can be copied across to the other columns.

Excel includes prewritten formulas called functions to help you compute these statistics. A **function** takes a value or values, performs an operation, and returns a result to the cell. The values that you use with a function are called **arguments**. All functions begin with an equal sign and include the arguments in parentheses after the function name. For example, in the function =AVERAGE(D4:D12), the function name is AVERAGE, and the argument is the range D4:D12.

With Excel, you can enter functions using one of six methods: (1) the keyboard or mouse; (2) the Insert Function box in the formula bar; (3) the AutoSum button menu; (4) the Function command on the Insert menu; (5) the Name box area in the formula bar (Figure 2-16); and (6) Voice Command mode. The method you choose will depend on your typing skills and whether you can recall the function name and required arguments.

The following pages uses each of the first three methods. The keyboard and mouse method will be used to determine the average number of shares (cell D14). The Insert Function button in the formula bar method will be used to determine the highest number of shares (cell D15). The AutoSum button menu method will be used to determine the lowest number of shares (cell D16).

Determining the Average of a Range of Numbers

The **AVERAGE function** sums the numbers in the specified range and then divides the sum by the number of non-zero cells in the range. To determine the average of the numbers in the range D4:D12, use the AVERAGE function, as shown in the following steps.

To Determine the Average of a Range of Numbers Using the Keyboard and Mouse

> **More About**
>
> ### Statistical Functions
>
> Excel usually considers a blank cell to be equal to 0. The statistical functions, however, ignore blank cells. Excel thus calculates the average of 3 cells with values of 7, blank, and 5 to be 6 or (7 + 5) / 2 and not 4 or (7 + 0 + 5) /3.

1

• **Select cell D14.**

• **Type** =average(**in the cell.**

• **Click cell D4, the first endpoint of the range to average and drag through cell D12, the second endpoint of the range to average. Do not release the mouse button.**

A marquee surrounds the range D4:D12. When you click cell D4, Excel appends cell D4 to the left parenthesis in the formula bar and surrounds cell D4 with a marquee. When you begin dragging, Excel appends to the argument a colon (:) and the cell reference of the cell where the mouse pointer is located (Figure 2-16).

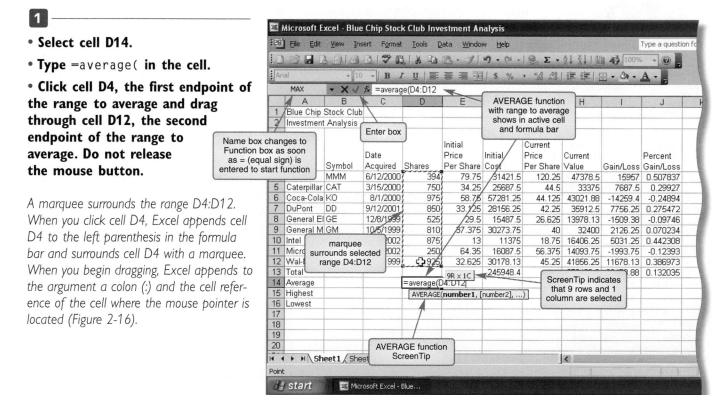

FIGURE 2-16

2

• **Release the mouse button and then click the Enter box.**

Excel computes the average of the nine numbers in the range D4:D12 and displays the result, 706, in cell D14 (Figure 2-17). Thus, the average number of shares owned in the nine companies is 706.

Callouts in figure:
- when cell D14 is active cell, formula bar displays AVERAGE function
- right parenthesis automatically appended when Enter box is clicked or ENTER key pressed
- average shares per stock

	A	B	C	D	E	F	G	H	I	J
1	Blue Chip Stock Club									
2	Investment Analysis									
3	Stock	Symbol	Date Acquired	Shares	Initial Price Per Share	Initial Cost	Current Price Per Share	Current Value	Gain/Loss	Percent Gain/Loss
4	3M	MMM	6/12/2000	394	79.75	31421.5	120.25	47378.5	15957	0.507837
5	Caterpillar	CAT	3/15/2000	750	34.25	25687.5	44.5	33375	7687.5	0.29927
6	Coca-Cola	KO	8/1/2000	975	58.75	57281.25	44.125	43021.88	-14259.4	-0.24894
7	DuPont	DD	9/12/2001	850	33.125	28156.25	42.25	35912.5	7756.25	0.275472
8	General El	GE	12/8/1999	525	29.5	15487.5	26.625	13978.13	-1509.38	-0.09746
9	General M	GM	10/5/1999	810	37.375	30273.75	40	32400	2126.25	0.070234
10	Intel	INTC	10/3/2002	875	13	11375	18.75	16406.25	5031.25	0.442308
11	Microsoft	MSFT	1/15/2002	250	64.35	16087.5	56.375	14093.75	-1993.75	-0.12393
12	Wal-Mart	WMT	7/9/1999	925	32.625	30178.13	45.25	41856.25	11678.13	0.386973
13	Total					245948.4		278422.3	32473.88	0.132035
14	Average			706						
15	Highest									
16	Lowest									

FIGURE 2-17

The AVERAGE function requires that the argument (in this case, the range D4:D12) be included within parentheses following the function name. Excel automatically appends the right parenthesis to complete the AVERAGE function when you click the Enter box or press the ENTER key. When you use Point mode, as in the previous steps, you cannot use the arrow keys to complete the entry. While in Point mode, the arrow keys change the selected cell reference in the range you are selecting.

Determining the Highest Number in a Range of Numbers

The next step is to select cell D15 and determine the highest (maximum) number in the range D4:D12. Excel has a function called the **MAX function** that displays the highest value in a range. Although you could enter the MAX function using the keyboard and Point mode as described in the previous steps, an alternative method to entering the function is to use the Insert Function box in the formula bar, as shown in the following steps.

To Determine the Highest Number in a Range of Numbers Using the Insert Function Box

1

- **Select cell D15.**
- **Click the Insert Function box in the formula bar.**
- **When Excel displays the Insert Function dialog box, click MAX in the Select a function list.**

Excel displays the Insert Function dialog box (Figure 2-18).

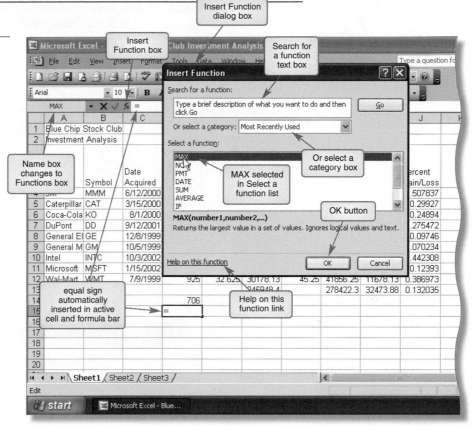

FIGURE 2-18

2

- **Click the OK button.**
- **When Excel displays the Function Arguments dialog box, type** d4:d12 **in the Number 1 box.**

Excel displays the Function Arguments dialog box with the range d4:d12 entered in the Number 1 box (Figure 2-19). The completed MAX function appears in the formula bar, and the last part of the function appears in the active cell, D15.

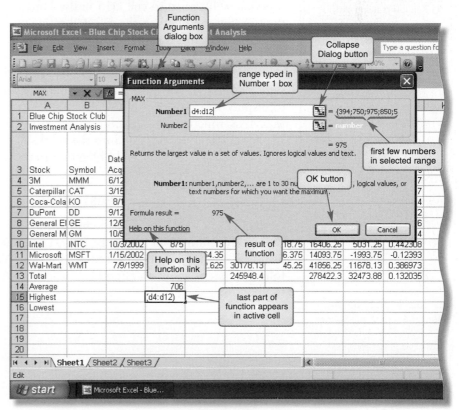

FIGURE 2-19

3

• **Click the OK button.**

Excel determines that the highest value in the range D4:D12 is 975 (value in cell D6) and displays it in cell D15 (Figure 2-20).

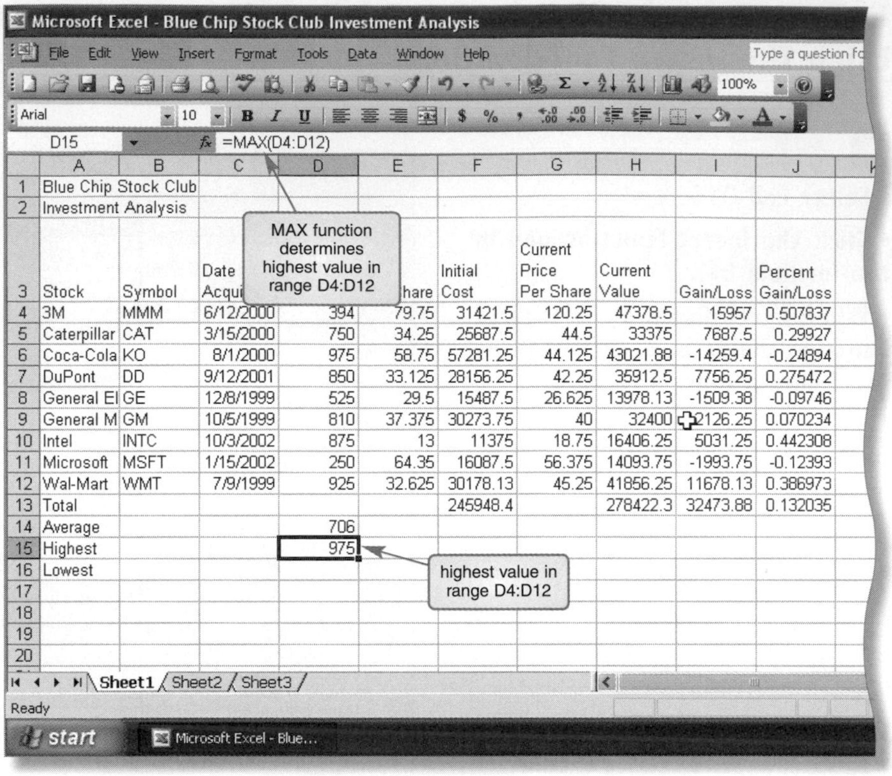

FIGURE 2-20

Other Ways

1. Click AutoSum button arrow on Standard toolbar, click Max function
2. On Insert menu click Function, click MAX in Select a function list
3. Type MAX function in cell
4. Type = (equal sign), click Functions box arrow, click MAX
5. In Voice command mode, say "Insert Function", [select Statistical category], say "Max, OK"

As shown in Figure 2-19 on the previous page, Excel displays the value the MAX function will return to cell D15 in the Function Arguments dialog box. It also lists the first few numbers in the selected range, next to the Number 1 box.

In this example, rather than entering the MAX function, you easily could scan the range D4:D12, determine that the highest number of shares is 975, and manually enter the number 975 as a constant in cell D15. Excel would display the number the same as in Figure 2-20. Because it contains a constant, however, Excel will continue to display 975 in cell D15, even if the values in the range D4:D12 change. If you use the MAX function, Excel will recalculate the highest value in the range D4:D12 each time a new value is entered into the worksheet. Manually determining the highest value in the range also would be more difficult if the club owned more stocks.

Determining the Lowest Number in a Range of Numbers

The next step is to enter the **MIN function** in cell D16 to determine the lowest (minimum) number in the range D4:D12. Although you can enter the MIN function using either of the methods used to enter the AVERAGE and MAX functions, the following steps show an alternative using the AutoSum button menu on the Standard toolbar.

To Determine the Lowest Number in a Range of Numbers Using the AutoSum Button Menu

1

• **Select cell D16.**

• **Click the AutoSum button arrow on the Standard toolbar.**

Excel displays the AutoSum button menu (Figure 2-21).

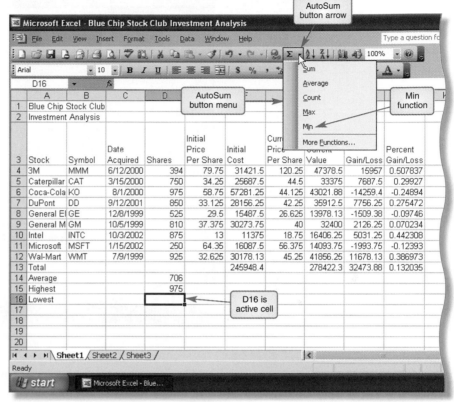

FIGURE 2-21

2

• **Click Min.**

The function =MIN(D14:D15) appears in the formula bar and in cell D16. A marquee surrounds the range D14:D15 (Figure 2-22). The range D14:D15 automatically selected by Excel is not correct.

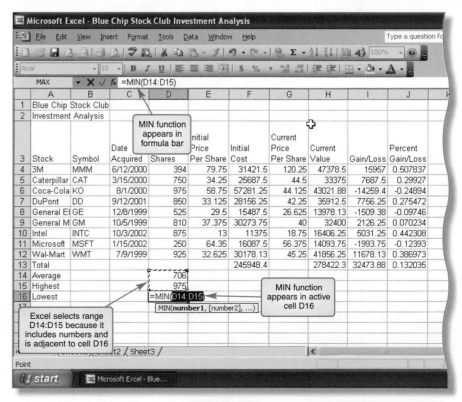

FIGURE 2-22

3

• **Click cell D4 and then drag through cell D12.**

Excel displays the function in the formula bar and in cell D14 with the new range D4:D12 (Figure 2-23).

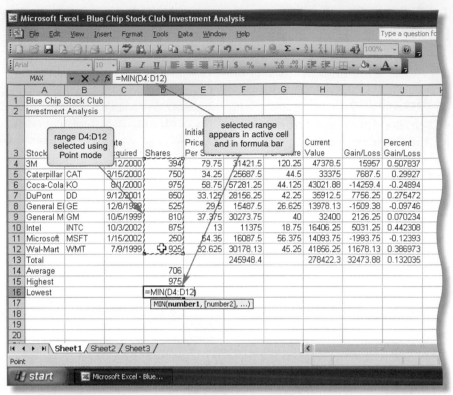

FIGURE 2-23

4

• **Click the Enter box.**

Excel determines that the lowest value in the range D4:D12 is 250 and displays it in cell D16 (Figure 2-24).

	A	B	C	D	E	F	G	H	I	J	K
1	Blue Chip Stock Club										
2	Investment Analysis										
3	Stock	Symbol	Date Acquired	Shares	Initial Price Per Share	Initial Cost	Current Price Per Share	Current Value	Gain/Loss	Percent Gain/Loss	
4	3M	MMM	6/12/2000	394	79.75	31421.5	120.25	47378.5	15957	0.507837	
5	Caterpillar	CAT	3/15/2000	750	34.25	25687.5	44.5	33375	7687.5	0.29927	
6	Coca-Cola	KO	8/1/2000	975	58.75	57281.25	44.125	43021.88	-14259.4	-0.24894	
7	DuPont	DD	9/12/2001	850	33.125	28156.25	42.25	35912.5	7756.25	0.275472	
8	General El	GE	12/8/1999	525	29.5	15487.5	26.625	13978.13	-1509.38	-0.09746	
9	General M	GM	10/5/1999	810	37.375	30273.75	40	32400	2126.25	0.070234	
10	Intel	INTC	10/3/2002	875	13	11375	18.75	16406.25	5031.25	0.442308	
11	Microsoft	MSFT	1/15/2002	250	64.35	16087.5	56.375	14093.75	-1993.75	-0.12393	
12	Wal-Mart	WMT	7/9/1999	925	32.625	30178.13	45.25	41856.25	11678.13	0.386973	
13	Total					245948.4		278422.3	32473.88	0.132035	
14	Average			706							
15	Highest			975							
16	Lowest			250							

FIGURE 2-24

Other Ways

1. Click Insert Function box in formula bar, click MIN function
2. On Insert menu click Function, click MIN in Select a function list
3. Type MIN function in cell
4. Type = (equal sign), click Functions box arrow, click MIN
5. In Voice command mode, say "Insert Function", [select Statistical category], say "Min, OK"

You can see from the previous example that using the AutoSum button menu allows you to enter one of five often-used functions easily into a cell, without having to memorize its name or the required arguments. If you need to enter a function not available on the AutoSum button menu and cannot remember its name, then click More Functions on the AutoSum button menu or click the Insert Function box in the formula bar.

Thus far, you have learned to use the SUM, AVERAGE, MAX, and MIN functions. In addition to these four functions, Excel has more than 400 additional functions that perform just about every type of calculation you can imagine. These functions are categorized in the Insert Function dialog box shown in Figure 2-18 on page EX 83. To view the categories, click the Or select a category box arrow. To obtain a description of a selected function, select its name in the Insert Function dialog box. Excel displays the description of the function below the Select a function list in the dialog box.

Copying the AVERAGE, MAX, and MIN Functions

The next step is to copy the AVERAGE, MAX, and MIN functions in the range D14:D16 to the adjacent range E14:J16. The fill handle again will be used to complete the copy. The following steps illustrate this procedure.

To Copy a Range of Cells across Columns to an Adjacent Range Using the Fill Handle

1

• **Select the range D14:D16.**

• **Drag the fill handle in the lower-right corner of the selected range through cell J16 and continue to hold down the mouse button.**

Excel displays an outline around the source and destination areas (range D14:J16) as shown in Figure 2-25.

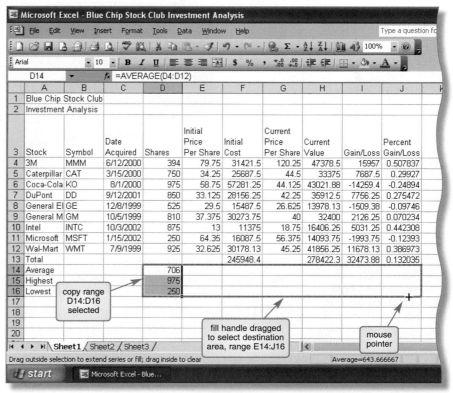

FIGURE 2-25

2

• **Release the mouse button.**

Excel copies the three functions to the range E14:J16 (Figure 2-26). The Auto Fill Options button appears to allow you to refine the copy.

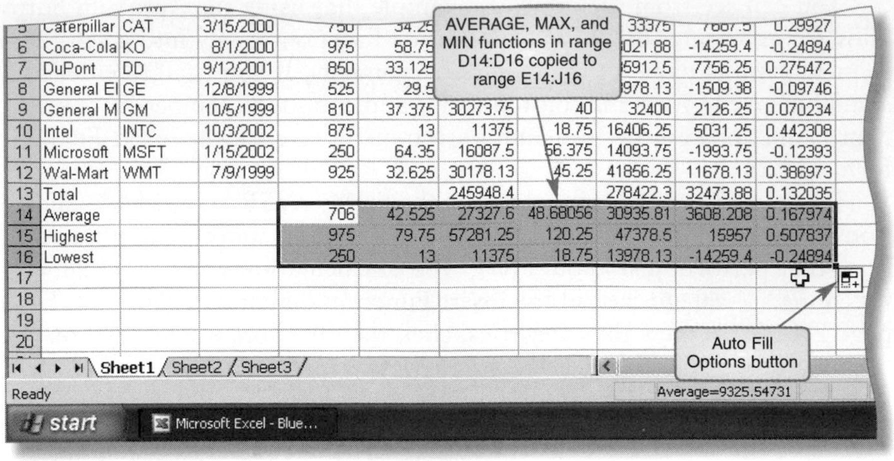

5	Caterpillar	CAT	3/15/2000	750	34.25			33375	7667.5	0.29927
6	Coca-Cola	KO	8/1/2000	975	58.75	AVERAGE, MAX, and		021.88	-14259.4	-0.24894
7	DuPont	DD	9/12/2001	850	33.125	MIN functions in range		5912.5	7756.25	0.275472
8	General El	GE	12/8/1999	525	29.5	D14:D16 copied to		978.13	-1509.38	-0.09746
9	General M	GM	10/5/1999	810	37.375	30273.75	40	32400	2126.25	0.070234
10	Intel	INTC	10/3/2002	875	13	11375	18.75	16406.25	5031.25	0.442308
11	Microsoft	MSFT	1/15/2002	250	64.35	16087.5	56.375	14093.75	-1993.75	-0.12393
12	Wal-Mart	WMT	7/9/1999	925	32.625	30178.13	45.25	41856.25	11678.13	0.386973
13	Total					245948.4		278422.3	32473.88	0.132035
14	Average			706	42.525	27327.6	48.68056	30935.81	3608.208	0.167974
15	Highest			975	79.75	57281.25	120.25	47378.5	15957	0.507837
16	Lowest			250	13	11375	18.75	13978.13	-14259.4	-0.24894
17										
18										
19										
20										

Auto Fill
Options button

FIGURE 2-26

3

• **Select cell J14 and press the DELETE key to delete the average of the percent gain/loss.**

Cell J14 is blank (Figure 2-27).

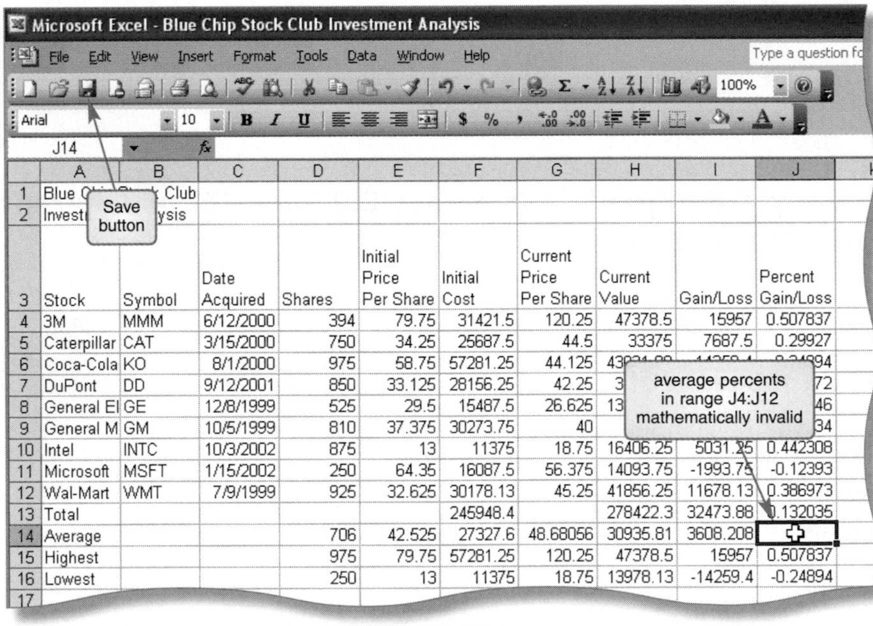

Microsoft Excel - Blue Chip Stock Club Investment Analysis

File   Edit   View   Insert   Format   Tools   Data   Window   Help

	A	B	C	D	E	F	G	H	I	J
1	Blue Chip Stock Club									
2	Investment Analysis									
3	Stock	Symbol	Date Acquired	Shares	Initial Price Per Share	Initial Cost	Current Price Per Share	Current Value	Gain/Loss	Percent Gain/Loss
4	3M	MMM	6/12/2000	394	79.75	31421.5	120.25	47378.5	15957	0.507837
5	Caterpillar	CAT	3/15/2000	750	34.25	25687.5	44.5	33375	7687.5	0.29927
6	Coca-Cola	KO	8/1/2000	975	58.75	57281.25	44.125	43		
7	DuPont	DD	9/12/2001	850	33.125	28156.25	42.25	3	average percents in range J4:J12 mathematically invalid	72
8	General El	GE	12/8/1999	525	29.5	15487.5	26.625	13		46
9	General M	GM	10/5/1999	810	37.375	30273.75	40			34
10	Intel	INTC	10/3/2002	875	13	11375	18.75	16406.25	5031.25	0.442308
11	Microsoft	MSFT	1/15/2002	250	64.35	16087.5	56.375	14093.75	-1993.75	-0.12393
12	Wal-Mart	WMT	7/9/1999	925	32.625	30178.13	45.25	41856.25	11678.13	0.386973
13	Total					245948.4		278422.3	32473.88	0.132035
14	Average			706	42.525	27327.6	48.68056	30935.81	3608.208	
15	Highest			975	79.75	57281.25	120.25	47378.5	15957	0.507837
16	Lowest			250	13	11375	18.75	13978.13	-14259.4	-0.24894
17										

Save button

FIGURE 2-27

Other Ways

1. Select source area and point to border of range, while holding down CTRL key, drag source area to destination area
2. Select source area, on Edit menu click Copy, select destination area, on Edit menu click Paste
3. Right-click source area, click Copy on shortcut menu, right-click destination area, click Paste on shortcut menu
4. Select source area, press CTRL+C, select destination area, press CTRL+V
5. In Voice Command mode, [select source area], say "Copy", [select destination area], say "Paste"

Remember that Excel adjusts the cell references in the copied functions so each function refers to the range of numbers above it in the same column. Review the numbers in rows 14 through 16 in Figure 2-26. You should see that the functions in each column return the appropriate values, based on the numbers in rows 4 through 12 of that column.

The average of the percent gain/loss in cell J14 was deleted in Step 3 because an average of percentages of this type is mathematically invalid.

Saving a Workbook Using the Same File Name

Earlier in this project, an intermediate version of the workbook was saved using the file name, Blue Chip Stock Club Investment Analysis. The following step saves the workbook a second time using the same file name.

To Save a Workbook Using the Same File Name

1 **Click the Save button on the Standard toolbar.**

Excel saves the workbook on the floppy disk in drive A using the file name Blue Chip Stock Club Investment Analysis.

Excel automatically stores the latest version of the workbook using the same file name, Blue Chip Stock Club Investment Analysis. When you save a workbook a second time using the same file name, Excel will not display the Save As dialog box as it does the first time you save the workbook. You also can click Save on the File menu or press SHIFT+F12 or CTRL+S to save a workbook again.

If you want to save the workbook using a new name or on a different drive, click Save As on the File menu. Some Excel users, for example, use the Save button to save the latest version of the workbook on the default drive. Then, they use the Save As command to save a copy of the workbook on another drive.

> *More About*
>
> ### File Types
>
> Excel lets you save a workbook in over 30 different file formats, such as Microsoft Excel Workbook, text, Web page, XML Spreadsheet, Unicode Text, Lotus 1-2-3 format, dBASE format, Text (Macintosh), and many more. You select the desired file format in the Save as type list in the Save As dialog box. The different file formats come in handy when you need to transfer the data in a workbook to another application or to non-PC hardware.

Verifying Formulas Using Range Finder

One of the more common mistakes made with Excel is to include a wrong cell reference in a formula. An easy way to verify that a formula references the cells you want it to reference is to use Excel's Range Finder. **Range Finder** can be used to check which cells are referenced in the formula assigned to the active cell. Range Finder allows you to make immediate changes to the cells referenced in a formula.

To use Range Finder to verify that a formula contains the intended cell references, double-click the cell with the formula you want to check. Excel responds by highlighting the cells referenced in the formula so you can check that the cell references are correct. The following steps use Range Finder to check the formula in cell J4.

To Verify a Formula Using Range Finder

1

• **Double-click cell J4.**

Excel responds by displaying different colored borders around the cells referenced by the formula in cell J4 (Figure 2-28). The different colors allow you to see easily which cells are referenced by the formula in cell J4.

2

• **Press the ESC key to quit Range Finder.**

• **Select cell A18.**

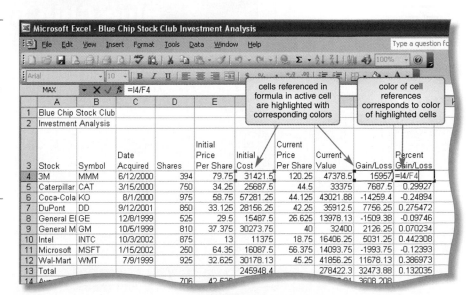

FIGURE 2-28

Not only does Range Finder show you the cells referenced in the formula in cell J4, but it also allows you to drag the colored borders to other cells to instruct Excel to change the cell references in the formula to the newly selected cells. If you use Range Finder to change the cells referenced in a formula, press the ENTER key to complete the edit.

More About

Checking Formulas

A useful command on the Tools menu is the Error Checking command, which checks all formulas in a workbook to ensure they are referencing valid data.

Formatting the Worksheet

Although the worksheet contains the appropriate data, formulas, and functions, the text and numbers need to be formatted to improve their appearance and readability.

In Project 1, the AutoFormat command was used to format the majority of the worksheet. This section describes how to change the unformatted worksheet in Figure 2-29a to the formatted worksheet in Figure 2-29b using the Formatting toolbar and Format Cells command.

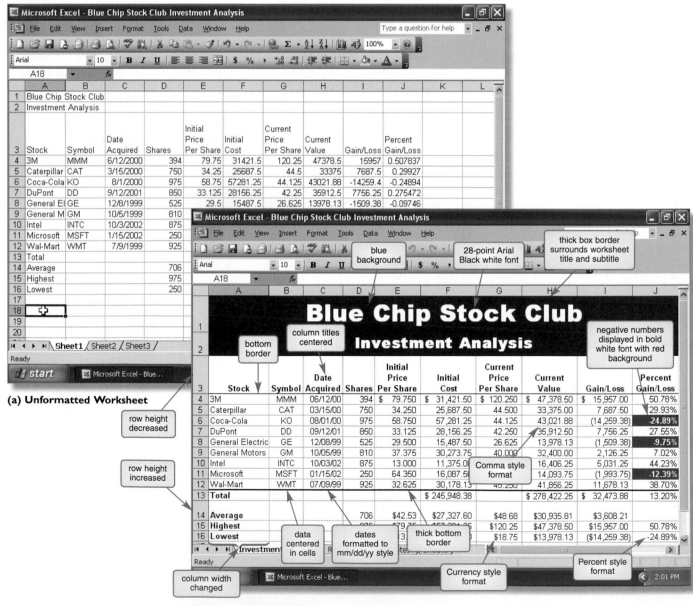

(a) **Unformatted Worksheet**

(b) **Formatted Worksheet**

FIGURE 2-29

The following outlines the formatting suggested in the sketch of the worksheet in Figure 2-3 on page EX 69:

1. Worksheet title and subtitle
   a. Font type — Arial Black
   b. Font size — title 28; subtitle 18
   c. Font style — bold
   d. Alignment — center across columns A through J and center vertically
   e. Background color (range A1:J2) — blue
   f. Font color — white
   g. Border — thick box border around range A1:J2
2. Column titles
   a. Font style — bold
   b. Alignment — center
   c. Border — bottom border on row 3
3. Data
   a. Alignment — center data in column B
   b. Dates in column C — mm/dd/yy format
   c. Numbers in top row (range E4:I4) — Currency style
   d. Numbers below top row (range E5:I12) — Comma style
   e. Border — thick bottom border on row 12
4. Total line
   a. Font style of row title in cell A13 — bold
   b. Numbers — Currency style
5. Average, Highest, and Lowest lines
   a. Font style of row titles in range A14:A16 — bold
   b. Numbers — Currency style with floating dollar sign in the range E14:I16
6. Percentages in column J
   a. Numbers — Percent style with two decimal places; if a cell in range J4:J12 is less than 0, then cell appears with bold white font and background color of red
7. Column widths
   a. Column A — 13.00 characters
   b. Columns B through D — best fit
   c. Column E, G, and J — 10.00 characters
   d. Columns F, H, and I — 12.00 characters
8. Row heights
   a. Row 3 — 45.00 points
   b. Row 14 — 24.00 points
   c. Remaining rows — default

Except for vertically centering the worksheet title in row 1, the Date format assigned to the dates in column C, the Currency style assigned to the functions in rows 14 through 16, and the conditional formatting in column J, all of the listed formats can be assigned to cells using the Formatting toolbar and mouse.

Changing the Font and Centering the Worksheet Title and Subtitle

When developing presentation-quality worksheets, different fonts often are used in the same worksheet. Excel allows you to change the font of individual characters in a cell or all the characters in a cell, in a range of cells, or in the entire worksheet. To emphasize the worksheet title and subtitle in cells A1 and A2, the font type, size, and style are changed and the title and subtitle are centered as described in the following two sets of steps.

More About

Colors

Knowing how people perceive colors helps you emphasize parts of your worksheet. Warmer colors (red and orange) tend to reach toward the reader. Cooler colors (blue, green, and violet) tend to pull away from the reader. Bright colors jump out of a dark background and are easiest to see. White or yellow text on a dark blue, green, purple, or black background is ideal.

More About

Toolbars

You can remove a button from a toolbar by holding down the ALT key and dragging the button off the toolbar. See Appendix D for information on resetting a toolbar to its default settings.

To Change the Font and Center the Worksheet Title

• **Click cell A1.**

• **Click the Font box arrow on the Formatting toolbar.**

Excel displays the Font list with Arial highlighted (Figure 2-30).

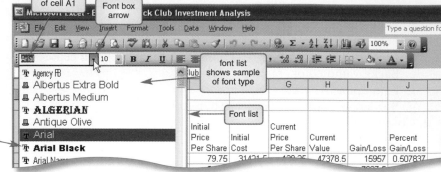

FIGURE 2-30

2

• **Click Arial Black (or Impact if Arial Black is not available).**

• **Click the Font Size box arrow on the Formatting toolbar and then click 28 in the Font Size list.**

• **Click the Bold button on the Formatting toolbar.**

• **Select the range A1:J1. Right-click the selection.**

Excel displays the text in cell A1 in 28-point Arial Black bold font. Excel automatically increases the height of row 1 so that the taller characters fit in the cell. Excel displays the shortcut menu for the selected range A1:J1 (Figure 2-31).

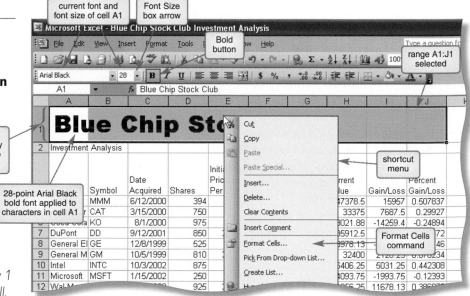

FIGURE 2-31

3

• **Click Format Cells on the shortcut menu.**

• **When Excel displays the Format Cells dialog box, click the Alignment tab.**

• **Click the Horizontal box arrow and select Center in the Horizontal list.**

• **Click the Vertical box arrow and select Center in the Vertical list.**

• **Click Merge cells in the Text control area.**

Excel displays the Format Cells dialog box as shown in Figure 2-32.

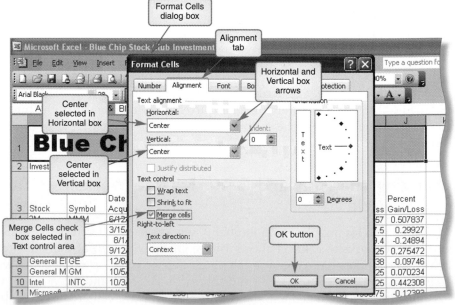

FIGURE 2-32

4
- **Click the OK button.**

Excel merges the cells A1 through J1 to create a new cell A1 and then centers the worksheet title horizontally across columns A through J and centers it vertically in row 1 (Figure 2-33).

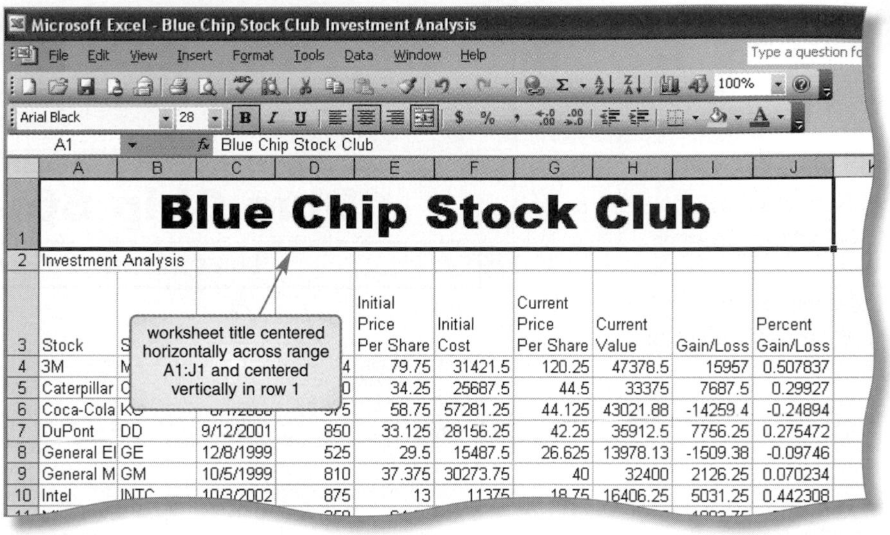

FIGURE 2-33

You can change a font type, size, or style at any time while the worksheet is active. Some Excel users prefer to change fonts before they enter any data. Others change the font while they are building the worksheet or after they have entered all the data.

In Project 1, the Merge and Center button on the Formatting toolbar was used to center the worksheet title across columns. In Step 3 of the previous steps, the Alignment tab in the Format Cells dialog box is used to center the worksheet title across columns, because the project also called for vertically centering the worksheet title in row 1.

The next step is to format the worksheet subtitle in the same fashion as the worksheet title, except that the font size will be changed to 18 rather than 28.

To Change the Font and Center the Worksheet Subtitle

1 Click cell A2. Click the Font box arrow on the Formatting toolbar.

2 Click Arial Black (or Impact if Arial Black is not available).

3 Click the Font Size box arrow on the Formatting toolbar and then click 18 in the Font Size list.

4 Click the Bold button on the Formatting toolbar.

5 Select the range A2:J2. Right-click the selection. Click Format Cells on the shortcut menu. When Excel displays the Format Cells dialog box, click the Alignment tab. Click the Horizontal box arrow and select Center in the Horizontal list. Click the Vertical box arrow and select Center in the Vertical list. Click Merge cells in the Text control area. Click the OK button.

Excel increases the font size of the worksheet subtitle to 18, centers it horizontally across columns A through J, centers it vertically in row 2, and merges the cells A2 through J2 to create a new cell A2 (Figure 2-34 on the next page).

Other Ways

1. On Format menu click Cells, click appropriate tab, select formats, click OK button
2. Press CTRL+I, click appropriate tab, select formats, click OK button
3. In Voice Command mode, say "Format Cells, [desired tab], [desired format], OK"

Q&A

Q: What is the most popular background color?

A: Blue. Research shows that the color blue is used most often because this color connotes serenity, reflection, and proficiency.

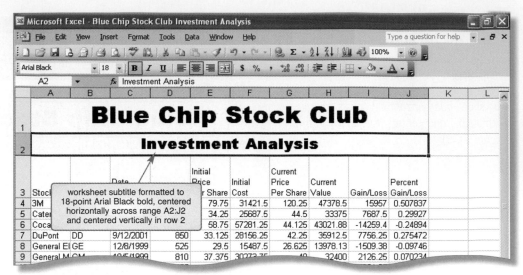

FIGURE 2-34

Some of the formatting, such as the font type, font style, and alignment, could have been done to both titles at the same time by selecting the range A1:A2 before assigning the formats. The font size, which is different, and the merging of cells, however, cannot be done to both titles at the same time.

Changing the Background and Font Colors and Applying a Box Border to the Worksheet Title and Subtitle

The final formats to be assigned to the worksheet title and subtitle are the blue background color, white font color, and thick box border (Figure 2-29b on page EX 90). The following steps complete the formatting of the worksheet titles.

To Change the Background and Font Colors and Apply a Box Border to the Worksheet Title and Subtitle

1

• **Select the range A1:A2, and then click the Fill Color button arrow on the Formatting toolbar.**

Excel displays the Fill Color palette (Figure 2-35).

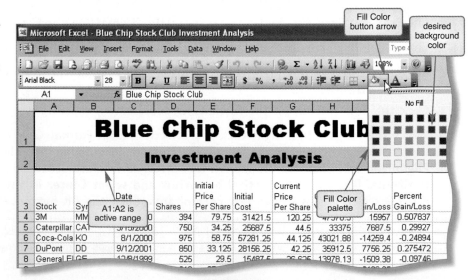

FIGURE 2-35

2

• **Click Blue (column 6, row 2) on the Fill Color palette.**

• **Click the Font Color button arrow on the Formatting toolbar.**

Excel changes the background color of cells A1 and A2 from white to blue and displays the Font Color palette (Figure 2-36).

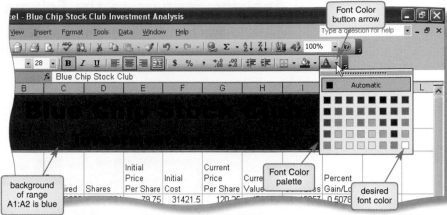

FIGURE 2-36

3

• **Click White (column 8, row 5) on the Font Color palette.**

• **Click the Borders button arrow on the Formatting toolbar.**

Excel changes the font in the worksheet titles from black to white and displays the Borders palette (Figure 2-37).

FIGURE 2-37

4

• **Click the Thick Box Border button (column 4, row 3) on the Borders palette.**

• **Click cell B16 to deselect the range A1:A2.**

Excel displays a thick box border around the range A1:A2 (Figure 2-38).

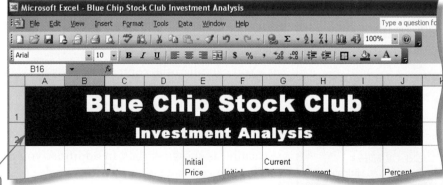

thick box border surrounds worksheet title in cell A1

FIGURE 2-38

You can remove borders, such as the thick box border around the range A1:A2, by selecting the range and clicking the No Border button on the Borders palette. You can remove a background color by selecting the range, clicking the Fill Color button arrow on the Formatting toolbar, and then clicking the No Fill button on the Fill Color palette. The same technique allows you to change the font color back to Excel's default color, except you use the Font Color button arrow and click the Automatic button on the Font Color palette.

Other Ways

1. On Format menu click Cells, click appropriate tab, click desired format, click OK button
2. Right-click range, click Format Cells on shortcut menu, click appropriate tab, click desired format, click OK button
3. In Voice Command mode, say "Format Cells, [desired tab], [desired format], OK"

Applying Formats to the Column Titles

As shown in Figure 2-29b on page EX 90, the column titles are bold, centered, and have a bottom border (underline). The following steps assign these formats to the column titles.

To Bold, Center, and Apply a Bottom Border to the Column Titles

1

• **Select the range A3:J3.**

• **Click the Bold button on the Formatting toolbar.**

• **Click the Center button on the Formatting toolbar.**

• **Click the Borders button arrow on the Formatting toolbar.**

The column titles in row 3 are bold and centered (Figure 2-39). Excel displays the Borders palette. Excel also displays the column titles in columns E and G on four lines. In cell J3, the last letter of the column title appears on a line by itself.

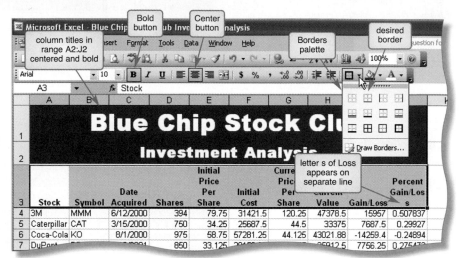

FIGURE 2-39

2

• **Click the Bottom Border button (column 2, row 1) on the Borders palette.**

Excel adds a bottom border to the range A3:J3.

Other Ways

1. On Format menu click Cells, click appropriate tab, click desired format, click OK button
2. Right-click range, click Format Cells on shortcut menu, click appropriate tab, click desired format, click OK button
3. Press CTRL+I, click appropriate tab, click desired format, click OK button
4. In Voice Command mode, say "Bold, Center, Borders, Bottom Border"

You can align the contents of cells in several different ways. Left alignment, center alignment, and right alignment are the more frequently used horizontal alignments. In fact, these three horizontal alignments are used so often that Excel has Align Left, Center, and Align Right buttons on the Formatting toolbar. In addition to aligning the contents of a cell horizontally, you also can align the contents of a cell vertically, as shown earlier. In addition, you can change the orientation of a cell to display the cell contents at various angles (see the Format Cells dialog box in Figure 2-32 on page EX 92).

Centering the Stock Symbols and Formatting the Dates and Numbers in the Worksheet

With the column titles formatted, the next step is to center the stock symbols in column B and format the dates in column C. If a cell entry is short, such as the stock symbols in column B, centering the entries within their respective columns improves the appearance of the worksheet. The following steps center the data in the range B4:B12 and format the dates in the range C4:C12.

To Center Data in Cells and Format Dates

1

- **Select the range B4:B12.**
- **Click the Center button on the Formatting toolbar.**

Excel centers the stock symbols in column B.

2

- **Select the range C4:C12.**
- **Right-click the selected range and then click Format Cells on the shortcut menu.**
- **When Excel displays the Format Cells dialog box, click the Number tab, click Date in the Category list, and then click 03/14/01 in the Type list.**

Excel displays the Format Cells dialog box as shown in Figure 2-40.

3

- **Click the OK button.**
- **Select cell E4 to deselect the range C4:C12.**

Excel displays the dates in column C using the date format style, mm/dd/yy (Figure 2-41).

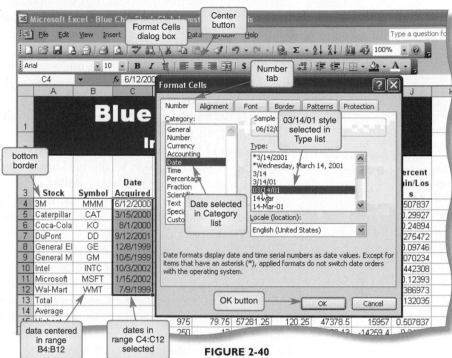

FIGURE 2-40

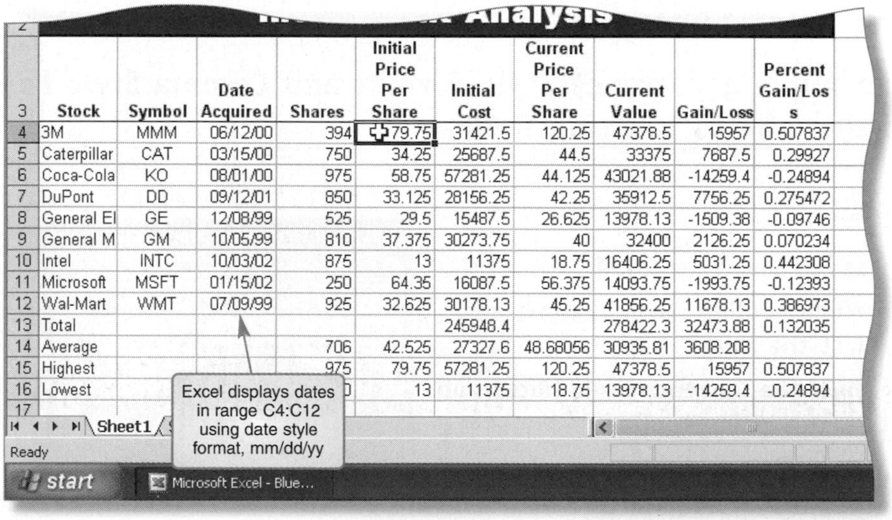

FIGURE 2-41

Rather than selecting the range B4:B12 in Step 1, you could have clicked the column B heading immediately above cell B1, and then clicked the Center button on the Formatting toolbar. In this case, all cells in column B down to cell B65536 would have been formatted to use center alignment. This same procedure could have been used to format the dates in column C.

Formatting Numbers Using the Formatting Toolbar

Microsoft Office
Excel 2003

As shown in Figure 2-29b on page EX 90, the worksheet is formatted to resemble an accounting report. For example, in columns E through I, the numbers in the first row (row 4), the totals row (row 13), and the rows below the totals (rows 14 through 16) have dollar signs, while the remaining numbers (rows 5 through 12) in columns E through I do not.

To append a dollar sign to a number, you should use the Currency style format. Excel displays numbers using the **Currency style format** with a dollar sign to the left of the number, inserts a comma every three positions to the left of the decimal point, and displays numbers to the nearest cent (hundredths place). Clicking the Currency Style button on the Formatting toolbar assigns the desired Currency style format. When you use the Currency Style button to assign the Currency style format, Excel displays a **fixed dollar sign** to the far left in the cell, often with spaces between it and the first digit. To assign a **floating dollar sign** that appears immediately to the left of the first digit with no spaces, you must use the Cells command on the Format menu or the Format Cells command on the shortcut menu. The sketch of the worksheet in Figure 2-3 on page EX 69 calls for the Currency style format with a fixed dollar sign to be assigned to the numbers in the ranges E4:I4 and F13:I13, and the Currency style format with a floating dollar sign to be assigned to the numbers in the range E14:I16.

The Comma style format is used to instruct Excel to display numbers with commas and no dollar signs. The **Comma style format**, which can be assigned to a range of cells by clicking the Comma Style button on the Formatting toolbar, inserts a comma every three positions to the left of the decimal point and causes numbers to be displayed to the nearest hundredths.

The following steps show how to assign formats using the Currency Style button and the Comma Style button on the Formatting toolbar.

To Apply a Currency Style Format and Comma Style Format Using the Formatting Toolbar

1

• **Select the range E4:I4.**

• **While holding down the CTRL key, select the range F13:I13.**

• **Click the Currency Style button on the Formatting toolbar.**

Excel applies the Currency style format with fixed dollar signs to the nonadjacent ranges E4:I4 and F13:I13 as shown in Figure 2-42. Excel automatically increases the width of columns F, H, and I to best fit, so the numbers assigned the Currency style format will fit in the cells.

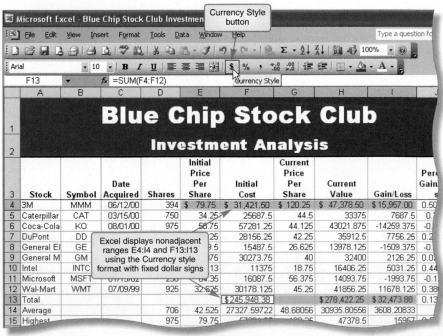

FIGURE 2-42

2

* Select the range E5:I12.
* Click the Comma Style button on the Formatting toolbar.

Excel assigns the Comma style format to the range E5:I12 (Figure 2-43).

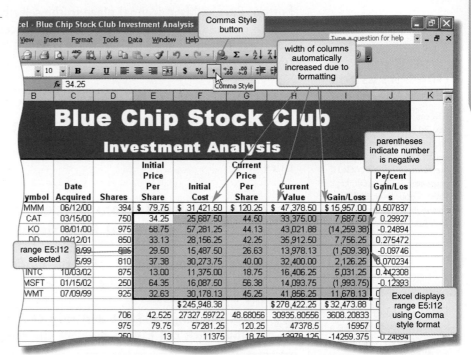

FIGURE 2-43

3

* Click cell E4.
* While holding down the CTRL key, select cell G4.
* Click the Increase Decimal button on the Formatting toolbar.
* Select the range E5:E12. While holding down the CTRL key, select the range G5:G12.
* Click the Increase Decimal button on the Formatting toolbar.
* Click cell A12 to deselect the range G5:G12.

Excel displays the initial prices and current prices with three decimal positions (Figure 2-44).

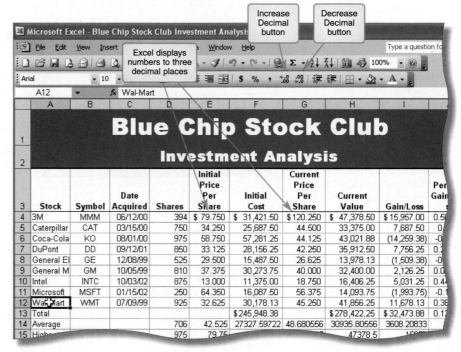

FIGURE 2-44

The Currency Style button assigns a fixed dollar sign to the numbers in the ranges E4:I4 and F13:I13. In each cell in these ranges, Excel displays the dollar sign to the far left with spaces between it and the first digit in the cell. Excel automatically rounds a number to fit the selected format.

Using the Increase Decimal button on the Formatting toolbar instructs Excel to display additional decimal places in a cell. Each time you click the Increase Decimal

More About

Formatting Numbers as You Enter Them

You can format numbers as you enter them by entering a dollar sign ($), comma (,), or percent sign (%) as part of the number. For example, if you enter 1500, Excel displays 1500. If you enter $1500, however, Excel displays $1,500.

Q&A

Q: What causes the sum of a group of numbers to be a penny or two off from an expected result?

A: If the numbers being summed are the result of multiplication or division of decimal fraction numbers, or the sum or difference of numbers with different numbers of decimal places, then the numbers you see on your screen may not be the same as the numbers used in calculations. When a number has more decimal places than Excel displays on the screen, the actual number (not the displayed number) is used in the computation. This can cause the sum to be a penny or two off from an expected result. You can eliminate this problem by using the ROUND function in formulas involving decimal fraction numbers.

button, Excel adds a decimal place to the selected cell. Using the Decrease Decimal button on the Formatting toolbar instructs Excel to display fewer decimal places in a cell. Each time you click the Decrease Decimal button, Excel removes a decimal place to the selected cell.

Applying a Thick Bottom Border to the Row above the Total Row and Bolding the Total Row Titles

The following steps add a thick bottom border to row 12 and bold the total row titles.

To Apply a Thick Bottom Border to the Row above the Total Row and Bold the Total Row Titles

1 Select the range A12:J12, click the Borders button arrow on the Formatting toolbar, and then click the Thick Bottom Border button (column 2, row 2) on the Borders palette.

2 Select the range A13:A16 and then click the Bold button on the Formatting toolbar. Click cell E14 to deselect the range A13:A16.

The row immediately above the total row (row 12) has a thick bottom border, signifying the last stock in the worksheet. The row titles in the range A13:A16 are bold (Figure 2-45).

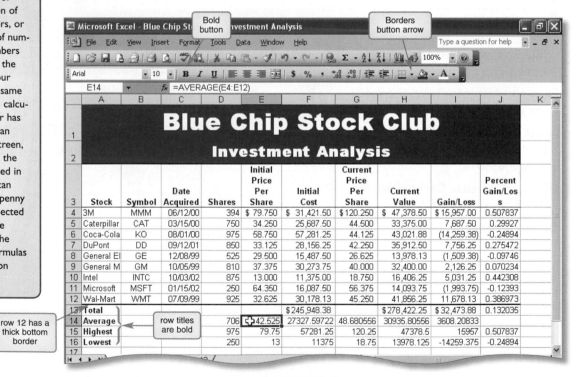

FIGURE 2-45

Formatting Numbers Using the Format Cells Command on the Shortcut Menu

The following steps show you how to use the Format Cells command on the shortcut menu to apply the Currency style format with a floating dollar sign to the numbers in the range E14:I16.

To Apply a Currency Style Format with a Floating Dollar Sign Using the Format Cells Command

1

• **Select the range E14:I16. Right-click the selected range.**

Excel displays the shortcut menu (Figure 2-46).

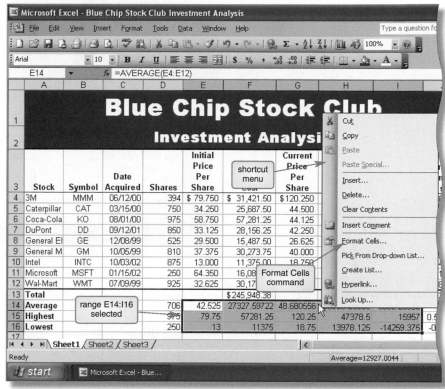

FIGURE 2-46

2

• **Click Format Cells on the shortcut menu.**

• **Click the Number tab in the Format Cells dialog box.**

• **Click Currency in the Category list and then click the third style ($1,234.10) in the Negative numbers list.**

Excel displays the Format Cells dialog box as shown in Figure 2-47.

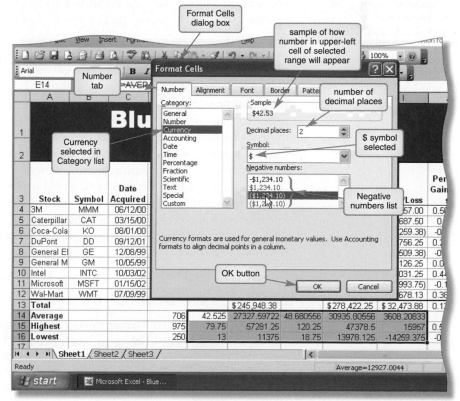

FIGURE 2-47

3

• Click the OK button.

Excel displays the worksheet with the numbers in rows 14 through 16 assigned the Currency style format with a floating dollar sign (Figure 2-48).

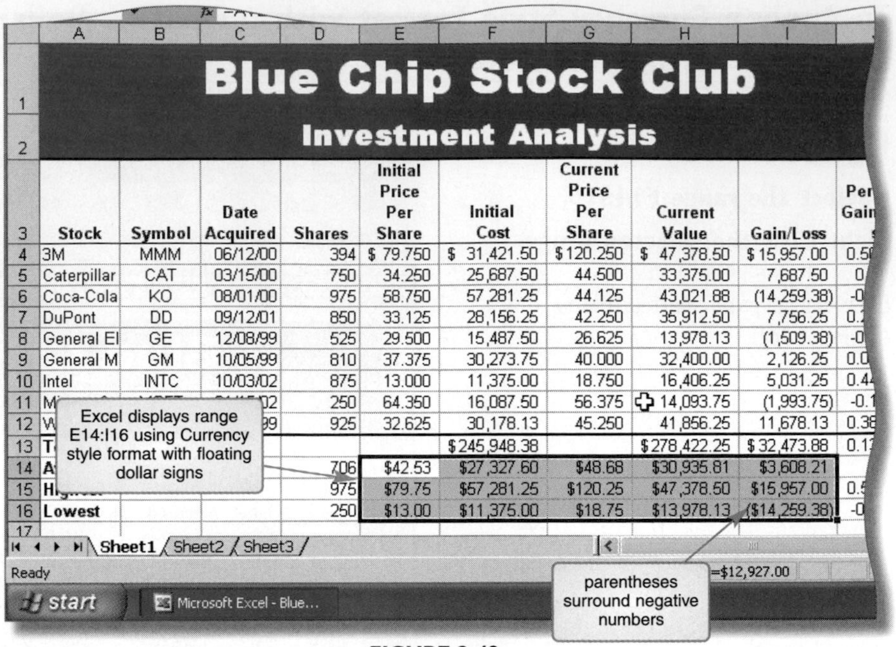

FIGURE 2-48

Other Ways

1. On Format menu click Cells, click Number tab, click Currency in Category list, select format, click OK button
2. Press CTRL+I, click Number tab, click Currency in Category list, select format, click OK button
3. Press CTRL+SHIFT+DOLLAR SIGN
4. In Voice Command mode, say "Format Cells, Number, Currency, OK"

Recall that a floating dollar sign always appears immediately to the left of the first digit, and the fixed dollar sign always appears on the left side of the cell. Cell E4, for example, has a fixed dollar sign, while cell E14 has a floating dollar sign. Also recall that, while cells E4 and E14 both were assigned a Currency style format, the Currency style was assigned to cell E4 using the Currency Style button on the Formatting toolbar and the result is a fixed dollar sign. The Currency style was assigned to cell E14 using the Format Cells dialog box and the result is a floating dollar sign.

As shown in Figure 2-47 on the previous page, you can choose from 12 categories of formats. Once you select a category, you can select the number of decimal places, whether or not a dollar sign should be displayed, and how negative numbers should appear. Selecting the appropriate negative numbers format in Step 2 on the previous page is important, because doing so adds a space to the right of the number in order to align the numbers in the worksheet on the decimal points (as do the Currency Style and Comma Style buttons). Some of the available negative number formats do not align the numbers in the worksheet on the decimal points.

The negative number format selected in the previous set of steps causes the negative entry in cell I16 to appear with parentheses surrounding the number. The third selection in the Negative numbers list (Figure 2-47) purposely was chosen to agree with the negative number format assigned to cell I6 using the Comma Style button.

Formatting Numbers Using the Percent Style Button and Increase Decimal Button

The next step is to format the percent gain/loss in column J. Currently, Excel displays the numbers in column J as a decimal fraction (for example, 0.507837 in cell J4). The following steps format the range J4:J16 to the Percent style format with two decimal places.

To Apply a Percent Style Format

1

- **Select the range J4:J16.**
- **Click the Percent Style button on the Formatting toolbar.**

Excel displays the numbers in column J as a rounded whole percent.

2

- **Click the Increase Decimal button on the Formatting toolbar twice.**

Excel displays the numbers in column J with the Percent style format with two decimal places (Figure 2-49).

FIGURE 2-49

The Percent Style button on the Formatting toolbar is used to instruct Excel to display a value as a percentage, determined by multiplying the cell entry by 100, rounding the result to the nearest percent, and adding a percent sign. For example, when cell J4 is formatted using the Percent Style and Increase Decimal buttons, Excel displays the actual value -0.507836990595611 as 50.78%.

Conditional Formatting

The next step is to emphasize the negative percentages in column J by formatting them to appear with white bold text on a red background. The Conditional Formatting command on the Format menu will be used to complete this task.

Excel lets you apply formatting that appears only when the value in a cell meets conditions that you specify. This type of formatting is called **conditional formatting**. You can apply conditional formatting to a cell, a range of cells, the entire worksheet, or the entire workbook. Usually, you apply conditional formatting to a range of cells that contains values you want to highlight, if conditions warrant. For example, you can instruct Excel to use the bold font style and change the color of the background of a cell if the value in the cell meets a condition, such as being less than 0 as shown below.

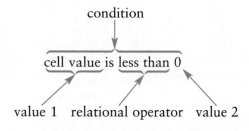

Other Ways

1. On Format menu click Cells, click Number tab, click Percentage in Category list, select format, click OK button
2. Right-click range, click Format Cells on shortcut menu, click Number tab, click Percentage in Category list, select format, click OK button
3. Press CTRL+1, click Number tab, click Percentage in Category list, select format, click OK button
4. Click CTRL+SHIFT+PERCENT SIGN (%)
5. In Voice Command mode, say "Format Cells, Number, Percentage, OK"

A **condition**, which is made up of two values and a relational operator, is true or false for each cell in the range. If the condition is true, then Excel applies the formatting. If the condition is false, then Excel suppresses the formatting. What makes conditional formatting so powerful is that the cell's appearance can change as you enter new values in the worksheet.

The following steps show how to assign conditional formatting to the range J4:J12, so that any cell value less than 0 will cause Excel to display the number in the cell in white bold text with a red background.

To Apply Conditional Formatting

1

• **Select the range J4:J12.**

• **Click Format on the menu bar.**

Excel displays the Format menu (Figure 2-50).

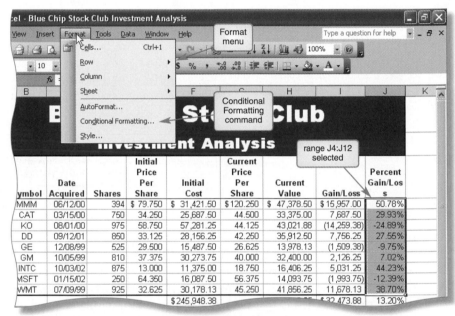

FIGURE 2-50

2

• **Click Conditional Formatting.**

• **When the Conditional Formatting dialog box appears, if necessary, click the leftmost text box arrow and then click Cell Value Is.**

• **Click the middle text box arrow and then click less than.**

• **Type 0 in the rightmost text box.**

Excel displays the Conditional Formatting dialog box as shown in Figure 2-51.

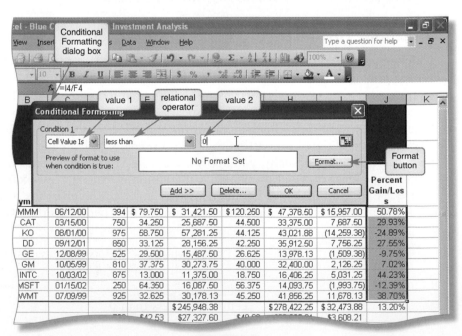

FIGURE 2-51

3

• **Click the Format button.**

• **When Excel displays the Format Cells dialog box, click the Patterns tab and then click Red (column 1, row 3).**

• **Click the Font tab and then click Bold in the Font style list.**

• **Click the Color box arrow.**

Excel displays the Format Cells dialog box as shown in Figure 2-52.

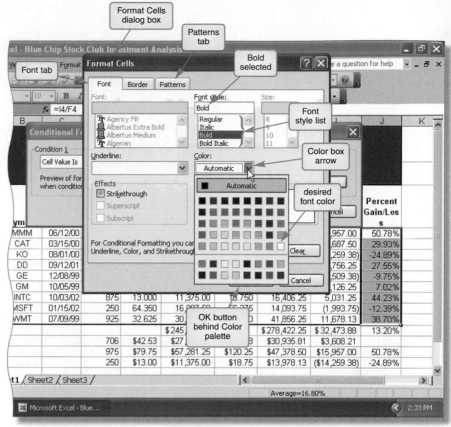

FIGURE 2-52

4

• **Click White (column 8, row 5) and then click the OK button.**

Excel displays the Conditional Formatting dialog box as shown in Figure 2-53. In the middle of the dialog box, Excel displays a preview of the format that Excel will use when the condition is true.

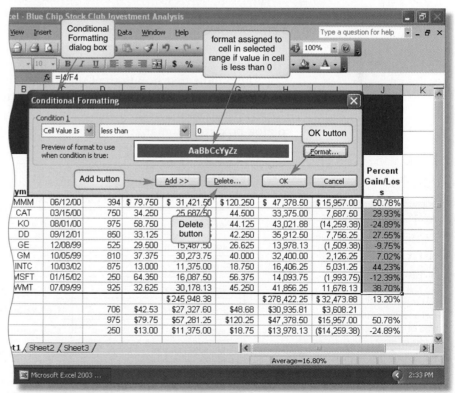

FIGURE 2-53

5

- **Click the OK button.**
- **Click cell B16 to deselect the range J4:J12.**

Excel assigns the conditional format to the range J4:J12. Excel displays any negative value in this range in bold with a red background (Figure 2-54).

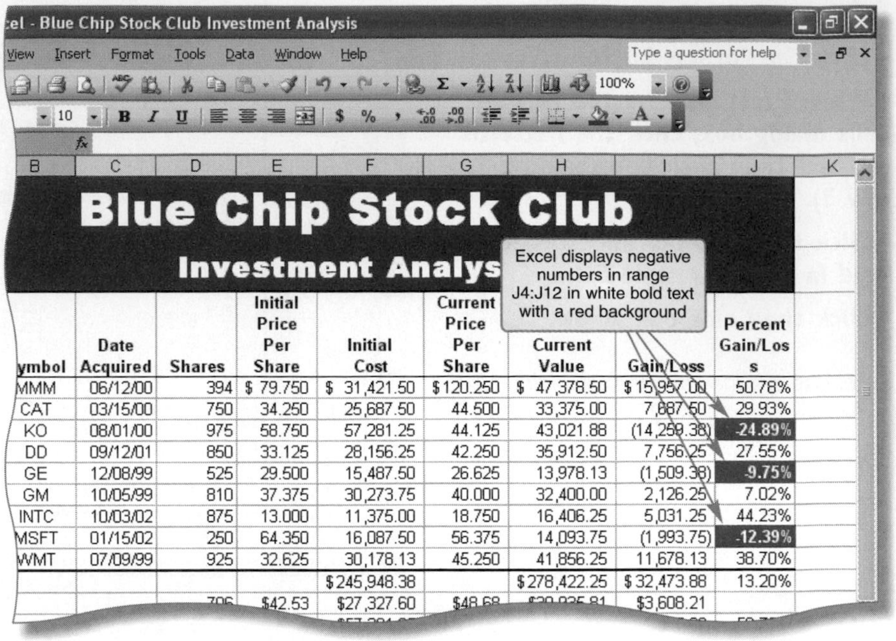

FIGURE 2-54

Other Ways

1. Press ALT+O, D
2. In Voice Command mode, say "Format, Conditional Formatting"

In Figure 2-53 on the previous page, the preview box in the Conditional Formatting dialog box shows the format that will be assigned to all cells in the range J4:J12 that have a value less than 0. This preview allows you to review the format before you click the OK button. The Add button in the Conditional Formatting dialog box allows you to add two additional conditions for a total of three conditions. The Delete button allows you to delete one or more active conditions.

The middle text box in the Conditional Formatting dialog box allows you to select a relational operator, such as less than, to use in the condition. The eight different relational operators from which you can choose in the Conditional Formatting dialog box are summarized in Table 2-5.

More About

Conditional Formatting

You can assign any format to a cell, a range of cells, a worksheet, or an entire workbook conditionally. If the value of the cell changes and no longer meets the specified condition, Excel suppresses the conditional formatting.

Table 2-5 Summary of Conditional Formatting Relational Operators

RELATIONAL OPERATOR	DESCRIPTION
Between	Cell value is between two numbers
Not between	Cell value is not between two numbers
Equal to	Cell value is equal to a number
Not equal to	Cell value is not equal to a number
Greater than	Cell value is greater than a number
Less than	Cell value is less than a number
Greater than or equal to	Cell value is greater than or equal to a number
Less than or equal to	Cell value is less than or equal to a number

With the conditional formatting complete, the next step is to change the column widths and row heights to make the worksheet easier to read.

Changing the Widths of Columns and Heights of Rows

When Excel starts and displays a blank worksheet on the screen, all of the columns have a default width of 8.43 characters, or 64 pixels. A **character** is defined as a letter, number, symbol, or punctuation mark in 10-point Arial font, the default font used by Excel. An average of 8.43 characters in 10-point Arial font will fit in a cell.

Another measure is pixels, which is short for picture element. A **pixel** is a dot on the screen that contains a color. The size of the dot is based on your screen's resolution. At a common resolution of 800 × 600, 800 pixels appear across the screen and 600 pixels appear down the screen for a total of 480,000 pixels. It is these 480,000 pixels that form the font and other items you see on the screen.

The default row height in a blank worksheet is 12.75 points (or 17 pixels). Recall from Project 1 that a point is equal to 1/72 of an inch. Thus, 12.75 points is equal to about 1/6 of an inch. You can change the width of the columns or height of the rows at any time to make the worksheet easier to read or to ensure that Excel displays an entry properly in a cell.

Changing the Widths of Columns

When changing the column width, you can set the width manually or you can instruct Excel to size the column to best fit. **Best fit** means that the width of the column will be increased or decreased so the widest entry will fit in the column. Sometimes, you may prefer more or less white space in a column than best fit provides. Excel thus allows you to change column widths manually.

When the format you assign to a cell causes the entry to exceed the width of a column, Excel automatically changes the column width to best fit. This happened earlier when the Currency style format was used (Figure 2-43 on page EX 99). If you do not assign a format to a cell or cells in a column, the column width will remain 8.43 characters, as is the case in columns A and B. To set a column width to best fit, double-click the right boundary of the column heading above row 1.

The following steps change the column widths: column A to 13.00 characters; columns B through D to best fit; columns E, G, and J to 10.00 characters; and columns F, H, and I to 12.00 characters.

To Change the Widths of Columns

1

• **Point to the boundary on the right side of the column A heading above row 1.**

• **When the mouse pointer changes to a split double arrow, drag to the right until the ScreenTip indicates Width: 13.00 (96 pixels). Do not release the mouse button.**

A dotted line shows the proposed right border of column A (Figure 2-55).

FIGURE 2-55

2

• **Release the mouse button.**

• **Drag through column headings B through D above row 1.**

• **Point to the boundary on the right side of column heading D.**

The mouse pointer becomes a split double arrow (Figure 2-56).

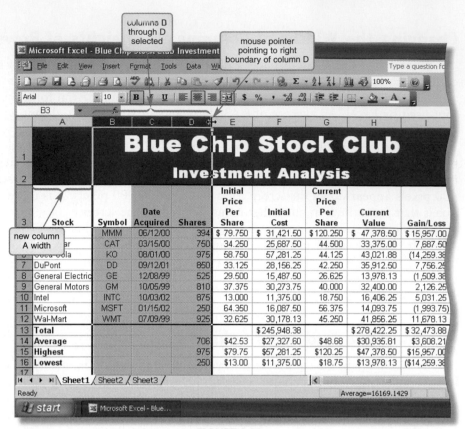

FIGURE 2-56

3

• **Double-click the right boundary of column heading D to change the width of columns B, C, and D to best fit.**

• **Click the column E heading above row 1.**

• **While holding down the CTRL key, click the column G heading and then the column J heading above row 1 so that columns E, G, and J are selected.**

• **Point to the boundary on the right side of the column J heading above row 1.**

• **Drag until the ScreenTip indicates Width: 10.00 (75 pixels). Do not release the mouse button.**

A dotted line shows the proposed right border of column J (Figure 2-57).

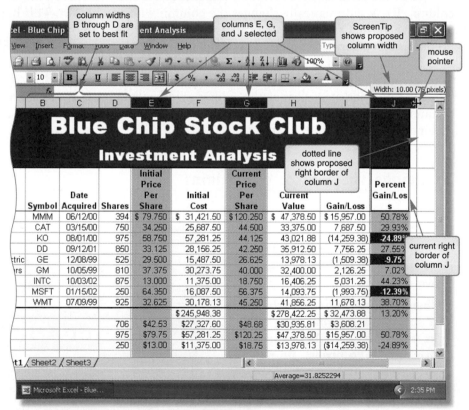

FIGURE 2-57

4

• **Release the mouse button.**

• **Click the column F heading above row 1 to select column F.**

• **While holding down the CTRL key, click the column H and I headings above row 1 so that columns F, H, and I are selected.**

• **Point to the boundary on the right side of the column I heading above row 1.**

• **Drag to the right until the ScreenTip indicates Width: 12.00 (89 pixels). Do not release the mouse button.**

A dotted line shows the proposed right border of column I (Figure 2-58).

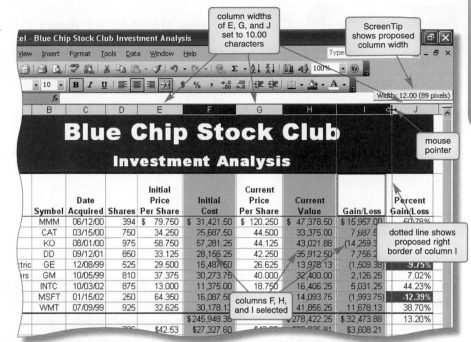

FIGURE 2-58

5

• **Release the mouse button.**

• **Click cell B16 to deselect columns F, H, and I.**

Excel displays the worksheet with the new column widths (Figure 2-59).

FIGURE 2-59

If you want to increase or decrease column width significantly, you can right-click a column heading and then use the Column Width command on the shortcut menu to change the column's width. To use this command, however, you must select one or more entire columns. As shown in the previous set of steps, you select entire columns by dragging through the column headings above row 1.

A column width can vary from zero (0) to 255 characters. If you decrease the column width to 0, the column is hidden. **Hiding cells** is a technique you can use to hide data that might not be relevant to a particular report or sensitive data that you do not want others to see. When you print a worksheet, hidden columns do not print. To instruct Excel to display a hidden column, position the mouse pointer to the right of the column heading boundary where the hidden column is located and then drag to the right.

Other Ways

1. Select cell or range of cells, on Format menu point to Column, click Width on Column sub-menu, enter desired column width, click OK button
2. Right-click column heading or drag through multiple column headings and right-click, click Column Width on shortcut menu, enter desired column width, click OK button
3. In Voice Command mode, say Format, Column, Width, [enter width], OK"

Microsoft Office
Excel 2003

More About

Hidden Columns

Trying to unhide a range of columns using the mouse can be frustrating. An alternative is to use the keyboard, by selecting the columns to the right and left of the hidden columns and then pressing CTRL+SHIFT+RIGHT PARENTHESIS. To use the keyboard to hide a range of columns, press CTRL+0.

Changing the Heights of Rows

When you increase the font size of a cell entry, such as the title in cell A1, Excel automatically increases the row height to best fit so it can display the characters properly. Recall that Excel did this earlier when multiple lines were entered in a cell in row 3 and when the font size of the worksheet title and subtitle were increased.

You also can increase or decrease the height of a row manually to improve the appearance of the worksheet. The following steps show how to improve the appearance of the worksheet by decreasing the height of row 3 to 45.00 points and increasing the height of row 14 to 24.00 points.

To Change the Heights of Rows

1

• **Point to the boundary below row heading 3.**

• **Drag up until the ScreenTip indicates Height: 45.00 (60 pixels). Do not release the mouse button.**

Excel displays a horizontal dotted line (Figure 2-60). The distance between the dotted line and the top of row 3 indicates the proposed height for row 3.

FIGURE 2-60

2

• **Release the mouse button.**

• **Point to the boundary below row heading 14.**

• **Drag down until the ScreenTip indicates Height: 24.00 (32 pixels). Do not release the mouse button.**

Excel displays a horizontal dotted line (Figure 2-61). The distance between the dotted line and the top of row 14 indicates the proposed height for row 14.

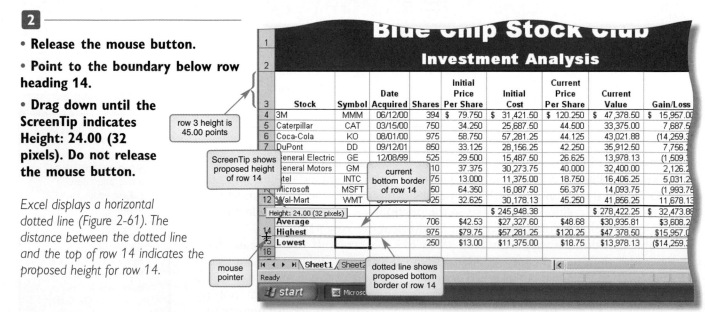

FIGURE 2-61

3

• **Release the mouse button and then select cell B16.**

The Total row and the Average row have additional white space between them, which improves the appearance of the worksheet (Figure 2-62). The formatting of the worksheet is complete.

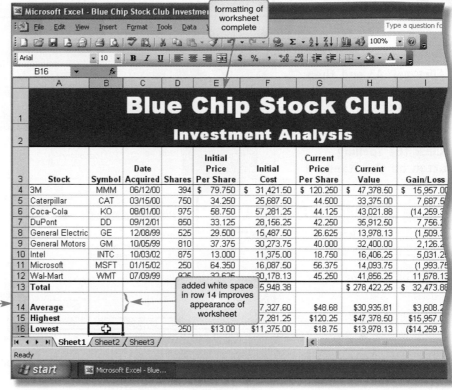

row 14 height is 24.00 points

added white space in row 14 improves appearance of worksheet

FIGURE 2-62

The row height can vary between 0 and 409 points. As with column widths, when you decrease the row height to 0, the row is hidden. To instruct Excel to display a hidden row, position the mouse pointer just below the row heading boundary where the row is hidden and then drag down. To set a row height to best fit, double-click the bottom boundary of the row heading.

The task of formatting the worksheet is complete. The next step is to check the spelling of the worksheet.

Checking Spelling

Excel has a **spell checker** you can use to check the worksheet for spelling errors. The spell checker looks for spelling errors by comparing words on the worksheet against words contained in its standard dictionary. If you often use specialized terms that are not in the standard dictionary, you may want to add them to a custom dictionary using the Spelling dialog box.

When the spell checker finds a word that is not in either dictionary, it displays the word in the Spelling dialog box. You then can correct it if it is misspelled.

To illustrate how Excel responds to a misspelled word, the word, Stock, in cell A3 is misspelled purposely as the word, Stcok, as shown in Figure 2-63 on the next page.

To Check Spelling on the Worksheet

1

• **Click cell A3 and then type** Stcok **to misspell the word Stock.**

• **Click cell A1.**

• **Click the Spelling button on the Standard toolbar.**

When the spell checker identifies the misspelled word, Stcok, in cell A3 it displays the Spelling dialog box (Figure 2-63).

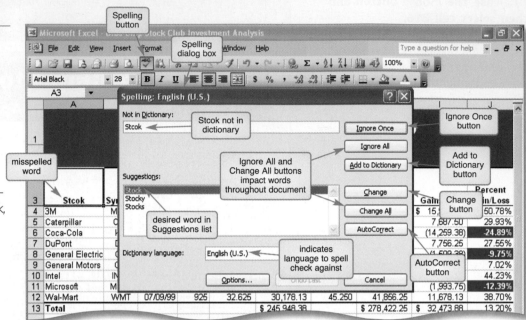

FIGURE 2-63

2

• **With the word Stock highlighted in the Suggestions list, click the Change button.**

• **As the spell checker checks the remainder of the worksheet, click the Ignore All and Change buttons as needed.**

The spell checker changes the misspelled word, Stcok, to the correct word, Stock, and continues spell checking the worksheet. When the spell checker is finished, it displays the Microsoft Office Excel dialog box with a message indicating that the spell check is complete (Figure 2-64).

3

• **Click the OK button.**

• **Click the Save button on the Standard toolbar to save the workbook.**

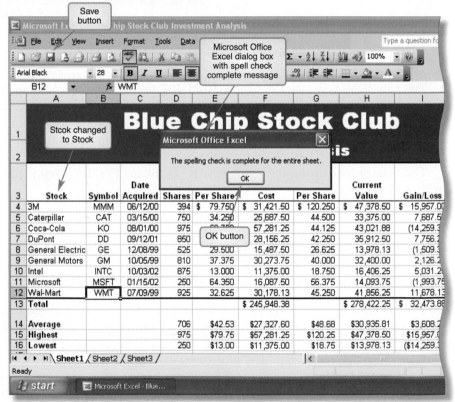

FIGURE 2-64

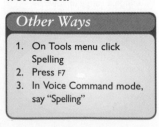

Other Ways

1. On Tools menu click Spelling
2. Press F7
3. In Voice Command mode, say "Spelling"

When the spell checker identifies that a cell contains a word not in its standard or custom dictionary, it selects that cell as the active cell and displays the Spelling dialog box. The Spelling dialog box (Figure 2-63) lists the word not found in the dictionary, a suggested correction, and a list of alternative suggestions. If one of the words in the Suggestions list is correct, click it and then click the Change button. If none of the suggestions is correct, type the correct word in the Not in Dictionary text box and then click the Change button. To change the word throughout the worksheet, click the Change All button instead of the Change button. To skip correcting the word, click the Ignore Once button. To have Excel ignore the word for the remainder of the worksheet, click the Ignore All button.

Consider these additional guidelines when using the spell checker:

- To check the spelling of the text in a single cell, double-click the cell to make the formula bar active and then click the Spelling button on the Standard toolbar.

- If you select a single cell so that the formula bar is not active and then start the spell checker, Excel checks the remainder of the worksheet, including notes and embedded charts.

- If you select a range of cells before starting the spell checker, Excel checks the spelling of the words only in the selected range.

- To check the spelling of all the sheets in a workbook, click Select All Sheets on the sheet tab shortcut menu and then start the spell checker. To instruct Excel to display the sheet tab shortcut menu, right-click any sheet tab.

- If you select a cell other than cell A1 before you start the spell checker, Excel will display a dialog box when the spell checker reaches the end of the worksheet, asking if you want to continue checking at the beginning.

- To add words to the dictionary such as your last name, click the Add to Dictionary button in the Spelling dialog box (Figure 2-63) when Excel identifies the word as not in the dictionary.

- Click the AutoCorrect button (Figure 2-63) to add the misspelled word and the correct version of the word to the AutoCorrect list. For example, suppose you misspell the word, do, as the word, dox. When the spell checker displays the Spelling dialog box with the correct word, do, in the Change to box, click the AutoCorrect button. Then, anytime in the future that you type the word, dox, Excel automatically will change it to the word, do.

Previewing and Printing the Worksheet

In Project 1, the worksheet was printed without first previewing it on the screen. By **previewing the worksheet**, however, you see exactly how it will look without generating a printout. Previewing allows you to see if the worksheet will print on one page in portrait orientation. **Portrait orientation** means the printout is printed across the width of the page. **Landscape orientation** means the printout is printed across the length of the page. Previewing a worksheet using the Print Preview command on the File menu or Print Preview button on the Standard toolbar can save time, paper, and the frustration of waiting for a printout only to discover it is not what you want.

The steps on the next page preview and then print the worksheet.

To Preview and Print a Worksheet

1

• **Point to the Print Preview button on the Standard toolbar (Figure 2-65).**

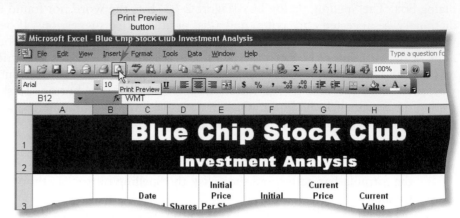

FIGURE 2-65

2

• **Click the Print Preview button.**

Excel displays a preview of the worksheet in portrait orientation, because portrait is the default orientation. In portrait orientation, the worksheet does not fit on one page (Figure 2-66).

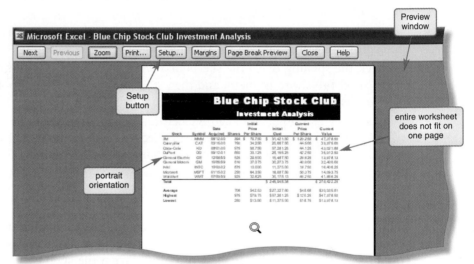

FIGURE 2-66

3

• **Click the Setup button.**

• **When Excel displays the Page Setup dialog box, click the Page tab and then click Landscape in the Orientation area.**

Excel displays the Page Setup dialog box. The Orientation area contains two option buttons, Portrait and Landscape. The Landscape option button is selected (Figure 2-67).

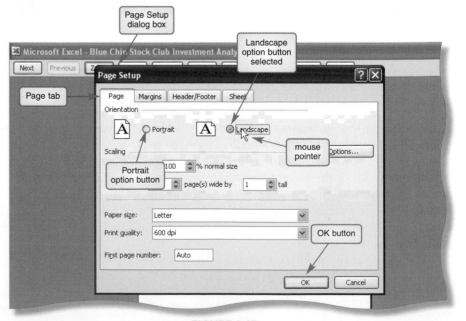

FIGURE 2-67

4

• **Click the OK button.**

Excel displays the worksheet in the Preview window. In landscape orientation, the entire worksheet fits on one page (Figure 2-68).

worksheet fits on one page in landscape orientation

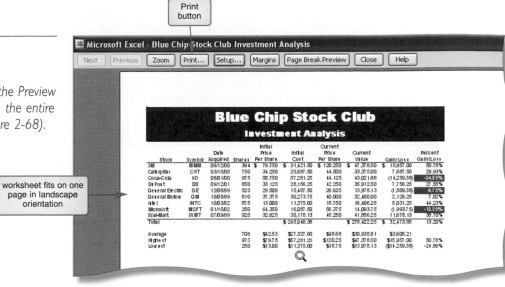

Print button

FIGURE 2-68

5

• **Click the Print button.**

Excel displays the Print dialog box as shown in Figure 2-69.

Print dialog box

All option button in Print range area instructs Excel to print entire worksheet

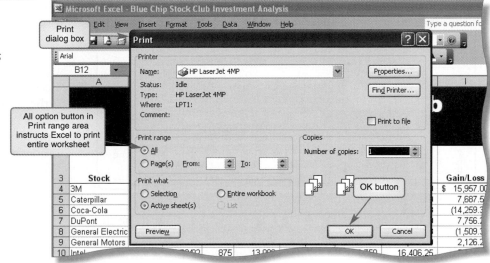

FIGURE 2-69

6

• **Click the OK button.**

• **Click the Save button on the Standard toolbar.**

Excel prints the worksheet (Figure 2-70). Excel saves the workbook with the landscape orientation print setting.

landscape orientation

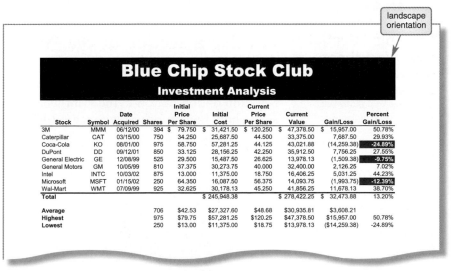

FIGURE 2-70

Other Ways

1. On File menu click Print Preview
2. On File menu click Page Setup, click Print Preview button
3. On File menu click Print, click Entire Workbook, click Preview button
4. In Voice Command mode, say "Print Preview"

Once you change the orientation and save the workbook, Excel will save the orientation setting for that workbook until you change it. When you open a new workbook, Excel sets the orientation to portrait.

Several buttons are at the top of the Preview window (Figure 2-68 on the previous page). The functions of these buttons are summarized in Table 2-6.

Table 2-6	Print Preview Buttons
BUTTON	**FUNCTION**
Next	Previews the next page
Previous	Previews the previous page
Zoom	Magnifies or reduces the print preview
Print...	Prints the worksheet
Setup...	Instructs Excel to display the Print Setup dialog box
Margins	Changes the print margins
Page Break Preview	Previews page breaks
Close	Closes the Preview window
Help	Instructs Excel to display Help about the Preview window

Rather than click the Next and Previous buttons to move from page to page as described in Table 2-6, you can press the PAGE UP and PAGE DOWN keys on your keyboard. You also can click the previewed page in the Preview window when the mouse pointer shape is a magnifying glass to carry out the function of the Zoom button.

The Page Setup dialog box shown in Figure 2-67 on page EX 114 allows you to make changes to the default settings for a printout. For example, on the Page tab, you can set the page orientation, as shown in the previous set of steps; scale the printout so it fits on one page; and set the page size and print quality. Scaling, which can be used to fit a wide worksheet on one page, will be discussed later in the project. The Margins tab, Header/Footer tab, and Sheet tab in the Page Setup dialog box provide additional options that allow for even more control of the way the printout will appear. These tabs will be discussed when they are used.

When you click the Print command on the File menu or a Print button in a dialog box or Preview window, Excel displays the Print dialog box shown in Figure 2-69 on the previous page. Excel does not display the Print dialog box when you use the Print button on the Standard toolbar, as was the case in Project 1. The Print dialog box allows you to select a printer, instruct Excel what to print, and indicate how many copies of the printout you want.

Printing a Section of the Worksheet

You might not always want to print the entire worksheet. You can print portions of the worksheet by selecting the range of cells to print and then clicking the Selection option button in the Print what area in the Print dialog box. The following steps show how to print the range A3:F16.

To Print a Section of the Worksheet

1

- **Select the range A3:F16.**
- **Click File on the menu bar and then click Print.**
- **Click Selection in the Print what area.**

Excel displays the Print dialog box (Figure 2-71). Because the Selection option button is selected, Excel will print only the selected range.

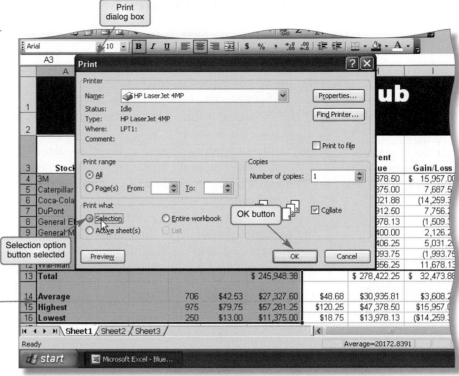

FIGURE 2-71

2

- **Click the OK button.**
- **Click cell B16 to deselect the range A3:F16.**

Excel prints the selected range of the worksheet on the printer (Figure 2-72).

Stock	Symbol	Date Acquired	Shares	Initial Price Per Share	Initial Cost
3M	MMM	06/12/00	394	$ 79.750	$ 31,421.50
Caterpillar	CAT	03/15/00	750	34.250	25,687.50
Coca-Cola	KO	08/01/00	975	58.750	57,281.25
DuPont	DD	09/12/01	850	33.125	28,156.25
General Electric	GE	12/08/99	525	29.500	15,487.50
General Motors	GM	10/05/99	810	37.375	30,273.75
Intel	INTC	10/03/02	875	13.000	11,375.00
Microsoft	MSFT	01/15/02	250	64.350	16,087.50
Wal-Mart	WMT	07/09/99	925	32.625	30,178.13
Total					**$ 245,948.38**
Average			706	$42.53	$27,327.60
Highest			975	$79.75	$57,281.25
Lowest			250	$13.00	$11,375.00

only selected range prints

FIGURE 2-72

The Print what area of the Print dialog box includes three option buttons (Figure 2-71). As shown in the previous steps, the Selection option button instructs Excel to print the selected range. The Active sheet(s) option button instructs Excel to print the active worksheet (the worksheet currently on the screen) or the selected worksheets. Finally, the Entire workbook option button instructs Excel to print all of the worksheets in the workbook.

Other Ways

1. Select range to print, on File menu point to Print Area, click Set Print Area, click Print button on Standard toolbar; on File menu point to Print Area, click Clear Print Area
2. Select range to print, in Voice Command mode, say "File, Print Area, Set Print Area"

Displaying and Printing the Formulas Version of the Worksheet

Microsoft Office
Excel 2003

More About

Values versus Formulas

When completing class assignments, do not enter numbers in cells that require formulas. Most instructors require their students to hand in both the values version and formulas version of the worksheet. The formulas version verifies that you entered formulas, rather than numbers, in formula-based cells.

Thus far, you have been working with the **values version** of the worksheet, which shows the results of the formulas you have entered, rather than the actual formulas. Excel also can display and print the **formulas version** of the worksheet, which shows the actual formulas you have entered, rather than the resulting values. You can toggle between the values version and formulas version by holding down the CTRL key while pressing the ACCENT MARK (`) key, which is located to the left of the number 1 key on the keyboard.

The formulas version is useful for debugging a worksheet. **Debugging** is the process of finding and correcting errors in the worksheet. Viewing and printing the formulas version instead of the values version makes it easier to see if any mistakes were made in the formulas.

When you change from the values version to the formulas version, Excel increases the width of the columns so the formulas and text do not overflow into adjacent cells on the right. The formulas version of the worksheet thus usually is significantly wider than the values version. To fit the wide printout on one page, you can use landscape orientation and the Fit to option in the Page sheet in the Page Setup dialog box. The following steps change the view of the worksheet from the values version to the formulas version of the worksheet and then print the formulas version on one page.

To Display the Formulas in the Worksheet and Fit the Printout on One Page

1

• Press CTRL+ACCENT MARK (`).

• When Excel displays the formulas version of the worksheet, click the right horizontal scroll arrow until column J appears.

• If the Formula Auditing toolbar appears, click its Close button.

Excel changes the display of the worksheet from values to formulas (Figure 2-73). It displays the formulas in the worksheet showing unformatted numbers, formulas, and functions that were assigned to the cells. Excel automatically increases the column widths.

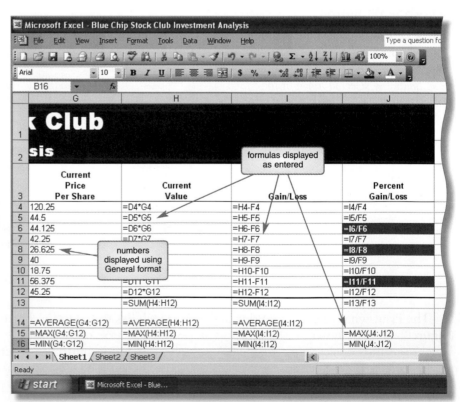

FIGURE 2-73

2

• **Click File on the menu bar and then click Page Setup.**

• **When Excel displays the Page Setup dialog box, click the Page tab.**

• **If necessary, click Landscape to select it and then click Fit to in the Scaling area.**

Excel displays the Page Setup dialog box with the Landscape and Fit to option buttons selected (Figure 2-74).

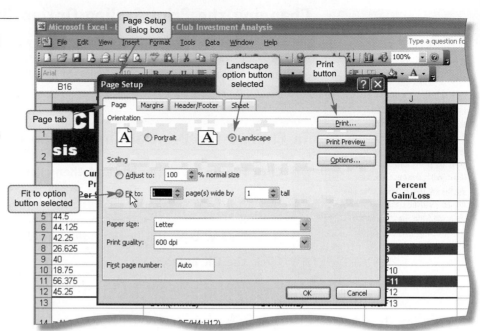

FIGURE 2-74

3

• **Click the Print button in the Page Setup dialog box.**

• **When Excel displays the Print dialog box, click the OK button.**

• **After viewing and printing the formulas version, press CTRL+ACCENT mark (`) to instruct Excel to display the values version.**

Excel prints the formulas in the worksheet on one page in landscape orientation (Figure 2-75). Excel displays the values version of the worksheet.

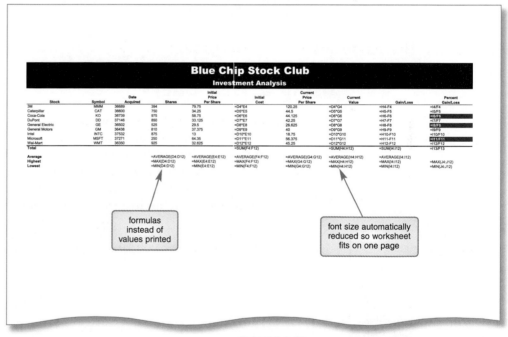

FIGURE 2-75

Although the formulas version of the worksheet was printed in the previous example, you can see from Figure 2-73 that you can review the formulas on the screen.

Other Ways

1. On Tools menu click Options, click View tab, click Formulas check box, click OK button
2. In Voice Command mode, say "Tools, Options, View, Formulas, OK"

More About

The Fit To Option

Do not take the Fit To option lightly. Most applications involve worksheets that extend well beyond the 8½"-by-11" page. Most users, however, want the information to print on one page, at least with respect to the width of the worksheet. The Fit To option thus is a valuable tool for Excel users.

Changing the Print Scaling Option Back to 100%

Depending on your printer driver, you may have to change the Print Scaling option back to 100% after using the Fit to option. The following steps reset the Print Scaling option so future worksheets print at 100%, instead of being resized to print on one page.

To Change the Print Scaling Option Back to 100%

1 Click File on the menu bar and then click Page Setup.

2 Click the Page tab in the Page Setup dialog box. Click Adjust to in the Scaling area.

3 If necessary, type 100 in the Adjust to box.

4 Click the OK button.

The print scaling is set to normal.

The Adjust to box allows you to specify the percentage of reduction or enlargement in the printout of a worksheet. The default percentage is 100%. When you click the Fit to option, this percentage automatically changes to the percentage required to fit the printout on one page.

Importing External Data from a Web Source Using a Web Query

One of the major features of Excel is its capability of importing external data from Web sites. To import external data from a Web site, you must have access to the Internet. You then can import data stored on a Web site using a **Web query**. When you run a Web query, Excel imports the external data in the form of a worksheet. As described in Table 2-7, three Web queries are available when you first install Excel. All three Web queries relate to investment and stock market activities.

More About

Web Queries

Most Excel specialists that build Web queries use the worksheet returned from the Web query as an engine to supply data to another worksheet in the workbook. With 3-D cell references, you can create a worksheet similar to the Blue Chip Stock Club worksheet to feed the Web query stock symbols and get refreshed stock prices in return.

Table 2-7 Excel Web Queries	
QUERY	**EXTERNAL DATA RETURNED**
MSN MoneyCentral Investor Currency Rates	Currency rates
MSN MoneyCentral Investor Major Indices	Major indices
MSN MoneyCentral Investor Stock Quotes	Up to 20 stocks of your choice

The data returned by the stock-related Web queries is real time in the sense that it is no more than 20 minutes old during the business day. The following steps show how to get the most recent stock quotes for the nine stocks owned by the Blue Chip Stock Club — 3M, Caterpillar, Coca-Cola, DuPont, General Electric, General Motors, Intel, Microsoft, and Wal-Mart. Although you can have a Web query return data to a blank workbook, the following steps have the data returned to a blank worksheet in the Blue Chip Stock Club Investment Analysis workbook.

To Import Data from a Web Source Using a Web Query

1

• **With the Blue Chip Stock Club Investment Analysis workbook open, click the Sheet2 tab at the bottom of the window.**

• **With cell A1 active, click Data on the menu bar, and then point to Import External Data on the Data menu.**

Excel displays the Data menu and Import External Data submenu as shown in Figure 2-76.

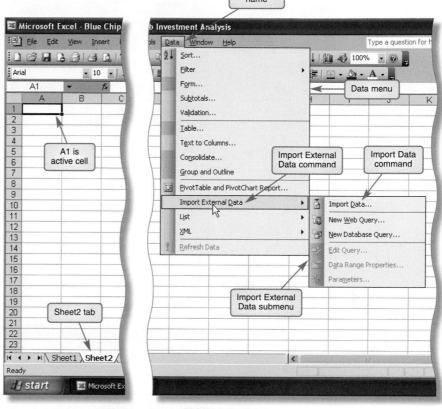

FIGURE 2-76

2

• **Click Import Data on the Import External Data submenu.**

Excel displays the Select Data Source dialog box (Figure 2-77). If your screen is different, ask your instructor for the folder location of the Web queries.

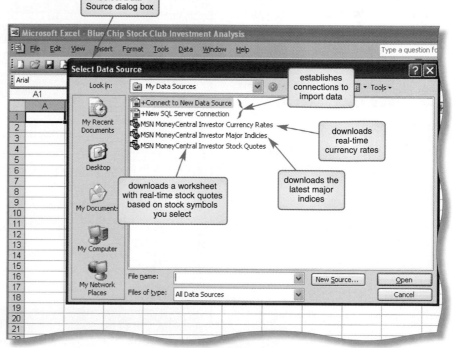

FIGURE 2-77

3

- **Double-click MSN MoneyCentral Investor Stock Quotes.**

- **When Excel displays the Import Data dialog box, if necessary, click Existing worksheet to select it.**

Excel displays the Import Data dialog box (Figure 2-78).

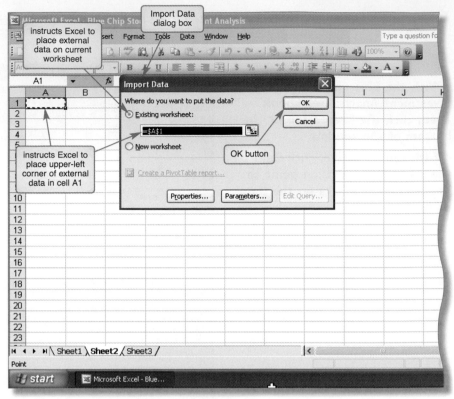

FIGURE 2-78

4

- **Click the OK button.**

- **When Excel displays the Enter Parameter Value dialog box, type the eight stock symbols** mmm cat ko dd ge gm intc msft wmt **in the text box.**

- **Click Use this value/reference for future refreshes to select it.**

Excel displays the Enter Parameter Value dialog box (Figure 2-79). You can enter up to 20 stock symbols separated by spaces (or commas).

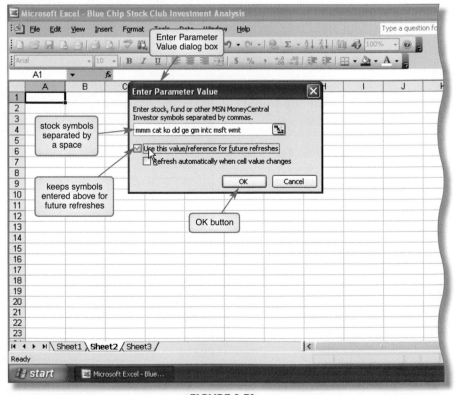

FIGURE 2-79

5

• **Click the OK button.**

Once your computer connects to the Internet, a message appears informing you that Excel is getting external data. After a short period, Excel displays a new worksheet with the desired data (Figure 2-80). The complete worksheet is shown in Figure 2-1b on page EX 67.

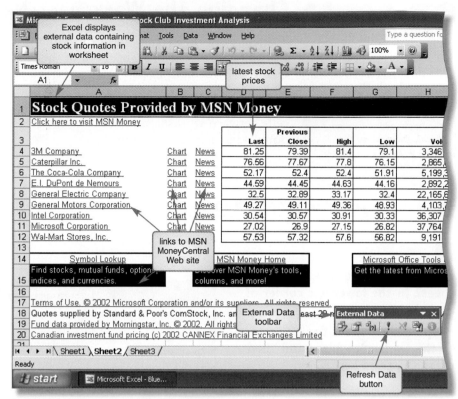

FIGURE 2-80

As shown in Figure 2-80, Excel displays the data returned from the Web query in an organized, formatted worksheet, which has a worksheet title, column titles, and a row of data for each stock symbol entered. Other than the first column, which contains the stock name and stock symbol, you have no control over the remaining columns of data returned. The latest price of each stock appears in column D.

Once Excel displays the worksheet, you can refresh the data as often as you want. To refresh the data for all the stocks, click the Refresh All button on the External Data toolbar (Figure 2-81). Because the Use this value/reference for future refreshes check box was selected in Step 4 of the previous steps (Figure 2-79), Excel will continue to use the same stock symbols each time it refreshes. You can change the symbols by clicking the Query Parameters button on the External Data toolbar.

If the External Data toolbar does not appear, right-click any toolbar and then click External Data. Instead of using the External Data toolbar, you also can invoke any Web query command by right-clicking any cell in the returned worksheet to display a shortcut menu with several of the same commands as the External Data toolbar.

FIGURE 2-81

This section gives you an idea of the potential of Web queries by having you use just one of Excel's Web queries. To reinforce the topics covered here, work through In the Lab 3 on page EX 136.

The workbook is nearly complete. The final step is to change the names of the sheets located on the sheet tabs at the bottom of the Excel window.

More About

Sheets Tabs

The name of the active sheet is bold on a white background. Using its shortcut menu, you can rename the sheets, color the tab, reorder the sheets, add and delete sheets, and move or copy sheets within a workbook or to another workbook.

Changing the Worksheet Names

The sheet tabs at the bottom of the window allow you to view any worksheet in the workbook. You click the sheet tab of the worksheet you want to view in the Excel window. By default, Excel presets the names of the worksheets to Sheet1, Sheet2, and so on. The worksheet names become increasingly important as you move towards more sophisticated workbooks, especially those in which you reference cells between worksheets. The following steps show how to rename worksheets by double-clicking the sheet tabs.

To Change the Worksheet Names

1

• **Double-click the sheet tab labeled Sheet2 in the lower-left corner of the window.**

• **Type** Real-Time Stock Quotes **as the worksheet name and then press the ENTER key.**

The new worksheet name appears on the sheet tab (Figure 2-82).

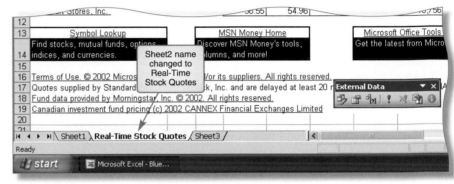

FIGURE 2-82

2

• **Double-click the sheet tab labeled Sheet1 in the lower-left corner of the window.**

• **Type** Investment Analysis **as the worksheet name and then press the ENTER key.**

Excel changes the worksheet name from Sheet1 to Investment Analysis (Figure 2-83).

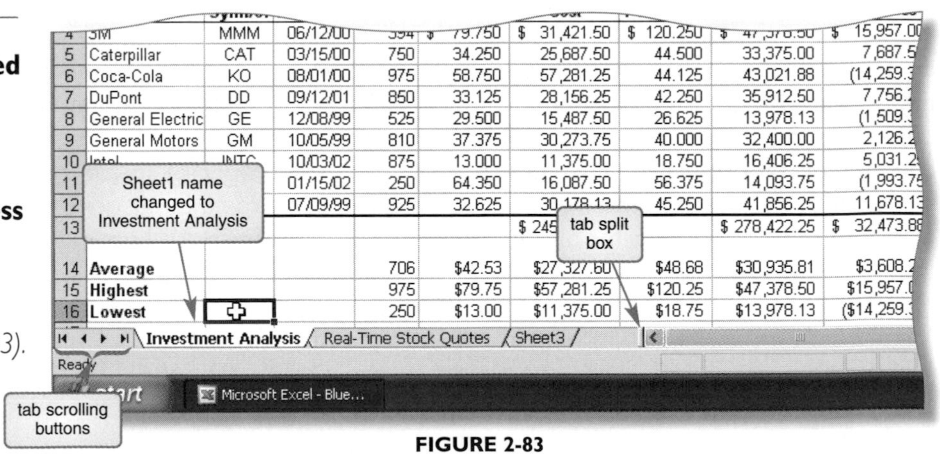

FIGURE 2-83

Worksheet names can be up to 31 characters (including spaces) in length. Longer worksheet names, however, mean that fewer sheet tabs will show. To view more sheet tabs, you can drag the tab split box (Figure 2-83) to the right. This will reduce the size of the scroll bar at the bottom of the screen. Double-click the tab split box to reset it to its normal position.

You also can use the tab scrolling buttons to the left of the sheet tabs (Figure 2-83) to move between worksheets. The leftmost and rightmost scroll buttons move to the first or last worksheet in the workbook. The two middle scroll buttons move one worksheet to the left or right.

E-Mailing a Workbook from within Excel

The most popular service on the Internet is electronic mail, or **e-mail**, which is the electronic transmission of messages and files to and from other computers using the Internet. Using e-mail, you can converse with friends across the room or on another continent. One of the features of e-mail is the ability to attach Office files, such as Word documents or Excel workbooks, to an e-mail message and send it to a coworker. In the past, if you wanted to e-mail a workbook, you saved the workbook, closed the file, started your e-mail program, and then attached the workbook to the e-mail message before sending it. With Excel you have the capability of e-mailing a worksheet or workbook directly from within Excel. For these steps to work properly, you must have an e-mail address and one of the following as your e-mail program: Microsoft Outlook, Microsoft Outlook Express, Microsoft Exchange Client, or another 32-bit e-mail program compatible with Messaging Application Programming Interface. The following steps show how to e-mail the Blue Chip Stock Club Investment Analysis workbook from within Excel to Alisha Wright at the e-mail address wright_alisha@hotmail.com.

More About

Obtaining an E-Mail Account

Several Web sites that allow you to sign up for free e-mail are available. For more information on signing up for free e-mail, visit the Excel 2003 More About Web page (scsite.com/ex2003/more) and click Signing Up for E-mail.

To E-Mail a Workbook from within Excel

1

• **With the Blue Chip Stock Club Investment Analysis workbook open, click File on the menu bar and then point to Send To.**

Excel displays the File menu and Send To submenu as shown in Figure 2-84.

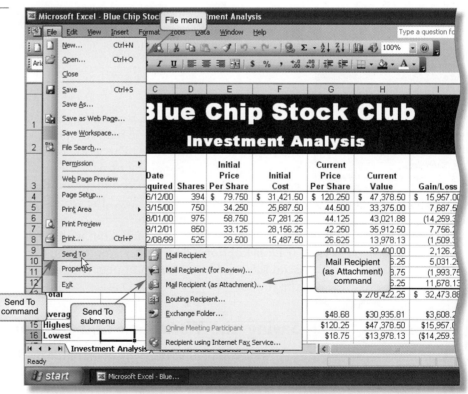

FIGURE 2-84

2

• **Click Mail Recipient (as Attachment) on the Send To submenu.**

• **When the e-mail Message window appears, type** wright_alisha@hotmail.com **in the To text box.**

• **Type the message shown in the message area in Figure 2-85.**

Excel displays the e-mail Message window. The workbook is included as an attachment (Figure 2-85).

3

• **Click the Send button.**

The e-mail with the attached workbook is sent to wright_alisha@hotmail.com.

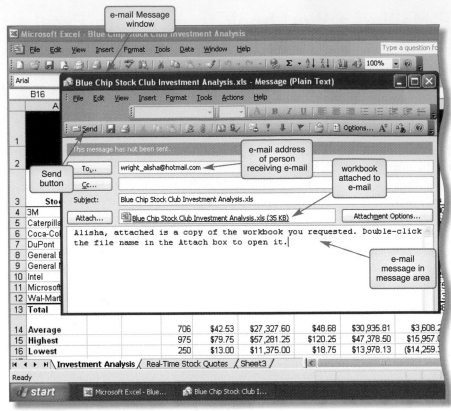

FIGURE 2-85

Because the workbook was sent as an attachment, Alisha Wright can double-click the attachment in the e-mail to open it in Excel, or she can save it on disk and then open it at a later time. The worksheet also could have been sent as part of the text portion of the e-mail by using the E-mail button on the Standard toolbar or by clicking the Mail Recipient command on the Send To submenu. In this case, the recepient would be able to read the worksheet in the e-mail message, but would not be able to open it in Excel.

When you send an e-mail from within Excel, you can choose from many other available options. The Options button on the toolbar, for example, allows you to send the e-mail to a group of people in a particular sequence and get responses along the route.

Saving the Workbook and Quitting Excel

After completing the workbook and e-mailing a copy of the workbook, the final steps are to save the workbook and quit Excel.

To Save the Workbook and Quit Excel

1 Click the Save button on the Standard toolbar.

2 Click the Close button on the upper-right corner of the title bar.

Project Summary

In creating the Blue Chip Stock Club Investment Analysis workbook, you learned how to enter formulas, calculate an average, find the highest and lowest numbers in a range, verify formulas using Range Finder, change fonts, draw borders, align text, format numbers, change column widths and row heights, and add conditional formatting to a range of numbers. You learned how to spell check a worksheet, preview a worksheet, print a worksheet, print a section of a worksheet, and display and print the formulas version of the worksheet using the Fit to option. You also learned how to complete a Web query to generate a worksheet using external data obtained from the Web and rename sheet tabs. Finally, you learned how to send an e-mail directly from within Excel with the opened workbook as an attachment.

 If you have a SAM user profile, you may have access to hands-on instruction, practice, and assessment of the skills covered in this project. Log in to your SAM account and go to your assignments page to see what your instructor has assigned.

What You Should Know

Having completed this project, you should be able to perform the tasks below. The tasks are listed in the same order they were presented in this project. For a list of the buttons, menus, toolbars, and commands introduced in this project, see the Quick Reference Summary at the back of this book and refer to the Page Number column.

1. Start and Customize Excel   (EX 70)
2. Enter the Worksheet Title and Subtitle   (EX 70)
3. Enter the Column Titles   (EX 71)
4. Enter the Stock Data   (EX 72)
5. Enter the Row Titles   (EX 72)
6. Save the Workbook   (EX 72)
7. Enter a Formula Using the Keyboard   (EX 73)
8. Enter Formulas Using Point Mode   (EX 75)
9. Copy Formulas Using the Fill Handle   (EX 77)
10. Determine Totals Using the AutoSum Button   (EX 79)
11. Determine the Total Percent Gain/Loss   (EX 80)
12. Determine the Average of a Range of Numbers Using the Keyboard and Mouse   (EX 81)
13. Determine the Highest Number in a Range of Numbers Using the Insert Function Box (EX 83)
14. Determine the Lowest Number in a Range of Numbers Using the AutoSum Button Menu (EX 85)
15. Copy a Range of Cells across Columns to an Adjacent Range Using the Fill Handle   (EX 87)

16. Save a Workbook Using the Same File Name   (EX 89)
17. Verify a Formula Using Range Finder   (EX 89)
18. Change the Font and Center the Worksheet Title   (EX 92)
19. Change the Font and Center the Worksheet Subtitle   (EX 93)
20. Change the Background and Font Colors and Apply a Box Border to the Worksheet Title and Subtitle   (EX 94)
21. Bold, Center, and Apply a Bottom Border to the Column Titles   (EX 96)
22. Center Data in Cells and Format Dates   (EX 97)
23. Apply a Currency Style Format and Comma Style Format Using the Formatting Toolbar   (EX 98)
24. Apply a Thick Bottom Border to the Row above the Total Row and Bold the Total Row Titles   (EX 100)
25. Apply a Currency Style Format with a Floating Dollar Sign Using the Format Cells Command   (EX 101)
26. Apply a Percent Style Format   (EX 103)
27. Apply Conditional Formatting   (EX 104)

(continued)

What You Should Know *(continued)*

28. Change the Widths of Columns   (EX 107)
29. Change the Heights of Rows   (EX 110)
30. Check Spelling on the Worksheet   (EX 112)
31. Preview and Print a Worksheet   (EX 114)
32. Print a Section of the Worksheet   (EX 117)
33. Display the Formulas in the Worksheet and Fit the Printout on One Page   (EX 118)
34. Change the Print Scaling Option Back to 100%   (EX 120)
35. Import Data from a Web Source Using a Web Query   (EX 121)
36. Change the Worksheet Names   (EX 124)
37. E-Mail a Workbook from within Excel   (EX 125)
38. Save the Workbook and Quit Excel   (EX 126)

More About

The Quick Reference

For a table that lists how to complete the tasks covered in this book using the mouse, menu, shortcut menu, and keyboard, see the Quick Reference Summary at the back of this book or visit the Excel 2003 Quick Reference Web page (scsite.com/ex2003/qr).

Learn It Online

Instructions: To complete the Learn It Online exercises, start your browser, click the Address bar, and then enter the Web address scsite.com/ex2003/learn. When the Excel 2003 Learn It Online page is displayed, follow the instructions in the exercises below. Each exercise has instructions for printing your results, either for your own records or for submission to your instructor.

1 Project Reinforcement TF, MC, and SA

Below Excel Project 2, click the Project Reinforcement link. Print the quiz by clicking Print on the File menu for each page. Answer each question.

2 Flash Cards

Below Excel Project 2, click the Flash Cards link and read the instructions. Type 20 (or a number specified by your instructor) in the Number of playing cards text box, type your name in the Enter your Name text box, and then click the Flip Card button. When the flash card is displayed, read the question and then click the ANSWER box arrow to select an answer. Flip through Flash Cards. If your score is 15 (75%) correct or greater, click Print on the File menu to print your results. If your score is less than 15 (75%) correct, then redo this exercise by clicking the Replay button.

3 Practice Test

Below Excel Project 2, click the Practice Test link. Answer each question, enter your first and last name at the bottom of the page, and then click the Grade Test button. When the graded practice test is displayed on your screen, click Print on the File menu to print a hard copy. Continue to take practice tests until you score 80% or better.

4 Who Wants To Be a Computer Genius?

Below Excel Project 2, click the Computer Genius link. Read the instructions, enter your first and last name at the bottom of the page, and then click the PLAY button. When your score is displayed, click the PRINT RESULTS link to print a hard copy.

5 Wheel of Terms

Below Excel Project 2, click the Wheel of Terms link. Read the instructions, and then enter your first and last name and your school name. Click the PLAY button. When your score is displayed, right-click the score and then click Print on the shortcut menu to print a hard copy.

6 Crossword Puzzle Challenge

Below Excel Project 2, click the Crossword Puzzle Challenge link. Read the instructions, and then enter your first and last name. Click the SUBMIT button. Work the crossword puzzle. When you are finished, click the Submit button. When the crossword puzzle is redisplayed, click the Print Puzzle button to print a hard copy.

7 Tips and Tricks

Below Excel Project 2, click the Tips and Tricks link. Click a topic that pertains to Project 2. Right-click the information and then click Print on the shortcut menu. Construct a brief example of what the information relates to in Excel to confirm you understand how to use the tip or trick.

8 Newsgroups

Below Excel Project 2, click the Newsgroups link. Click a topic that pertains to Project 2. Print three comments.

9 Expanding Your Horizons

Below Excel Project 2, click the Expanding Your Horizons link. Click a topic that pertains to Project 2. Print the information. Construct a brief example of what the information relates to in Excel to confirm you understand the contents of the article.

10 Search Sleuth

Below Excel Project 2, click the Search Sleuth link. To search for a term that pertains to this project, select a term below the Project 2 title and then use the Google search engine at google.com (or any major search engine) to display and print two Web pages that present information on the term.

11 Excel Online Training

Below Excel Project 2, click the Excel Online Training link. When your browser displays the Microsoft Office Online Web page, click the Excel link. Click one of the Excel courses that covers one or more of the objectives listed at the beginning of the project on page EX 66. Print the first page of the course before stepping through it.

12 Office Marketplace

Below Excel Project 2, click the Office Marketplace link. When your browser displays the Microsoft Office Online Web page, click the Office Marketplace link. Click a topic that relates to Excel. Print the first page.

Apply Your Knowledge

1 Profit Analysis Worksheet

Instructions Part 1: Start Excel. Open the workbook Apply 2-1 e-cove Profit Analysis from the Data Disk. See the inside back cover of this book for instructions for downloading the Data Disk or see your instructor for information on accessing the files required in this book. The purpose of this exercise is to open a partially completed workbook, enter formulas and functions, copy the formulas and functions, and then format the worksheet titles and numbers. As shown in Figure 2-86, the completed worksheet analyzes profits by item. Use the following formulas:

Total Sales (cell F3) = Units Sold * (Unit Cost + Unit Profit) or =C3 * (D3 + E3)
Total Profit (cell G3) = Units Sold * Unit Profit or = C3 * E3
% Total Profit (cell H3) = Total Profit / Total Sales or = G3 / F3

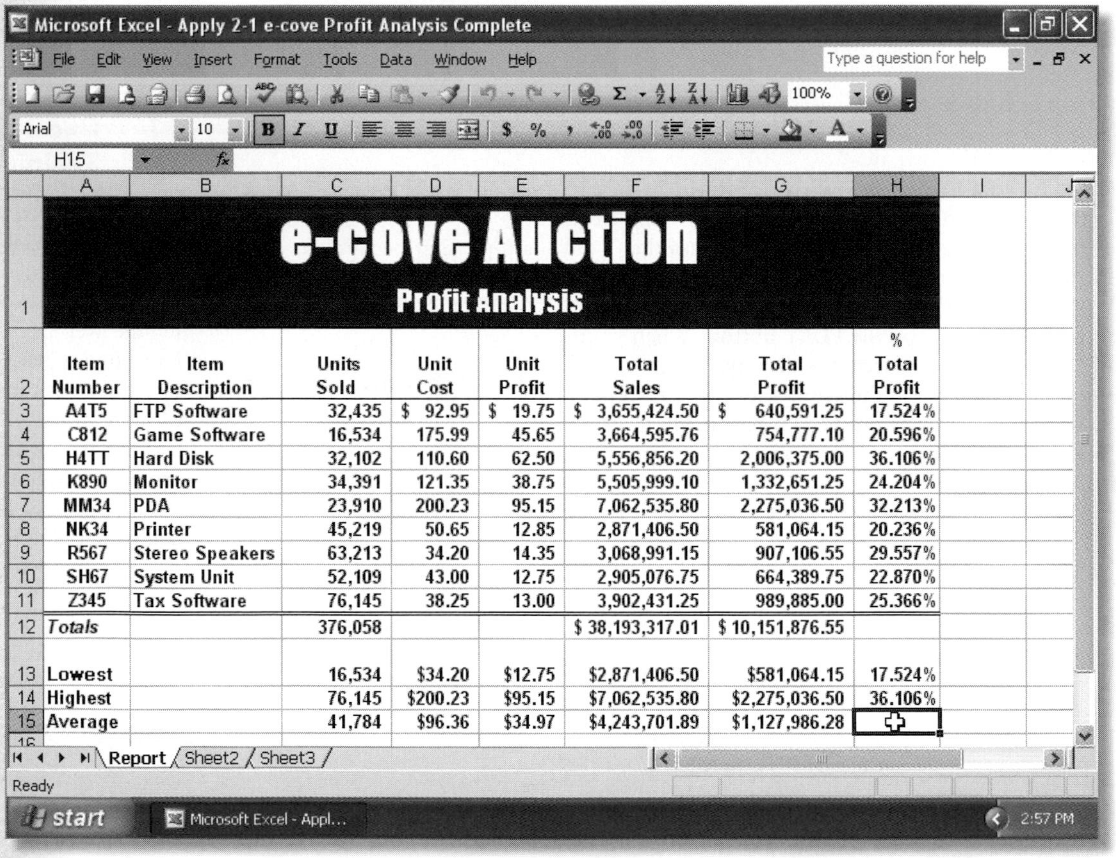

	A	B	C	D	E	F	G	H
1	e-cove Auction Profit Analysis							
2	Item Number	Item Description	Units Sold	Unit Cost	Unit Profit	Total Sales	Total Profit	% Total Profit
3	A4T5	FTP Software	32,435	$ 92.95	$ 19.75	$ 3,655,424.50	$ 640,591.25	17.524%
4	C812	Game Software	16,534	175.99	45.65	3,664,595.76	754,777.10	20.596%
5	H4TT	Hard Disk	32,102	110.60	62.50	5,556,856.20	2,006,375.00	36.106%
6	K890	Monitor	34,391	121.35	38.75	5,505,999.10	1,332,651.25	24.204%
7	MM34	PDA	23,910	200.23	95.15	7,062,535.80	2,275,036.50	32.213%
8	NK34	Printer	45,219	50.65	12.85	2,871,406.50	581,064.15	20.236%
9	R567	Stereo Speakers	63,213	34.20	14.35	3,068,991.15	907,106.55	29.557%
10	SH67	System Unit	52,109	43.00	12.75	2,905,076.75	664,389.75	22.870%
11	Z345	Tax Software	76,145	38.25	13.00	3,902,431.25	989,885.00	25.366%
12	*Totals*		376,058			$ 38,193,317.01	$ 10,151,876.55	
13	Lowest		16,534	$34.20	$12.75	$2,871,406.50	$581,064.15	17.524%
14	Highest		76,145	$200.23	$95.15	$7,062,535.80	$2,275,036.50	36.106%
15	Average		41,784	$96.36	$34.97	$4,243,701.89	$1,127,986.28	

FIGURE 2-86

Use the fill handle to copy the three formulas in the range F3:H3 to the range F4:H11. After the copy is complete, click the Auto Fill Options button and then click the Fill Without Formatting command to maintain the bottom double border in the range F11:H11. Determine totals for the units sold, total sales, and total profit in row 12. In the range C13:C15, determine the lowest value, highest value, and average value, respectively, for the values in the range C3:C11. Use the fill handle to copy the three functions to the range D13:H15. Delete the average from cell H15, because an average of percentages of this type is mathematically invalid.

Apply Your Knowledge

Format the worksheet as follows:

(1) cell A1 – change to Impact font (or a font of your choice) with a dark red (column 1, row 2) background
(2) cells D3:G3 and F12:G12 – apply Currency style format with fixed dollar signs
(3) cells C3, C4:G11, and C13:C15 – apply Comma style format
(4) cells C3:C15 – format numbers to appear with no decimal places
(5) cells H3:H14 – apply Percent style format with three decimal places
(6) cells D13:G15 – apply Currency style format with floating dollar signs

Enter your name, course, laboratory assignment number (Apply 2-1), date, and instructor name in the range A20:A24. Preview and print the worksheet in landscape orientation. Save the workbook using the file name, Apply 2-1 e-cove Profit Analysis Complete.

Use Range Finder to verify the formula in cell G3. Print the range A2:F15. Press CTRL+ACCENT MARK (`) to change the display from the values version of the worksheet to the formulas version. Print the formulas version in landscape orientation on one page with gridlines showing (Figure 2-87) by (1) using the Fit to option in the Page sheet in the Page Setup dialog box and (2) clicking Gridlines on the Sheet sheet in the Page Setup dialog box. Press CTRL+ACCENT MARK (`) to change the display of the worksheet back to the values version. Do not save the workbook. Hand in the three printouts to your instructor.

Instructions Part 2: In column E, use the keyboard to add manually $3.00 to the profit of each product with a unit profit less than $40.00 and $4.00 to the profits of all other products. You should end up with $11,352,596.55 in cell G12. Print the worksheet. Do not save the workbook. Hand in the printout to your instructor.

Report

e-cove Auction
Profit Analysis

Item Number	Item Description	Units Sold	Unit Cost	Unit Profit	Total Sales	Total Profit	% Total Profit
A4T5	FTP Software	32435	92.95	19.75	=C3*(D3+E3)	=C3*E3	=G3/F3
C812	Game Software	16534	175.99	45.65	=C4*(D4+E4)	=C4*E4	=G4/F4
H4TT	Hard Disk	32102	110.6	62.5	=C5*(D5+E5)	=C5*E5	=G5/F5
K890	Monitor	34391	121.35	38.75	=C6*(D6+E6)	=C6*E6	=G6/F6
MM34	PDA	23910	200.23	95.15	=C7*(D7+E7)	=C7*E7	=G7/F7
NK34	Printer	45219	50.65	12.85	=C8*(D8+E8)	=C8*E8	=G8/F8
R567	Stereo Speakers	63213	34.2	14.35	=C9*(D9+E9)	=C9*E9	=G9/F9
SH67	System Unit	52109	43	12.75	=C10*(D10+E10)	=C10*E10	=G10/F10
Z345	Tax Software	76145	38.25	13	=C11*(D11+E11)	=C11*E11	=G11/F11
Totals		=SUM(C3:C11)			=SUM(F3:F11)	=SUM(G3:G11)	
Lowest		=MIN(C3:C11)	=MIN(D3:D11)	=MIN(E3:E11)	=MIN(F3:F11)	=MIN(G3:G11)	=MIN(H3:H11)
Highest		=MAX(C3:C11)	=MAX(D3:D11)	=MAX(E3:E11)	=MAX(F3:F11)	=MAX(G3:G11)	=MAX(H3:H11)
Average		=AVERAGE(C3:C11)	=AVERAGE(D3:D11)	=AVERAGE(E3:E11)	=AVERAGE(F3:F11)	=AVERAGE(G3:G11)	

FIGURE 2-87

1 Weekly Payroll Worksheet

Problem: Illiana Custom Homes has hired you as an intern in its software applications department. Because you took an Excel course last semester, the assistant manager has asked you to prepare a weekly payroll report for the six employees listed in Table 2-8.

Table 2-8 Illiana Custom Homes Weekly Payroll Data			
Employee	Rate	Hours	Dep.
Jedi, Hubert	24.90	40.00	3
Kaden, Hadef	33.50	38.75	5
Pancer, Dion	12.90	66.00	8
Rifken, Felix	29.75	27.25	3
Sanchez, Maria	21.35	45.00	5
Scarff, Heidi	17.85	39.75	1

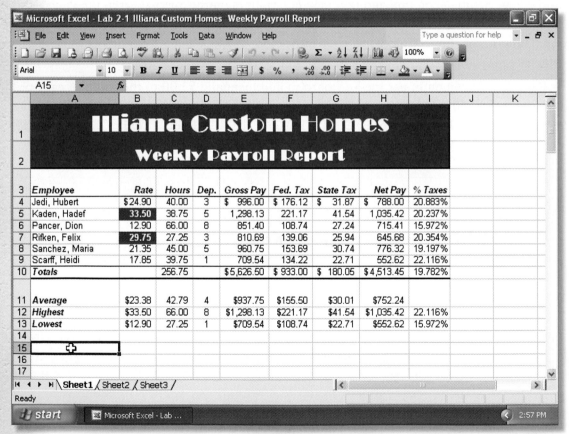

FIGURE 2-88

Instructions Part 1: Perform the following tasks to create a worksheet similar to the one shown in Figure 2-88.

1. Enter the worksheet titles Illiana Custom Homes in cell A1 and Weekly Payroll Report in cell A2. Enter the column titles in row 3, the data in Table 2-8 in columns A through D, and the row titles in the range A10:A13.

In the Lab

2. Use the following formulas to determine the gross pay, federal tax, state tax, and net pay for the first employee:
   a. Gross Pay (cell E4) = Rate*Hours or =B4 * C4
   b. Fed. Tax (cell F4) = 20% * (Gross Pay – Dep. * 38.46) or =20% *(E4 – D4 * 38.46)
   c. State Tax (cell G4) = 3.2% * Gross Pay or =3.2% * E4
   d. Net Pay (cell H4) = Gross Pay – (Fed. Tax + State Tax) or =E4 – (F4 + G4)
   e. % Taxes (I4) = (Fed. Tax + State Tax) / Gross Pay or =(F4 + G4) / E4
   Copy the formulas for the first employee to the remaining employees.

3. Calculate totals for hours, gross pay, federal tax, state tax, net pay, and % taxes paid in row 10.

4. Use the appropriate functions to determine the average, highest, and lowest values of each column in rows 11 through 13. Delete the value in cell I11.

5. Use Range Finder to verify each of the formulas entered in row 4.

6. Select the range A1:A2 and change its background color to red. Change the worksheet title to 26-point Broadway white, bold font (or a font of your choice). Center the worksheet title across columns A through I. Vertically center the worksheet title. Format the worksheet subtitle in a similar fashion, except change its font size to 18. Assign the range A1:A2 a border (column 4, row 4 on the Borders palette). Assign the Comma style format with two decimal places to the ranges B5:H9 and C4:C13. Assign a Currency style format with a fixed dollar sign to the ranges B4, E4:H4, and E10:H10. Assign a Currency style format with a floating dollar sign to the ranges B11:B13 and E11:H13. Assign the Number style format with 0 decimals to the range D4:D13 and center the range. Assign a Percent style format with three decimal places to the range I4:I13. Bold, italicize, and assign a bottom border (column 2, row 1 on the Borders palette) to the range A3:I3. Align right the column titles in the range B3:I3. Bold and italicize the range A10:A13. Assign a top and thick bottom border (column 1, row 3 on the Borders palette) to the range A10:I10.

7. Change the width of column A to 18.00 characters. If necessary, change the widths of columns B through H to best fit. Change the heights of row 1 to 39.75 points and rows 2, 3, and 11 to 30.00 points.

8. Use the Conditional Formatting command on the Format menu to display white, bold font on a blue background for any rate in the range B4:B9 greater than $25.00.

9. Enter your name, course, laboratory assignment number (Lab 2-1), date, and instructor name in the range A15:A19.

10. Spell check the worksheet. Save the workbook using the file name Lab 2-1 Illiana Custom Homes Weekly Payroll Report. Preview and then print the worksheet.

11. Press CTRL+ACCENT MARK (`) to change the display from the values version to the formulas version. Print the formulas version of the worksheet in landscape orientation using the Fit to option in the Page sheet in the Page Setup dialog box. After the printer is finished, press CTRL+ACCENT MARK (`) to reset the worksheet to the values version. Reset the Scaling option to 100% by clicking the Adjust to option button in the Page sheet in the Page Setup dialog box and then setting the percent value to 100%. Hand in the printouts to your instructor.

Instructions Part 2: Use the keyboard to increase manually the number of hours worked for each employee by 12 hours. The total net pay in cell H10 should equal $5,806.00. If necessary, increase the width of column F to best fit to view the new federal tax total. Preview and print the worksheet with the new values. Do not save the workbook. Hand in the printout to your instructor.

2 Accounts Receivable Balance Sheet

Problem: You are a spreadsheet specialist in the Accounting department of Fife's Finer Furniture, a popular Virginia Beach-based furniture company with several outlets in major cities across the United States. You have been asked to use Excel to generate a report (Figure 2-89) that summarizes the monthly accounts receivable balance. A graphic breakdown of the data also is desired. The customer accounts receivable data in Table 2-9 is available for test purposes.

Table 2-9   Fife's Finer Furniture Accounts Receivable Data

Customer ID	Customer Name	Beginning Balance	Purchases	Payments	Credits
A421	Sri, Oranu	32548.30	3291.50	6923.00	785.25
H861	Agarwall, Bikash	9351.55	4435.10	5000.00	75.00
K190	Amigo, Julio	5909.50	750.30	2350.00	0.00
M918	Wang, Shiela	18761.60	5560.00	1875.00	905.25
P415	Davis, Jasmine	14098.20	1596.10	3250.00	236.45
R623	Smith, John	18433.60	200.20	1375.00	196.00
U111	Gupta, Arjun	13462.75	2026.00	750.00	25.00

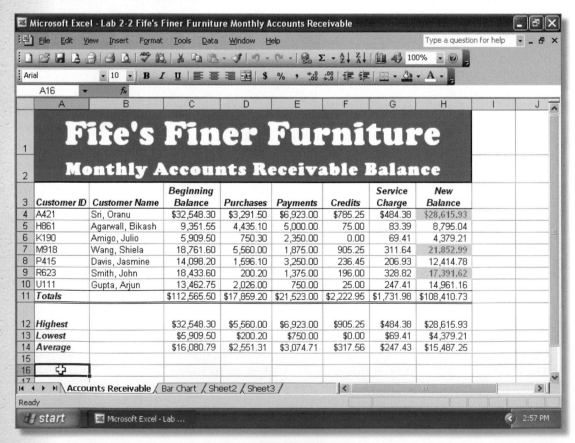

FIGURE 2-89

In the Lab

Instructions Part 1: Create a worksheet similar to the one shown in Figure 2-89. Include the six columns of customer data in Table 2-9 in the report, plus two additional columns to compute a service charge and a new balance for each customer. Assume no negative unpaid monthly balances. Perform the following tasks.

1. Enter and format the worksheet title, worksheet subtitle, column titles and row titles. Use a font type of your choice for the worksheet titles. The Cooper Black font is shown in Figure 2-89. Bold and italicize the column titles in row 3. Add a bottom border to the column titles in row 3. Center the column titles in the range B3:H3. Bold and italicize the titles in the range A11:A14. Add a top and double bottom border to the range A11:H11.
2. Enter the data in Table 2-9.
3. Use the following formulas to determine the service charge in column G and the new balance in column H for the first customer. Copy the two formulas down through the remaining customers.
   a. Service Charge (cell G4) = 1.95% * (Beginning Balance – Payments – Credits) or = 0.0195 * (C4 - E4 - F4)
   b. New Balance (H4) = Beginning Balance + Purchases – Payments – Credits + Service Charge or C4 + D4 - E4 - F4 + G4
4. Determine the totals in row 11.
5. Determine the maximum, minimum, and average values in cells C12:C14 for the range C4:C10 and then copy the range C12:C14 to D12:H14.
6. Change the width of column A to 11.00 characters. Change the widths of columns B through H to best fit. Change the heights of row 3 to 27.75 and row 12 to 30.00 points.
7. Assign the Currency style with a floating dollar sign to the cells containing numeric data in the ranges C4:H4 and C11:H14. Assign the Comma style (currency with no dollar sign) to the range C5:H10.
8. Use conditional formatting to change the formatting to green bold font on a yellow background in any cell in the range H4:H10 that contains a value greater than or equal to 15000.
9. Change the widths of columns C through H to best fit again, if necessary.
10. Change the worksheet name from Sheet1 to Accounts Receivable.
11. Enter your name, course, laboratory assignment number (Lab 2-2), date, and instructor name in the range A16:A20.
12. Spell check the worksheet. Preview and then print the worksheet in landscape orientation. Save the workbook using the file name Lab 2-2 Fife's Finer Furniture Monthly Accounts Receivable.
13. Print the range A3:D14. Print the formulas version on one page. Close the workbook without saving the changes. Hand in the three printouts to your instructor.

Instructions Part 2: This part requires that you use the Chart Wizard button on the Standard toolbar to draw a 3-D Bar chart. If necessary, use the Type a question for help box on the menu bar to obtain information on drawing a Bar chart on a separate sheet in the workbook.

With the Lab 2-2 Fife's Finer Furniture Monthly Accounts Receivable workbook open, draw the 3-D Bar chart showing each customer's total new balance as shown in Figure 2-90 on the next page. Use the CTRL key and mouse to select the nonadjacent chart ranges B4:B10 and H4:H10. The customer names in the range B4:B10 will identify the bars, while the data series in the range H4:H10 will determine the length of the bars. Click the Chart Wizard button on the Standard toolbar. When the Chart Wizard - Step 1 of 4 - Chart Type dialog box is displayed, select the Bar Chart type and Chart sub-type Clustered bar with a 3-D visual effect (column 1, row 2). Click the Next button twice to display the Chart Wizard - Step 3 of 4 - Chart Options dialog box. Add the chart title Accounts Receivable. Click the Next button and select As new sheet to draw the bar chart on a new worksheet.

(continued)

In the Lab

Accounts Receivable Balance Sheet (*continued*)

Change the worksheet name from Chart1 to Bar Chart. Drag the Accounts Receivable tab to the left of the Bar Chart tab to reorder the sheets in the workbook. Save the workbook using the same file name as in Part 1. Preview and print the chart. Hand in the printout to your instructor.

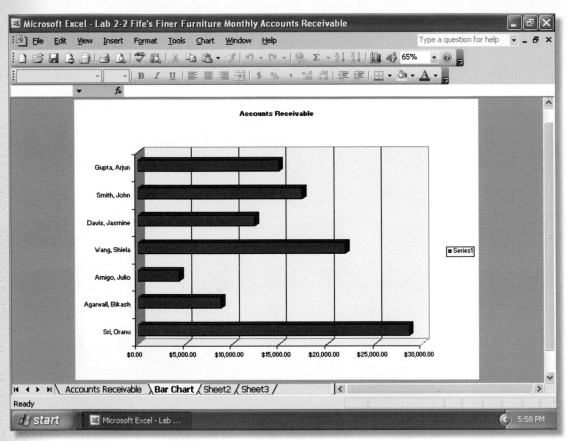

FIGURE 2-90

Instructions Part 3: With the Lab 2-2 Fife's Finer Furniture Monthly Accounts Receivable workbook open, click the Accounts Receivable tab. Change the following purchases: account number K190 to $6,500.00; account number R623 to $3,000.00. The total new balance in cell H11 should equal $116,960.23. Select both sheets by holding down the SHIFT key and then clicking the Bar Chart tab. Preview and print the selected sheets. Hand in the printouts to your instructor. Save the worksheet using the file name Lab 2-2 Fife's Finer Furniture Monthly Accounts Receivable 2.

Instructions Part 4: With your instructor's permission, e-mail the workbook created in this exercise with the changes indicated in Part 2 as an attachment to your instructor. Close the workbook without saving the changes.

3 Equity Web Queries

Problem: Esmeralda Dominga, president of Pro Cards, Inc., recently attended a Microsoft Office seminar at the local community college and learned that Excel can connect to the Web, download real-time stock data into

In the Lab

a worksheet, and then refresh the data as often as needed. Because you have had courses in Excel and the Internet, she has hired you as a consultant to develop a stock analysis workbook. Her portfolio is listed in Table 2-10.

Instructions Part 1: If necessary, connect to the Internet. Open a new Excel workbook and select cell A1. Perform a Web query to obtain multiple stock quotes (Figure 2-91), using the stock symbols in Table 2-10. Enter your name, course, laboratory assignment number (Lab 2-3a), date, and instructor

Table 2-10 Esmeralda Dominga's Stock Portfolio

Company	Stock Symbol
International Business Machines	IBM
Oracle	ORCL
Johnson & Johnson	JNJ
Boeing	BA
Home Depot	HD
Citigroup	C

name in the range A22:A26. Rename the worksheet Multiple Quotes. Save the workbook using the file name Lab 2-3 Esmeralda Dominga Equities Online. Preview and then print the worksheet in landscape orientation using the Fit to option.

Click the following links and print the Web page that appears in the browser window: Click here to visit MSN Money; Oracle Corporation; Chart to the right of Home Depot, Inc., and News to the right of Citigroup Inc. Hand in the printouts to your instructor.

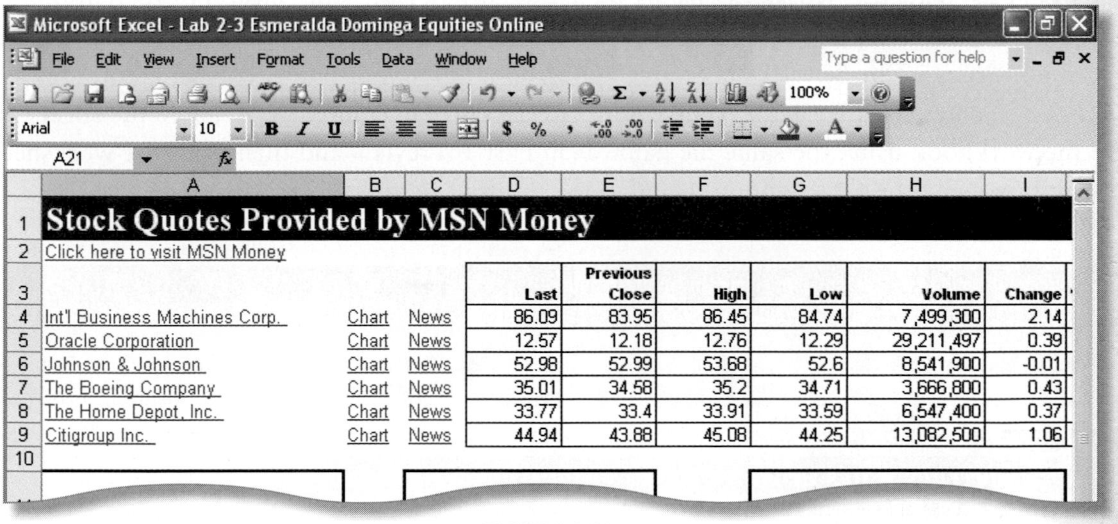

FIGURE 2-91

Instructions Part 2: Create a worksheet listing the major indices and their current values on Sheet 2 of the Lab 2-3 Esmeralda Dominga Equities Online workbook (Figure 2-92 on the next page). To create this worksheet, double-click MSN MoneyCentral Investor Major Indices in the Select Data Source dialog box. Enter your name, course, laboratory assignment number (Lab 2-3b), date, and instructor name below the last entry in column A. Rename the worksheet Major Indices. Save the workbook using the same file name as in Part 1. Preview and then print the worksheet in landscape orientation using the Fit to option. Hand in the printout to your instructor.

(continued)

Equity Web Queries (continued)

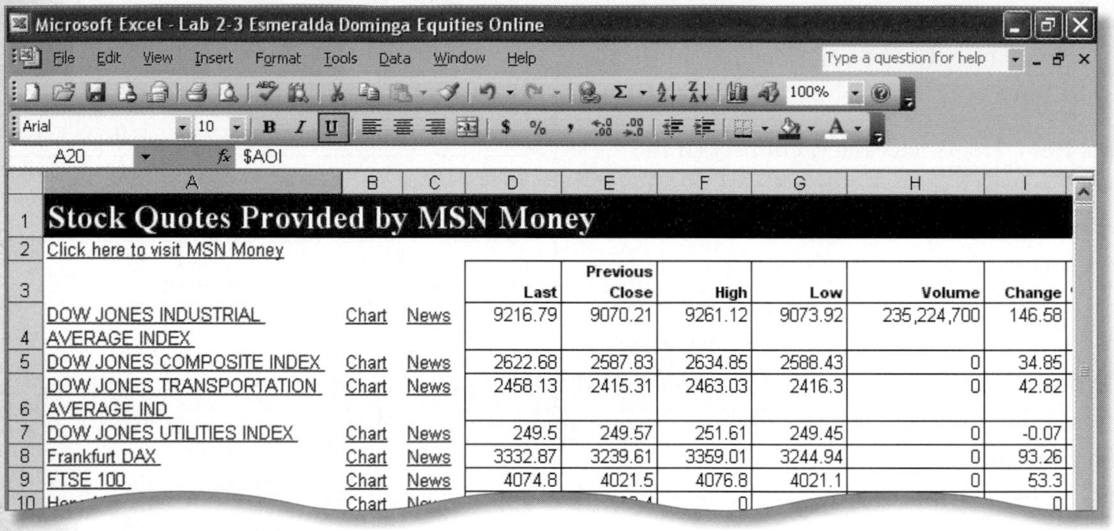

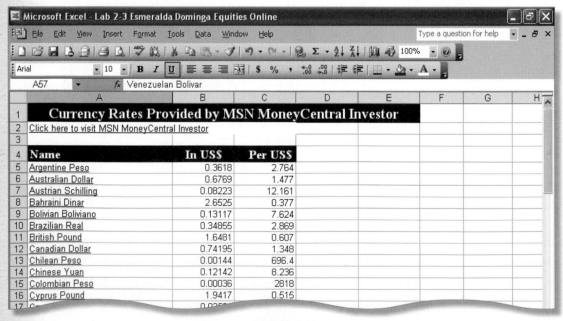

FIGURE 2-92

Instructions Part 3: Create a worksheet listing the latest currency rates on Sheet 3 of the Lab 2-3 Esmeralda Dominga Equities Online workbook (Figure 2-93). To create this worksheet, double-click MSN MoneyCentral Investor Currency Rates in the Select Data Source dialog box. Enter your name, course, laboratory assignment number (Lab 2-3c), date, and instructor name below the last entry in column A. Rename the sheet Currency Rates. Save the workbook using the same file name as in Part 1. Preview and then print the worksheet in portrait orientation using the Fit to option. Hand in the printout to your instructor.

FIGURE 2-93

In the Lab

Instructions Part 4: Excel recognizes certain types of data in a cell, such as stock symbols. To indicate that it recognizes the data, Excel then inserts a smart tag indicator (a small purple triangle) in the lower-right corner of those cells. If you click the cell with the smart tag indicator, Excel displays the Smart Tag Actions button. If you click the Smart Tag Actions button arrow, Excel displays a menu (Figure 2-94) that can be used to gain instant access to information about the data. To ensure Excel options are set to label data with smart tags, click AutoCorrect Options on the Tools menu and then click the Smart Tags tab when the AutoCorrect dialog box appears. If necessary, select the three check boxes, Label data with smart tags, Smart tag lists (MSN MoneyCentral Financial Symbols), and Embed smart tags in this workbook.

With a new workbook opened, enter the column title, Stock Symbols, in cell A1 as shown in Figure 2-94. Enter the three stock symbols, JPM (J.P. Morgan Chase), MCD (McDonald's Corporation), and SBC (SBC Communications) in the range A2:A4. Save the workbook using the file name Lab 2-3 Smart Tags.

Click cell A4. When Excel displays the Smart Tag Actions button, click the arrow to display the Smart Tag Actions list (Figure 2-94). One at a time, click the first three commands below Financial Symbol: SBC. Print the Web pages that your browser displays when you click these three commands and then print the worksheet. Repeat these steps, clicking the first three commands in the Smart Tag Actions list for the stock symbols in cells A2 and A3. Hand in the printouts to your instructor.

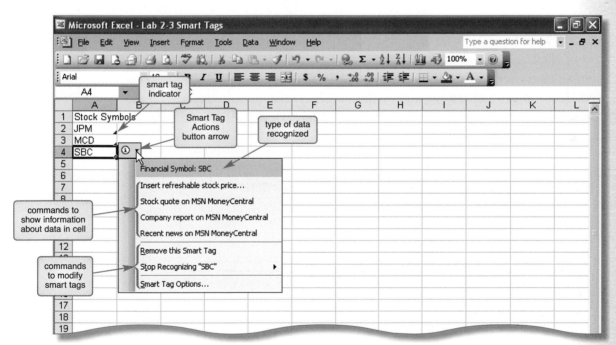

FIGURE 2-94

Cases and Places

The difficulty of these case studies varies:
■ are the least difficult and ■■ are more difficult. The last exercise is a group exercise.

1 ■ You are the cochairman of the fund-raising committee for the school's band. You want to compare various fund-raising ideas to determine which will give you the best profit. You obtain information from six businesses about their products (Table 2-11). Using the formulas in Table 2-12 and the general worksheet layout in Table 2-11, produce a worksheet to share the information with your committee. Use the concepts and techniques presented in this project to create and format the worksheet.

Table 2-11   Band Fund-Raising Data and Worksheet Layout

Company	Product	Cost Per Unit	Margin	Selling Price	Profit Per 3000 Sales
T&S	T-shirts	$2.50	60%	Formula A	Formula B
Aunt Mame's	Coffee	2.00	55%		
Wong Lo	Green Tea	1.75	65%		
Pen & Pencil	Pens	1.60	50%		
Gum-It	Gum	1.75	53%		
Dip-N-Donuts	Donuts	2.60	45%		
Minimum	Formula C				
Maximum	Formula D				

Table 2-12   Band Fund-Raising Formulas

Formula A = Cost Per Unit / (1 − Margin)

Formula B = 3000 * (Selling Price − Cost Per Unit)

Formula C = MIN function

Formula D = MAX function

Cases and Places

2 ■■ To determine the effectiveness of their endangered species recovery plan, the Fish and Wildlife Department traps and releases red wolves in selected sections of the state and records how many are pregnant. To obtain a representative sample, the department tries to trap and release approximately 20% of the population. The sample for eight sections is shown in Table 2-13. Use the following formula to determine the total red wolf population for each section:

Wolves in a Section = 5 * (Wolves Caught + Pregnant Wolves) – 5 * Death Rate * (Wolves Caught + Pregnant Wolves)

Use the concepts and techniques presented in this project to create the worksheet. Determine appropriate totals. Finally, estimate the total state red wolf population if 925 sections are in the state.

Table 2-13 Red Wolf Catch Data			
Section	**Wolves Caught**	**Wolves Pregnant**	**Annual Death Rate**
1	7	3	51%
2	8	6	67%
3	7	1	51%
4	6	4	61%
5	3	1	60%
6	4	2	54%
7	4	2	44%
8	4	1	53%

Cases and Places

3 ■■ You are a spreadsheet specialist consultant for Super Store Furniture. The owners of the store want to know the profit potential of their furniture inventory. The data and the format of the desired report are shown in Table 2-14. The required formulas are shown in Table 2-15.

Use the concepts and techniques developed in this project to create and format the worksheet and chart. Hand in a printout of the values version and formulas version of the worksheet. The company just received a shipment of 100 additional loveseats and 250 end tables. Update the appropriate cells in the Units on Hands column. The additional inventory yields a total profit potential of $3,878,742.96.

Table 2-14   Super Store Profit Potential Data and Worksheet Layout

Item	Units On Hand	Unit Cost	Total Cost	Average Unit Price	Total Value	Potential Profit
Rugs	983	$89.00	Formula A	Formula B	Formula C	Formula D
Sofas	1,980	678.00				
Loveseats	2,187	189.00				
End Tables	2,354	65.45				
Lamps	2,346	23.85				
Total	—		—		—	—
Average	Formula E					
Lowest	Formula F					
Highest	Formula G					

Table 2-15   Super Store Profit Potential Formulas

Formula A = Units on Hand * Unit Cost

Formula B = Unit Cost * (1 / (1 − .65))

Formula C = Units on Hand * Average Unit Price

Formula D = Total Value − Total Cost

Formula E = AVERAGE function

Formula F = MIN function

Formula G = MAX function

Cases and Places

4 ■■ LUV Steel Company pays a 3.25% commission to its salespeople to stimulate sales. The company also pays each employee a base salary. The management has projected each employee's sales for the next quarter. This information — employee name, employee base salary, and projected sales — is as follows: Meeks, Tyrone, $12,500.00, $542,413.00; Mandinka, Al-Jabbar, $10,250.00, $823,912.00; Silverstein, Aaron, $9,150.00, $362,750.00; Chronowski, John, $6,950.00, $622,165.00; Putin, Nikita, $9,500.00, $750,450.00.

With this data, you have been asked to develop a worksheet calculating the amount of commission and the projected quarterly salary for each employee. The following formulas can be used to obtain this information:

Commission Amount = 3.25% × Projected Sales

Quarterly Salary = Base Salary + Commission Amount

Include a total, average value, highest value, and lowest value for employee base salary, commission amount, and quarterly salary. Use the concepts and techniques presented in this project to create and format the worksheet.

Create a 3-D Pie chart on a separate sheet illustrating the portion each employee's quarterly salary contributes to the total quarterly salary. Use the Microsoft Excel Help system to create a professional looking 3-D Pie chart with title and data labels.

5 ■■ **Working Together** Have each member of your team select six stocks — two technology stocks, two bank stocks, and two retail stocks. Each member should submit the stock names, stock symbols, and an approximate 12-month-old price. Create a worksheet that lists the stock names, symbols, price, and number of shares for each stock (use 500 shares as number of shares for all stocks). Format the worksheet so that it has a professional appearance and is as informative as possible.

Have the group do research on the use of 3-D references, which is a reference to a range that spans two or more worksheets in a workbook (use Microsoft Excel Help). Use what the group learns to create a Web query on the Sheet2 worksheet by referencing the stock symbols on the Sheet1 worksheet. Change the cells that list current price per share numbers on the Sheet1 worksheet to use 3-D cell references that refer to the worksheet created by the Web query on the Sheet2 worksheet. Present your workbook and findings to the class.

What-If Analysis, Charting, and Working with Large Worksheets

CASE PERSPECTIVE

Aquatics Wear is a global provider of swimming accessories, including swimsuits, water exercise gear, swim caps, goggles, and water polo equipment. The Aquatics Wear sales force sells these products in bulk to large retail stores. The company also sells directly to customers via catalog sales and the Web.

Each June and December, the chief financial officer (CFO) of Aquatics Wear, Adriana Romaro, submits a plan to the board of directors to show projected monthly revenues, cost of goods sold, expenses, and operating income for the next six months.

Last December, Adriana used pencil, paper, and a calculator to complete the report and draw a Pie chart. When she presented her report, the directors asked for the effect on the projected operating income if the percentage of expenses allocated to the marketing department was changed. While the directors anxiously waited, Adriana calculated the answers by hand. Once she changed the percentage of expenses allocated to marketing, the Pie chart no longer matched the projections and thus was meaningless. Adriana now wants to use a computer and spreadsheet software to address what-if questions so she can take advantage of its instantaneous recalculation feature.

Adriana has asked you to assist her in preparing an easy-to-read worksheet that shows financial projections for the next six months (Figure 3-1a). In addition, she wants a 3-D Pie chart (Figure 3-1b) that shows the projected operating income contribution for each of the six months, because the directors prefer a graphical representation to numbers.

As you read through this project, you will learn how to create large worksheets, develop professional looking charts, and complete what-if analyses.

What-If Analysis, Charting, and Working with Large Worksheets

P R O J E C T

3

Objectives

You will have mastered the material in this project when you can:

- Rotate text in a cell
- Create a series of month names
- Use the Format Painter button to format cells
- Copy, paste, insert, and delete cells
- Format numbers using format symbols
- Freeze and unfreeze titles
- Show and format the system date

- Use absolute cell references in a formula
- Use the IF function to perform a logical test
- Show and dock toolbars
- Create a 3-D Pie chart on a separate chart sheet
- Color and rearrange worksheet tabs
- Change the worksheet view
- Goal seek to answer what-if questions

Introduction

Worksheets normally are much larger than those created in the previous projects, often extending beyond the size of the window (Figure 3-1a). Because you cannot see the entire worksheet on the screen at one time, working with a large worksheet sometimes can be frustrating to work with. This project introduces several Excel commands that allow you to control what displays on the screen so you can view critical parts of a large worksheet at one time. One command lets you freeze the row and column titles so Excel always displays them on the screen. Another command splits the worksheet into separate window panes so you can view different parts of a worksheet on the screen at one time.

When you set up a worksheet, you should use as many cell references in formulas as possible, rather than constant values. The cell references in a formula are called assumptions. **Assumptions** are values in cells that you can change to determine new values for formulas. This project emphasizes the use of assumptions and shows how to use Excel to answer what-if questions such as, what happens to the six-month total operating income (cell H16 in Figure 3-1a) if you decrease the marketing expenses assumption (cell B22 in Figure 3-1a) by 2%? Being able to analyze quickly the effect of changing values in a worksheet is an important skill in making business decisions.

This project also introduces you to techniques that will enhance your ability to create worksheets and draw charts. From your work in Project 1, you are aware of how easily charts can be created. This project covers additional charting techniques that allow you to convey your message in a dramatic pictorial fashion (Figure 3-1b). This project also covers other methods for entering values in cells and formatting these values. In addition, you will learn how to use absolute cell references and how to use the IF function to assign a value to a cell based on a logical test.

In the previous projects, you learned how to use the Standard and Formatting toolbars. Excel has several other toolbars that can make your work easier. One such toolbar is the Drawing toolbar, which allows you to draw shapes and arrows and add drop shadows to cells you want to emphasize.

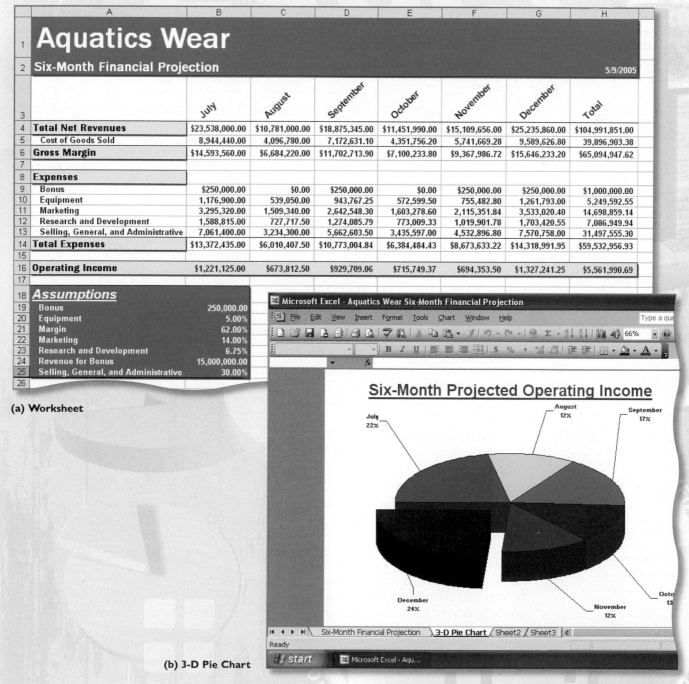

(a) Worksheet

(b) 3-D Pie Chart

FIGURE 3-1

More About

Correctness

Studies have shown that more than 25 percent of all business worksheets have errors. If you are not careful entering data and formulas, then your worksheet is prone to errors. You can ensure correctness in your formulas by carefully checking them using Range Finder and the Error Checking command on the Tools menu. The Formula Auditing command on the Tools menu also can be helpful when verifying formulas.

Project Three — Aquatics Wear Six-Month Financial Projection

The requirements document for the Aquatics Wear Six-Month Financial Projection worksheet is shown in Figure 3-2. It includes the needs, source of data, summary of calculations, chart requirements, and other facts about its development.

REQUEST FOR NEW WORKBOOK

Date Submitted:	May 2, 2005
Submitted By:	Adriana Romaro
Worksheet Title:	Aquatics Wear Six-Month Financial Projection
Needs:	The needs are: (1) a worksheet (Figure 3-3a) that shows Aquatics Wear's projected monthly total net revenues, cost of goods sold, gross margin, expenses, and operating income for a six-month period; and (2) a 3-D Pie chart (Figure 3-3b) that shows the expected contribution of each month's operating income to the six-month period operating income.
Source of Data:	The data supplied by the Finance department includes the projected monthly total net revenues and expense assumptions (Table 3-1). The six projected monthly total net revenues (row 4 of Figure 3-3a) and the seven assumptions at the bottom of Figure 3-3a are based on the company's historical data. All the remaining numbers in the worksheet are determined from these 13 numbers using formulas.
Calculations:	The following calculations must be made for each month: 1. Cost of Goods Sold = Total Net Revenues - Total Net Revenues * Margin 2. Gross Margin = Total Net Revenues - Cost of Goods Sold 3. Bonus = $250,000.00 if the Total Net Revenues exceeds the Revenue for Bonus; otherwise, Bonus = 0 4. Equipment = Total Net Revenues × Equipment Assumption 5. Marketing = Total Net Revenues × Marketing Assumption 6. Research and Development = Total Net Revenues × Research and Development Assumption 7. Selling, General, and Administrative = Total Net Revenues × Selling, General, and Administrative Assumption 8. Total Expenses = Sum of Expenses 9. Operating Income = Gross Margin - Total Expenses
Chart Requirements:	A 3-D Pie chart is required on a separate sheet (Figure 3-3b) to show the contribution of each month's operating income to the six-month period operating income. The chart also should emphasize the month with the greatest operating income.

Approvals

Approval Status:	X	Approved
		Rejected
Approved By:	Adriana Romaro	
Date:	May 3, 2005	
Assigned To:	J. Quasney, Spreadsheet Specialist	

FIGURE 3-2

More About

Excel's Usefulness

Just a few short years ago, a what-if question of any complexity only could be answered using a large, expensive computer programmed by highly paid computer professionals. Generating a result could take days. Excel gives the noncomputer professional the ability to get complex business-related questions answered instantaneously and economically.

The sketch of the worksheet (Figure 3-3a) consists of titles, column and row headings, location of data values, calculations, and a rough idea of the desired formatting. The sketch of the 3-D Pie chart (Figure 3-3b) shows the expected contribution of each month's operating income to the six-month period operating income.

Table 3-1 includes the company's projected monthly total net revenues and expense assumptions for the six months based on historical sales. The projected monthly total net revenues will be entered in row 4 of the worksheet. The

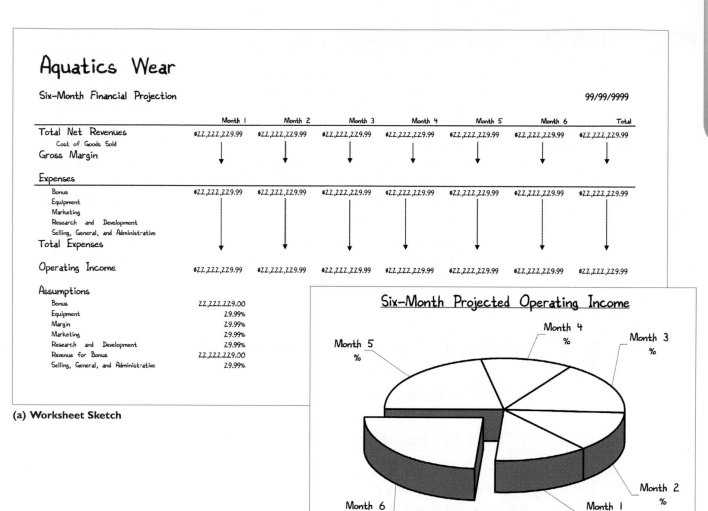

Aquatics Wear

Six-Month Financial Projection   99/99/9999

	Month 1	Month 2	Month 3	Month 4	Month 5	Month 6	Total
Total Net Revenues	$ZZ,ZZZ,ZZ9.99	$ZZ,ZZZ,ZZ9.99	$ZZ,ZZZ,ZZ9.99	$ZZ,ZZZ,ZZ9.99	$ZZ,ZZZ,ZZ9.99	$ZZ,ZZZ,ZZ9.99	$ZZ,ZZZ,ZZ9.99
Cost of Goods Sold							
Gross Margin							
Expenses							
Bonus	$ZZ,ZZZ,ZZ9.99	$ZZ,ZZZ,ZZ9.99	$ZZ,ZZZ,ZZ9.99	$ZZ,ZZZ,ZZ9.99	$ZZ,ZZZ,ZZ9.99	$ZZ,ZZZ,ZZ9.99	$ZZ,ZZZ,ZZ9.99
Equipment							
Marketing							
Research and Development							
Selling, General, and Administrative							
Total Expenses							
Operating Income	$ZZ,ZZZ,ZZ9.99	$ZZ,ZZZ,ZZ9.99	$ZZ,ZZZ,ZZ9.99	$ZZ,ZZZ,ZZ9.99	$ZZ,ZZZ,ZZ9.99	$ZZ,ZZZ,ZZ9.99	$ZZ,ZZZ,ZZ9.99

Assumptions

Bonus	ZZ,ZZZ,ZZ9.00
Equipment	Z9.99%
Margin	Z9.99%
Marketing	Z9.99%
Research and Development	Z9.99%
Revenue for Bonus	ZZ,ZZZ,ZZ9.00
Selling, General, and Administrative	Z9.99%

(a) Worksheet Sketch

Six-Month Projected Operating Income

Month 5 %   Month 4 %   Month 3 %   Month 2 %   Month 1 %   Month 6 %

(b) 3-D Pie Chart Sketch

FIGURE 3-3

assumptions will be entered in the range A18:B25 below the operating income (Figure 3-3a). The projected monthly total revenues and the assumptions will be used to calculate the remaining numbers in the worksheet.

Starting and Customizing Excel

With the requirements document and sketch of the worksheet and chart complete, the next step is to start and customize Excel. If you are stepping through this project on a computer and you want your screen to agree with the figures in this book, then you should change your computer's resolution to 800 × 600. For information on changing the resolution on your computer, see Appendix B. The steps on the next page start Excel and customize the Excel window.

Table 3-1 Aquatics Wear Six-Month Financial Projections Data and Assumptions	
PROJECTED MONTHLY TOTAL NET REVENUES	
July	$23,538,000
August	10,781,000
September	18,875,345
October	11,451,990
November	15,109,656
December	25,235,860
ASSUMPTIONS	
Bonus	$250,000.00
Equipment	5.00%
Margin	62.00%
Marketing	14.00%
Research and Development	6.75%
Revenue for Bonus	$15,000,000.00
Selling, General, and Administrative	30.00%

More About

The Startup Submenu

Any application on the Startup submenu starts automatically when you turn your computer on. To add Excel to the Startup submenu, do the following: (1) Click the Start button on the Windows taskbar, point to All Programs on the Start menu, and then point to Microsoft Office on the All Programs submenu; (2) Right-drag Microsoft Office Excel 2003 from the Microsoft Office submenu to the Startup submenu; (3) When the shortcut menu appears, click Copy Here. The next time you turn your computer on, Excel will start automatically.

To Start and Customize Excel

1 Click the Start button on the Windows taskbar, point to All Programs on the Start menu, point to Microsoft Office on the All Programs submenu, and then click Microsoft Office Excel 2003 on the Microsoft Office submenu.

2 If the Excel window is not maximized, double-click its title bar to maximize it.

3 If the Language bar appears, right-click it and then click Close the Language bar on the shortcut menu.

4 If the Getting Started task pane appears in your Excel window, click its Close button in the upper-right corner.

5 If the Standard and Formatting toolbars are positioned on the same row, click the Toolbar Options button on the right side of either toolbar and then click Show Buttons on Two Rows.

Excel displays its window with the Standard and Formatting toolbars on two rows.

Bolding the Font of the Entire Worksheet

The following steps show how to assign a bold format to the font for the entire worksheet so that all entries will be emphasized.

To Bold the Font of the Entire Worksheet

1 Click the Select All button immediately above row heading 1 and to the left of column heading A (Figure 3-4).

2 Click the Bold button on the Formatting toolbar.

No immediate change takes place on the screen. As you enter text and numbers into the worksheet, however, Excel will display them in bold.

Q: What are three alternatives to bolding to make it easier for users to read a worksheet on the screen?

A: Select easy-to-read font styles, increase the font size, or increase the percentage in the Zoom box. The latter is particularly useful if users have less-than-average eyesight.

Entering the Worksheet Titles and Saving the Workbook

The worksheet contains two titles, one in cell A1 and another in cell A2. In the previous projects, titles were centered across the worksheet. With large worksheets that extend beyond the size of a window, it is best to enter titles in the upper-left corner as shown in the sketch of the worksheet in Figure 3-3a on the previous page. The following steps enter the worksheet titles and save the workbook.

To Enter the Worksheet Titles and Save the Workbook

1 Click cell A1 and then enter Aquatics Wear as the worksheet title.

2 Click cell A2 and then enter Six-Month Financial Projection as the worksheet subtitle.

3 With a floppy disk in drive A, click the Save button on the Standard toolbar.

4 When Excel displays the Save As dialog box, type Aquatics Wear Six-Month Financial Projection in the File name text box.

5 If necessary, click 3½ Floppy (A:) in the Save in list. Click the Save button in the Save As dialog box.

Excel responds by displaying the worksheet titles in cells A1 and A2 in bold as shown in Figure 3-4. Excel saves the workbook on the floppy disk in drive A using the file name Aquatics Wear Six-Month Financial Projection.

Rotating Text and Using the Fill Handle to Create a Series

When you first enter text, its angle is zero degrees (0°), and it reads from left to right in a cell. Text in a cell can be rotated counterclockwise by entering a number between 1° and 90° on the Alignment sheet in the Format Cells dialog box.

Projects 1 and 2 used the fill handle to copy a cell or a range of cells to adjacent cells. The fill handle also can be used to create a series of numbers, dates, or month names automatically. The following steps illustrate how to enter the month name, July, in cell B3; format cell B3 (including rotating the text); and then use the fill handle to enter the remaining month names in the range C3:G3.

To Rotate Text and Use the Fill Handle to Create a Series of Month Names

1

• **Select cell B3.**

• **Type** July **as the cell entry and then click the Enter box.**

• **Click the Font Size box arrow on the Formatting toolbar and then click 11 in the Font Size list.**

• **Click the Borders button arrow on the Formatting toolbar and then click the Bottom Border button (column 2, row 1) on the Borders palette.**

• **Right-click cell B3.**

Excel displays the text, July, in cell B3 using the assigned formats and it displays the shortcut menu (Figure 3-4).

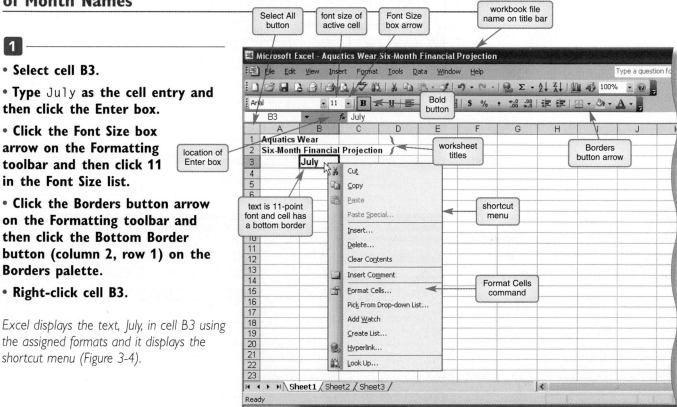

FIGURE 3-4

2

• **Click Format Cells on the shortcut menu.**

• **When the Format Cells dialog box is displayed, click the Alignment tab.**

• **Click the 45° point in the Orientation area.**

Excel displays the Alignment sheet in the Format Cells dialog box. The Text hand in the Orientation area points to the 45° point and 45 appears in the Degrees box (Figure 3-5).

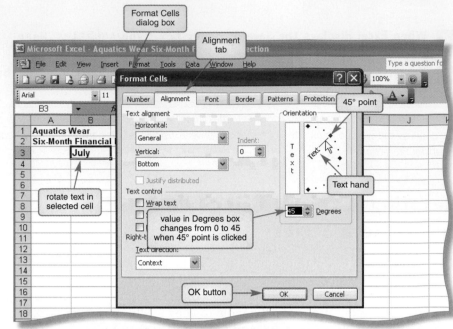

FIGURE 3-5

3

• **Click the OK button.**

• **Point to the fill handle on the lower-right corner of cell B3.**

Excel displays the text, July, in cell B3 at a 45° angle and automatically increases the height of row 3 to best fit the rotated text (Figure 3-6). The mouse pointer changes to a crosshair.

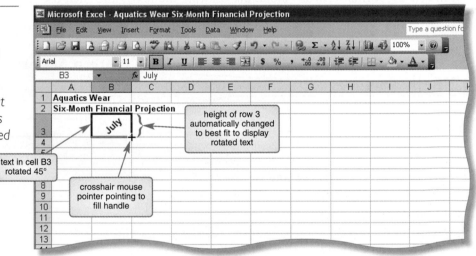

FIGURE 3-6

4

• **Drag the fill handle to the right to select the range C3:G3. Do not release the mouse button.**

Excel displays a light border that surrounds the selected range and a ScreenTip indicating the month of the last cell in the selected range (Figure 3-7).

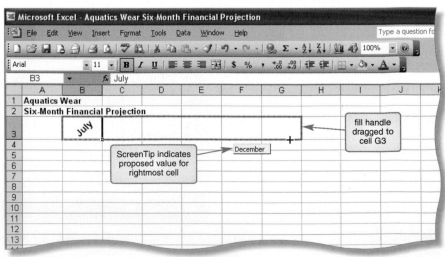

FIGURE 3-7

Release the mouse button.

Click the Auto Fill Options button below the lower-right corner of the fill area.

Using July in cell B3 as the basis, Excel creates the month name series August through December in the range C3:G3 (Figure 3-8). The formats assigned to cell B3 earlier in the previous steps (11-point font, bottom border, and text rotated 45°) also are copied to the range C3:G3. The Auto Fill Options menu shows the available fill options.

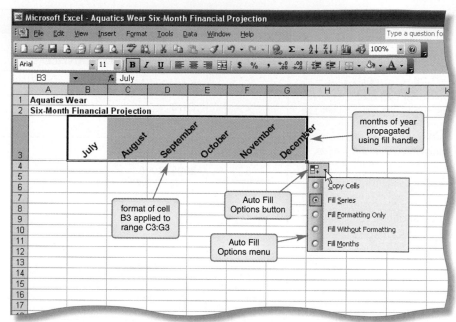

FIGURE 3-8

6

Click the Auto Fill Options button to hide the Auto Fill Options menu.

Other Ways

1. Enter start month in cell, right-drag fill handle in direction to fill, click Fill Months on shortcut menu
2. Select range to fill, in Voice Command mode, say "Edit, Fill, Series, AutoFill"

In addition to creating a series of values, dragging the fill handle instructs Excel to copy the format of cell B3 to the range C3:G3. With some fill operations, you may not want to copy the formats of the source cell or range to the destination cell or range. If this is the case, click the Auto Fill Options button after the range fills (Figure 3-8) and then select the option you desire on the Auto Fill Options menu. As shown in Figure 3-8, Fill Series is the default option that Excel uses to fill the area, which means it fills the destination area with a series, using the same formatting as the source area. If you choose another option on the Auto Fill Options menu, then Excel immediately changes the contents of the destination range. Following the use of the fill handle, the Auto Fill Options button remains active until you begin the next Excel operation. Table 3-2 summarizes the options on the Auto Fill Options menu.

You can use the fill handle to create a series longer than the one shown in Figure 3-8. If you drag the fill handle past cell G3 in Step 4, Excel continues to increment the months and logically will repeat July, August, and so on, if you extend the range far enough to the right.

You can create several different types of series using the fill handle. Table 3-3 on the next page illustrates several examples. Notice in examples 4 through 7 that, if you use the fill handle to create a series of numbers or non-sequential months, you must enter the first item in the series in one cell and the second item in the series in an adjacent cell. Next, select both cells and drag the fill handle through the destination area.

Table 3-2 Options Available on the Auto Fill Options Menu	
AUTO FILL OPTION	**DESCRIPTION**
Copy Cells	Fill destination area with contents using format of source area. Do not create a series.
Fill Series	Fill destination area with series using format of source area. This option is the default.
Fill Formatting Only	Fill destination area using format of source area. No content is copied unless fill is series.
Fill Without Formatting	Fill destination area with contents, without the formatting of source area.
Fill Months	Fill destination area with series of months using format of source area. Same as Fill Series and shows as an option only if source area contains a month.

More About

The Mighty Fill Handle

If you drag the fill handle to the left or up, Excel will decrement the series rather than increment the series. To copy a word, such as January or Monday, which Excel might interpret as the start of a series, hold down the CTRL key while you drag the fill handle to a destination area. If you drag the fill handle back into the middle of a cell, Excel erases the contents.

Table 3-3   Examples of Series Using the Fill Handle

EXAMPLE	CONTENTS OF CELL(S) COPIED USING THE FILL HANDLE	NEXT THREE VALUES OF EXTENDED SERIES
1	2:00	3:00, 4:00, 5:00
2	Qtr3	Qtr4, Qtr1, Qtr2
3	Quarter 1	Quarter 2, Quarter 3, Quarter 4
4	5-Jan, 5-Mar	5-May, 5-Jul, 5-Sep
5	2005, 2006	2007, 2008, 2009
6	1, 2	3, 4, 5
7	430, 410	390, 370, 350
8	Sun	Mon, Tue, Wed
9	Sunday, Tuesday	Thursday, Saturday, Monday
10	4th Section	5th Section, 6th Section, 7th Section
11	-205, -208	-211, -214, -217

More About

Painting a Format to Nonadjacent Ranges

Double-click the Format Painter button on the Standard toolbar and then drag through the nonadjacent ranges to paint the formats to the ranges. Click the Format Painter button to deactivate it.

Copying a Cell's Format Using the Format Painter Button

Because the last column title, Total, is not part of the series, it must be entered separately in cell H3 and formatted to match the other column titles. Imagine how many steps it would take, however, to assign the formatting of the other column titles to this cell — first, you have to change the font to 11 point, and then add a bottom border, and finally, rotate the text 45°. Using the Format Painter button on the Standard toolbar, however, you can format a cell quickly by copying a cell's format to another cell. The following steps enter the column title, Total, in cell H3 and format the cell using the Format Painter button.

To Copy a Cell's Format Using the Format Painter Button

1

• **Click cell H3.**

• **Type** Total **and then press the LEFT ARROW key.**

• **With cell G3 selected, click the Format Painter button on the Standard toolbar.**

• **Point to cell H3.**

The mouse pointer changes to a block plus sign with a paint brush (Figure 3-9).

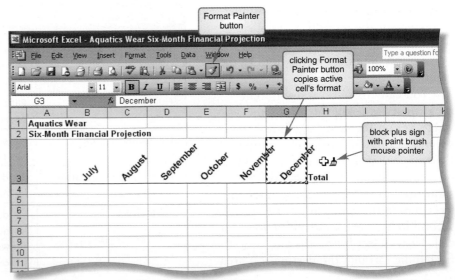

FIGURE 3-9

2

• **Click cell H3 to assign the format of cell G3 to cell H3.**

• **Click cell A4.**

Excel copies the format of cell G3 (11-point font, bottom border, text rotated 45°) to cell H3 (Figure 3-10). Cell A4 is now the active cell.

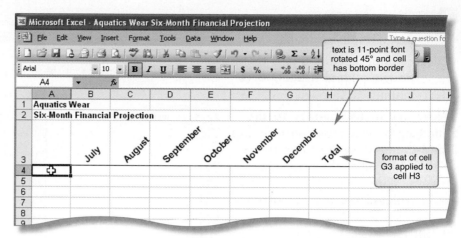

FIGURE 3-10

Other Ways

1. Click Copy button, select cell, on Edit menu click Paste Special, click Formats, click OK button
2. Select cell with desired format, in Voice Command mode, say "Format Painter" [select cell or range of cells]

The Format Painter button also can be used to copy the formats of a cell to a range of cells. To copy formats to a range of cells, select the cell or range with the desired format, click the Format Painter button on the Standard toolbar, and then drag through the range to which you want to paste the formats.

Increasing the Column Widths and Indenting Row Titles

In Project 2, the column widths were increased after the values were entered into the worksheet. Sometimes, you may want to increase the column widths before you enter the values and, if necessary, adjust them later. The following steps increase the column widths and then enter the row titles in column A down to Assumptions in cell A18.

To Increase Column Widths and Enter Row Titles

1

• **Move the mouse pointer to the boundary between column heading A and column heading B so that the mouse pointer changes to a split double arrow.**

• **Drag the mouse pointer to the right until the ScreenTip displays, Width: 35.00 (250 pixels). Do not release the mouse button.**

The distance between the left edge of column A and the vertical dotted line below the mouse pointer shows the proposed column width (Figure 3-11). The ScreenTip displays the proposed width in points and pixels.

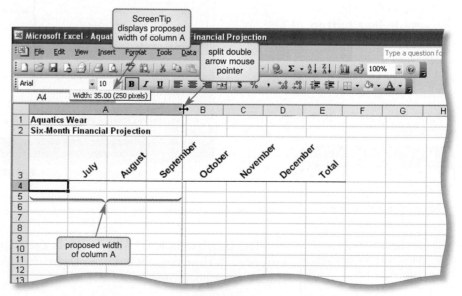

FIGURE 3-11

2

• **Release the mouse button.**

• **Click column heading B and then drag through column heading G to select columns B through G.**

• **Move the mouse pointer to the boundary between column headings B and C and then drag the mouse to the right until the ScreenTip displays, Width: 14.00 (103 pixels). Do not release the mouse button.**

The distance between the left edge of column B and the vertical line below the mouse pointer shows the proposed width of columns B through G (Figure 3-12). The ScreenTip displays the proposed width in points and pixels.

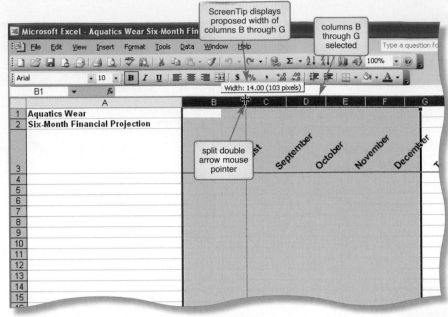

FIGURE 3-12

3

• **Release the mouse button.**

• **Use the technique described in Step 1 to increase the width of column H to 15.00.**

• **Enter the row titles in the range A4:A18 as shown in Figure 3-13, but without the indents.**

• **Click cell A5 and then click the Increase Indent button on the Formatting toolbar.**

• **Select the range A9:A13 and then click the Increase Indent button on the Formatting toolbar.**

• **Click cell A19.**

Excel displays the row titles as shown in Figure 3-13.

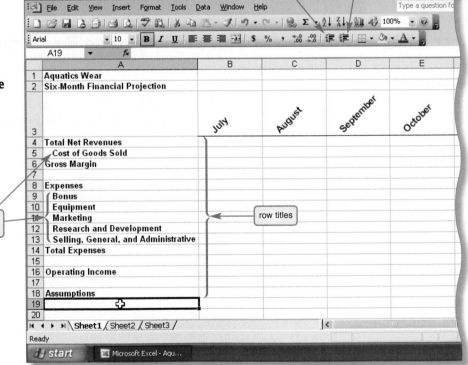

FIGURE 3-13

Other Ways

1. To indent, right-click range, click Format cells on shortcut menu, click Alignment tab, click Left (Indent) in Horizontal list, type number of spaces to indent in Indent text box, click OK button
2. To indent, in Voice Command mode, say "Increase Indent"

The Increase Indent button indents the contents of a cell to the right by three spaces each time you click it. The Decrease Indent button decreases the indent by three spaces each time you click it.

Copying a Range of Cells to a Nonadjacent Destination Area

As shown in the sketch of the worksheet (Figure 3-3a on page EX 149), the row titles in the range A9:A13 are the same as the row titles in the Assumptions table in the range A19:A25, with the exception of the two additional entries in cells A21 (Margin) and A24 (Revenue for Bonus). Hence, the Assumptions table row titles can be created by copying the range A9:A13 to the range A19:A23 and then inserting two rows for the additional entries in cells A21 and A24. The source area (range A9:A13) is not adjacent to the destination area (range A19:A23). The first two projects used the fill handle to copy a source area to an adjacent destination area. To copy a source area to a nonadjacent destination area, however, you cannot use the fill handle.

A more versatile method of copying a source area is to use the Copy button and Paste button on the Standard toolbar. You can use these two buttons to copy a source area to an adjacent or nonadjacent destination area.

The Copy button copies the contents and format of the source area to the **Office Clipboard**, a special place in the computer's memory that allows you to collect text and graphic items from an Office document and then paste them into any Office document. The Copy command on the Edit menu or shortcut menu works the same as the Copy button. The Paste button copies the item from the Office Clipboard to the destination area. The Paste command on the Edit menu or shortcut menu works the same as the Paste button.

The following steps use the Copy and Paste buttons to copy the range A9:A13 to the nonadjacent range A19:A23.

More About

Fitting Entries in a Cell

An alternative to increasing the column widths or row heights is to shrink the characters in the cell to fit the current width of the column. To shrink to fit, click Format on the menu bar, click Cells on the Format menu, click the Alignment tab, and click Shrink to fit in the Text control area. After shrinking entries to fit in a cell, consider using the Zoom box on the Standard toolbar to make the entries more readable.

Q&A

Q: Can you copy a range of cells from one workbook to another workbook?

A: Yes. You can copy a range of cells from one workbook to another by opening the source workbook, selecting the range, clicking the Copy button to place the range of cells on the Office Clipboard, activating the destination workbook, selecting the destination area, and then clicking the Paste button.

To Copy a Range of Cells to a Nonadjacent Destination Area

1

• **Select the range A9:A13 and then click the Copy button on the Standard toolbar.**

• **Click cell A19, the top cell in the destination area.**

Excel surrounds the source area A9:A13 with a marquee (Figure 3-14). Excel also copies the values and formats of the range A9:A13 to the Office Clipboard.

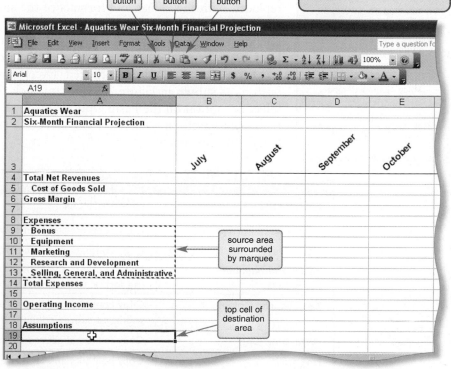

FIGURE 3-14

2

- **Click the Paste button on the Standard toolbar.**
- **Scroll down so row 5 appears at the top of the window.**

Excel copies the values and formats of the last item placed on the Office Clipboard (range A9:A13) to the destination area A19:A23 (Figure 3-15). The Paste Options button appears.

3

- **Press the ESC key.**

Excel removes the marquee from the source area and disables the Paste button on the Standard toolbar.

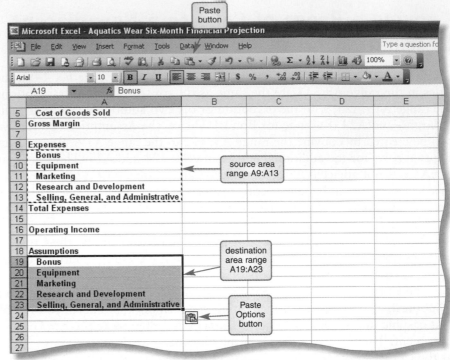

FIGURE 3-15

Other Ways

1. Select source area, on Edit menu click Copy, select destination area, on Edit menu click Paste
2. Right-click source area, click Copy on shortcut menu, right-click destination area, click Paste on shortcut menu
3. Select source area and point to border of range; while holding down CTRL key, drag source area to destination area
4. Select source area, press CTRL+C, select destination area, press CTRL+V
5. Select source area, in Voice Command mode, say "Copy" [select destination area], in Voice Command mode, say "Paste"

As shown in Step 1 and Figure 3-14 on the previous page, you are not required to select the entire destination area (range A19:A23) before clicking the Paste button. Excel only needs to know the upper-left cell of the destination area. In the case of a single column range, such as A19:A23, the top cell of the destination area (cell A19) also is the upper-left cell of the destination area.

When you complete a copy, the values and formats in the destination area are replaced with the values and formats of the source area. Any data contained in the destination area prior to the copy and paste is lost. If you accidentally delete valuable data, immediately click the Undo button on the Standard toolbar or click the Undo Paste command on the Edit menu to undo the paste.

After the Paste button is clicked, Excel immediately displays the Paste Options button, as shown in Figure 3-15. If you click the Paste Options button arrow and select an option on the Paste Options menu, Excel modifies the most recent paste operation based on your selection. Table 3-4 summarizes the options available on the Paste Options menu.

Table 3-4 Options Available on the Paste Options Menu	
PASTE OPTION	**DESCRIPTION**
Keep Source Formatting	Copy contents and format of source area. This option is the default.
Match Destination Formatting	Copy contents of source area, but not the format.
Values and Numbers Formatting	Copy contents and format of source area for numbers or formulas, but use format of destination area for text.
Keep Source Column Widths	Copy contents and format of source area. Change destination column widths to source column widths.
Formatting Only	Copy format of source area, but not the contents.
Link Cells	Copy contents and format and link cells so that a change to the cells in source area updates the corresponding cells in destination area.

The Paste button on the Standard toolbar (Figure 3-15) includes an arrow, which displays a list of advanced paste options (Formulas, Values, No Borders, Transpose, Paste Link, and Paste Special). These options will be discussed when they are used.

An alternative to clicking the Paste button is to press the ENTER key. The ENTER key completes the paste operation, removes the marquee from the source area, and disables the Paste button so that you cannot paste the copied source area to other destination areas. The ENTER key was not used in the previous set of steps so that the capabilities of the Paste Options button could be discussed. The Paste Options button does not appear on the screen when you use the ENTER key to complete the paste operation.

As previously indicated, the Office Clipboard allows you to collect text and graphic items from an Office document and then paste them into any Office document. You can use the Office Clipboard to collect up to 24 different items. To collect multiple items, you first must display the Clipboard task pane by clicking Office Clipboard on the Edit menu. If you want to paste an item on the Office Clipboard into a document, such as a spreadsheet, click the icon representing the item in the Clipboard task pane.

Using Drag and Drop to Move or Copy Cells

You also can use the mouse to move or copy cells. First, you select the source area and point to the border of the cell or range. You know you are pointing to the border of the cell or range when the mouse pointer changes to a block arrow. To move the selected cell or cells, drag the selection to the destination area. To copy a selection, hold down the CTRL key while dragging the selection to the destination area. You know Excel is in copy mode when a small plus sign appears next to the block arrow mouse pointer. Be sure to release the mouse button before you release the CTRL key. Using the mouse to move or copy cells is called **drag and drop**.

Using Cut and Paste to Move or Copy Cells

Another way to move cells is to select them, click the Cut button on the Standard toolbar (Figure 3-14 on page EX 157) to remove them from the worksheet and copy them to the Office Clipboard, select the destination area, and then click the Paste button on the Standard toolbar or press the ENTER key. You also can use the Cut command on the Edit menu or shortcut menu, instead of the Cut button.

Inserting and Deleting Cells in a Worksheet

At anytime while the worksheet is on the screen, you can insert cells to enter new data or delete cells to remove unwanted data. You can insert or delete individual cells, a range of cells, entire rows, entire columns, or entire worksheets.

Inserting Rows

The Rows command on the Insert menu or the Insert command on the shortcut menu allows you to insert rows between rows that already contain data. According to the sketch of the worksheet in Figure 3-3a on page EX 149, two rows must be inserted in the Assumptions table, one between rows 20 and 21 for the Margin assumption and another between rows 22 and 23 for the Revenue for Bonus assumption. The steps on the next page show how to accomplish the task of inserting the new rows into the worksheet.

More About

Move It or Copy It

You may hear someone say, "move it or copy it, it's all the same." No, it is not the same! When you move a cell, the data in the original location is cleared and the format is reset to the default. When you copy a cell, the data and format of the copy area remains intact. In short, you should copy cells to duplicate entries and move cells to rearrange entries.

More About

Cutting

When you cut a cell or range of cells using the Cut command or Cut button, Excel copies the cells to the Office Clipboard, but does not remove the cells from the source area until you paste the cells in the destination area by clicking the Paste button or pressing the ENTER key. When you complete the paste, Excel clears the cell entry and its formats from the source area.

More About

Inserting Multiple Rows

If you want to insert multiple rows, you have two choices. First, you can insert a single row by using the Insert command on the shortcut menu and then repeatedly press F4 to keep inserting rows. Alternatively, you can select any number of existing rows before inserting new rows. For instance, if you want to insert five rows, select five existing rows in the worksheet, right-click the rows, and then click Insert on the shortcut menu.

To Insert a Row

1

• **Right-click row heading 21, the row below where you want to insert a row.**

Excel highlights row 21 and displays the shortcut menu (Figure 3-16).

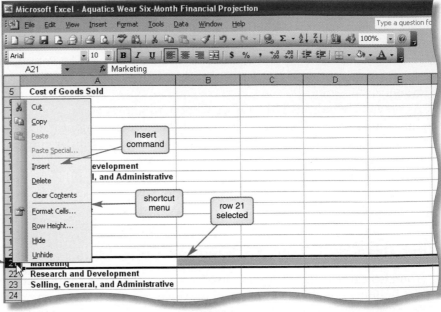

FIGURE 3-16

2

• **Click Insert on the shortcut menu.**

• **Click cell A21 in the new row and then enter** `Margin` **as the row title.**

Excel inserts a new row in the worksheet by shifting the selected row 21 and all rows below it down one row (Figure 3-17). Excel displays the new row title in cell A21. The cells in the new row inherit the formats of the cells in the row above them.

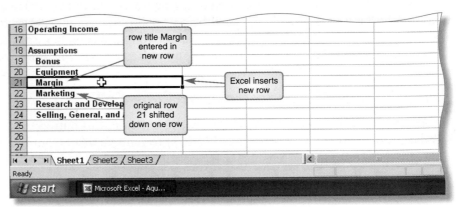

FIGURE 3-17

3

• **Right-click row heading 24 and then click Insert on the shortcut menu.**

• **Click cell A24 in the new row and then enter** `Revenue for Bonus` **as the row title.**

Excel inserts a new row in the worksheet and displays the new row title in cell A24 (Figure 3-18).

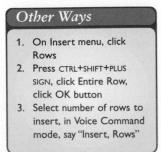

Other Ways

1. On Insert menu, click Rows
2. Press CTRL+SHIFT+PLUS SIGN, click Entire Row, click OK button
3. Select number of rows to insert, in Voice Command mode, say "Insert, Rows"

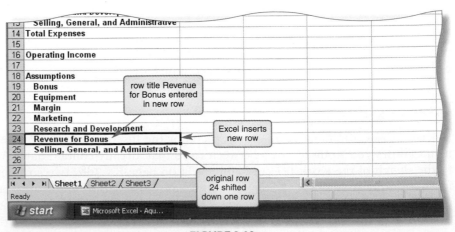

FIGURE 3-18

To insert multiple adjacent rows, first select as many rows as you want to insert by dragging through the row headings immediately below where you want the new rows inserted before invoking the Insert command.

When you insert a row, it inherits the format of the row above it. You can change this by clicking the Insert Options button that appears immediately above the inserted row. Following the insertion of a row, the Insert Options button lets you select from the following options: (1) Format Same As Above; (2) Format Same As Below; and (3) Clear Formatting. The Format Same as Above option is the default. The Insert Options button remains active until you begin the next Excel operation.

If the rows that are shifted down include cell references in formulas located in the worksheet, Excel automatically adjusts the cell references in the formulas to their new locations. Thus, in Step 2 in the previous steps, if a formula in the worksheet references a cell in row 21 before the insert, then the cell reference in the formula is adjusted to row 22 after the insert.

The primary difference between the Insert command on the shortcut menu and the Rows command on the Insert menu is that the Insert command on the shortcut menu requires that you select an entire row (or rows) in order to insert a row (or rows). The Rows command on the Insert menu requires that you select a single cell in a row to insert one row or a range of cells to insert multiple rows.

Inserting Columns

You insert columns into a worksheet in the same way you insert rows. To insert columns, select one or more columns immediately to the right of where you want Excel to insert the new column or columns. Select the number of columns you want to insert. Next, click Columns on the Insert menu or click Insert on the shortcut menu. The primary difference between these two commands is this: The Columns command on the Insert menu requires that you select a single cell in a column to insert one column or a range of cells to insert multiple columns. The Insert command on the shortcut menu, however, requires that you select an entire column (or columns) to insert a column (or columns). Following the insertion of a column, Excel displays the Insert Options button, which allows you to modify the insertion in a fashion similar to that discussed earlier when inserting rows.

Inserting Single Cells or a Range of Cells

The Insert command on the shortcut menu or the Cells command on the Insert menu allows you to insert a single cell or a range of cells. You should be aware that if you shift a single cell or a range of cells, however, it no longer may be lined up with its associated cells. To ensure that the values in the worksheet do not get out of order, it is recommended that you insert only entire rows or entire columns. When you insert a single cell or a range of cells, Excel displays the Insert Options button so that you can change the format of the inserted cell, using options similar to those for inserting rows and columns.

Deleting Columns and Rows

The Delete command on the Edit menu or shortcut menu removes cells (including the data and format) from the worksheet. Deleting cells is not the same as clearing cells. The Clear command, which was described earlier in Project 1 on page EX 52, clears the data from the cells, but the cells remain in the worksheet. The Delete command removes the cells from the worksheet and shifts the remaining

More About

Dragging Ranges

You can move and insert a selected cell or range between existing cells by holding down the SHIFT key while you drag the selection to the gridline where you want to insert. You also can copy and insert by holding down the CTRL+SHIFT keys while you drag the selection to the desired gridline.

More About

The Insert Options Button

When you insert columns or rows, Excel only displays the Insert Options button if formats are assigned to the leftmost column or top row of the selection.

Q&A

Q: Can you undo copying, deleting, inserting, and moving ranges of cells?

A: Yes. Copying, deleting, inserting, and moving ranges of cells have the potential to render a worksheet useless. Carefully review these actions before continuing on to the next task. If you are not sure the action is correct, click the Undo button on the Standard toolbar.

rows up (when you delete rows) or shifts the remaining columns to the left (when you delete columns). If formulas located in other cells reference cells in the deleted row or column, Excel does not adjust these cell references. Excel displays the error message **#REF!** in those cells to indicate a cell reference error. For example, if cell A7 contains the formula =A4+A5 and you delete row 5, Excel assigns the formula =A4+#REF! to cell A6 (originally cell A7) and displays the error message #REF! in cell A6. It also displays an Error Options button when you select the cell containing the error message #REF!, which allows you to select options to determine the nature of the problem.

Deleting Individual Cells or a Range of Cells

Although Excel allows you to delete an individual cell or range of cells, you should be aware that if you shift a cell or range of cells on the worksheet, it no longer may be lined up with its associated cells. For this reason, it is recommended that you delete only entire rows or entire columns.

Entering Numbers with Format Symbols

The next step in creating the Six-Month Financial Projection worksheet is to enter the assumption values in the range B19:B25. The assumption numbers can be entered and then formatted as in Projects 1 and 2, or each one can be entered with format symbols. When a number is entered with a **format symbol**, Excel immediately displays it with the assigned format. Valid format symbols include the dollar sign ($), comma (,), and percent sign (%).

If you enter a whole number, it appears without any decimal places. If you enter a number with one or more decimal places and a format symbol, Excel displays the number with two decimal places. Table 3-5 illustrates several examples of numbers entered with format symbols. The number in parentheses in column 4 indicates the number of decimal places.

Table 3-5	Numbers Entered with Format Symbols		
FORMAT SYMBOL	**TYPED IN FORMULA BAR**	**DISPLAYS IN CELL**	**COMPARABLE FORMAT**
,	83,341	83,341	Comma (0)
	1,675.8	1,675.80	Comma (2)
$	$278	$278	Currency (0)
	$3818.54	$3,818.54	Currency (2)
	$45,612.3	$45,612.3	Currency (2)
%	23%	23%	Percent (0)
	97.5%	97.50%	Percent (2)
	39.833%	39.83%	Percent (2)

The following step enters the numbers in the Assumptions table with format symbols.

To Enter Numbers with Format Symbols

1

• **Enter** 250,000.00 **in cell B19,** 5.00% **in cell B20,** 62.00% **in cell B21,** 14.00% **in cell B22,** 6.75% **in cell B23,** 15,000,000.00 **in cell B24, and** 30.00% **in cell B25.**

Excel displays the entries using a format based on the format symbols entered with the numbers (Figure 3-19).

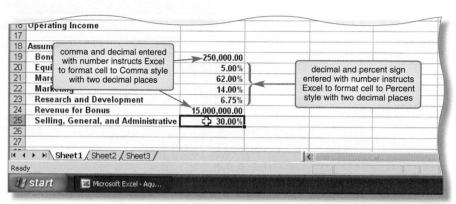

FIGURE 3-19

Freezing Worksheet Titles

Freezing worksheet titles is a useful technique for viewing large worksheets that extend beyond the window. Normally, when you scroll down or to the right, the column titles in row 3 and the row titles in column A that define the numbers no longer appear on the screen. This makes it difficult to remember what the numbers in these rows and columns represent. To alleviate this problem, Excel allows you to **freeze the titles,** so that Excel displays the titles on the screen, no matter how far down or to the right you scroll.

The following steps show how to use the Freeze Panes command on the Window menu to freeze the worksheet title and column titles in rows 1, 2, and 3, and the row titles in column A.

To Freeze Column and Row Titles

1

• **Press CTRL+HOME to select cell A1 and ensure that Excel displays row 1 and column A on the screen.**

• **Select cell B4.**

• **Click Window on the menu bar.**

Excel displays the Window menu (Figure 3-20).

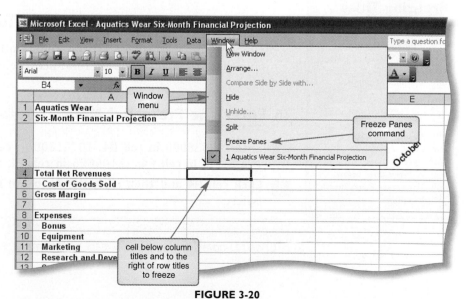

FIGURE 3-20

Other Ways

1. On Format menu click Cells, click Number tab, click category in Category list, [select desired format], click OK button
2. Right-click range, click Format Cells on shortcut menu, click Number tab, click category in Category list, [select desired format], click OK button
3. Press CTRL+1, click Number tab, click category in Category list, [select desired format], click OK button
4. In Voice Command mode, say "Format, Cells, Number, [desired category and format], OK"

2

• Click Freeze Panes on the Window menu.

Excel displays a thin black line on the right side of column A, indicating the split between the frozen row titles in column A and the rest of the worksheet. It also displays a thin black line below row 3, indicating the split between the frozen column titles in rows 1 through 3 and the rest of the worksheet (Figure 3-21).

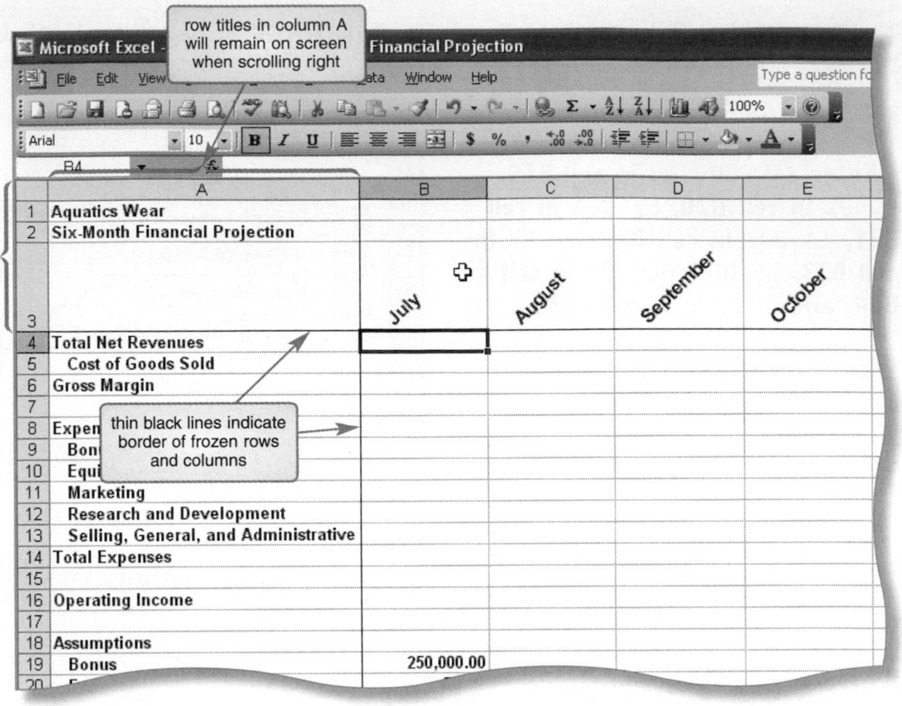

FIGURE 3-21

Other Ways

1. Press ALT+W, F
2. In Voice Command mode, say "Window, Freeze Panes"

Once frozen, the column titles in rows 1 through 3 and the row titles in column A will remain on the screen even when you scroll to the right. The titles remain frozen until you unfreeze them. You unfreeze the titles by clicking the Unfreeze Panes command on the Window menu. You will learn how to use the Unfreeze Panes command later in this project.

Before freezing the titles, it is important that Excel displays cell A1 in the upper-left corner of the screen. For example, if in Step 1 on the previous page, cell B4 was selected without first selecting cell A1 to ensure Excel displays the upper-left corner of the screen, then Excel would have frozen the titles and also hidden rows 1 and 2. Excel thus would not be able to display rows 1 and 2 until they are unfrozen.

More About

Freezing Titles

If you only want to freeze column headings, select the appropriate cell in column A before you click Freeze Panes on the Window menu. If you only want to freeze row titles, then select the appropriate cell in row 1. To freeze both column headings and row titles, select the cell that is the intersection of the column and row titles before you click Freeze Panes on the Window menu.

Entering the Projected Monthly Total Net Revenues

The next step is to enter the projected monthly total net revenues in row 4 and compute the projected six-month total net revenue in cell H4.

To Enter the Projected Monthly Total Net Revenue

1 **Enter** 23538000 **in cell B4,** 10781000 **in cell C4,** 18875345 **in cell D4,** 11451990 **in cell E4,** 15109656 **in cell F4, and** 25235860 **in cell G4.**

2 **Click cell H4 and then click the AutoSum button on the Standard toolbar twice.**

The projected six-month total net revenue (104991851) appears in cell H4 (Figure 3-22). Columns B, C, and D have scrolled off the screen, but column A remains because it was frozen earlier.

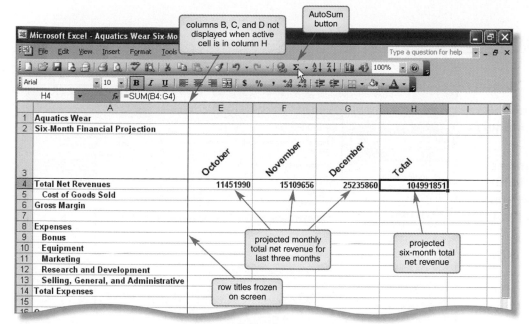

FIGURE 3-22

Recall from Projects 1 and 2 that if you select a single cell below or to the right of a range of numbers, you must click the AutoSum button twice to instruct Excel to display the sum. If you select a range of cells below or to the right of a range of numbers, you only need to click the AutoSum button once to instruct Excel to display the sums.

Displaying a System Date

The sketch of the worksheet in Figure 3-3a on page EX 149 includes a date stamp on the right side of the heading section. A **date stamp** shows the date a workbook, report, or other document was created or the period it represents. In business, a report often is meaningless without a date stamp. For example, if a printout of the worksheet in this project were distributed to the company's analysts, the date stamp would show when the six-month projections were made, as well as what period the report represents.

A simple way to create a date stamp is to use the NOW function to enter the system date tracked by your computer in a cell in the worksheet. The **NOW function** is one of 14 date and time functions available in Excel. When assigned to a cell, the NOW function returns a number that corresponds to the system date and time beginning with December 31, 1899. For example, January 1, 1900 equals 1, January 2, 1900 equals 2, and so on. Noon equals .5. Thus, noon on January 1, 1900 equals 1.5 and 6 P.M. on January 1, 1900 equals 1.75. If the computer's system date is set to the current date, which normally it is, then the date stamp is equivalent to the current date.

Excel automatically formats this number as a date, using the date and time format, mm/dd/yyyy hh:mm, where the first mm is the month, dd is the day of the month, yyyy is the year, hh is the hour of the day, and mm is the minutes past the hour.

The steps on the next page show how to enter the NOW function and change the format from mm/dd/yyyy hh:mm to mm/dd/yyyy.

To Enter and Format the System Date

1

• **Click cell H2 and then click the Insert Function box in the formula bar.**

• **When Excel displays the Insert Function dialog box, click the Or select a category box arrow, and then select Date & Time in the list.**

• **Scroll down in the Select a function list and then click NOW.**

An equal sign appears in the active cell and in the formula bar. Excel displays the Insert Function dialog box as shown in Figure 3-23.

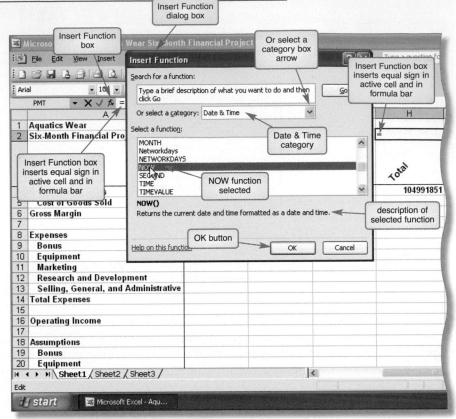

FIGURE 3-23

2

• **Click the OK button.**

• **When Excel displays the Function Arguments dialog box, click the OK button.**

• **Right-click cell H2.**

Excel displays the system date and time in cell H2, using the default date and time format mm/dd/yyyy hh:mm. It also displays the shortcut menu (Figure 3-24). The system date on your computer may be different.

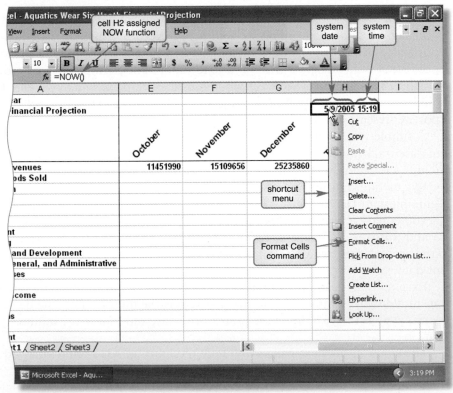

FIGURE 3-24

3

• **Click Format Cells on the shortcut menu.**

• **When Excel displays the Format Cells dialog box, if necessary, click the Number tab.**

• **Click Date in the Category list. Scroll down in the Type list and then click 3/14/2001.**

Excel displays the Format Cells dialog box with Date selected in the Category list and 3/14/2001 (mm/dd/yyyy) selected in the Type list (Figure 3-25). A sample of the data in the active cell (H2) using the selected format appears in the Sample area.

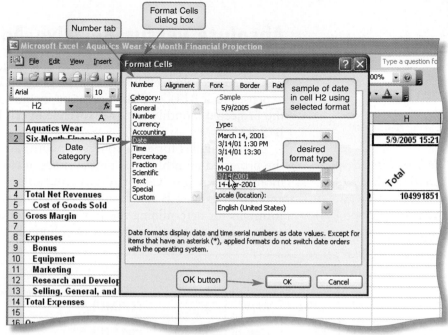

FIGURE 3-25

4

• **Click the OK button.**

Excel displays the system date in the form mm/dd/yyyy (Figure 3-26).

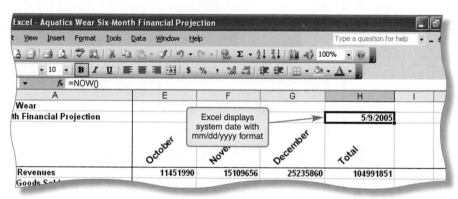

FIGURE 3-26

In Figure 3-26, the date is displayed right-aligned in the cell because Excel treats a date as a number formatted to display as a date. If you assign the General format (Excel's default format for numbers) to a date in a cell, the date is displayed as a number with two decimal places. For example, if the system time and date is 6:00 P.M. on September 12, 2005 and the cell containing the NOW function is assigned the General format, then Excel displays the following number in the cell:

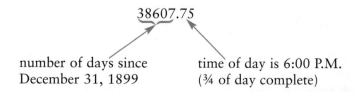

number of days since   time of day is 6:00 P.M.
December 31, 1899   (¾ of day complete)

The whole number portion of the number (38607) represents the number of days since December 31, 1899. The decimal portion of the number (.75) represents 6:00 P.M. as the time of day, at which point ¾ of the day is complete. To assign the General format to a cell, click General in the Category list in the Format Cells dialog box (Figure 3-25).

Other Ways

1. On Insert menu click Function, click Date & Time in Or select a category list, click NOW, click OK button
2. Press CTRL+SEMICOLON (not a volatile date)
3. Press CTRL+SHIFT+# to format date to day-month-year
4. In Voice Command mode, say "Insert, Function, [select Date & Time category], NOW, OK"

Absolute versus Relative Addressing

The next step is to enter the formulas that calculate the following values for July: cost of goods sold (cell B5), gross margin (cell B6), expenses (range B9:G13), total expenses (cell B14), and the operating income (cell B16). The formulas are based on the projected monthly total net revenue in cell B4 and the assumptions in the range B19:B25.

The formulas for each column (month) are the same, except for the reference to the projected monthly total net revenues in row 4, which varies according to the month (B4 for July, C4 for August, and so on). Thus, the formulas for July can be entered in column B and then copied to columns C through G. Table 3-6 shows the formulas for determining the July costs of goods sold, gross margin, expenses, total expenses, and operating income in column B.

Table 3-6 Formulas for Determining Cost of Goods Sold, Gross Margin, Expenses, Total Expenses, and Operating Income for July

CELL	ROW TITLE	FORMULA	COMMENT
B5	Cost of Goods Sold	=B4 * (1 − B21)	Total Net Revenues * (1 − Margin %)
B6	Gross Margin	= B4 − B5	Total Net Revenues minus Cost of Goods Sold
B9	Bonus	=IF(B4 >= B24, B19, 0)	Bonus equals value in B19 or 0
B10	Equipment	=B4 * B20	Total Net Revenues times Equipment %
B11	Marketing	=B4 * B22	Total Net Revenues times Marketing %
B12	Research and Development	=B4 * B23	Total Net Revenues times Research and Development %
B13	Selling, General, and Administrative	=B4 * B25	Total Net Revenues times Selling, General, and Administrative %
B14	Total Expenses	=SUM(B9:B13)	Sum of July Expenses
B16	Operating Income	=B6 − B14	Gross Margin minus Total Expenses

If the formulas are entered as shown in Table 3-6 in column B for July and then copied to columns C through G (August through December) in the worksheet, Excel will adjust the cell references for each column automatically. Thus, after the copy, the August Equipment expense in cell C10 would be =C4 * C20. While the cell reference C4 (August Revenue) is correct, the cell reference C20 references an empty cell. The formula for cell C7 should read =C4 * B20, rather than =C4 * C20, because B20 references the Equipment % value in the Assumptions table. In this instance, a way is needed to keep a cell reference in a formula the same, or constant, when it is copied.

To keep a cell reference constant when copying a formula or function, Excel uses a technique called absolute cell referencing. To specify an absolute cell reference in a formula, enter a dollar sign ($) before any column letters or row numbers you want to keep constant in formulas you plan to copy. For example, $B$20 is an absolute cell reference, while B20 is a relative cell reference. Both reference the same cell. The difference becomes apparent when they are copied to a destination area. A formula using the **absolute cell reference** $B$20 instructs Excel to keep the cell reference B20 constant (absolute) in the formula as it copies it to the destination area. A formula using the **relative cell reference** B20 instructs Excel to adjust the cell reference as it copies it to the destination area. A cell reference with only one dollar sign before either the column or the row is called a **mixed cell reference**. Table 3-7 gives some additional examples of absolute, relative, and mixed cell references.

Table 3-7 Examples of Absolute, Relative, and Mixed Cell References

CELL REFERENCE	TYPE OF REFERENCE	MEANING
$B$20	Absolute cell reference	Both column and row references remain the same when you copy this cell, because the cell references are absolute.
B$20	Mixed reference	This cell reference is mixed. The column reference changes when you copy this cell to another column because it is relative. The row reference does not change because it is absolute.
$B20	Mixed reference	This cell reference is mixed. The row reference changes when you copy this cell reference to another row because it is relative. The column reference does not change because it is absolute.
B20	Relative cell reference	Both column and row references are relative. When copied to another cell, both the row and column in the cell reference are adjusted to reflect the new location.

Entering a Formula Containing Absolute Cell References

The following steps show how to enter the cost of goods sold formula =B4 * (1 – $B$21) in cell B5 using Point mode. To enter an absolute cell reference, you can type the dollar sign ($) as part of the cell reference or enter it by pressing F4 with the insertion point in or to the right of the cell reference to change to absolute.

To Enter a Formula Containing Absolute Cell References

1

• **Press CTRL+HOME and then click cell B5.**

• **Type = (equal sign), click cell B4, type *(1–b21 and then press F4 to change b21 from a relative cell reference to an absolute cell reference.**

• **Type) to complete the formula.**

Excel displays the formula =B4*(1–$B$21) in cell B5 and in the formula bar (Figure 3-27). The formula always will reference the Margin value in cell B21, even if it is copied.

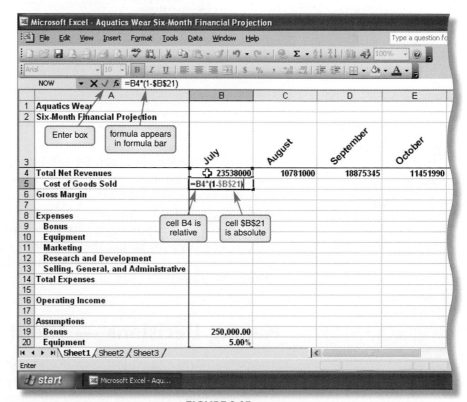

FIGURE 3-27

2

• **Click the Enter box in the formula bar.**

Excel displays the result, 8944440, in cell B5, instead of the formula (Figure 3-28). With cell B5 selected, the formula assigned to it appears in the formula bar.

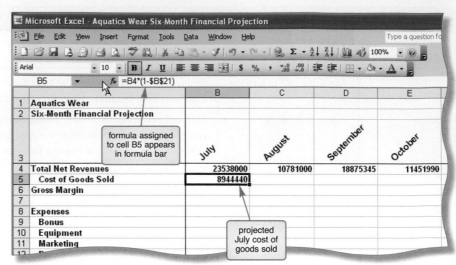

FIGURE 3-28

3

• **Click cell B6, type = (equal sign), click cell B4, type − and then click cell B5.**
• **Click the Enter box in the formula bar.**

Excel displays the gross margin for July, 14593560, in cell B6.

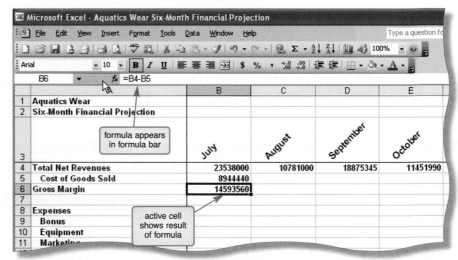

FIGURE 3-29

Because the formula in cell B4 will be copied across columns, rather than down rows, the formula entered in cell B4 in Step 1 on the previous page could have been entered as =B4*(1−$B21), rather than =B4*(1−$B$21). That is, the formula could have included the mixed cell reference $B21, rather than the absolute cell reference $B$21. When you copy a formula across columns, the row does not change anyway. The key is to ensure that column B remains constant as you copy the formula across rows. To change the absolute cell reference to a mixed cell reference, continue to press the F4 key until you get the desired cell reference.

Making Decisions — The If Function

According to the Request for New Workbook in Figure 3-2 on page EX 148, if the projected July total net revenues in cell B4 is greater than or equal to the revenue for bonus in cell B24 (15,000,000.00), then the July bonus value in cell B9 is equal to the bonus value in cell B19 (250,000.00); otherwise, cell B9 is equal to 0. One way to assign the monthly bonus value in cell B9 is to check to see if the total net revenues in cell B4 equal or exceed the revenue for bonus amount in cell B24 and, if so, then to enter 250,000.00 in cell B9. You can use this manual process for all six months by checking the values for the corresponding month.

Because the data in the worksheet changes each time a report is prepared or the figures are adjusted, however, it is preferable to have Excel assign the monthly bonus to the entries in the appropriate cells automatically. To do so, cell B9 must include a formula or function that displays 250,000.00 or 0.00 (zero), depending on whether the projected July total net revenues in cell B4 is greater than or equal to or less than the revenue for bonus value in cell B24.

The **IF function** is useful when you want to assign a value to a cell based on a logical test. For example, using the IF function, cell B9 can be assigned the following IF function:

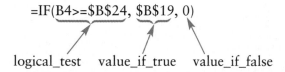

$$=IF(B4>=\$B\$24, \$B\$19, 0)$$

logical_test   value_if_true   value_if_false

The IF function instructs Excel that, if the projected July total net revenues in cell B4 is greater than or equal to the revenue for bonus value in cell B24, then Excel should display the value 250000 in cell B19, in cell B9. If the projected July total net revenues in cell B4 is less than the revenue for bonus value in cell B24, then Excel displays a 0 (zero) in cell B9.

The general form of the IF function is:

$$=IF(logical\_test, value\_if\_true, value\_if\_false)$$

The argument, logical_test, is made up of two expressions and a comparison operator. Each expression can be a cell reference, a number, text, a function, or a formula. Valid comparison operators, their meaning, and examples of their use in IF functions are shown in Table 3-8. The argument, value_if_true, is the value you want Excel to display in the cell when the logical test is true. The argument, value_if_false, is the value you want Excel to display in the cell when the logical test is false.

Table 3-8	Comparison Operators	
COMPARISON OPERATOR	**MEANING**	**EXAMPLE**
=	Equal to	=IF(H7 = 0, J6 ^ H4, L9 + D3)
<	Less than	=IF(C34 * W3 < K7, $K$6, L33 − 5)
>	Greater than	=IF(MIN(K8:K12) > 75, 1, 0)
>=	Greater than or equal to	=IF(P8 >= $H$6, J7 / V4, 7.5)
<=	Less than or equal to	=IF(G7 − G2 <= 23, L$9, 35 / Q2)
<>	Not equal to	=IF(B1 <> 0, ''No'',''Yes'')

The steps on the next page assign the IF function =IF(B4>=$B$24,$B$19,0) to cell B9. This IF function determines whether or not the worksheet assigns a bonus for July.

More About

Logical Operators in IF Functions

IF functions can use logical operators, such as AND, OR, and NOT. For example, the three IF functions =IF(AND(B3>C3, D3<C5), "OK", "Not OK") and =IF(OR(C3>G5, D2<X3), "OK", "Not OK") and =IF(NOT(A6<H7), "OK", "Not OK") use logical operators. In the first example, both logical tests must be true for the value_if_true OK to be assigned to the cell. In the second example, one or the other logical tests must be true for the value_if_true OK to be assigned to the cell. In the third example, the logical test A6<H7 must be false for the value_if_true OK to be assigned to the cell.

To Enter an IF Function

1

• **Click cell B9. Type**
`=if(b4>=$b$24,$b$19,0)` **in the cell.**

Excel displays the IF function in the formula bar and in the active cell B9. Excel also displays a ScreenTip showing the general form of the IF function (Figure 3-30).

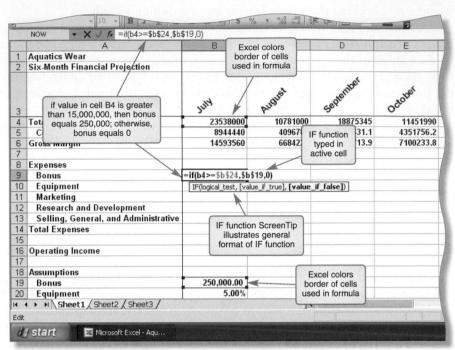

FIGURE 3-30

2

• **Click the Enter box in the formula bar.**

Excel displays 250000 in cell B9 (Figure 3-31), because the value in cell B4 (23538000) is greater than or equal to the value in cell B24 (15,000,000.00).

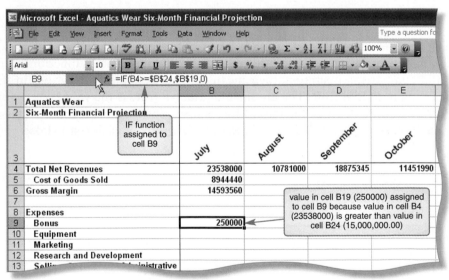

FIGURE 3-31

Other Ways

1. On Insert menu click Function, click Logical in Or select a category list, click IF, click OK button
2. Click Insert Function box in formula bar, click Logical in Or select a category list, click IF, click OK button
3. In Voice Command mode, say "Insert, Function", [select Logical category], in Voice Command mode, say "IF, OK"

The value that Excel displays in cell B9 depends on the values assigned to cells B4, B19, and B24. For example, if the value for July total net revenues in cell B4 is reduced below 15,000,000.00, then the IF function in cell B9 will cause Excel to display a 0. If you change the bonus in cell B19 from 250,000.00 to another number and the value in cell B4 greater than or equal to the value in cell B24, it will change the results in cell B9 as well. Finally, increasing the revenue for bonus in cell B24 so that it is greater than the value in cell B4 will change the result in cell B9.

Entering the Remaining Formulas

The July equipment expense in cell B10 is equal to the total net revenues in cell B4 times the equipment assumption in cell B20 (5.00%). The July marketing expense in cell B11 is equal to the projected July total net revenue in cell B4 times the marketing assumption in cell B22 (14.00%). Similar formulas determine the remaining July expenses in cells B12 and B13.

The total expenses value in cell B14 is equal to the sum of the expenses in the range B9:B13. The operating income in cell B16 is equal to the gross margin in cell B6 minus the total expenses in cell B14. The formulas are short, and therefore, they are typed in the following steps, rather than entered using Point mode.

More About

Replacing a Formula with a Constant

You can replace a formula with its result so it remains constant. Do the following: (1) click the cell with the formula; (2) press F2 or click in the formula bar; (3) press F9 to display the value in the formula bar; and (4) press the ENTER key.

To Enter the Remaining July Formulas

1 **Click cell B10. Type** =b4*b20 **and then press the DOWN ARROW key. Type** =b4*b22 **and then press the down arrow key. Type** =b4*b23 **and then press the DOWN ARROW key. Type** =b4*b25 **and then press the DOWN ARROW key.**

2 **With cell B14 selected, click the AutoSum button on the Standard toolbar twice. Click cell B16. Type** =b6-b14 **and then press the ENTER key.**

3 **Press CTRL+ACCENT MARK(`) to instruct Excel to display the formulas version of the worksheet.**

4 **When you are finished viewing the formulas version, press CTRL+ACCENT MARK(`) to instruct Excel to display the values version of the worksheet.**

Following Step 2 and Step 4, Excel displays the results of the remaining July formulas (Figure 3-32a). Following Step 3, Excel displays the formulas version of the worksheet (Figure 3-32b).

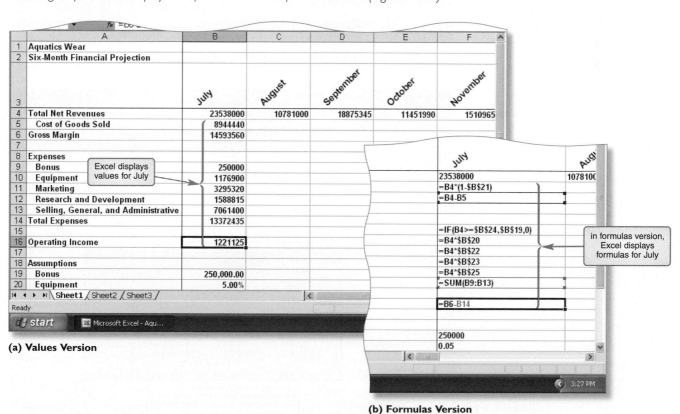

(a) Values Version

(b) Formulas Version

FIGURE 3-32

Viewing the formulas version (Figure 3-32b on the previous page) of the worksheet allows you to check the formulas assigned to the range B5:B16. You can see that Excel converts all the formulas from lowercase to uppercase.

Copying Formulas with Absolute Cell References

The following steps show how to use the fill handle to copy the July formulas in column B to the other five months in columns C through G.

To Copy Formulas with Absolute Cell References Using the Fill Handle

1

• **Select the range B5:B16 and then point to the fill handle in the lower-right corner of cell B16.**

Excel highlights the range B5:B16 and the mouse pointer changes to a crosshair (Figure 3-33).

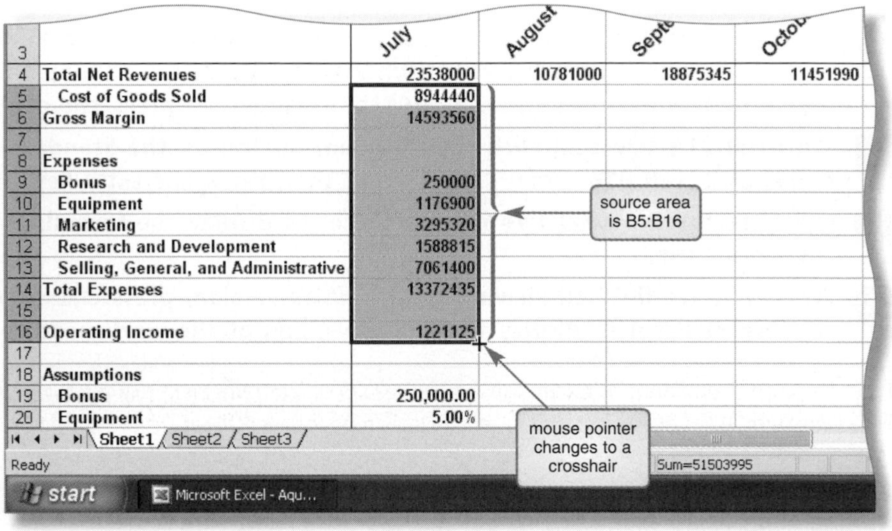

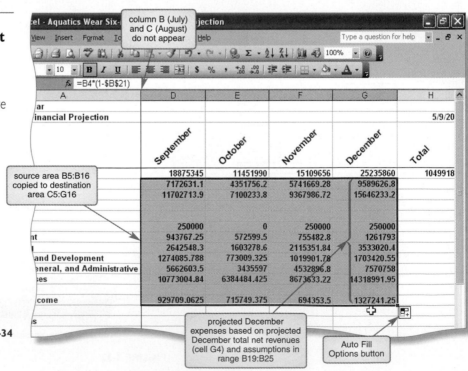

FIGURE 3-33

2

• **Drag the fill handle to the right to select the destination area C5:G16.**

Excel copies the formulas from the source area (B5:B16) to the destination area (C5:G16) and displays the calculated amounts (Figure 3-34). The Auto Fill Options button appears below the fill area.

FIGURE 3-34

Because the formulas in the range B5:B16 use absolute cell references, the formulas still refer to the current values in the Assumptions table when the formulas are copied to the range C5:G16.

As shown in Figure 3-34, as the fill handle is dragged to the right, columns B and C no longer appear on the screen. Column A, however, remains on the screen, because the row titles were frozen earlier in this project.

Determining Row Totals in Nonadjacent Cells

The following steps determine the row totals in column H. To determine the row totals using the AutoSum button, select only the cells in column H containing numbers in adjacent cells to the left. If, for example, you select the range H5:H16, Excel will display 0s as the sum of empty rows in cells H7, H8, and H15.

To Determine Row Totals in Nonadjacent Cells

1 Select the range H5:H6. Hold down the CTRL key and select the range H9:H14 and cell H16 as shown in Figure 3-35.

2 Click the AutoSum button on the Standard toolbar.

Excel displays the row totals in column H (Figure 3-35).

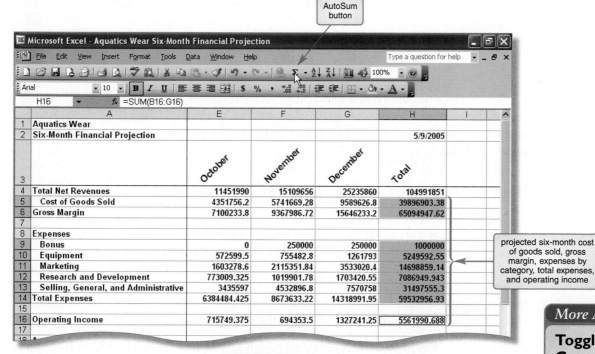

FIGURE 3-35

Unfreezing Worksheet Titles and Saving the Workbook

All the text, data, and formulas have been entered into the worksheet. The steps on the next page unfreeze the titles and save the workbook using its current file name, Aquatics Wear Six-Month Financial Projection.

To Unfreeze the Worksheet Titles and Save the Workbook

1 Press CTRL+HOME to select cell B4 and view the upper-left corner of the screen.

2 Click Window on the menu bar (Figure 3-36) and then click Unfreeze Panes.

3 Click the Save button on the Standard toolbar.

Excel unfreezes the titles so that column A scrolls off the screen when you scroll to the right and the first three rows scroll off the screen when you scroll down. The latest changes to the workbook are saved on disk using the file name, Aquatics Wear Six-Month Financial Projection.

More About

Work Days

Assume that you have two dates: one in cell F3 and the other in cell F4. The date in cell F3 is your starting date and the date in cell F4 is the ending date. To calculate the work days between the two dates (excludes weekends), use the following formula: =NETWORKDAYS(F3, F4). For this function to work, make sure the Analysis ToolPak add-in is installed. You can install it by clicking Add-Ins on the Tools menu.

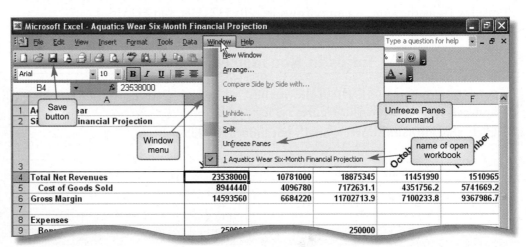

FIGURE 3-36

When the titles are frozen and you press CTRL+HOME, Excel selects the upper-left cell of the unfrozen section of the worksheet. For example, in Step 1 of the previous steps, Excel selected cell B4. When the titles are unfrozen, then pressing CTRL+HOME selects cell A1.

Nested Forms of the IF function

A **nested IF function** is one in which the action to be taken for the true or false case includes yet another IF function. The second IF function is considered to be nested, or layered, within the first. Study the nested IF function below, which determines the eligibility of a person to vote. Assume the following in this example: (1) the nested IF function is assigned to cell K12, which instructs Excel to display one of three messages in the cell; (2) cell H12 contains a person's age; and (3) cell I12 contains a Y or N, based on whether the person is registered to vote.

=IF(H12>=18, IF(I12="Y","Registered","Eligible and Not Registered"),"Not Eligible to Register")

The nested IF function instructs Excel to display one, and only one, of the following three messages in cell K12: (1) Registered; or (2) Eligible and Not Registered; or (3) Not Eligible to Register.

You can nest IF functions as deep as you want, but after you get beyond a nest of three IF functions, the logic becomes difficult to follow and alternative solutions, such as the use of multiple cells and simple IF functions, should be considered.

Formatting the Worksheet

The worksheet created thus far shows the financial projections for the six-month period, from July to December. Its appearance is uninteresting, however, even though some minimal formatting (bolding the worksheet, formatting assumptions numbers, changing the column widths, and formatting the date) was performed earlier. This section will complete the formatting of the worksheet to make the numbers easier to read and to emphasize the titles, assumptions, categories, and totals. The worksheet will be formatted in the following manner so it appears as shown in Figure 3-37: (1) format the numbers; (2) format the worksheet title, column titles, row titles, and operating income row; and (3) format the assumptions table.

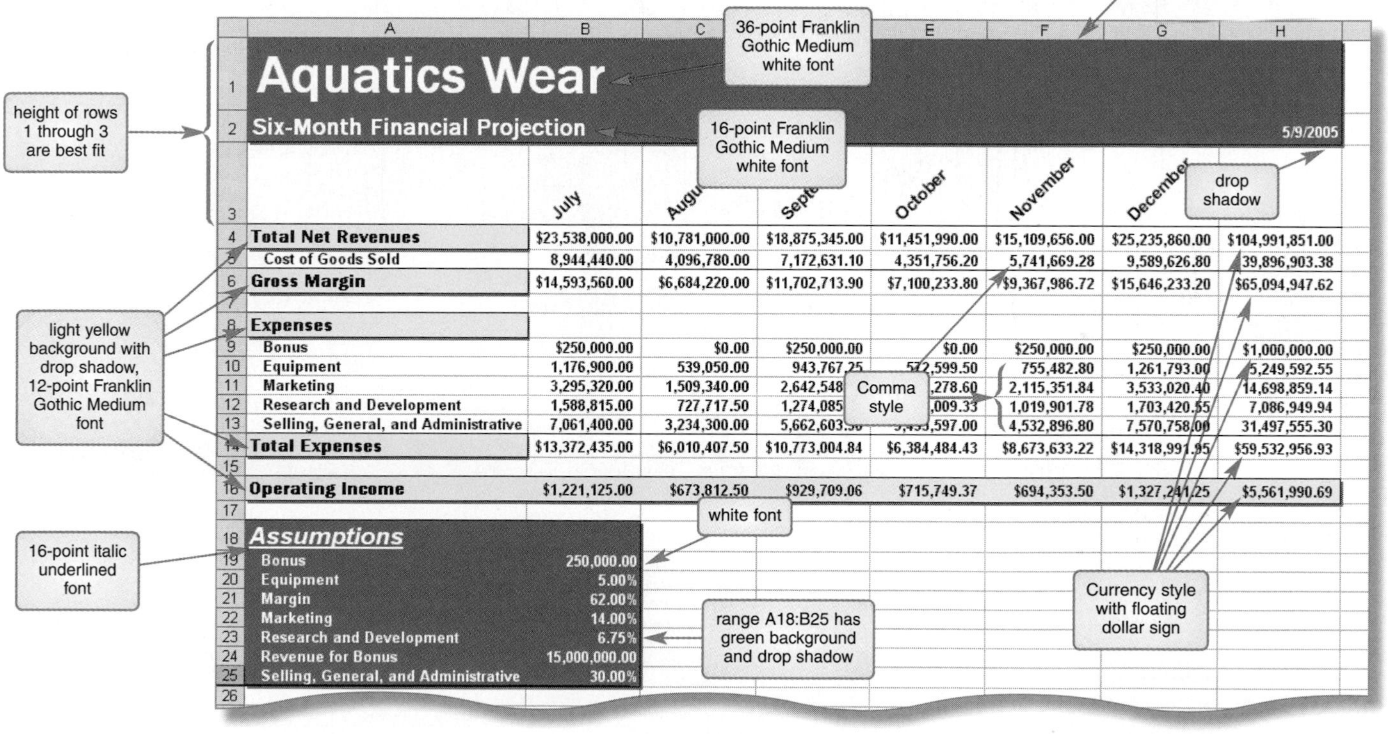

FIGURE 3-37

Formatting the Numbers

The numbers in the range B4:H16 are to be formatted as follows:

1. Assign the Currency style with a floating dollar sign to rows 4, 6, 9, 14, and 16.
2. Assign a customized Comma style to rows 5 and 10 through 13.

To assign a Currency style with a floating dollar sign, the Format Cells command will be used, rather than the Currency Style button on the Formatting toolbar, which assigns a fixed dollar sign. The Comma style also must be assigned using the Format Cells command, because the Comma Style button on the Formatting toolbar assigns a format that displays a dash (-) when a cell has a value of 0. The specifications for this worksheet call for displaying a value of 0 as 0.00 (see cell C9 in Figure 3-37), rather than as a dash. To create a Comma style using the Format Cells command, you can assign a Currency style with no dollar sign. The steps on the next page show how to assign formats to the numbers in rows 4 through 16.

More About

Selecting Nonadjacent Ranges

One of the more difficult tasks to learn is selecting nonadjacent ranges. To complete this task, do not hold down the CTRL key when you select the first range because Excel will consider the current active cell to be the first selection. Once the first range is selected, hold down the CTRL key and drag through the nonadjacent ranges. If a desired range is not visible in the window, use the scroll arrows to view the range. It is not necessary to hold down the CTRL key while you scroll.

To Assign Formats to Nonadjacent Ranges

1

• **Select the range B4:H4.**

• **While holding down the CTRL key, select the nonadjacent ranges B6:H6, B9:H9, B14:H14, and B16:H16, and then release the CTRL key.**

• **Right-click the selected range.**

Excel highlights the selected nonadjacent ranges and displays the shortcut menu as shown in Figure 3-38.

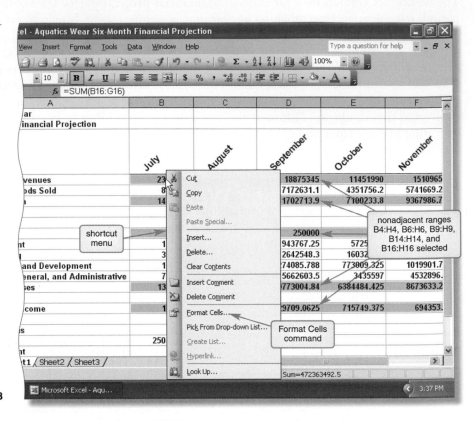

FIGURE 3-38

2

• **Click Format Cells on the shortcut menu.**

• **When Excel displays the Format Cells dialog box, click the Number tab, click Currency in the Category list, select 2 in the Decimal places box, click $ in the Symbol list to ensure a dollar sign shows, and click ($1,234.10) in the Negative numbers list.**

Excel displays the cell format settings in the Number sheet in the Format Cells dialog box as shown in Figure 3-39.

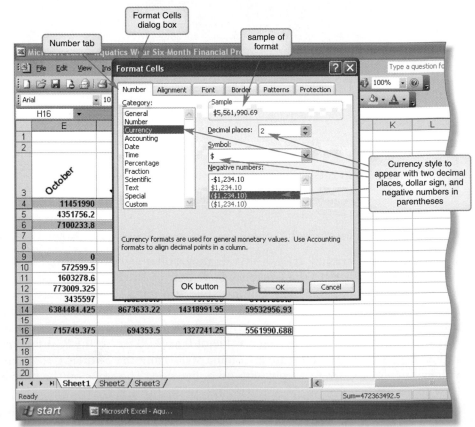

FIGURE 3-39

3

- Click the OK button.
- Select the range B5:H5.
- While holding down the CTRL key, select the range B10:H13, and then release the CTRL key.
- Right-click the selected range.
- Click Format Cells on the shortcut menu.

nonadjacent ranges B5:H5 and B10:H13 selected

4

- When Excel displays the Format Cells dialog box, click Currency in the Category list, select 2 in the Decimal places box, click None in the Symbol list so a dollar sign does not show, click (1,234.10) in the Negative numbers list.

Excel displays the format settings in the Number sheet in the Format Cells dialog box as shown in Figure 3-40.

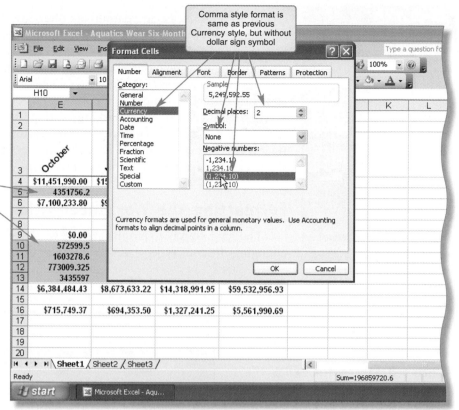

FIGURE 3-40

5

- Click the OK button.
- Press CTRL+HOME to select cell A1.

Excel displays the formatted numbers as shown in Figure 3-41.

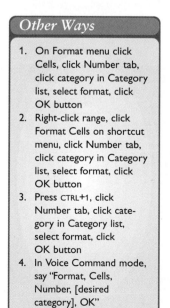

Other Ways

1. On Format menu click Cells, click Number tab, click category in Category list, select format, click OK button
2. Right-click range, click Format Cells on shortcut menu, click Number tab, click category in Category list, select format, click OK button
3. Press CTRL+1, click Number tab, click category in Category list, select format, click OK button
4. In Voice Command mode, say "Format, Cells, Number, [desired category], OK"

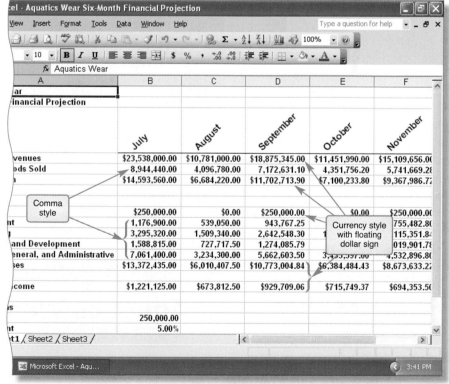

FIGURE 3-41

More About

The Fill and Font Color Buttons

You may have noticed that the color bar at the bottom of the Fill Color and Font Color buttons on the Formatting toolbar (Figure 3-44) changes to the most recently selected color. To apply this same color to a cell background or text, select a cell and then click the Fill Color button to use the color as a background or click the Font Color button to use the color as a font color.

In accounting, negative numbers often are shown with parentheses surrounding the value rather than with a negative sign preceding the value. Thus, in Step 2 and Step 4 of the previous steps, the format (1,234.10) in the Negative numbers list was clicked. The data being used in this project contains no negative numbers. You must, however, select a format for negative numbers, and you must be consistent if you are choosing different formats in a column, otherwise the decimal points may not line up.

In Step 2 (Figure 3-39) and Step 4 (Figure 3-40), the Accounting category could have been selected to generate the same format, rather than Currency. You should review the formats available in each category. Thousands of combinations of format styles can be created using the options in the Format Cells dialog box.

Formatting the Worksheet Titles

The next step is to emphasize the worksheet titles in cells A1 and A2 by changing the font type, size, and color as described in the following steps.

To Format the Worksheet Titles

1

• **Click cell A1 and then click the Font box arrow on the Formatting toolbar.**

• **Scroll down and point to Franklin Gothic Medium (or a similar font) in the Font list.**

Excel displays the Font list as shown in Figure 3-42. The names in the Font list are displayed in the font type they represent, allowing you to view the font type before you assign it to a cell or range of cells.

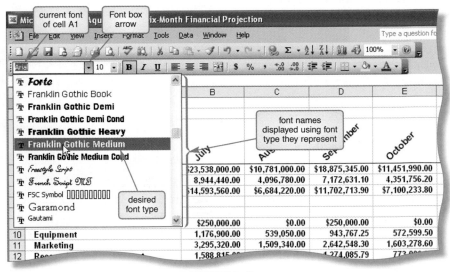

FIGURE 3-42

2

• **Click Franklin Gothic Medium.**

• **Click the Font Size box arrow on the Formatting toolbar and then click 36 in the Font Size list.**

• **Click cell A2 and then click the Font box arrow.**

• **Click Franklin Gothic Medium (or a similar font) in the Font list.**

• **Click the Font Size box arrow and then click 16 in the Font Size list.**

Excel displays the worksheet titles in cells A1 and A2 as shown in Figure 3-43.

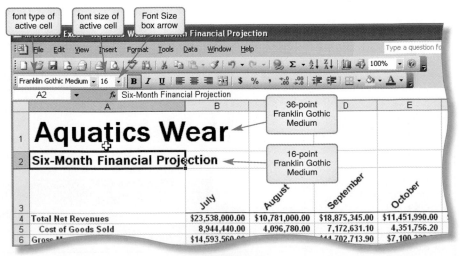

FIGURE 3-43

3

* Select the range **A1:H2** and then click the **Fill Color button arrow** on the Formatting toolbar.

* Click **Green (column 4, row 2)** on the Fill Color palette and then click the **Font Color button arrow** on the Formatting toolbar.

Excel assigns a green background to the selected range and displays the Font Color palette (Figure 3-44).

4

* Click **White (column 8, row 5)** on the Font Color palette.

Excel changes the color of the font in the range A1:H2 from black to white (see Figure 3-37 on page EX 177).

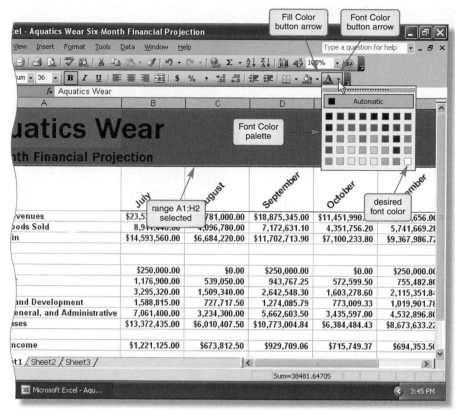

FIGURE 3-44

Showing the Drawing Toolbar

The next step is to add a drop shadow to the selected range A1:H2 using the Shadow button on the Drawing toolbar. The Drawing toolbar currently is hidden. Before using the Drawing toolbar, Excel must be instructed to display the Drawing toolbar on the screen. This section describes how to show an inactive (hidden) toolbar and then dock it.

Excel has hundreds of toolbar buttons, most of which it displays on 22 built-in toolbars. Two of these 22 built-in toolbars are the Standard toolbar and Formatting toolbar, which usually appear at the top of the screen. Another built-in toolbar is the Drawing toolbar. The **Drawing toolbar** provides tools that can simplify adding lines, boxes, and other geometric figures to a worksheet. You also can create customized toolbars containing the buttons that you use often.

To show or hide any Excel toolbar, you can use the shortcut menu that Excel displays when you right-click a toolbar, or you can use the Toolbars command on the View menu. The Drawing toolbar also can be displayed or hidden by clicking the Drawing button on the Standard toolbar.

The step on the next page illustrates how to show the Drawing toolbar.

Other Ways

1. On Format menu click Cells, click Patterns tab to color background (or click Font tab to color font), click OK button
2. Right-click range, click Format Cells on shortcut menu, click Patterns tab to color background (or click Font tab to color font), click OK button
3. Press CTRL+1, click Patterns tab to color background (or click Font tab to color font), click OK button
4. In Voice Command mode, say "Format, Cells, Patterns (or Font), [desired color], OK"

To Show the Drawing Toolbar

1

• **Click the Drawing button on the Standard toolbar.**

Excel displays the Drawing toolbar in the same location and with the same shape as it displayed the last time it was used (Figure 3-45).

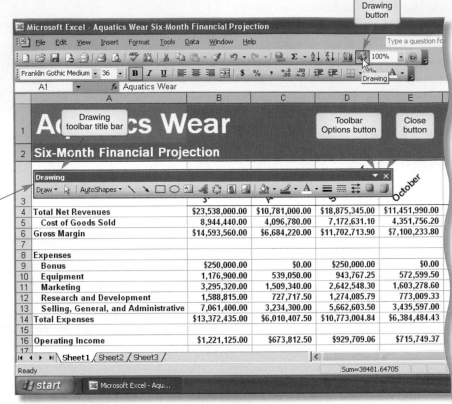

FIGURE 3-45

Other Ways

1. On View menu point to Toolbars, click Drawing
2. Right-click Standard or Formatting toolbar, click Drawing on shortcut menu
3. In Voice Command mode, say "View, Toolbars, Drawing"

Q: What happens when you dock a toolbar with a box or a button with a list on the left or right edge of the window?

A: If you dock a toolbar that includes a box or a button with a list on the left or right edge of the window, the box and its list will not appear on the toolbar and will not be available.

When a toolbar is displayed in the middle of the screen as shown in Figure 3-45, the toolbar includes a title bar. The Toolbar Options button and Close button are on the right side of the title bar.

Moving and Docking a Toolbar

The Drawing toolbar in Figure 3-45 is called a **floating toolbar** because it is displayed in its own window and can be moved anywhere in the Excel window. You move the toolbar by pointing to the toolbar title bar or to a blank area within the toolbar window (not a button) and then dragging the toolbar to its new location. As with any window, you also can resize the toolbar by dragging the toolbar window borders.

Sometimes a floating toolbar gets in the way no matter where you move it or how you resize it. You can hide the floating toolbar by clicking the Close button on the toolbar title bar. At times, however, you will want to keep the toolbar available for use. For this reason, Excel allows you to position toolbars on the edge of its window. If you drag the toolbar close to the edge of the window, Excel positions the toolbar in a **toolbar dock**.

Excel has four toolbar docks, one on each of the four sides of the window. You can add as many toolbars to a toolbar dock as you want. Each time you dock a toolbar, however, the Excel window slightly decreases in size to compensate for the room occupied by the toolbar. The following step shows how to dock the Drawing toolbar at the bottom of the screen below the scroll bar.

To Move and Dock a Toolbar

1

• **Point to the Drawing toolbar title bar or to a blank area in the Drawing toolbar.**

• **Drag the Drawing toolbar over the status bar at the bottom of the screen.**

Excel docks the Drawing toolbar at the bottom of the screen (Figure 3-46).

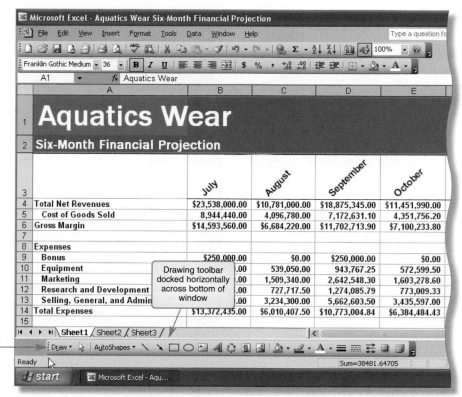

FIGURE 3-46

Compare Figure 3-46 with Figure 3-45. The heavy window border that surrounded the floating toolbar has changed to a light border and the title bar no longer appears.

To move a toolbar to any of the other three toolbar docks, drag the toolbar from its current position to the desired side of the window. To move a docked toolbar, it is easiest to point to the move handle and, when the mouse pointer changes to a cross with four arrowheads, drag it to the desired location.

Adding a Drop Shadow

With the Drawing toolbar docked at the bottom of the screen, the next step is to add the drop shadow to the range A1:H2, as shown in the steps on the next page.

More About

Creating Your Own Toolbar

You can create and add buttons to your own toolbar by clicking the Customize command on the shortcut menu that appears when you right-click a toolbar. When Excel displays the Customize dialog box, click the Toolbars tab, click the New button, name the toolbar, click the Commands tab, and then drag buttons to the new toolbar.

To Add a Drop Shadow

1

• **With the range A1:H2 selected, click the Shadow Style button on the Drawing toolbar.**

Excel displays the Shadow Style palette of drop shadows with varying shadow depths (Figure 3-47).

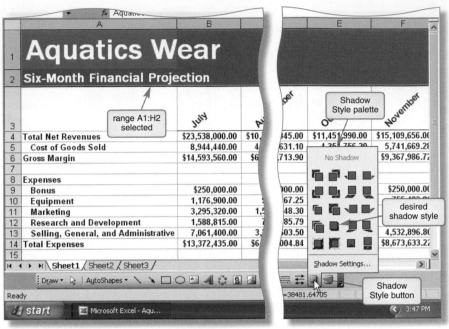

FIGURE 3-47

2

• **Click Shadow Style 14 (column 2, row 4) on the Shadow Style palette.**

• **Click cell A4 to deselect the range A1:H2.**

Excel adds a drop shadow to the range A1:H2 (Figure 3-48).

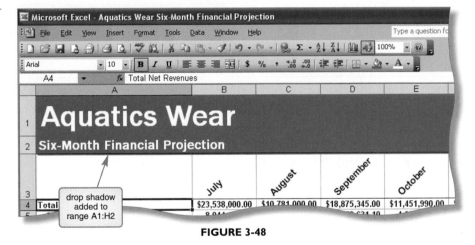

FIGURE 3-48

Other Ways

1. In Voice Command mode, say "Shadow, Shadow Style 14"

When you add a drop shadow to a range of cells, Excel selects the drop shadow and surrounds it with handles. To deselect the drop shadow, click any cell, as described in Step 2 above.

Formatting Nonadjacent Cells

The following steps change the font type and font size of the nonadjacent cells A4, A6, A8, A14, and A16 to 12-point Franklin Gothic Medium. The steps then add the light yellow background color and drop shadows to the nonadjacent cells A4, A6, A8, A14, and the range A16:H16.

To Change Font, Add Underlines, Add Background Colors, and Add Drop Shadows to Nonadjacent Cells

1

• With cell A4 selected, hold down the CTRL key, click cells A6, A8, A14, and A16.

• Click the Font box arrow on the Formatting toolbar, scroll down and click Franklin Gothic Medium (or a similar font) in the Font list.

• Click the Font Size box arrow on the Formatting toolbar and then click 12 in the Font Size list.

• Use the CTRL key to select the nonadjacent ranges B5:H5 and B13:H13 and then click the Borders button on the Formatting toolbar.

• Click cell A4 and then while holding down the CTRL key, click cells A6, A8, A14, and select the range A16:H16.

• Click the Fill Color button arrow on the Formatting toolbar and then click Light Yellow (column 3, row 5).

• Click the Shadow Style button on the Drawing toolbar

Excel displays the worksheet with the new formats (Figure 3-49). The Shadow Style palette appears at the bottom of the window.

2

• Click Shadow Style 14 (column 2, row 4) on the Shadow palette.

Excel adds a drop shadow to cells A4, A6, A8, A14, and the range A16:H16 (Figure 3-50).

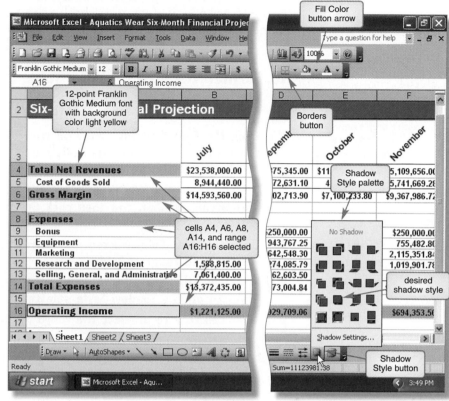

FIGURE 3-49

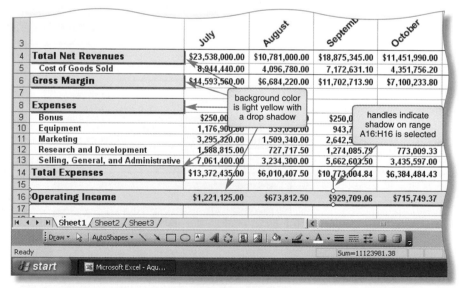

FIGURE 3-50

An alternative to formatting the nonadjacent ranges at once is to select each range separately and then apply the formats.

Formatting the Assumptions Table

The last step to improving the appearance of the worksheet is to format the Assumptions table in the range A18:B25. The specifications in Figure 3-37 on page EX 177 require a 16-point italic underlined font for the title in cell A18. The range A18:B25 has a white font, green background color, and a drop shadow that surrounds it. The following steps format the Assumptions table.

To Format the Assumptions Table

1 Scroll down to view rows 18 through 25 and then click cell A18.

2 Click the Font Size box arrow on the Formatting toolbar and then click 16 in the Font Size list. Click the Italic button and then click the Underline button on the Formatting toolbar.

3 Select the range A18:B25, click the Fill Color button arrow on the Formatting toolbar, and then click Green (column 4, row 2) on the Fill Color palette.

4 Click the Font Color button on the Formatting toolbar to change the font in the selected range to white.

5 Click the Shadow Style button on the Drawing toolbar and then click Shadow Style 14 on the Shadow Style palette.

6 Click cell D25 to deselect the range A18:B25.

Excel displays the Assumptions table as shown in Figure 3-51.

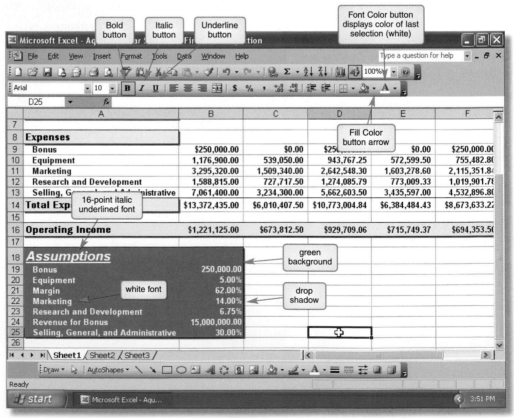

FIGURE 3-51

The previous steps introduced you to two new formats: italic and underline. When you assign the **italic** font style to a cell, Excel slants the characters slightly to the right as shown in cell A18 in Figure 3-51. The **underline** format underlines only the characters in the cell, rather than the entire cell, as is the case when you assign a cell a bottom border.

Hiding the Drawing Toolbar and Saving the Workbook

The formatting of the worksheet is complete. The following steps hide the Drawing toolbar and save the workbook.

To Hide the Drawing Toolbar and Save the Workbook

1 Click the Drawing button on the Standard toolbar.

2 Click the Save button on the Standard toolbar.

Excel hides the Drawing toolbar (Figure 3-52) and saves the workbook using the file name Aquatics Wear Six-Month Financial Projection.

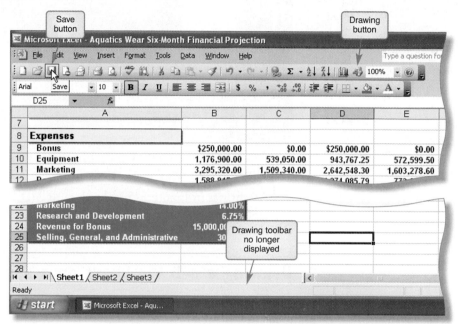

FIGURE 3-52

Adding a 3-D Pie Chart to the Workbook

The next step in the project is to draw the 3-D Pie chart on a separate sheet in the workbook, as shown in Figure 3-53 on the next page. A **Pie chart** is used to show the relationship or proportion of parts to a whole. Each slice (or wedge) of the pie shows what percent that slice contributes to the total (100%). The 3-D Pie chart in Figure 3-53 shows the contribution of each month's projected operating income to the six-month projected operating income. The 3-D Pie chart makes it easy to evaluate the contribution of one month to the six-month projected operating income in comparison to the other months.

Unlike the 3-D Column chart created in Project 1, the 3-D Pie chart shown in Figure 3-53 is not embedded in the worksheet. Instead, the Pie chart resides on a separate sheet, called a **chart sheet**, which contains only the chart.

In this worksheet, the ranges to chart are the nonadjacent ranges B3:G3 (month names) and B16:G16 (monthly operating incomes). The month names in the range B3:G3 will identify the slices of the Pie chart; these entries are called **category names**. The range B16:G16 contains the data that determines the size of the slices in the pie; these entries are called the **data series**. Because six months are being charted, the 3-D Pie chart contains six slices.

The sketch of the 3-D Pie chart in Figure 3-3b on page EX 149 also calls for emphasizing the month with the greatest contribution to the six-month projected operating income (in this case, December) by offsetting its slice from the main portion. A Pie chart with one or more slices offset is called an **exploded Pie chart**.

> ## More About
>
> ### Charts
>
> You are aware that, when you change a value on which a chart is dependent, Excel immediately redraws the chart based on the new value. Did you know that, with bar charts, you can drag the bar in the chart in one direction or another to change the corresponding value in the worksheet, as well?

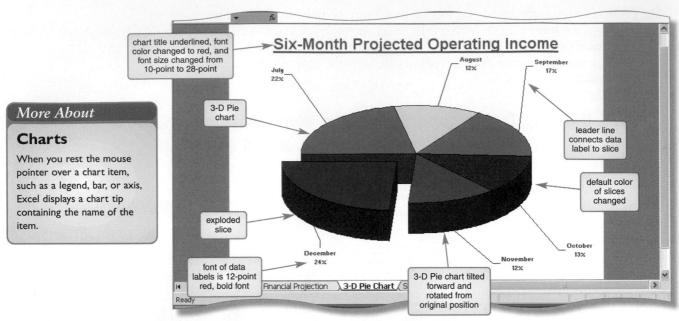

chart title underlined, font color changed to red, and font size changed from 10-point to 28-point

3-D Pie chart

leader line connects data label to slice

default color of slices changed

More About

Charts

When you rest the mouse pointer over a chart item, such as a legend, bar, or axis, Excel displays a chart tip containing the name of the item.

exploded slice

font of data labels is 12-point red, bold font

3-D Pie chart tilted forward and rotated from original position

FIGURE 3-53

As shown in Figure 3-53, the default 3-D Pie chart also has been enhanced by rotating and tilting the pie forward, changing the colors of the slices, and modifying the chart title and labels that identify the slices.

Drawing a 3-D Pie Chart on a Separate Chart Sheet

The following steps show how to draw the 3-D Pie chart on a separate chart sheet using the Chart Wizard button on the Standard toolbar.

To Draw a 3-D Pie Chart on a Separate Chart Sheet

1

• **Select the range B3:G3.**

• **While holding down the CTRL key, select the range B16:G16.**

• **Click the Chart Wizard button on the Standard toolbar.**

• **When Excel displays the Chart Wizard - Step 1 of 4 - Chart Type dialog box, click Pie in the Chart type list and then click the 3-D Pie chart (column 2, row 1) in the Chart sub-type box.**

Excel displays the Chart Wizard - Step 1 of 4 - Chart Type dialog box, which allows you to select one of the 14 types of charts available in Excel (Figure 3-54).

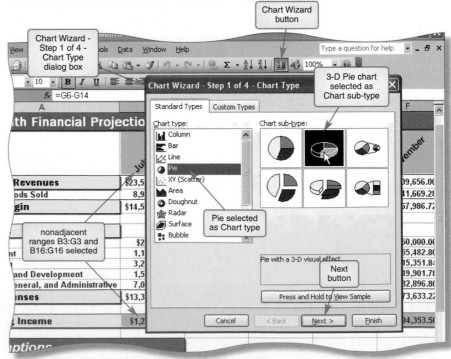

FIGURE 3-54

2

- **Click the Next button.**

Excel displays the Chart Wizard - Step 2 of 4 - Chart Source Data dialog box showing a sample of the 3-D Pie chart and the chart data range. A marquee surrounds the selected nonadjacent ranges on the worksheet (Figure 3-55).

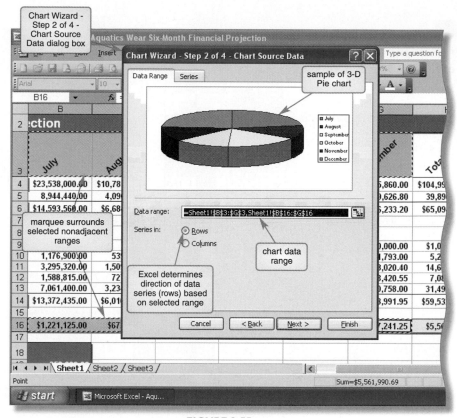

FIGURE 3-55

3

- **Click the Next button.**
- **When Excel displays the Chart Wizard - Step 3 of 4 - Chart Options dialog box, type** Six-Month Projected Operating Income **in the Chart title text box.**

Excel redraws the sample 3-D Pie chart with the chart title, Six-Month Projected Operating Income (Figure 3-56). Excel automatically bolds the chart title.

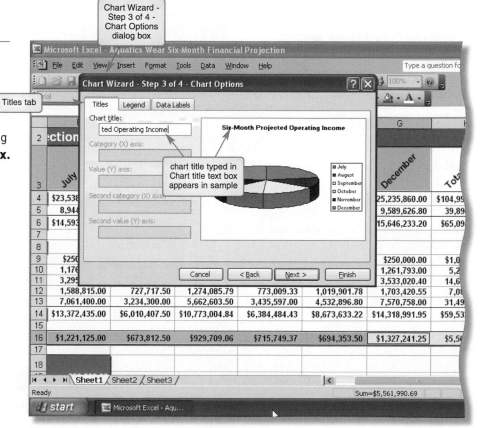

FIGURE 3-56

4

• **Click the Legend tab and then click Show legend to remove the check mark.**

Excel displays the Legend tab. Excel redraws the sample 3-D Pie chart without the legend (Figure 3-57).

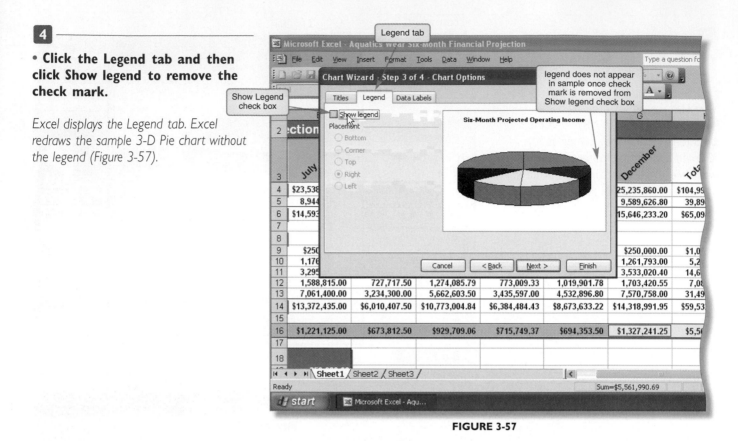

FIGURE 3-57

5

• **Click the Data Labels tab.**

• **In the Label Contains area, click Category name and click Percentage to select them.**

• **If necessary, click Show leader lines to select it.**

Excel displays the Data Labels sheet. Excel redraws the sample 3-D Pie chart with data labels and percentages (Figure 3-58). Because some of the data labels are close to the slices, the leader lines do not appear.

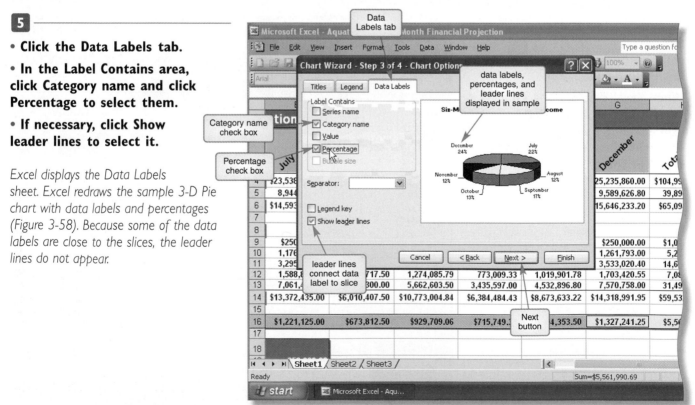

FIGURE 3-58

6

• **Click the Next button.**

• **When Excel displays the Chart Wizard - Step 4 of 4 - Chart Location dialog box, click As new sheet.**

Excel displays the Chart Wizard - Step 4 of 4 - Chart Location dialog box (Figure 3-59). It offers two chart location options: to draw the chart on a new sheet in the workbook or to draw it as an object in an existing worksheet.

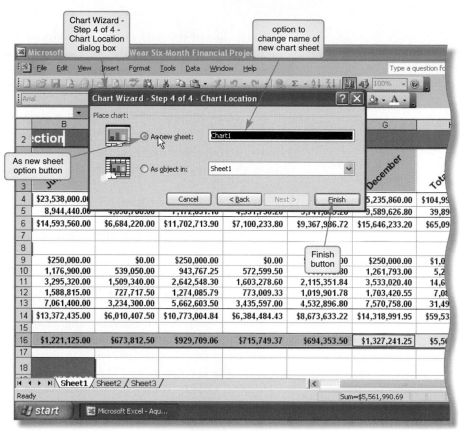

FIGURE 3-59

7

• **Click the Finish button.**

• **If the Chart toolbar appears, click its Close button.**

Excel draws the 3-D Pie chart on a separate chart sheet (Chart1) in the Aquatics Wear Six-Month Financial Projection workbook (Figure 3-60).

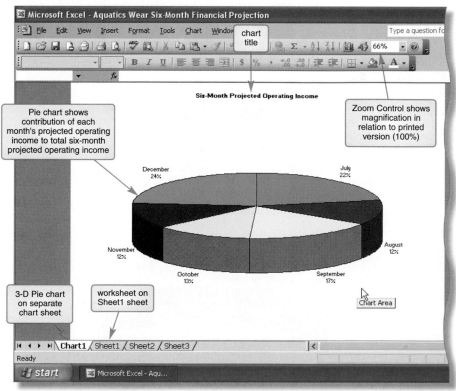

FIGURE 3-60

Each slice of the 3-D Pie chart in Figure 3-60 on the previous page represents one of the six months — July, August, September, October, November, and December. Excel displays the names of the months and the percent contribution to the total value outside the slices. The chart title, Six-Month Projected Operating Income, appears immediately above the 3-D Pie chart.

Excel determines the direction of the data series range (down a column or across a row) on the basis of the selected range. Because the range selected for the 3-D Pie chart is across the worksheet (ranges B3:G3 and B16:G16), Excel automatically selects the Rows option button in the Data Range sheet as shown in Figure 3-55 on page EX 189.

In any of the four Chart Wizard dialog boxes (Figure 3-54 through Figure 3-59), a Back button is available to return to the previous Chart Wizard dialog box. Clicking the Finish button in any of the dialog boxes creates the 3-D Pie chart with the options selected up to that point.

Formatting the Chart Title and Data Labels

The next step is to format the chart title and labels that identify the slices. Before you can format a chart item, such as the chart title or data labels, you must select it. Once a chart item is selected, you can format it using the Formatting toolbar, shortcut menu, or the Format menu. The following steps use the Formatting toolbar to format chart items similar to the way cell entries were formatted earlier in this project.

To Format the Chart Title and Data Labels

1 Click the chart title. On the Formatting toolbar, click the Font Size box arrow, click 28 in the Font Size list, click the Underline button, click the Font Color button arrow, and then click Red (column 1, row 3) on the Font Color palette.

2 Click one of the five data labels that identify the slices. On the Formatting toolbar, click the Font Size box arrow, click 12 in the Font Size list, click the Bold button, and then click the Font Color button to change the font to the color red.

Excel increases the font size of the chart title, underlines the chart title, and displays the chart title and data labels in red as shown in Figure 3-61. The data labels are selected.

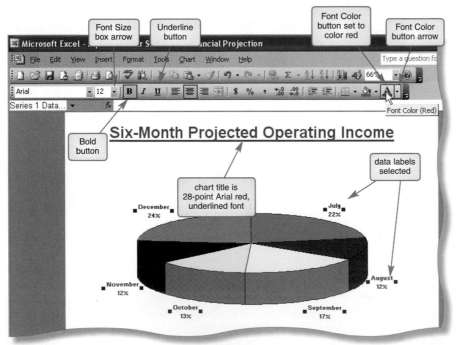

FIGURE 3-61

If you compare Figure 3-61 with Figure 3-60, you can see that the labels and chart title are easier to read and make the chart sheet look more professional.

Changing the Colors of Slices in a Pie Chart

The next step is to change the colors of the slices of the pie. The colors shown in Figure 3-61 are the default colors Excel uses when you first create a 3-D Pie chart. Project 3 requires that the colors be changed to those shown in Figure 3-53 on page EX 188. The following steps show how to change the colors of the slice by selecting them one at a time and using the Fill Color button arrow on the Formatting toolbar.

Other Ways

1. Click slice twice, on Format menu click Selected Data Point, click Patterns tab, click color, click OK button
2. Click slice twice, right-click selected slice, click Format Data Point on shortcut menu, click Patterns tab, click color, click OK button

To Change the Colors of Slices in a Pie Chart

1

• **Click the July slice twice (do not double-click). Click the Fill Color button arrow on the Formatting toolbar.**

Excel displays sizing handles around the July slice. Excel also displays the Fill Color palette (Figure 3-62).

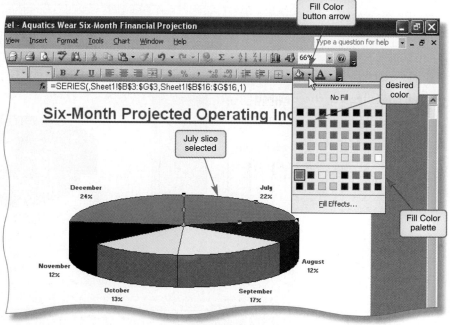

FIGURE 3-62

2

• **Click Orange (column 2, row 2). One at a time, click the remaining slices and then use the Fill Color button arrow on the Formatting toolbar to change each slice to the following colors: August – Yellow (column 3, row 4); September – Green (column 4, row 2); October – Plum (column 7, row 4); November – Red (column 1, row 3); and December – Blue (column 6, row 2). Click outside the chart area.**

Excel displays the 3-D Pie chart as shown in Figure 3-63.

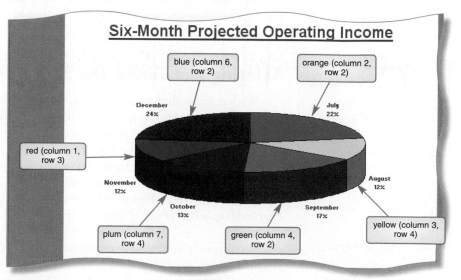

FIGURE 3-63

Exploding the 3-D Pie Chart

The next step is to emphasize the slice representing December, the month with the greatest contribution to the operating income, by **offsetting**, or exploding, it from the rest of the slices so that it stands out. The following steps show how to explode a slice of the 3-D Pie chart.

To Explode the 3-D Pie Chart

1

• **Click the slice labeled December twice (do not double-click).**

Excel displays sizing handles around the December slice.

2

• **Drag the slice to the desired position.**

Excel redraws the 3-D Pie chart with the December slice offset from the rest of the slices (Figure 3-64).

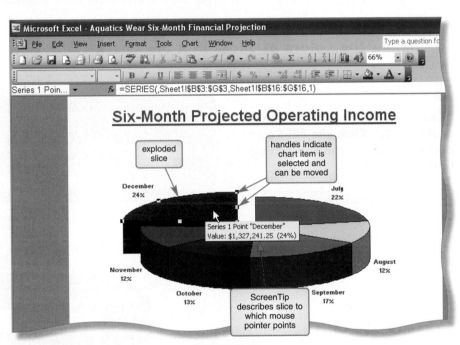

FIGURE 3-64

You can offset as many slices as you want, but remember that the reason for offsetting a slice is to emphasize it. Offsetting multiple slices tends to reduce the impact on the reader and reduces the overall size of the Pie chart.

Rotating and Tilting the 3-D Pie Chart

With a three-dimensional chart, you can change the view to better show the section of the chart you are trying to emphasize. Excel allows you to control the rotation angle, elevation, perspective, height, and angle of the axes by using the 3-D View command on the Chart menu.

When Excel initially draws a Pie chart, it always positions the chart so that one of the dividing lines between two slices is a straight line pointing to 12 o'clock (or 0°). As shown in Figure 3-64, the line that divides the July and December slices currently is set to 0°. It is this line that defines the rotation angle of the 3-D Pie chart.

To obtain a better view of the offset December slice, the 3-D Pie chart can be rotated 90° to the left. The following steps show how to rotate the 3-D Pie chart and change, or tilt, the elevation so the 3-D Pie chart is at less of an angle to the viewer.

To Rotate and Tilt the 3-D Pie Chart

1

• **With the December slice selected, click Chart on the menu bar.**

Excel displays the Chart menu (Figure 3-65).

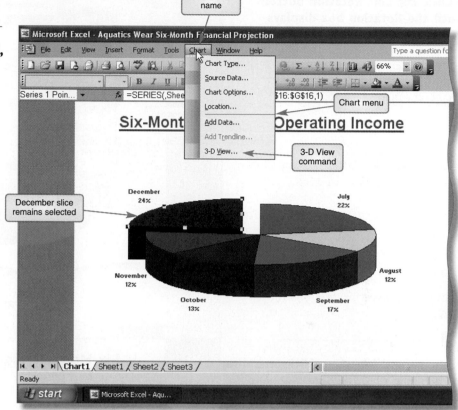

FIGURE 3-65

2

• **Click 3-D View.**

• **When Excel displays the 3-D View dialog box, click the Up Arrow button until 25 shows in the Elevation box.**

Excel displays the 3-D View dialog box, which includes a sample of the 3-D Pie chart (Figure 3-66). Increasing the elevation of the 3-D Pie chart causes it to tilt forward.

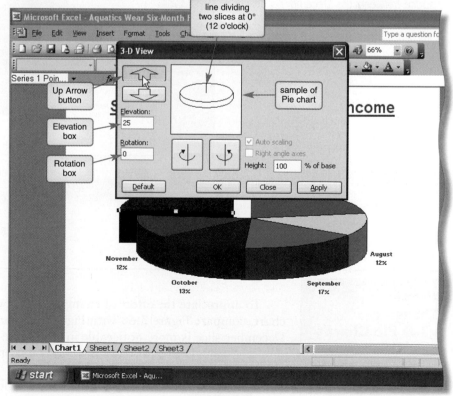

FIGURE 3-66

3

• **Click the Left Rotation button until the Rotation box displays 270.**

The new rotation setting (270) shows in the Rotation box (Figure 3-67). A sample of the rotated Pie chart appears in the dialog box.

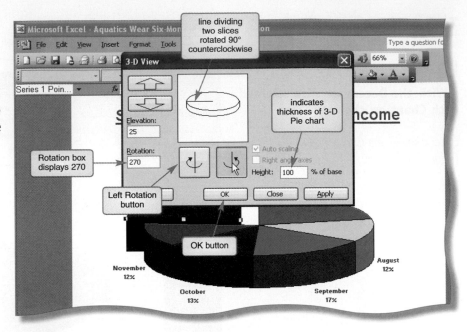

FIGURE 3-67

4

• **Click the OK button. Click outside the chart area.**

Excel displays the 3-D Pie chart tilted forward and rotated to the left, which makes the space between the December slice and the main portion of the pie more prominent (Figure 3-68).

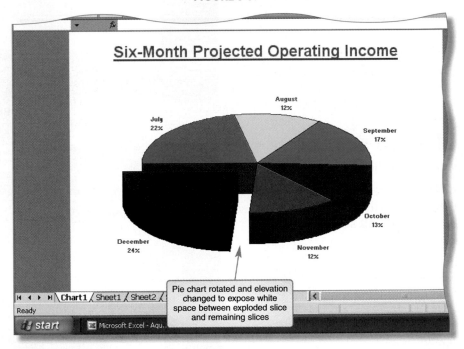

FIGURE 3-68

To appreciate the effect of changing the elevation and rotation of the 3-D Pie chart, compare Figure 3-68 with Figure 3-65 on the previous page. The offset of the December slice is more noticeable in Figure 3-68, because the Pie chart has been tilted and rotated to expose the white space between the December slice and the rest of the Pie chart.

In addition to controlling the rotation angle and elevation, you also can control the thickness of the 3-D Pie chart by entering a percent smaller or larger than the default 100% in the Height box (Figure 3-67).

Showing Leader Lines with the Data Labels

In Step 5 on page EX 190 in the Data Labels sheet of the Chart Wizard - Step 3 of 4 - Chart Options dialog box, the Show leader lines option was selected to instruct Excel to display leader lines. As the data labels are dragged away from each slice, Excel draws thin leader lines that connect each data label to its corresponding slice. The following steps show how to add leader lines to the data labels.

To Show Leader Lines with the Data Labels

1

• **Click the December data label twice (do not double-click).**

Excel displays a box with handles around the December data label.

2

• **Point to the upper-left sizing handle on the box border and drag the December data label away from the December slice.**

• **Select and drag the remaining data labels away from their corresponding slices as shown in Figure 3-69.**

• **Click outside the chart area.**

Excel displays the data labels with leader lines as shown in Figure 3-69.

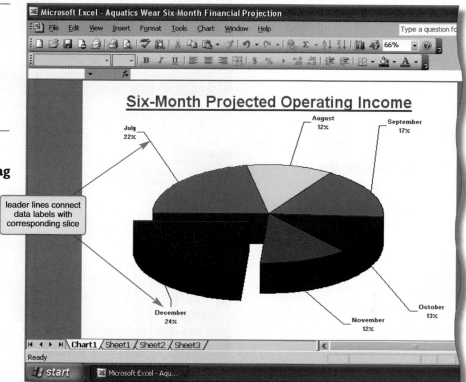

FIGURE 3-69

You also can select and format individual labels by clicking a specific data label after all the data labels have been selected. Making an individual data label larger or a different color, for example, helps emphasize a small or large slice in a Pie chart.

Renaming and Reordering the Sheets and Coloring Their Tabs

The final step in creating the workbook is to reorder the sheets and modify the tabs at the bottom of the screen. The steps on the next page show how to rename the sheets, color the tabs, and reorder the sheets so the worksheet precedes the chart sheet in the workbook.

To Rename and Reorder the Sheets and Color Their Tabs

1

- **Double-click the tab labeled Chart1 at the bottom of the screen.**
- **Type** 3-D Pie Chart **and then press the ENTER key.**
- **Right-click the tab.**

The label on the Chart1 tab changes to 3-D Pie Chart (Figure 3-70). Excel displays the tab's shortcut menu.

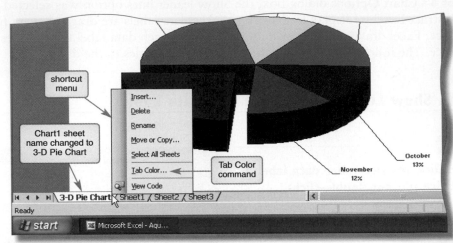

FIGURE 3-70

2

- **Click Tab Color on the shortcut menu.**
- **When Excel displays the Format Tab Color dialog box, click Red (column 1, row 3) in the Tab Color area.**

Excel displays the Format Tab Color dialog box as shown in Figure 3-71.

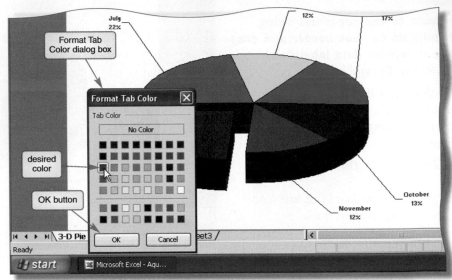

FIGURE 3-71

3

- **Click the OK button.**

Excel displays the name on the tab with a red underline (Figure 3-72). The red underline indicates the sheet is active. When the sheet is inactive, Excel displays the tab with a red background.

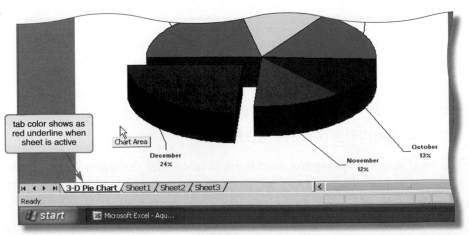

FIGURE 3-72

4

- **Double-click the tab labeled Sheet1 at the bottom of the screen.**

- **Type** Six-Month Financial Projection **as the new sheet name and then press the ENTER key.**

- **Right-click the tab and then click Tab Color on the shortcut menu.**

- **When Excel displays the Format Tab Color dialog box, click Light Yellow (column 3, row 5) in the Tab Color area, and then click the OK button.**

- **Drag the Six-Month Financial Projection tab to the left in front of the 3-D Pie Chart tab and then click cell E18.**

Excel rearranges the sequence of the sheets and displays the Six-Month Financial Projection worksheet (Figure 3-73). The yellow underline indicates the sheet is active.

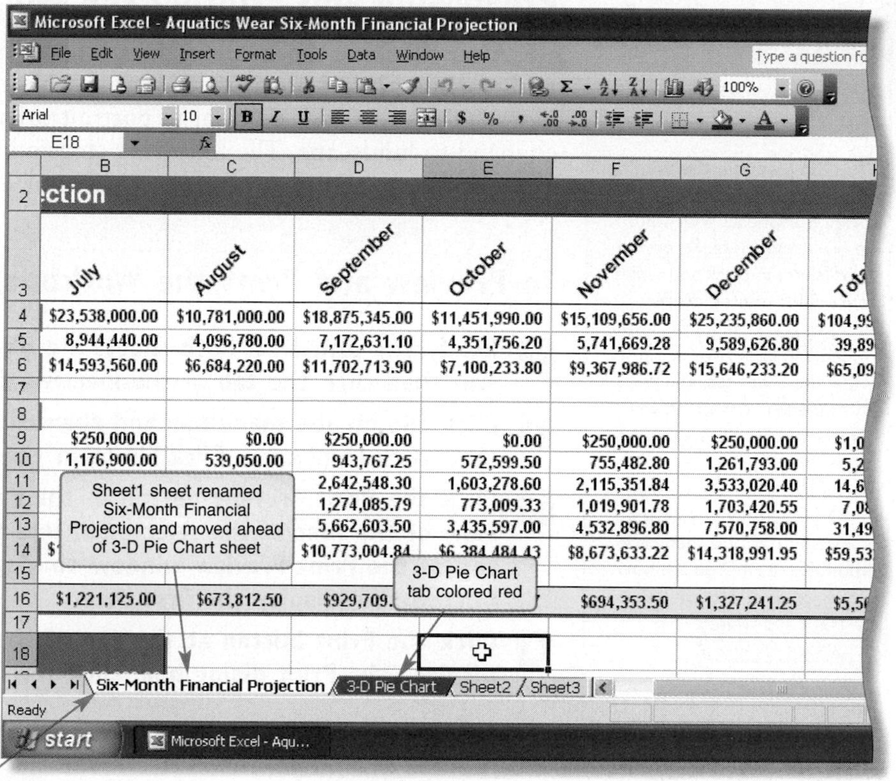

FIGURE 3-73

Checking Spelling, Saving, Previewing, and Printing the Workbook

With the workbook complete, this section checks spelling, saves, previews, and then prints the workbook. Each set of steps concludes with saving the workbook to ensure that the latest changes are saved.

Checking Spelling in Multiple Sheets

By default, the spell checker checks the spelling only in the selected sheets. It will check all the cells in the selected sheets, unless you select a range of two or more cells. Before checking the spelling, the following steps select the 3-D Pie Chart sheet so that the entire workbook is checked for spelling errors.

To Check Spelling in Multiple Sheets

1 **With the Six-Month Financial Projection sheet active, hold down the CTRL key and then click the 3-D Pie Chart tab.**

2 **Click the Spelling button on the Standard toolbar.**

3 **Correct any errors and then click the OK button when the spell check is complete.**

4 **Click the Save button on the Standard toolbar.**

Other Ways

1. To rename sheet, right-click sheet tab, click Rename on shortcut menu
2. To move sheet, on Edit menu click Move or Copy
3. To move sheet, right-click sheet tab, click Move or Copy on shortcut menu
4. To move sheet, in Voice Command mode, say "Edit, Move" or "Edit, Copy"

More About

Checking Spelling

Unless you first select a range of cells or an object before starting the spell checker, Excel checks the selected worksheet, including all cell values, cell comments, embedded charts, text boxes, buttons, and headers and footers.

Microsoft Office
Excel 2003

Previewing and Printing the Workbook

After checking the spelling, the next step is to preview and print the sheets. As with spelling, Excel previews and prints only the selected sheets. Also, because the worksheet is too wide to print in portrait orientation, the orientation must be changed to landscape. The following steps adjust the orientation and scale, preview the workbook, and then print the workbook.

To Preview and Print the Workbook

1 Ready the printer. If both sheets are not selected, hold down the CTRL key and then click the tab of the inactive sheet.

2 Click File on the menu bar and then click Page Setup. Click the Page tab and then click Landscape. Click Fit to in the Scaling area.

3 Click the Print Preview button in the Page Setup dialog box. When the preview of the first of the selected sheets appears, click the Next button at the top of the Print Preview window to view the next sheet. Click the Previous button to redisplay the first sheet.

4 Click the Print button at the top of the Print Preview window. When Excel displays the Print dialog box, click the OK button.

5 Right-click the Six-Month Financial Projection tab. Click Ungroup Sheets on the shortcut menu to deselect the 3-D Pie Chart tab.

6 Click the Save button on the Standard toolbar.

The worksheet and 3-D Pie chart print as shown in Figures 3-74a and 3-74b. Excel saves the print settings with the workbook.

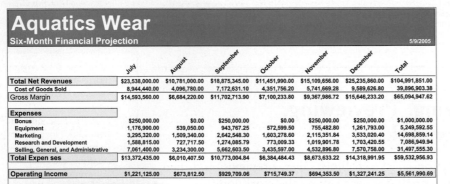

Aquatics Wear
Six-Month Financial Projection
5/9/2005

	July	August	September	October	November	December	Total
Total Net Revenues	$23,538,000.00	$10,781,000.00	$18,875,345.00	$11,451,990.00	$15,109,656.00	$25,235,860.00	$104,991,851.00
Cost of Goods Sold	8,944,440.00	4,096,780.00	7,172,631.10	4,351,756.20	5,741,669.28	9,589,626.80	39,896,903.38
Gross Margin	$14,593,560.00	$6,684,220.00	$11,702,713.90	$7,100,233.80	$9,367,986.72	$15,646,233.20	$65,094,947.62
Expenses							
Bonus	$250,000.00	$0.00	$250,000.00	$0.00	$250,000.00	$250,000.00	$1,000,000.00
Equipment	1,176,900.00	539,050.00	943,767.25	572,599.50	755,482.80	1,261,793.00	5,249,592.55
Marketing	3,295,320.00	1,509,340.00	2,642,548.30	1,603,278.60	2,115,351.84	3,533,020.40	14,698,859.14
Research and Development	1,588,815.00	727,717.50	1,274,085.79	773,009.33	1,019,901.78	1,703,420.55	7,086,949.94
Selling, General, and Administrative	7,061,400.00	3,234,300.00	5,662,603.50	3,435,597.00	4,532,896.80	7,570,758.00	31,497,555.30
Total Expenses	$13,372,435.00	$6,010,407.50	$10,773,004.84	$6,384,484.43	$8,673,633.22	$14,318,991.95	$59,532,956.93
Operating Income	$1,221,125.00	$673,812.50	$929,709.06	$715,749.37	$694,353.50	$1,327,241.25	$5,561,990.69

Assumptions	
Bonus	250,000.00
Equipment	5.00%
Margin	62.00%
Marketing	14.00%
Research and Development	6.75%
Revenue for Bonus	15,000,000.00
Selling, General, and Administrative	30.00%

(a) Worksheet

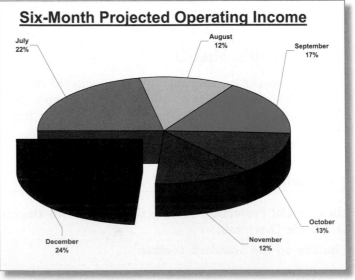

Six-Month Projected Operating Income

July 22%
August 12%
September 17%
October 13%
November 12%
December 24%

(b) 3-D Pie Chart

FIGURE 3-74

Changing the View of the Worksheet

With Excel, you easily can change the view of the worksheet. For example, you can magnify or shrink the worksheet on the screen. You also can view different parts of the worksheet through window panes.

Shrinking and Magnifying the View of a Worksheet or Chart

You can magnify (zoom in) or shrink (zoom out) the appearance of a worksheet or chart by using the Zoom box on the Standard toolbar. When you magnify a worksheet, Excel enlarges the view of the characters on the screen, but displays fewer columns and rows. Alternatively, when you shrink a worksheet, Excel is able to display more columns and rows. Magnifying or shrinking a worksheet affects only the view; it does not change the window size or printout of the worksheet or chart. The following steps shrink and magnify the view of the worksheet.

To Shrink and Magnify the View of a Worksheet or Chart

1

- **If cell A1 is not active, press** CTRL+HOME.
- **Click the Zoom box arrow on the Standard toolbar.**

Excel displays a list of percentages in the Zoom list (Figure 3-75).

FIGURE 3-75

2

- **Click 75%.**

Excel shrinks the display of the worksheet to 75% of its normal display (Figure 3-76). With the worksheet zoomed out to 75%, you can see more rows and columns than you did at 100% magnification. Some of the numbers, however, appear as a series of number signs (#), because the columns are not wide enough to show the formatted numbers.

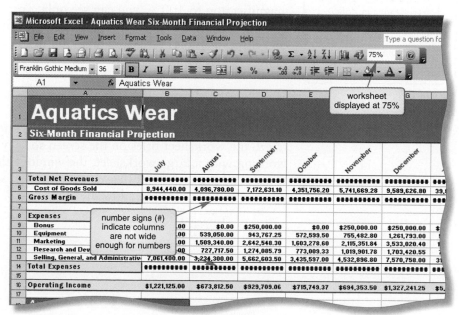

FIGURE 3-76

3

• **Click the Zoom box arrow on the Standard toolbar and then click 100%.**

Excel displays the worksheet at 100%.

4

• **Click the 3-D Pie Chart tab at the bottom of the screen. Click the Zoom box arrow on the Standard toolbar and then click 100%.**

Excel changes the magnification of the chart from 66% (shown in Figure 3-69 on page EX 197) to 100% (Figure 3-77). Excel displays the chart at the same size as the printout of the chart.

5

• **Enter 66 in the Zoom box to return the chart to its original magnification.**

Excel changes the magnification of the chart back to 66%.

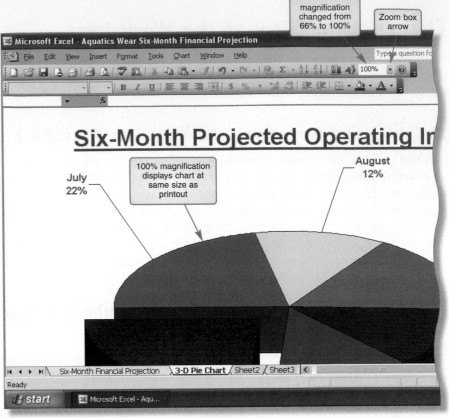

FIGURE 3-77

Other Ways

1. On View menu, click Zoom, click desired magnification, click OK button
2. Type desired percent magnification in Zoom box on Standard toolbar
3. In Voice Command mode, say "Zoom [desired percent magnification]"

At 800 × 600 resolution, Excel normally displays a chart in the range of 65% to 70% magnification, so that the entire chart appears on the screen. By changing the magnification to 100%, you can see only a part of the chart, but at a magnification that corresponds with the chart's size on a printout. Excel allows you to enter a percent magnification between 10 and 400 in the Zoom box for worksheets and chart sheets.

Splitting the Window into Panes

This project previously used the Freeze Panes command to instruct Excel to freeze the worksheet titles on the screen so they always show when you scroll. When working with a large worksheet, the window also can be split into two or four panes to view different parts of the worksheet at the same time. The following steps show how to split the Excel window into four panes.

To Split a Window into Panes

1

• **Click the Six-Month Financial Projection tab at the bottom of the screen.**

• **Select cell D7, the intersection of the four proposed panes.**

• **Click Window on the menu bar.**

Excel displays the Window menu (Figure 3-78). Cell D7 is the active cell.

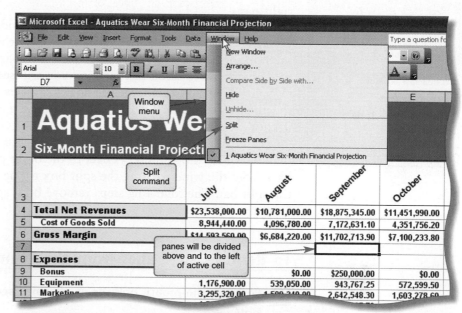

FIGURE 3-78

2

• **Click Split on the Window menu.**

• **Use the scroll arrows to show the four corners of the worksheet at the same time.**

Excel divides the window into four panes and displays the four corners of the worksheet (Figure 3-79).

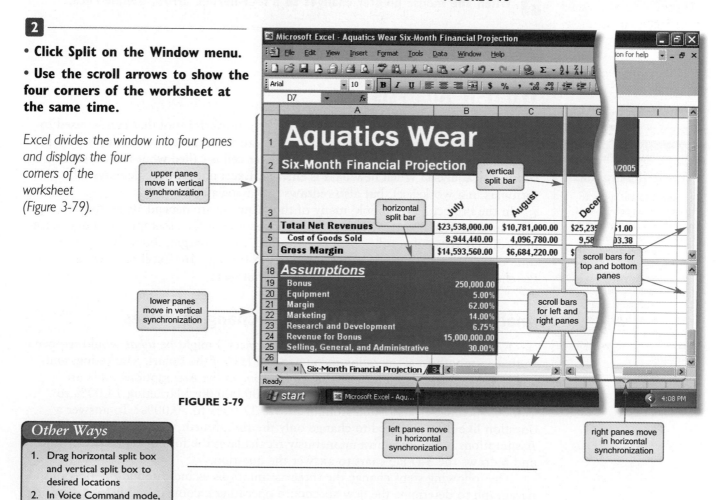

FIGURE 3-79

Other Ways

1. Drag horizontal split box and vertical split box to desired locations
2. In Voice Command mode, say "Window, Split"

More About

Window Panes

If you want to split the window into two panes, rather than four, drag the vertical split box to the far left of the window or horizontal split box to the top of the window (Figure 3-80). You also can drag the center of the four panes in any direction to change the size of the panes.

The four panes in Figure 3-79 on the previous page are used to show the following: (1) range A1:B6 in the upper-left pane; (2) range F1:I6 in the upper-right pane; (3) range A18:B26 in the lower-left pane; and (4) range F18:I26 in the lower-right pane.

The vertical bar going up and down the middle of the window is called the **vertical split bar**. The horizontal bar going across the middle of the window is called the **horizontal split bar**. If you use the scroll bars below the window and to the right of the window to scroll the window, you will see that the panes split by the horizontal split bar scroll together vertically. The panes split by the vertical split bar scroll together horizontally. To resize the panes, drag either split bar to the desired location in the window.

You can change the values of cells in any of the four panes. Any change you make in one pane also takes effect in the other panes. To remove one of the split bars from the window, drag the split box to the edge of the window or double-click the split bar. The following steps remove both split bars to remove the four panes from the window.

To Remove the Panes from the Window

1 Position the mouse pointer at the intersection of the horizontal and vertical split bars.

2 When the mouse pointer changes to a four-headed arrow, double-click.

Excel removes the four panes from the window.

What-If Analysis

The automatic recalculation feature of Excel is a powerful tool that can be used to analyze worksheet data. Using Excel to scrutinize the impact of changing values in cells that are referenced by a formula in another cell is called **what-if analysis** or **sensitivity analysis**. When new data is entered, Excel not only recalculates all formulas in a worksheet, but also redraws any associated charts.

In the Project 3 workbook, many of the formulas are dependent on the assumptions in the range B19:B25. Thus, if you change any of the assumption values, Excel immediately recalculates the cost of goods sold, gross margin, monthly expenses, total expenses, and operating income in rows 5 through 16. Excel redraws the 3-D Pie chart as well, because it is based on these numbers.

Analyze Data in a Worksheet by Changing Values

A what-if question for the worksheet in Project 3 might be *what* would happen to the six-month total operating income in cell H16 *if* the Bonus, Marketing, and Selling, General, and Administrative assumptions in the Assumptions table are changed as follows: Bonus $250,000.00 to $100,000.00; Marketing 14.00% to 10.00%; Selling, General, and Administrative 32.00% to 30.00%? To answer a question like this, you need to change only the first, fourth, and seventh values in the Assumptions table. Excel instantaneously recalculates the formulas in the worksheet and redraws the 3-D Pie chart to answer the question.

The following steps change the three assumptions as indicated in the previous paragraph to determine the new six-month operating income in cell H16. To ensure that the Assumptions table and the six-month operating income in cell H16 show on the screen at the same time, the steps also divide the window into two vertical panes.

More About

What-If Analysis

Instead of requiring you to change assumptions in a worksheet manually, Excel has additional methods for answering what-if questions, including Goal Seek, Solver, PivotTables, Scenario Manager, and the Analysis ToolPak. For more information, enter each of these what-if tools in the Type a question for help box on the menu bar.

To Analyze Data in a Worksheet by Changing Values

1

- Use the vertical scroll bar to move the window so cell A6 is in the upper-left corner of the screen.

- Drag the vertical split box from the lower-right corner of the screen to the left so that the vertical split bar is positioned as shown in Figure 3-80.

- Use the right scroll arrow to view the totals in column H in the right pane.

- Click cell B19 in the left pane.

Excel divides the window into two vertical panes and shows the totals in column H in the pane on the right side of the window (Figure 3-80).

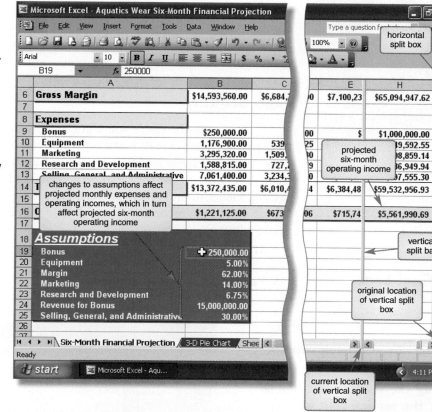

FIGURE 3-80

2

- Enter 100000 in cell B19, 10 in cell B22, and 32 in cell B25.

Excel immediately recalculates all the formulas in the worksheet (Figure 3-81).

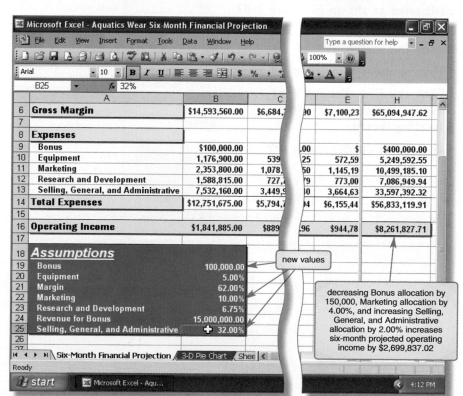

FIGURE 3-81

Each time you enter a new assumption, Excel recalculates the worksheet and redraws the 3-D Pie chart. This process usually takes less than one second, depending on how many calculations must be performed and the speed of your computer. Compare the six-month operating income in cell H16 in Figures 3-80 and 3-81 on the previous page. By changing the values of the three assumptions (Figure 3-81), the six-month operating income in cell H16 increases from $5,561,990.69 to $8,261,827.71. This translates into an increase of $2,699,837.71 for the six-month operating income.

Goal Seeking

If you know the result you want a formula to produce, you can use **goal seeking** to determine the value of a cell on which the formula depends. The following steps close and reopen the Aquatics Wear Six-Month Financial Projection workbook. They then show how to use the Goal Seek command on the Tools menu to determine the Selling, General, and Administrative percentage in cell B25 that will yield a six-month operating income of $7,000,000.00 in cell H16, rather than the original $5,561,990.69.

To Goal Seek

1

• **Close the workbook without saving changes and then reopen it.**

• **Drag the vertical split box so that the vertical split bar is positioned as shown in Figure 3-82.**

• **Scroll down so row 6 is at the top of the screen.**

• **Show column H in the right pane.**

• **Click cell H16, the cell that contains the six-month total operating income.**

• **Click Tools on the menu bar.**

Excel displays the Tools menu and the vertical split bar as shown in Figure 3-82.

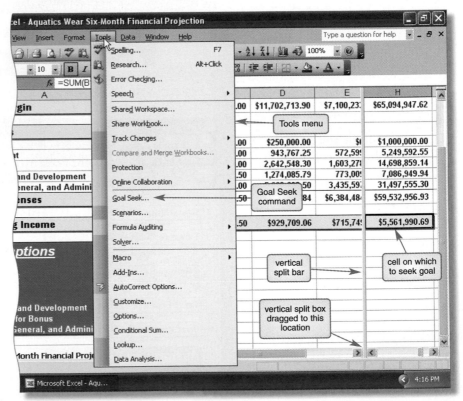

FIGURE 3-82

2

- **Click Goal Seek.**

- **When Excel displays the Goal Seek dialog box, click the To value text box, type** 7,000,000 **and then click the By changing cell box.**

- **Click cell B25 on the worksheet.**

Excel displays the Goal Seek dialog box as shown in Figure 3-83. Excel automatically assigns the Set cell box the cell reference of the active cell in the worksheet (cell H16). A marquee surrounds cell B25, which is set as the cell reference in the By changing cell box.

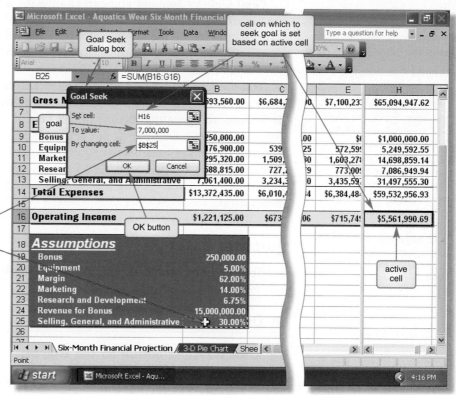

FIGURE 3-83

3

- **Click the OK button.**

Excel immediately changes cell H16 from $5,561,990.69 to the desired value of $7,000,000.00. More importantly, Excel changes the Selling, General, and Administrative assumption in cell B25 from 30.00% to 28.63% (Figure 3-84). Excel also displays the Goal Seek Status dialog box. If you click the OK button, Excel keeps the new values in the worksheet. If you click the Cancel button, Excel redisplays the original values.

4

- **Click the Cancel button in the Goal Seek Status dialog box.**

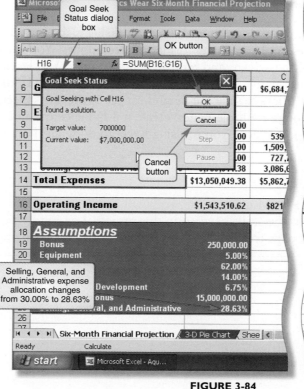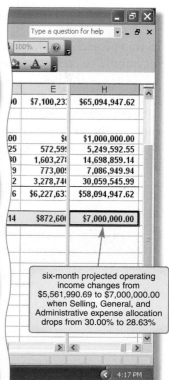

FIGURE 3-84

Other Ways

1. Press ALT+T, G
2. In Voice Command mode, say "Tools, Goal Seek", enter desired values, in Voice Command mode say, "OK"

More About

Goal Seeking

Goal seeking is a methodology in which you know the desired result of a formula in one cell, but you do not know what value to place in a cell used in the formula in order to reach that result, or goal. Goal seeking determines what value to use by changing the value in that cell, so that the formula returns the desired result in the first cell, as illustrated in Figures 3-83 and 3-84 on the previous page.

Goal seeking assumes you can change the value of only one cell referenced directly or indirectly to reach a specific goal for a value in another cell. In this example, to change the six-month operating income in cell H16 to $7,000,000.00, the Selling, General, and Administrative percentage in cell B25 must decrease by 1.37% from 30.00% to 28.63%.

You can see from this goal seeking example that the cell to change (cell B25) does not have to be referenced directly in the formula or function. For example, the six-month operating income in cell H16 is calculated by the function =SUM(B16:G16). Cell B25 is not referenced in this function. Instead, cell B25 is referenced in the formulas in rows 8 through 13, on which the monthly operating incomes in row 16 are based. Excel thus is capable of goal seeking on the six-month operating income by varying the value for the Selling, General, and Administrative assumption.

Quitting Excel

To quit Excel, complete the following steps.

To Quit Excel

1 Click the Close button on the title bar.

2 If the Microsoft Excel dialog box is displayed, click the No button.

Project Summary

In this project, you learned how to work with large worksheets that extend beyond the window, how to use the fill handle to create a series, and some new formatting techniques. You learned to show hidden toolbars, dock a toolbar at the bottom of the screen, and hide an active toolbar. You learned about the difference between absolute cell references and relative cell references and how to use the IF function. You also learned how to rotate text in a cell, freeze titles, change the magnification of the worksheet, show different parts of the worksheet at the same time through multiple panes, create a 3-D Pie chart, and improve the appearance of a 3-D Pie chart. Finally, this project introduced you to using Excel to do what-if analysis by changing values in cells and goal seeking.

If you have a SAM user profile, you may have access to hands-on instruction, practice, and assessment of the skills covered in this project. Log in to your SAM account and go to your assignments page to see what your instructor has assigned.

What You Should Know

Having completed this project, you should be able to perform the tasks below. The tasks are listed in the same order they were presented in this project. For a list of the buttons, menus, toolbars, and commands introduced in this project, see the Quick Reference Summary at the back of this book and refer to the Page Number column.

1. Start and Customize Excel   (EX 150)
2. Bold the Font of the Entire Worksheet   (EX 150)
3. Enter the Worksheet Titles and Save the Workbook   (EX 150)
4. Rotate Text and Use the Fill Handle to Create a Series of Month Names   (EX 151)
5. Copy a Cell's Format Using the Format Painter Button   (EX 154)
6. Increase Column Widths and Enter Row Titles   (EX 155)
7. Copy a Range of Cells to a Nonadjacent Destination Area   (EX 157)
8. Insert a Row   (EX 160)
9. Enter Numbers with Format Symbols   (EX 163)
10. Freeze Column and Row Titles   (EX 163)
11. Enter the Projected Monthly Total Net Revenue   (EX 164)
12. Enter and Format the System Date   (EX 166)
13. Enter a Formula Containing Absolute Cell References   (EX 169)
14. Enter an IF Function   (EX 172)
15. Enter the Remaining July Formulas   (EX 173)
16. Copy Formulas with Absolute Cell References Using the Fill Handle   (EX 174)
17. Determine Row Totals in Nonadjacent Cells   (EX 175)
18. Unfreeze the Worksheet Titles and Save the Workbook   (EX 176)
19. Assign Formats to Nonadjacent Ranges (EX 178)
20. Format the Worksheet Titles   (EX 180)
21. Show the Drawing Toolbar   (EX 182)
22. Move and Dock a Toolbar   (EX 183)
23. Add a Drop Shadow   (EX 184)
24. Change Font, Add Underlines, Add Background Colors, and Add Drop Shadows to Nonadjacent Cells   (EX 185)
25. Format the Assumptions Table   (EX 186)
26. Hide the Drawing Toolbar and Save the Workbook   (EX 187)
27. Draw a 3-D Pie Chart on a Separate Chart Sheet   (EX 188)
28. Format the Chart Title and Data Labels (EX 192)
29. Change the Colors of the Slices in a Pie Chart   (EX 193)
30. Explode the 3-D Pie Chart   (EX 194)
31. Rotate and Tilt the 3-D Pie Chart   (EX 195)
32. Show Leader Lines with the Data Labels (EX 197)
33. Rename and Reorder the Sheets and Color Their Tabs   (EX 198)
34. Check Spelling in Multiple Sheets   (EX 199)
35. Preview and Print the Workbook   (EX 200)
36. Shrink and Magnify the View of a Worksheet or Chart   (EX 201)
37. Split a Window into Panes   (EX 203)
38. Remove the Panes from the Window   (EX 204)
39. Analyze Data in a Worksheet by Changing Values   (EX 205)
40. Goal Seek   (EX 206)
41. Quit Excel   (EX 208)

More About

The Quick Reference

For a table that lists how to complete the tasks covered in this book using the mouse, menu, shortcut menu, and keyboard, see the Quick Reference Summary at the back of this book or visit the Excel 2003 Quick Reference Web page (scsite.com/ex2003/qr).

More About

Microsoft Certification

The Microsoft Office Specialist Certification program provides an opportunity for you to obtain a valuable industry credential — proof that you have the Excel 2003 skills required by employers. For more information, see Appendix E or visit the Excel 2003 Certification Web page (scsite.com/ex2003/cert).

Learn It Online

Instructions: To complete the Learn It Online exercises, start your browser, click the Address bar, and then enter the Web address scsite.com/ex2003/learn. When the Excel 2003 Learn It Online page is displayed, follow the instructions in the exercises below. Each exercise has instructions for printing your results, either for your own records or for submission to your instructor.

1 Project Reinforcement TF, MC, and SA

Below Excel Project 3, click the Project Reinforcement link. Print the quiz by clicking Print on the File menu for each page. Answer each question.

2 Flash Cards

Below Excel Project 3, click the Flash Cards link and read the instructions. Type 20 (or a number specified by your instructor) in the Number of playing cards text box, type your name in the Enter your Name text box, and then click the Flip Card button. When the flash card is displayed, read the question and then click the ANSWER box arrow to select an answer. Flip through Flash Cards. If your score is 15 (75%) correct or greater, click Print on the File menu to print your results. If your score is less than 15 (75%) correct, then redo this exercise by clicking the Replay button.

3 Practice Test

Below Excel Project 3, click the Practice Test link. Answer each question, enter your first and last name at the bottom of the page, and then click the Grade Test button. When the graded practice test is displayed on your screen, click Print on the File menu to print a hard copy. Continue to take practice tests until you score 80% or better.

4 Who Wants To Be a Computer Genius?

Below Excel Project 3, click the Computer Genius link. Read the instructions, enter your first and last name at the bottom of the page, and then click the PLAY button. When your score is displayed, click the PRINT RESULTS link to print a hard copy.

5 Wheel of Terms

Below Excel Project 3, click the Wheel of Terms link. Read the instructions, and then enter your first and last name and your school name. Click the PLAY button. When your score is displayed, right-click the score and then click Print on the shortcut menu to print a hard copy.

6 Crossword Puzzle Challenge

Below Excel Project 3, click the Crossword Puzzle Challenge link. Read the instructions, and then enter your first and last name. Click the SUBMIT button. Work the crossword puzzle. When you are finished, click the Submit button. When the crossword puzzle is redisplayed, click the Print Puzzle button to print a hard copy.

7 Tips and Tricks

Below Excel Project 3, click the Tips and Tricks link. Click a topic that pertains to Project 3. Right-click the information and then click Print on the shortcut menu. Construct a brief example of what the information relates to in Excel to confirm you understand how to use the tip or trick.

8 Newsgroups

Below Excel Project 3, click the Newsgroups link. Click a topic that pertains to Project 3. Print three comments.

9 Expanding Your Horizons

Below Excel Project 3, click the Expanding Your Horizons link. Click a topic that pertains to Project 3. Print the information. Construct a brief example of what the information relates to in Excel to confirm you understand the contents of the article.

10 Search Sleuth

Below Excel Project 3, click the Search Sleuth link. To search for a term that pertains to this project, select a term below the Project 3 title and then use the Google search engine at google.com (or any major search engine) to display and print two Web pages that present information on the term.

11 Excel Online Training

Below Excel Project 3, click the Excel Online Training link. When your browser displays the Microsoft Office Online Web page, click the Excel link. Click one of the Excel courses that covers one or more of the objectives listed at the beginning of the project on page EX 146. Print the first page of the course before stepping through it.

12 Office Marketplace

Below Excel Project 3, click the Office Marketplace link. When your browser displays the Microsoft Office Online Web page, click the Office Marketplace link. Click a topic that relates to Excel. Print the first page.

Apply Your Knowledge

1 Understanding the IF Function and Absolute Cell Referencing

Instructions: Fill in the correct answers.

1. Determine the truth value (true or false) of the following logical tests, given the following cell values: A2 = 20; B6 = 17; L8 = 100; S2 = 25; and W9 = 42. Enter true or false.

   a. B6 < A2   Truth value: _____

   b. 5 * A2 = L8 - 10   Truth value: _____

   c. W9 + 12 * S2 / 5 <> 2 * L8   Truth value: _____

   d. L8 / S2 > A2 – B6   Truth value: _____

   e. B6 * 2 – 42 < (S2 – W9 +8) / 4   Truth value: _____

   f. A2 + 300 <= B6 * S2 + 10   Truth value: _____

   g. W9 + L8 + 100 > 8 * (S2 + 10)   Truth value: _____

   h. A2 + B6 – 27 <> 2 * (S2 / 5)   Truth value: _____

2. Write an IF function for cell H3 that assigns the value of cell A7 to cell H3 if the value in cell J7 is less than the value in cell Q2; otherwise, have the IF function assign zero (0) to cell H3.

   Function: _____

3. Write an IF function for cell P8 that assigns the text "OK" if the value in cell S3 is five times greater than the value in cell F4; otherwise, have the IF function assign the text "Not OK" to cell P8.

   Function: _____

4. A nested IF function is an IF function that contains another IF function in the value_if_true or value_if_false arguments. For example, =IF(A1 = "IN","Region 1", IF(A1 = "OH", "Region 2", "Not Applicable")) is a valid nested IF function. Start Excel and enter this IF function in cell B1 and then use the fill handle to copy the function down through cell B7. Enter the following data in the cells in the range A1:A7 and then write down the results in cells B1 through B7 for each set. Set 1: A1 = IL; A2 = IN; A3 = IN; A4 = OH; A5 = IN; A6 = OH; A7 = IN. Set 2: A1= WI; A2 = KY; A3 = IN; A4 = IL; A5 = IN; A6 = IN; A7 = OH.

   Set 1 Results: _____

   Set 2 Results: _____

5. Write cell G3 as a relative cell reference, absolute cell reference, mixed cell reference with the row varying, and mixed cell reference with the column varying.

   _____   _____   _____   _____

6. Write the formula for cell B8 that divides cell D5 by the sum of cells N10 through N13. Write the formula so that when it is copied to cells C8 and D8, cell D5 remains absolute.

   Formula: _____

7. Write the formula for cell Y6 that divides cell P7 by the sum of cells H4, I4, and J4. Write the formula so that when it is copied to cells Y7, Y8, and Y9, cell P7 remains absolute.

   Formula: _____

8. Write the formula for cell M4 that multiplies cell T7 by the sum of cells D4 through D10. Write the formula so that when it is copied to cells M5 and M6, Excel adjusts all the cell references according to the new locations.

   Formula: _____

1 Seven-Year Financial Projection

Problem: As the spreadsheet specialist at Shawshank Manufacturing, you have been asked to create a worksheet that will project the annual gross margin, expenses, operating income, income taxes, and net income for the next seven years based on the assumptions in Table 3-9. The desired worksheet is shown in Figure 3-85.

Instructions Part 1: Complete the following steps to create the worksheet shown in Figure 3-85.

Table 3-9 Shawshank Manufacturing Assumptions	
Units Sold in Year 2003	12,459,713
Unit Cost	$12.96
Annual Sales Growth	4.25%
Annual Price Decrease	3.75%
Margin	39.25%

1. Bold the entire worksheet. Enter the worksheet titles in cells A1 and A2. Enter the system date in cell H2 using the NOW function. Format the date to the 3/14/2001 style.
2. Enter the seven column titles 2004 through 2010 in the range B3:H3 by entering 2004 in cell B3, and then, while holding down the CTRL key, dragging cell B3's fill handle. Format cell B3 as follows: (a) change the number in cell B3 to text by assigning it the format Text in the Format Cells dialog box; (b) center and italicize cell B3; (c) rotate its contents 45°. Use the Format Painter button to copy the format assigned to cell B3 to the range C3:H3.
3. Enter the row titles in the range A4:A24. Add heavy bottom borders to the ranges A3:H3 and B5:H5.
4. Change the following column widths: A = 24.71; B through H = 11.00. Change the heights of rows 7, 13, 15, 16, and 17 to 24.00.
5. Enter the assumptions values in Table 3-9 in the range B20:B24. Use format symbols.
6. Assign the Comma style format with no decimal places to the range B4:H17.
7. Complete the following entries:
   a. 2004 Total Net Revenue (cell B4) = Units Sold in Year 2003 * (Unit Cost / (1 – Margin)) or =B20 * (B21 / (1 – B24))
   b. 2005 Total Net Revenue (cell C4) = 2004 Total Net Revenue * (1 + Annual Sales Growth) * (1 – Annual Price Decrease) or =B4 * (1 + $B$22) * (1 – $B$23)
   c. Copy cell C4 to the range D4:H4.
   d. 2004 Cost of Goods Sold (cell B5) = 2004 Total Net Revenue – (2004 Total Net Revenue * Margin) or =B4 * (1 – $B$24)
   e. Copy cell B5 to the range C5:H5.
   f. 2004 Gross Margin (cell B6) = 2004 Total Net Revenue – 2004 Cost of Goods Sold or =B4 – B5
   g. Copy cell B6 to the range C6:H6.
   h. 2004 Advertising (cell B8) = 500 + 13% * 2004 Total Net Revenue or =500 + 13% * B4
   i. Copy cell B8 to the range C8:H8.
   j. Maintenance (row 9): 2004 = 1,900,000; 2005 = 5,397,000; 2006 = 4,200,000; 2007 = 5,150,000; 2008 = 2,500,000; 2009 = 3,150,000; 2010 = 2,960,000
   k. 2004 Rent (cell B10) = 1,800,000
   l. 2005 Rent (cell C10) = 2004 Rent + 10% * 2004 Rent or =B10 * (1 + 10%)
   m. Copy cell C10 to the range D10:H10.
   n. 2004 Salaries (cell B11) = 22% * 2004 Total Net Revenue or =22% * B4

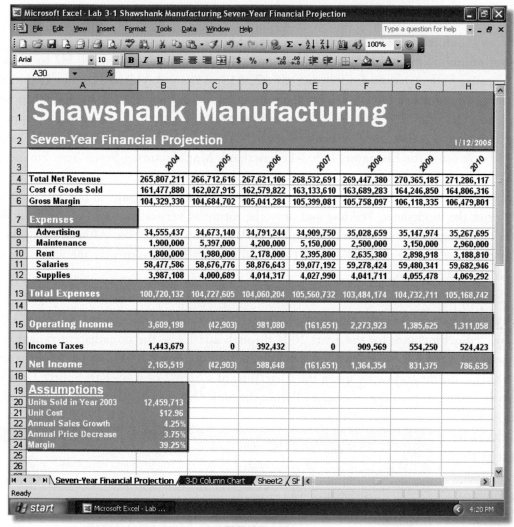

FIGURE 3-85

o. Copy cell B11 to the range C11:H11.

p. 2004 Supplies (cell B12) = 1.5% * 2004 Total Net Revenue or =1.5% * B4

q. Copy cell B12 to the range C12:H12.

r. 2004 Total Expenses (cell B13) = SUM(B8:B12)

s. Copy cell B13 to the range C13:H13.

t. 2004 Operating Income (cell B15) = 2004 Gross Margin – 2004 Total Expenses or =B6 – B13

u. Copy cell B15 to the range C15:H15.

v. 2004 Income Taxes (cell B16): If 2004 Operating Income is less than 0, then 2004 Income Taxes equal 0; otherwise 2004 Income Taxes equal 40% * 2004 Operating Income or =IF(B15 < 0, 0, 40% * B15)

w. Copy cell B16 to the range C16:H16.

x. 2004 Net Income (cell B17) = 2004 Operating Income – 2004 Income Taxes or =B15 – B16

y. Copy cell B17 to the range C17:H17.

(continued)

In the Lab

Seven-Year Financial Projection *(continued)*

8. Change the font in cell A1 to 36-point Franklin Gothic Medium (or a similar font). Change the font in cell A2 to 16-point Franklin Gothic Medium (or a similar font). Change the font in cell H2 to 10-point Century Gothic (or a similar font). Change the font in cells A7, A13, A15, and A17 to 12-point Franklin Gothic Medium. Change the font size in cell A19 to 14 point and underline the characters in the cell. Change the background and font colors and add drop shadows as shown in Figure 3-85 on the previous page.

9. Enter your name, course, laboratory assignment (Lab 3-1), date, and instructor name in the range A27:A31. Save the workbook using the file name, Lab 3-1 Shawshank Manufacturing Seven-Year Financial Projection.

10. Use the Page Setup command on the File menu to fit the printout on one page in portrait orientation. Preview and print the worksheet. Preview and print the formulas version (CTRL+`) of the worksheet in landscape orientation using the Fit to option button in the Page Setup dialog box. After printing the formulas version, reset the print scaling to 100%. Press CTRL+` to instruct Excel to display the values version of the worksheet. Save the workbook again.

11. Zoom to: (a) 200%; (b) 75%; (c) 25%; and (d) 100%.

Instructions Part 2: Open the workbook created in Part 1. Draw a 3-D Column chart (Figure 3-86) that compares the projected net incomes for the years 2004 through 2010. Use the nonadjacent ranges B3:H3 and B17:H17. Because the desired x-axis labels 2004 through 2010 in the range B3:H3 were entered as numbers in Step 2 on page EX 212, do the following when the ChartWizard – Step 2 of 4 – Chart Source Data dialog box appears: (1) click the Series tab; (2) remove Series 1 from the Series list if necessary; and (3) type =sheet1!b3:h3 in the Category (X) axis labels box. Add the chart title and format it as shown in Figure 3-86. To change the color of the columns, right-click a column and then click Format Data Series on the shortcut menu. To change the color of the walls behind and to the left of the columns, right-click a wall and then click Format Walls on the shortcut menu. Rename and rearrange the sheets, and color their tabs as shown in Figure 3-86. Save the workbook using the same file name (Lab 3-1 Shawshank Manufacturing Seven-Year Financial Projection) as defined in Part 1. Print both sheets.

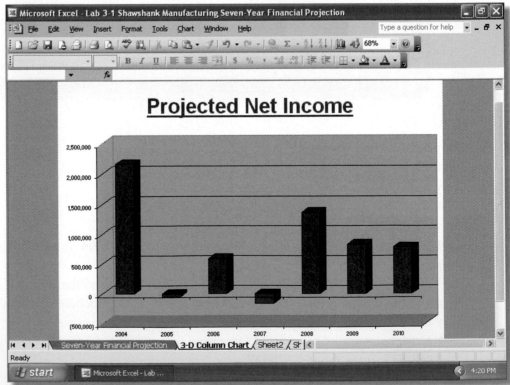

FIGURE 3-86

Instructions Part 3: Open the workbook created in Part 2. If the 3-D Column chart is on the screen, click the Seven-Year Financial Projection tab to view the worksheet. Divide the window into two panes by dragging the horizontal split box between rows 6 and 7. Use the scroll bars to show both the top and bottom of the worksheet.

Using the numbers in columns 2 and 3 of Table 3-10, analyze the effect of changing the annual sales growth (cell B22) and annual price decrease (cell B23) on the annual net incomes in row 17. The resulting answers are in column 4 of Table 3-10. Print both the worksheet and chart for each case.

Table 3-10 Shawshank Manufacturing Data to Analyze and Results			
Case	Annual Sales Growth	Annual Price Decrease	2010 Resulting Net Income
1	18.25%	2.75%	6,454,088
2	20.25%	−2.75%	11,914,998
3	34.35%	15.45%	5,732,746

Close the workbook without saving it, and then reopen it. Use the Goal Seek command to determine a margin (cell B24) that would result in a net income in 2010 of $5,000,000 (cell H17). You should end up with a margin of 41.63% in cell B24. After you complete the goal seeking, print only the worksheet. Do not save the workbook with the latest changes.

2 Profit Center Analysis of Indirect Expense Allocations

Problem: You are a summer intern at the elegant five-star Casa Grande Resort & Spa. Your work-study advisor at school and your supervisor have agreed on a challenging Excel project for you to do. They want you to create an indirect expense allocation worksheet (Figure 3-87 on the next page) that will help the resort and spa administration better evaluate the profit centers described in Table 3-11.

Table 3-11 Casa Grande Resort & Spa Worksheet Data								
	Spa	Lounge	Banquet Room	Restaurant	Business Center	Conference Rooms	Gift Shop	Children's Game Room
Total Net Revenue	78865	492800	486725	592500	225125	196475	88450	19450
Cost of Sales	36715	136500	106500	325600	14790	45125	37000	8650
Direct Expenses	14750	152975	53890	252975	8435	22475	31800	6940
Square Footage	2500	5100	8800	6000	900	5700	750	1200

(continued)

Profit Center Analysis of Indirect Expense Allocations *(continued)*

Casa Grande Resort & Spa
Profit Center Analysis of Indirect Expenses

1/12/2004

	Spa	Lounge	Banquet Room	Restaurant	Business Center	Conference Rooms	Gift Shop	Children's Game Room	Total
Total Net Revenue	$78,865.00	$492,800.00	$486,725.00	$592,500.00	$225,125.00	$196,475.00	$88,450.00	$19,450.00	$2,180,390.00
Cost of Sales	36,715.00	136,500.00	106,500.00	325,600.00	14,790.00	45,125.00	37,000.00	8,650.00	710,880.00
Direct Expenses	14,750.00	152,975.00	53,890.00	252,975.00	8,435.00	22,475.00	31,800.00	6,940.00	544,240.00
Indirect Expenses									
Administrative	$2,622.33	$16,386.06	$16,184.06	$19,701.18	$7,485.62	$6,532.98	$2,941.04	$646.73	$72,500.00
Depreciation	4,947.50	10,092.89	17,415.19	11,873.99	1,781.10	11,280.29	1,484.25	2,374.80	61,250.00
Energy	1,663.83	10,396.67	10,268.51	12,500.06	4,749.49	4,145.06	1,866.04	410.34	46,000.00
Insurance	1,009.69	2,059.77	3,554.12	2,423.26	363.49	2,302.10	302.91	484.65	12,500.00
Maintenance	2,100.16	4,284.33	7,392.57	5,040.39	756.06	4,788.37	630.05	1,008.08	26,000.00
Marketing	1,889.89	11,809.26	11,663.68	14,198.43	5,394.81	4,708.25	2,119.58	466.09	52,250.00
Total Indirect Expenses	$14,233.40	$55,028.99	$66,478.13	$65,737.31	$20,530.56	$33,757.05	$9,343.87	$5,390.69	$270,500.00
Net Income	$13,166.60	$148,296.01	$259,856.87	($51,812.31)	$181,369.44	$95,117.95	$10,306.13	($1,530.69)	$654,770.00
Square Footage	2,500	5,100	8,800	6,000	900	5,700	750	1,200	30,950
Planned Indirect Expenses									
Administrative	$72,500.00								
Depreciation	$61,250.00								
Energy	$46,000.00								
Insurance	$12,500.00								
Maintenance	$26,000.00								
Marketing	$52,250.00								

FIGURE 3-87

Instructions Part 1: Do the following to create the worksheet shown in Figure 3-87.

1. Bold the entire worksheet. Enter the worksheet titles in cells A1 and A2 and the system date in cell J2. Format the date to the 3/14/2001 style.

2. Enter the column titles and the first three rows of numbers in Table 3-11 on the previous page in rows 3 through 6. In row 3, use ALT+ENTER so the column titles show on two lines in a cell. Center and italicize the column headings in the range B3:J3. Add a bottom border to the range B3:J3. Select the range J4:J6 and click the AutoSum button. Freeze rows 1 through 3 and column A.

3. Enter the Square Footage row in Table 3-11 in row 16. Select cell J16 and use the AutoSum button to determine the sum of the values in the range B16:I16. Change the height of row 16 to 39.00 and vertically center the range A16:J16.

4. Change the following column widths: A = 26.00; B through I = 12.00, and J = 13.00.

5. Enter the remaining row titles in the range A7:A17 as shown in Figure 3-87. Increase the font size in cells A7, A14, and A15 to 12-point.

6. Copy the row titles in range A8:A13 to the range A18:A23. Enter the numbers shown in the range B18:B23 of Figure 3-87 with format symbols.

7. The planned indirect expenses in the range B18:B23 are to be prorated across the profit center as follows: Administrative (row 8), Energy (row 10), and Marketing (row 13) on the basis of Total Net Revenue (row 4); Depreciation (row 9), Insurance (row 11), and Maintenance (row 12) on the basis of Square Footage (row 16). Use the following formulas to accomplish the prorating.

In the Lab

    a. Spa Administrative (cell B8) = Administrative Expenses * Spa Total Net Revenue / Resort Total Net Revenue or =$B$18 * B4 / $J$4

    b. Spa Depreciation (cell B9) = Depreciation Expenses * Spa Square Footage / Total Square Footage or =$B$19 * B16 / $J$16

    c. Spa Energy (cell B10) = Energy Expenses * Spa Total Net Revenue / Resort Total Net Revenue or =$B$20 * B4 / $J$4

    d. Spa Insurance (cell B11) = Insurance Expenses * Spa Square Feet / Total Square Footage or =$B$21 * B16 / $J$16

    e. Spa Maintenance (cell B12) = Maintenance Expenses * Spa Square Footage / Total Square Footage or =$B$22 * B16 / $J$16

    f. Spa Marketing (cell B13) = Marketing Expenses * Spa Total Net Revenue / Resort Total Net Revenue or =$B$23 * B4 / $J$4

    g. Spa Total Indirect Expenses (cell B14) = SUM(B8:B13)

    h. Spa Net Income (cell B15) = Revenue – (Cost of Sales + Direct Expenses + Total Indirect Expenses) or =B4 – (B5 + B6 + B14)

    i. Use the fill handle to copy the range B8:B15 to the range C8:I15.

    j. Select the range J8:J15 and click the AutoSum button on the Standard toolbar.

8. Add a bottom border to the range B13:J13. Assign the Currency style with two decimal places and show negative numbers in parentheses to the following ranges: B4:J4; B8:J8; and B14:J15. Assign the Comma style with two decimal places and show negative numbers in parentheses to the following ranges: B5:J6 and B9:J13.

9. Change the font in cell A1 to 36-point Arial Black (or a similar font). Change the font in cell A2 to 18-point Arial Black (or a similar font). Change the font in cell A17 to 14-point italic underlined font.

10. Use the background color red, the font color white, and a drop shadow (Shadow Style 14) for the ranges A1:J2; A7; A15:J15; and A17:B23 as shown in Figure 3-87.

11. Rename the Sheet1 sheet, Indirect Expenses, and color its tab red. Unfreeze the worksheet.

12. Enter your name, course, laboratory assignment (Lab 3-2), date, and instructor name in the range A27:A31. Save the workbook using the file name, Lab 3-2 Casa Grande Profit Center Analysis of Indirect Expenses.

13. Use the Page Setup command on the File menu to change the orientation to landscape. Preview and print the worksheet. Preview and print the formulas version (CTRL+`) of the worksheet in landscape orientation using the Fit to option button in the Page Setup dialog box. After printing the formulas version, reset the print scaling to 100%. Press CTRL+` to show the values version of the worksheet. Save the workbook again.

14. Divide the window into four panes and show the four corners of the worksheet. Remove the four panes.

15. Add white space to the worksheet by inserting blank rows between rows 6 and 7 and 15 and 16. Move the range A19:B25 down three rows. Print the worksheet and then close the workbook without saving changes.

Instructions Part 2: Open the workbook created in Part 1. Draw a 3-D Pie chart (Figure 3-88 on the next page) that shows the contribution of each category of indirect expense to the total indirect expenses. That is, chart the nonadjacent ranges A8:A13 (category names) and J8:J13 (data series). Show labels that include category names and percentages. Do not show the legend. Format the 3-D Pie chart as shown in Figure 3-88. Rename the chart sheet 3-D Pie Chart and color the tab blue. Move the chart tab to the right of the worksheet tab. Save the workbook using the file name Lab 3-2 Casa Grande Profit Center Analysis of Indirect Expenses. Preview and print both sheets.

(continued)

In the Lab

Profit Center Analysis of Indirect Expense Allocations *(continued)*

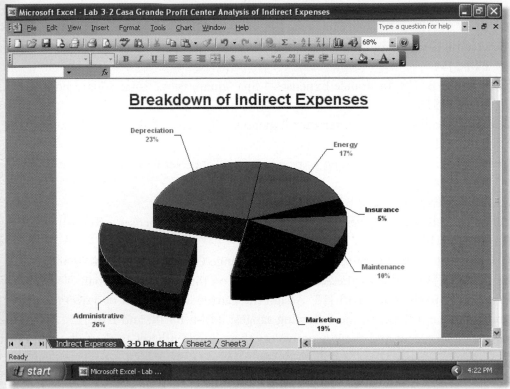

FIGURE 3-88

Instructions Part 3: Using the numbers in Table 3-12, analyze the effect of changing the planned indirect expenses in the range B18:B23 on the net incomes for each profit center. Print the worksheet for each case. You should end with the following totals in cell J15: Case 1 = $538,570.00 and Case 2 = $654,020.00. When you have finished, close the workbook without saving the latest changes.

Table 3-12 Casa Grande Resort & Spa What-If Data		
	Case 1	Case 2
Administrative	110000	66250
Depreciation	96500	63000
Energy	48750	31500
Insurance	32450	22500
Maintenance	38000	28000
Marketing	61000	60000

3 Modifying the Weekly Payroll Worksheet

Problem: Your supervisor in the Payroll department has asked you to modify the payroll workbook developed in Exercise 1 of the Project 2 In the Lab section on page EX 132, so that it appears as shown in Figure 3-89. If you did not complete Exercise 1 in Project 2, ask your instructor for a copy of Lab 2-1 Illiana Custom Homes Weekly Payroll Report workbook or complete that exercise before you begin this one.

In the Lab

	A	B	C	D	E	F	G	H	I	J	K	L	M
1	**Illiana Custom Homes**												
2	Weekly Payroll Report	2/7/2005											
3	Employee	Rate	Hours	Dep.	YTD Soc. Sec.	Gross Pay	Soc. Sec.	Medicare	Fed. Tax	State Tax	Net Pay	% Taxes	
4	Jedi, Hubert	24.90	40.00	3	4,974.00	996.00	61.75	14.44	176.12	31.87	711.81	28.53%	
5	Kaden, Hadef	8.00	38.75	10	5,340.20	310.00	19.22	4.50	0.00	9.92	276.37	10.85%	
6	Pancer, Dion	12.90	66.00	8	4,254.00	1,019.10	63.18	14.78	142.28	32.61	766.24	24.81%	
7	Sanchez, Maria	21.35	45.00	5	5,393.00	1,014.13	1.00	14.70	164.37	32.45	801.60	20.96%	
8	Scarff, Heidi	17.85	39.75	1	4,825.50	709.54	43.99	10.29	134.22	22.71	498.34	29.77%	
9	Ho, Lee	25.50	6.00	7	250.00	153.00	9.49	2.22	0.00	4.90	136.40	10.85%	
10	Mil, Tyrone	31.50	32.50	5	5,394.00	1,023.75	0.00	14.84	166.29	32.76	809.86	20.89%	
11	Totals		268.00			30,430.70	5,225.51	198.63	75.77	783.28	167.22	4,000.61	23.44%
12													
13	Social Security Tax	6.20%											
14	Medicare Tax	1.45%											
15	Maximum Social Security	$5,394.00											
16													

FIGURE 3-89

The major modifications requested by your supervisor include: (1) reformatting the worksheet; (2) adding computations of time-and-a-half for hours worked greater than 40; (3) removing the conditional formatting assigned to the range B4:B9; (4) adding calculations to charge no federal tax in certain situations; (5) adding Social Security and Medicare deductions; (6) adding and deleting employees; and (7) changing employee information.

Instructions Part 1: Open the workbook, Lab 2-1 Illiana Custom Homes Weekly Payroll Report, created in Project 2 (Figure 2-88 on page EX 132). Perform the following tasks.

1. Delete rows 11 through 13. Change all the row heights back to the default height (12.75). Select the entire sheet using the Select All button and then clear all remaining formats using the Formats command on the Clear submenu of the Edit menu. Bold the entire worksheet. Enhance the worksheet title as shown in Figure 3-89.

2. Insert a new column between columns D and E. Enter the new column E title YTD Soc. Sec. in cell E3. Insert two new columns between columns E and F. Enter the new column G title Soc. Sec. in cell G3. Enter the new column H title Medicare in cell H3.

3. Change the column widths as follows: A = 25.00; B = 9.43; C = 7.00; D = 6.00; E = 13.14; F through K = 9.71; and L = 8.43. Change the row heights as follows: row 1 = 41.25; rows 2 and 3 = 18.00.

4. Assign the NOW function to cell B2 and format it to the 3/14/2001 style.

5. Delete row 7 (Rifken, Felix). Change Hadef Kaden's (row 5) rate of pay to $8.00 and number of dependents to 10.

6. Freeze column A and rows 1 through 3. In column E, enter the YTD Soc. Sec. values listed in Table 3-13.

Table 3-13 Illiana Custom Homes Employee YTD Social Security Values

Employee	YTD Soc. Sec.
Jedi, Hubert	4,974.00
Kaden, Hadef	5,340.20
Pancer, Dion	4,254.00
Sanchez, Maria	5,393.00
Scarff, Heidi	4,825.50

(continued)

In the Lab

Modifying the Weekly Payroll Worksheet *(continued)*

7. Insert two new rows immediately above the Totals row. Add the new employee data as listed in Table 3-14.

Table 3-14 New Employee Data				
Employee	**Rate**	**Hours**	**Dep.**	**YTD Soc. Sec.**
Ho, Lee	25.50	6.00	7	250.00
Mil, Tyrone	31.50	32.50	5	5,394.00

8. Assign a Comma style with two decimal places to the ranges B4:C11 and E4:K11. Assign a Percent style and two decimal places to the range L4:L11. Center the range D4:D10.

9. As shown in Figure 3-89 on the previous page, enter and format the Social Security and Medicare tax information in the range A13:B15. Use format symbols where applicable.

10. Change the formulas to determine the gross pay in column F and the federal tax in column I as follows:

  a. In cell F4, enter an IF function that applies the following logic and then copy it to the range F5:F10.

   If Hours <= 40, then Gross Pay = Rate * Hours, otherwise Gross Pay = Rate * Hours + 0.5 * Rate * (Hours - 40)

  b. In cell I4, enter the IF function that applies the following logic and then copy it to the range I5:I10.

   If (Gross Pay – Dependents * 38.46) > 0, then Federal Tax = 20% * (Gross Pay – Dependents * 38.46), otherwise Federal Tax = 0

11. An employee pays Social Security tax only if his or her YTD Soc. Sec. in column E is less than the Maximum Social Security in cell B15. Use the following logic to determine the Social Security tax for Hubert Jedi in cell G4 and then copy it to the range G5:G10.

   If Social Security Tax * Gross Pay + YTD Soc. Sec. > Maximum Social Security, then Maximum Social Security – YTD Soc. Sec., otherwise Social Security Tax * Gross Pay

   Use absolute cell references for the Social Security Tax and Maximum Social Security values.

12. In cell H4, enter the following formula and then copy it to the range H5:H10:
   Medicare = Medicare Tax * Gross Pay
   Use absolute cell references for the Medicare Tax values.

13. In cell K4, enter the following formula and copy it to the range K5:K10:
   Gross Pay – (Soc. Sec. + Medicare + Fed. Tax + State Tax)

14. In cell L4, enter the following formula and copy it to the range L5:L11:
   (Soc. Sec. + Medicare + Fed. Tax + State Tax) / Gross Pay

15. Determine any new totals as shown in row 11 of Figure 3-89.

16. Use alignment, borders, and drop shadows to format the worksheet as shown in Figure 3-89.

17. Enter your name, course, laboratory assignment (Lab 3-3), date, and instructor name in the range A17:A21.

18. Save the workbook using the file name Lab 3-3 Illiana Custom Homes Weekly Payroll Report.

19. Use the Zoom box on the Standard toolbar to change the view of the worksheet. One by one, select all the percents in the Zoom list. When you are done, return the worksheet to 100% magnification.

20. Use the Page Setup command on the File menu to change the orientation to landscape. Preview the worksheet. If number signs appear in place of numbers in any columns, adjust the column widths. Print the worksheet. Save the worksheet using the same file name.

21. Preview and print the formulas version (CTRL+`) in landscape orientation using the Fit to option button in the Page Setup dialog box. Close the worksheet without saving the latest changes.

In the Lab

Instructions Part 2: Open Lab 3-3 Illiana Custom Homes Weekly Payroll Report. Using the numbers in Table 3-15, analyze the effect of changing the Social Security tax in cell B13 and the Medicare tax in cell B14. Print the worksheet for each case. The first case should result in a total Social Security tax in cell G11 of $240.07. The second case should result in a total Social Security tax of $319.76. Close the workbook and do not save any changes.

Table 3-15 Illiana Custom Homes Social Security and Medicare Tax Cases		
Case	Social Security Tax	Medicare Tax
1	7.50%	2.45%
2	10.00%	3.00%

Instructions Part 3: Hand in your handwritten results for this exercise to your instructor. Open Lab 3-3 Illiana Custom Homes Weekly Payroll Report.

1. Select cell F4. Write down the formula that Excel displays in the formula bar. Select the range C4:C10. Point to the border surrounding the range and drag the selection to the range D13:D19. Click cell F4, and write down the formula that Excel displays in the formula bar below the one you wrote down earlier. Compare the two formulas. What can you conclude about how Excel responds when you move cells involved in a formula? Click the Undo button on the Standard toolbar.
2. Right-click the range C4:C10 and then click Delete on the shortcut menu. When Excel displays the Delete dialog box, click Shift cells left and then click the OK button. What does Excel display in cell F4? Use the Type a question for help box on the menu bar to find a definition of the result in cell F4. Write down the definition. Click the Undo button on the Standard toolbar.
3. Right-click the range C4:C10 and then click Insert on the shortcut menu. When Excel displays the Insert dialog box, click Shift cells right and then click the OK button. What does Excel display in the formula bar when you click cell F4? What does Excel display in the formula bar when you click cell G4? What can you conclude about how Excel responds when you insert cells next to cells involved in a formula? Close the workbook without saving the changes.

Cases and Places

The difficulty of these case studies varies:
■ are the least difficult and ■■ are more difficult. The last exercise is a group exercise.

1 ■ Ester's Sweet Shop is open all year, but most of the shop's sales revolves around four holidays: Valentine's Day (18,330 pounds of candy), Easter (12,925 pounds of candy), Halloween (14,275 pounds of candy), and Christmas (15,975 pounds of candy). On and around these holidays, 31% of the store's output is Chocolate Creams, 27% is Gummy Bears, 18% is Jelly Beans, and the remaining 24% is Mints. The Chocolate Creams sell for $4.50 per pound, the Gummy Bears for $2.75 per pound, the Jelly Beans for $2.50 per pound, and the Mints for $1.75 per pound. Ester's management is considering revising its production figures. They have asked you to create a worksheet they can use in making this decision. The worksheet should show the total number of pounds of each candy ordered for each holiday, total candy ordered for the four holidays, potential dollar sales for each type of candy, total potential dollar sales for each holiday, and total potential dollar sales from each type of candy. Include an appropriate chart illustrating total potential dollar sales for each candy type. Use the concepts and techniques presented in this project to create and format the worksheet and chart.

2 ■ Vashon's IT Hardware & Services is one of the largest Information Technology hardware and services company in the Southwest. The company generates revenue from the sale of hardware and consulting. A fixed percentage of the total net revenue is spent on marketing, payroll, equipment, quarterly bonus if the total net revenue for the quarter exceeds $150,000,000, production, and administrative expenses. The company's projected receipts and expenditures for the next four quarters are shown in Table 3-16.

With this data, you have been asked to prepare a worksheet and chart similar to Figure 3-1 on page EX 147 for the next shareholders' meeting. The worksheet should show total net revenues, total expenditures, and operating income for each quarterly period. Include a 3-D Pie chart on a separate sheet that compares the quarterly contributions to the operating income. Use the concepts and techniques presented in this project to create and format the worksheet and chart. During the meeting, one shareholder lobbied to reduce marketing expenditures by 1.25% and payroll costs by 3.65%. Perform a what-if analysis reflecting the proposed changes in expenditures. The changes should result in an operating income of $153,310,217 for the year.

Table 3-16 Vashon's IT Hardware & Services Projected Revenues and Expenses				
Revenues	**Quarter 1**	**Quarter 2**	**Quarter 3**	**Quarter 4**
Sales	77,230,192	82,822,010	79,401,034	73,010,304
Consulting	67,023,910	62,912,013	80,771,819	62,010,498
Expenditures				
Marketing	13.25%			
Payroll	23.65%			
Equipment	21.75%			
Production	6.50%			
Bonus	300,000.00			
Revenue for Bonus	150,000,000.00			
Administrative	13.50%			

Cases and Places

3 ■ You are the product manager for JB Smyth Publishers, a company that produces textbooks for the career school market. One of your responsibilities is to submit income projections to your publisher for the books you plan to sign. The projected first year net sales for the three books you plan to sign are shown in Table 3-17. Also included in the table are the percent of net sales for payment of royalty, manufacturing, and administrative costs. Use the concepts and techniques presented in this project to create and format a worksheet that shows the projected royalty, manufacturing costs, administrative costs, net income for each book, and totals for the five columns in Table 3-17. The net income for a book is equal to the net sales minus the royalty, manufacturing, and administrative costs. Also create an embedded 3-D Pie chart that shows the contributions of each book to the total net income.

Table 3-17 JB Smyth Publishers 1st Year Net Sales and Cost Allocations					
Book Title	Net Sales	Royalty	Manu. Costs	Adm. Costs	Net Income
Book 1	4,123,489.00	—	—	—	—
Book 2	2,275,546.50	—	—	—	—
Book 3	1,678,925.75	—	—	—	—
Total	—	—	—	—	—
Assumptions					
Royalty	16.25%				
Manu. Costs	23.5%				
Adm. Costs	20.00%				

Your publisher reviewed your plan and returned it, requesting printouts of the worksheet for the following set of values: Set 1 – Royalty - 12.5%; Manu. Costs - 30.5%, and Adm. Costs - 18.50% (answer Total Net Income = $3,110,015.08); Set 2 – Royalty - 18.5%; Manu. Costs - 32%, and Adm. Costs - 20.50% (answer Total Net Income = $2,342,608.76).

4 ■■ Uncle Harry and Aunt Matilda own a plumbing company and run a farm part-time. They want to save enough money over the next six months to buy a used tractor for the spring planting season. They have job orders at their plumbing company for the next six months: $15,200 in January, $18,560 in February, $29,560 in March, $32,019 in April, $43,102 in May, and $29,955 in June. Each month, they spend 36.35% of the job order income on material, 3.15% on patterns, 5.25% on their retirement account, and 42.5% on food and clothing. 25% of the remaining profits (orders – total expenses) will be put aside for the tractor. Aunt Matilda's parents have agreed to provide a bonus of $150 whenever the monthly savings exceeds $750. Uncle Harry has asked you to create a worksheet that shows orders, expenses, profits, bonuses, and savings for the next six months, and totals for each category. Aunt Matilda would like you to (a) perform a what-if analysis to determine the total savings by reducing the percentage spent on material to 25% (answer total savings = $11,045.86), and (b) with the original assumptions, goal seek to determine what percentage of profits to spend on food and clothing if $7,000 is needed for the used tractor (answer = 40.05%). Use the concepts and techniques presented in this project to create and format the worksheet.

Cases and Places

5 ■■ **Working Together**   Your group has been asked to develop a worksheet that shows quarterly growth for the year based on Quarter 1 sales and growth data. The data and general layout of the worksheet, including the totals, are shown in Table 3-18.

Table 3-18 Working Together Data and General Layout					
	Qtr 1	Qtr 2	Qtr 3	Qtr 4	Total
Total Net Revenue	Formula A	Formula D		→	—
Cost of Goods Sold	Formula B			→	—
Gross Margin	Formula C			→	—
Assumptions					
Qtr 1 Revenue	$18,645,830.00				
Qtr Growth Rate	0.00%	−3.50%	5.00%	3.75%	
Qtr Cost Rate	42.50%	46.00%	52.00%	53.75%	
Extra	2.90%	3.10%	4.95%	2.50%	

Enter the formulas shown in Table 3-19 in the locations shown in Table 3-18. Copy Formula B, C, and D to the remaining quarters.

Table 3-19   Working Together Formulas
Formula A = Qtr 1 Revenue
Formula B = IF(Qtr Growth Rate < 0, Revenue * (Qtr Cost Rate + Extra), Revenue * Qtr Cost Rate)
Formula C = Revenue – Cost
Formula D = Qtr 1 Total Net Revenue * (1 + Qtr Growth Rate)

Have each member of your team submit a sketch of the proposed worksheet and 3-D Pie chart (see Figure 3-3b on page EX 149) and then implement the best one. The gross margin for the four quarters should equal $38,014,124.00. Include an embedded exploded 3-D Pie chart that shows the contribution of each quarter to the gross margin. Use the concepts and techniques developed in the first three projects to create and format the worksheet and embedded 3-D Pie chart. Use the Goal Seek command to determine the Qtr 1 Revenue (first value in the Assumptions area) that will generate a total gross margin of $40,000,000.00. Your team should end up with a Qtr 1 Revenue of $19,619,897.07. Hand in the sketches submitted by each team member and a printout of the modified worksheet and 3-D Pie chart.

Creating Static and Dynamic Web Pages Using Excel

Objectives

You will have mastered the material in this Web feature when you can:

- Publish a worksheet and chart as a static or a dynamic Web page
- Display Web pages published in Excel in a browser
- Manipulate the data in a published Web page using a browser
- Complete file management tasks within Excel

CASE PERSPECTIVE

Home Wireless Fidelity, a network company that specializes in the installation of wireless home networks, has experienced significant growth since it developed the first wireless home network system. In two years, the company has grown from a single owner, garage-based company to one with annual sales in the millions.

Sergio Autohbon is a spreadsheet specialist for Home Wireless Fidelity. One of Sergio's responsibilities is a workbook that summarizes quarterly sales by store location (Figure 1a on the next page). In the past, Sergio printed the worksheet and chart, sent it out to make copies of it, and then mailed it to his distribution list.

Home Wireless Fidelity recently upgraded to Office 2003 because of its Web and collaboration capabilities. After attending an Office 2003 training session, Sergio had a great idea and called you for help. He would like to save the Excel worksheet and Pie chart (Figure 1a) on the company's intranet as a static Web page (Figure 1b), so the lower-level management on the distribution list can display it using a browser. He also suggested publishing the same workbook on the company's intranet as a dynamic (interactive) Web page (Figure 1c), so the higher-level management could use its browser to manipulate the data in the worksheet without requiring Excel.

Finally, Sergio wants both the static and dynamic Web pages saved as single files, also called Single File Web Page format, rather than in the traditional file and folder format, called Web Page format.

As you read through this Web feature, you will learn how to create static and dynamic Web pages from workbooks in Excel and then display the results using a browser.

Introduction

Excel provides fast, easy methods for saving workbooks as Web pages that can be stored on the World Wide Web, a company's intranet, or a local hard disk. A user then can display the workbook using a browser, rather than Excel.

You can save a workbook, or a portion of a workbook, as a static Web page or a dynamic Web page. A **static Web page**, also called a **noninteractive Web page** or **view-only Web page**, is a snapshot of the workbook. It is similar to a printed report in that you can view it through your browser, but you cannot modify it. In the browser window, the workbook appears as it would in Microsoft Excel, including sheet tabs that you can click to switch between worksheets. A **dynamic Web page**, also called an **interactive Web page**, includes the interactivity and functionality of the workbook. For example, with a dynamic Web page, you can view a copy of the worksheet in your browser and then enter formulas, reformat cells, and change values in the worksheet to perform what-if analysis. A user does not need Excel on his or her computer to complete these tasks.

As illustrated in Figure 1, this Web feature shows you how to save a workbook (Figure 1a) as a static Web page (Figure 1b) and view it using your browser. Then, using the same workbook, the steps show how to save it as a dynamic Web page (Figure 1c), view it using your browser, and then change values to test the Web page's interactivity and functionality.

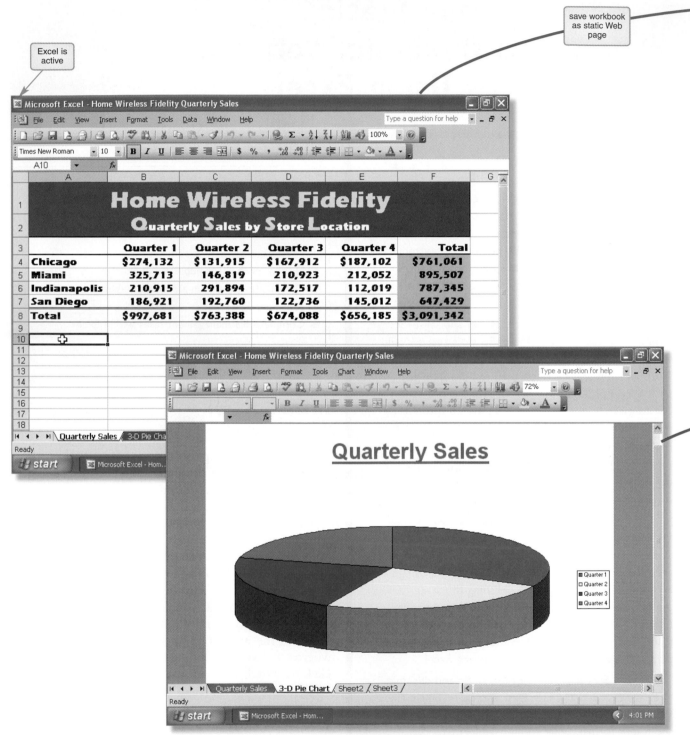

(a) Workbook Viewed in Excel

FIGURE 1

browser is active

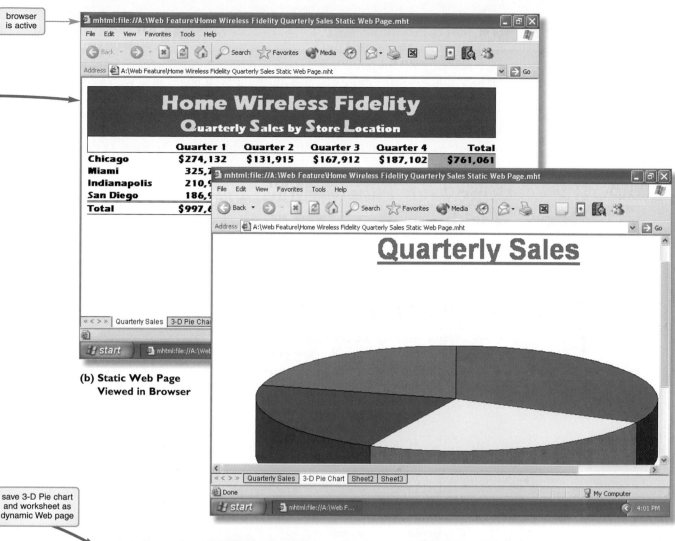

Home Wireless Fidelity
Quarterly Sales by Store Location

	Quarter 1	Quarter 2	Quarter 3	Quarter 4	Total
Chicago	$274,132	$131,915	$167,912	$187,102	$761,061
Miami	325,7				
Indianapolis	210,9				
San Diego	186,9				
Total	$997,6				

Quarterly Sales

« < > » | Quarterly Sales | 3-D Pie Chart | Sheet2 | Sheet3

(b) Static Web Page
Viewed in Browser

save 3-D Pie chart and worksheet as dynamic Web page

browser is active

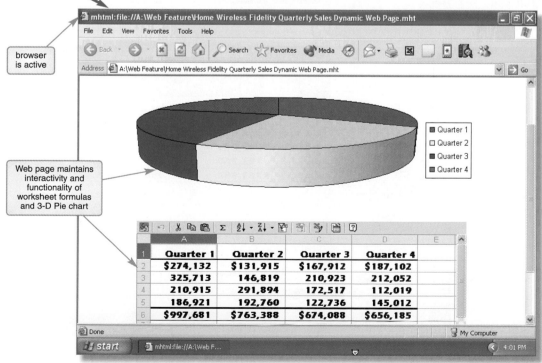

Web page maintains interactivity and functionality of worksheet formulas and 3-D Pie chart

Quarter 1
Quarter 2
Quarter 3
Quarter 4

	Quarter 1	Quarter 2	Quarter 3	Quarter 4	E
1	**Quarter 1**	**Quarter 2**	**Quarter 3**	**Quarter 4**	
2	**$274,132**	**$131,915**	**$167,912**	**$187,102**	
3	325,713	146,819	210,923	212,052	
4	210,915	291,894	172,517	112,019	
5	186,921	192,760	122,736	145,012	
6	**$997,681**	**$763,388**	**$674,088**	**$656,185**	

(c) Dynamic Web Page
Viewed in Browser

More About

Web Folders and FTP Locations

Web folders and FTP locations are particularly useful because they appear as standard folders in Windows Explorer or in the Save in list. You can save any type of file in a Web folder or on an FTP location, just as you would save in a folder on your hard disk. For additional information, see Appendix C.

The Save as Web Page command on the File menu allows you to **publish workbooks**, which is the process of making a workbook available to others; for example, on the World Wide Web or on a company's intranet. If you have access to a Web server, you can publish Web pages by saving them in a Web folder or on an FTP location. To learn more about publishing Web pages in a Web folder or on an FTP location using Microsoft Office applications, refer to Appendix C.

This Web feature illustrates how to create and save the Web pages on a floppy disk, rather than on a Web server. This feature also demonstrates how to preview a workbook as a Web page and create a new folder using the Save As dialog box.

Using Web Page Preview and Saving an Excel Workbook as a Static Web Page

After you have created an Excel workbook, you can preview it as a Web page. If the preview is acceptable, then you can save the workbook as a Web page.

Web Page Preview

At anytime during the construction of a workbook, you can preview it as a Web page by using the Web Page Preview command on the File menu. When you invoke the Web Page Preview command, it starts your browser and displays the active sheet in the workbook as a Web page. The following steps show how to use the Web Page Preview command.

To Preview the Workbook as a Web Page

1

- **Insert the Data Disk in drive A.**
- **Start Excel and then open the workbook, Home Wireless Fidelity Quarterly Sales, on drive A.**
- **Click File on the menu bar.**

Excel starts and opens the workbook, Home Wireless Fidelity Quarterly Sales. The workbook is made up of two sheets: a worksheet and a chart. Excel displays the File menu (Figure 2).

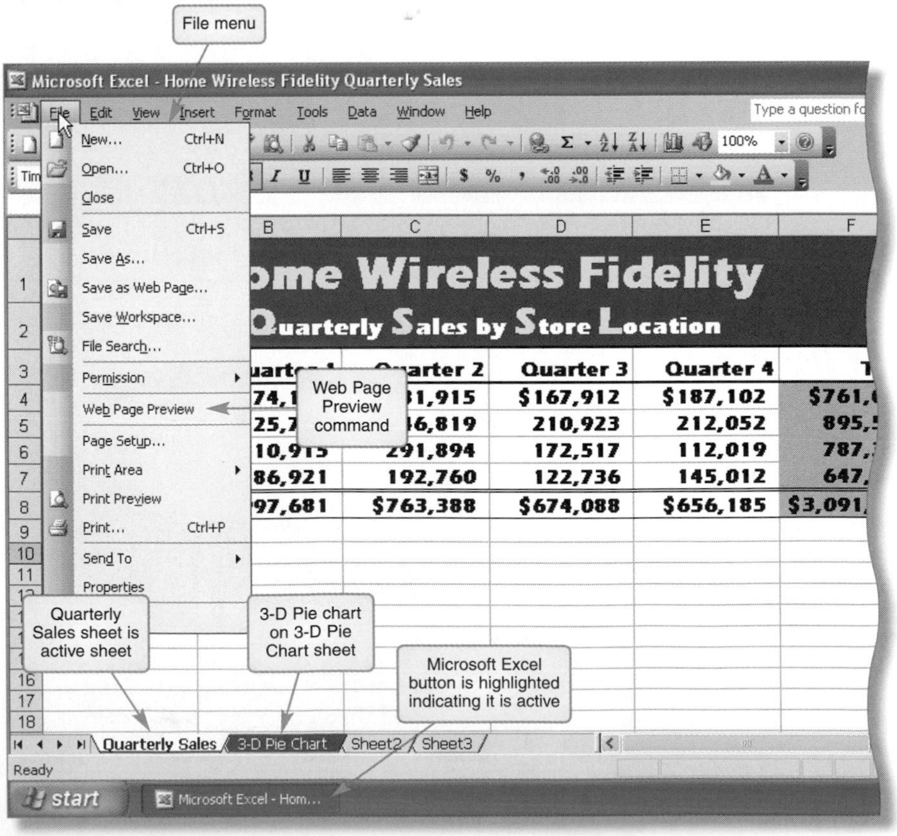

FIGURE 2

2

• **Click Web Page Preview.**

Excel starts your browser. The browser displays a preview of how the Quarterly Sales sheet will appear as a Web page (Figure 3). The Web page preview in the browser is nearly identical to the display of the worksheet in Excel. A highlighted browser button appears on the Windows taskbar indicating it is active. The Excel button on the Windows taskbar no longer is highlighted.

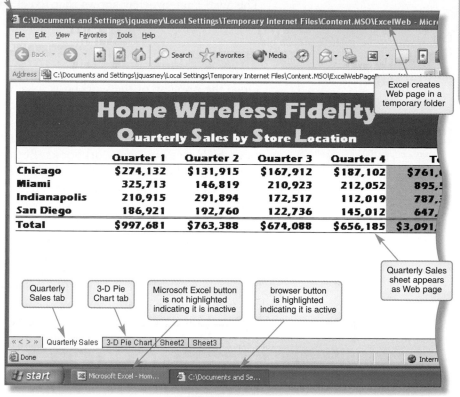

FIGURE 3

3

• **Click the 3-D Pie Chart tab at the bottom of the Web page.**

The browser displays the 3-D Pie chart (Figure 4).

4

• **After viewing the Web page preview of the Home Wireless Fidelity Quarterly Sales workbook, click the Close button on the right side of the browser title bar.**

The browser closes. Excel becomes active and again displays the Home Wireless Fidelity Quarterly Sales worksheet.

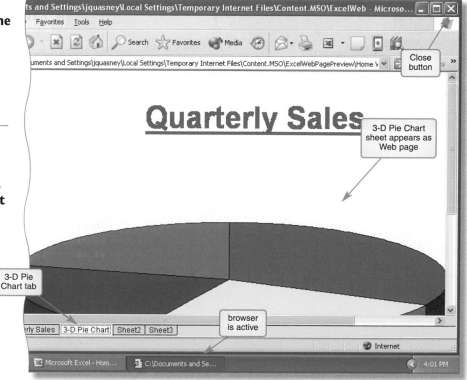

FIGURE 4

The Web Page preview shows that Excel has the capability of producing professional looking Web pages from workbooks.

Saving a Workbook as a Static Web Page in a New Folder

Once the preview of the workbook as a Web page is acceptable, you can save the workbook as a Web page so that others can view it using a Web browser, such as Internet Explorer or Netscape Navigator.

Whether you plan to save static or dynamic Web pages, two Web page formats exist in which you can save workbooks. Both formats convert the contents of the workbook into HTML (HyperText Markup Language), which is a language browsers can interpret. One format is called **Single File Web Page format**, which saves all of the components of the Web page in a single file with an .mht extension. This format is useful particularly for e-mailing workbooks in HTML format. The second format, called **Web Page format,** saves the Web page in a file and some of its components in a folder. This format is useful if you need access to the components, such as images, that make up the Web page.

Experienced users organize the files saved on a storage medium, such as a floppy disk or hard disk, by creating folders. They then save related files in a common folder. Excel allows you to create folders before saving a file using the Save As dialog box. The following steps create a new folder on the Data Disk in drive A and save the workbook as a static Web page in the new folder.

More About

Publishing Web Pages

For more information about publishing Web pages using Excel, visit the Excel 2003 More About Web page (scsite.com/ex2003/more) and then click Publishing Web Pages Using Excel.

To Save an Excel Workbook as a Static Web Page in a Newly Created Folder

1

• **With the Home Wireless Fidelity Quarterly Sales workbook open, click File on the menu bar.**

Excel displays the File menu (Figure 5).

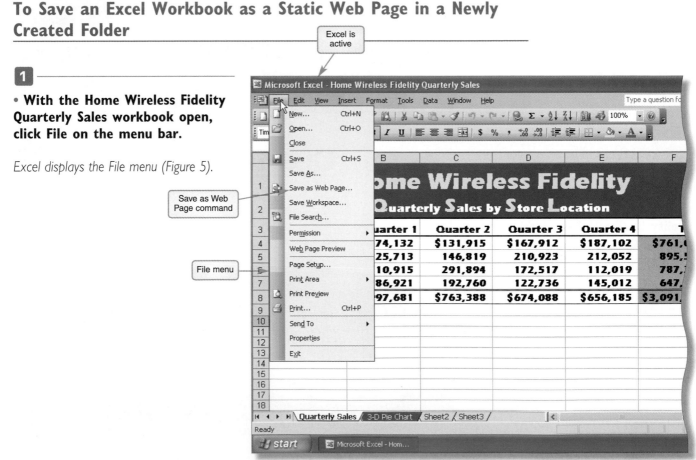

FIGURE 5

2

- **Click Save as Web Page.**

- **When Excel displays the Save As dialog box, type** Home Wireless Fidelity Quarterly Sales Static Web Page **in the File name text box.**

- **Click the Save as type box arrow and then click Single File Web Page.**

- **Click the Save in box arrow, select 3½ Floppy (A:), and then click the Create New Folder button.**

- **When Excel displays the New Folder dialog box, type** Web Feature **in the Name text box.**

Excel displays the Save As dialog box and New Folder dialog box as shown in Figure 6.

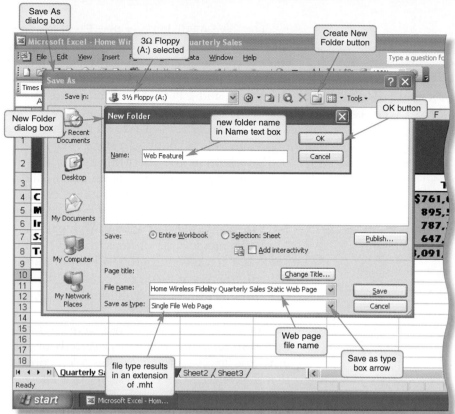

FIGURE 6

3

- **Click the OK button in the New Folder dialog box.**

Excel automatically selects the new folder Web Feature in the Save in box (Figure 7). The Entire Workbook option in the Save area instructs Excel to save all sheets in the workbook as static Web pages.

4

- **Click the Save button in the Save As dialog box.**

- **Click the Close button on the right side of the Excel title bar to quit Excel.**

Excel saves the workbook in a single file in HTML format in the Web Feature folder on the Data Disk in drive A.

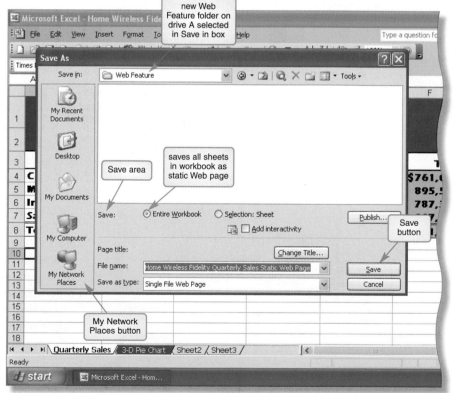

FIGURE 7

More About

Viewing Web Pages Created in Excel

To view static Web pages created in Excel, you can use any browser. To view dynamic Web pages created in Excel, you must have the Microsoft Office Web Components and Microsoft Internet Explorer 4.01 or later installed on your computer.

The Save As dialog box that Excel displays when you use the Save as Web Page command is slightly different from the Save As dialog box that Excel displays when you use the Save As command. When you use the Save as Web Page command, a Save area appears in the dialog box. Within the Save area are two option buttons, a check box, and a Publish button (Figure 7 on the previous page). You can select only one of the option buttons. The Entire Workbook option button is selected by default. This indicates Excel will save all the active sheets (Quarterly Sales and 3-D Pie Chart) in the workbook as a static Web page. The alternative is the Selection Sheet option button. If you select this option, Excel will save only the active sheet (the one that currently is displaying in the Excel window) in the workbook. If you add a check mark to the Add interactivity check box, then Excel saves the active sheet as a dynamic Web page. If you leave the Add interactivity check box unchecked, Excel saves the active sheet as a static Web page.

In the previous set of steps, the Save button was used to save the Excel workbook as a static Web page. The Publish button in the Save As dialog box in Figure 7 is an alternative to the Save button. It allows you to customize the Web page further. Later in this feature, the Publish button will be used to explain how you can customize a Web page further.

If you have access to a Web server and it allows you to save files in a Web folder, then you can save the Web page directly on the Web server by clicking the My Network Places button in the lower-left corner of the Save As dialog box (Figure 7). If you have access to a Web server that allows you to save on an FTP site, then you can select the FTP site below FTP locations in the Save in box just as you select any folder on which to save a file. To learn more about publishing Web pages in a Web folder or on an FTP location using Office applications, refer to Appendix C.

After Excel saves the workbook in Step 4 on the previous page, it displays the HTML file in the Excel window. Excel can continue to display the workbook in HTML format, because, within the HTML file that it created, it also saved the Excel formats that allow it to display the HTML file in Excel. This is referred to as **round tripping** the HTML file back to the application in which it was created.

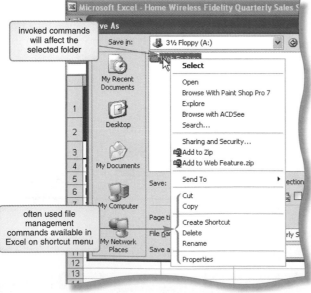

invoked commands will affect the selected folder

often used file management commands available in Excel on shortcut menu

FIGURE 8

File Management Tools in Excel

It was not necessary to create a new folder in the previous set of steps. The Web page could have been saved on the Data Disk in drive A in the same manner files were saved on the Data Disk in drive A in the previous projects. Creating a new folder, however, allows you to organize your work.

Another point concerning the new folder created in the previous set of steps is that Excel automatically inserts the new folder name in the Save in box when you click the OK button in the New Folder dialog box (Figure 7).

Finally, once you create a folder, you can right-click it while the Save As dialog box is active and perform many file management tasks directly in Excel (Figure 8). For example, once the shortcut menu appears, you can rename the selected folder, delete it, copy it, display its properties, and perform other file management functions.

Viewing the Static Web Page Using a Browser

With the static Web page saved in the Web Feature folder on drive A, the next step is to view it using a browser as shown in the following steps.

To View and Manipulate the Static Web Page Using a Browser

1

• **If necessary, insert the Data Disk in drive A.**

• **Click the Start button on the Windows taskbar, point to All Programs on the Start menu, and then click Internet Explorer on the All Programs submenu.**

• **When the Internet Explorer window appears, type** a:\web feature\home wireless fidelity quarterly sales static web page.mht **in the Address box and then press the ENTER key.**

The browser displays the Web page, Home Wireless Fidelity Quarterly Sales Static Web Page.mht, with the Quarterly Sales sheet active (Figure 9).

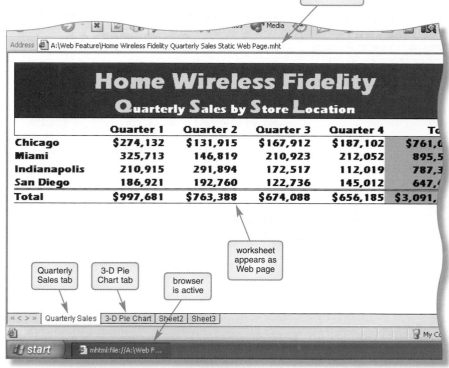

FIGURE 9

2

• **Click the 3-D Pie Chart tab at the bottom of the window.**

• **Use the scroll arrows to display the lower portion of the chart.**

The browser displays the 3-D Pie chart as shown in Figure 10.

3

• **Click the Close button on the right side of the browser title bar to close the browser.**

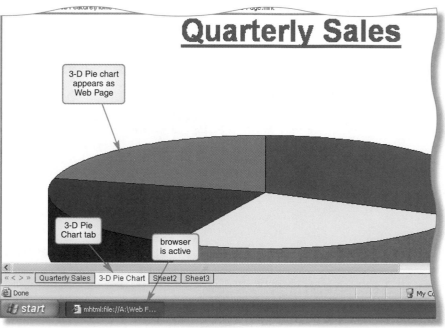

FIGURE 10

You can see from Figures 9 and 10 on the previous page that a static Web page is an ideal way to distribute information to a large group of people. For example, the static Web page could be published on a Web server connected to the Internet and made available to anyone with a computer, browser, and the address of the Web page. It also can be e-mailed easily, because the Web page resides in a single file, rather than in a file and folder. Publishing a static Web page of a workbook thus is an excellent alternative to distributing printed copies of the workbook.

Figures 9 and 10 show that, when you instruct Excel to save the entire workbook (see the Entire Workbook option button in Figure 7 on page EX 231), it creates a Web page with tabs for each sheet in the workbook. Clicking a tab displays the corresponding sheet. If you want, you can use the Print command on the File menu in your browser to print the sheets one at a time.

Saving an Excel Chart as a Dynamic Web Page

This section shows how to publish a dynamic Web page that includes Excel functionality and interactivity. The objective is to publish the 3-D Pie chart that is on the 3-D Pie Chart sheet in the Home Wireless Fidelity Quarterly Sales workbook. The following steps use the Publish button in the Save As dialog box, rather than the Save button, to illustrate the additional publishing capabilities of Excel.

To Save an Excel Chart as a Dynamic Web Page

1

• **If necessary, insert the Data Disk in drive A.**

• **Start Excel and then open the workbook, Home Wireless Fidelity Quarterly Sales, on drive A.**

• **Click File on the menu bar.**

Excel opens the workbook and displays the File menu (Figure 11).

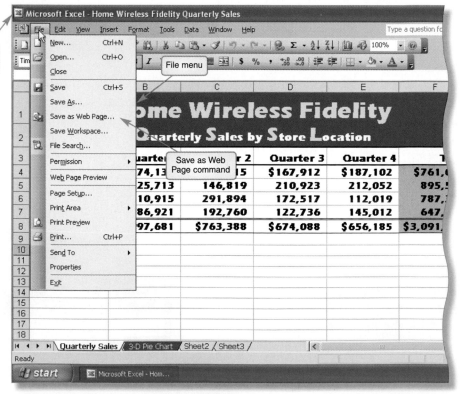

FIGURE 11

2

- **Click Save as Web Page.**

- **When Excel displays the Save As dialog box, type** Home Wireless Fidelity Quarterly Sales Dynamic Web Page **in the File name text box.**

- **Click the Save as type box arrow and then click Single File Web Page.**

- **If necessary, click the Save in box arrow, select 3½ Floppy (A:) in the Save in list, and then select the Web Feature folder.**

Excel displays the Save As dialog box as shown in Figure 12.

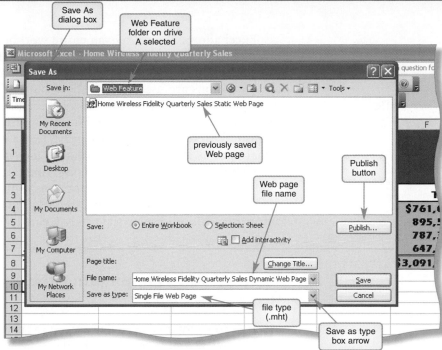

FIGURE 12

3

- **Click the Publish button.**

- **When Excel displays the Publish as Web Page dialog box, click the Choose box arrow and then click Items on 3-D Pie Chart.**

- **Click the Add interactivity with check box in the Viewing options area.**

- **If necessary, click the Add interactivity with box arrow and then click Chart functionality.**

Excel displays the Publish as Web Page dialog box as shown in Figure 13.

4

- **Click the Publish button, click the Close button on the right side of the Excel title bar, and if necessary, click the No button in the Microsoft Excel dialog box.**

Excel saves the dynamic Web page in the Web Feature folder on the Data Disk in drive A. The Excel window is closed.

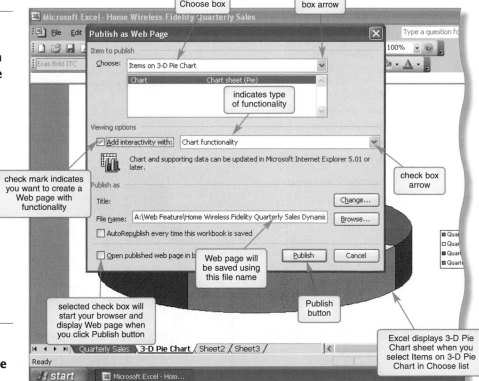

FIGURE 13

More About

Dynamic Web Pages

When you change a value in a dynamic Web page, it does not affect the saved workbook or the saved HTML file. If you change a value on a dynamic Web page and then save the Web page using the Save As command on the browser's File menu, Excel will save the original version, not the modified one that appears on the screen.

Excel allows you to save an entire workbook, a sheet in the workbook, or a range on a sheet as a Web page. In Figure 12 on the previous page, the Save area provides options that allow you to save the entire workbook or only a sheet. These option buttons are used with the Save button. If you want to be more selective in what you save, then you can disregard the option buttons in the Save area in Figure 12 and click the Publish button as described in Step 3. The Choose box in the Publish as Web Page dialog box in Figure 13 on the previous page provides additional options for you to select what to include on the Web page. You also may save the Web page as a dynamic Web page (interactive) or a static Web page (noninteractive) by selecting the appropriate options in the Viewing options area. The check box at the bottom of the dialog box gives you the opportunity to start your browser automatically and display the newly created Web page when you click the Publish button.

Viewing and Manipulating the Dynamic Web Page Using a Browser

With the dynamic Web page saved in the Web Feature folder on drive A, the next step is to view and manipulate the dynamic Web page using a browser, as shown in the following steps.

To View and Manipulate the Dynamic Web Page Using a Browser

1

• **Click the Start button on the Windows taskbar, point to All Programs on the Start menu, and then click Internet Explorer on the All Programs submenu.**

• **When the Internet Explorer window appears, type** a:\web feature\home wireless fidelity quarterly sales dynamic web page.mht **in the Address box, and then press the ENTER key.**

The browser displays the Web page, Home Wireless Fidelity Quarterly Sales Dynamic Web Page.mht, as shown in Figure 14. The 3-D Pie chart appears at the top of the Web page. The rows and columns of the worksheet that determine the size of the slices appear immediately below the 3-D Pie chart.

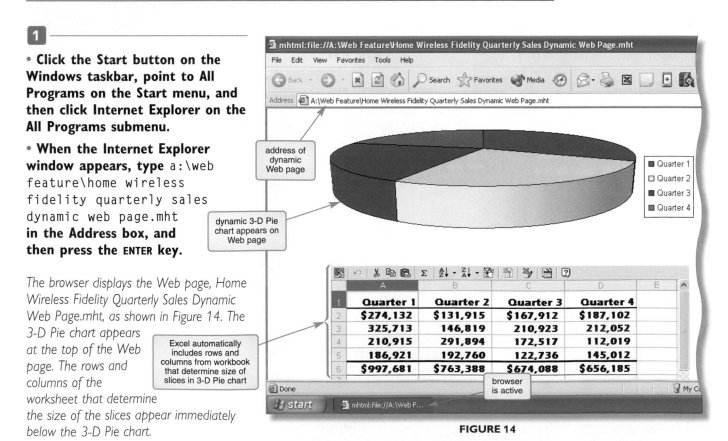

FIGURE 14

Excel Web Feature

2

• **Click cell A2 and then enter** 1600000 **as the new value.**

The number 1,600,000 replaces the number 274,132 in cell A2. The formulas in the worksheet portion recalculate the totals in row 6 and the slices in the 3-D Pie chart change to agree with the new totals (Figure 15).

3

• **Click the Close button on the right side of the browser title bar to close the browser.**

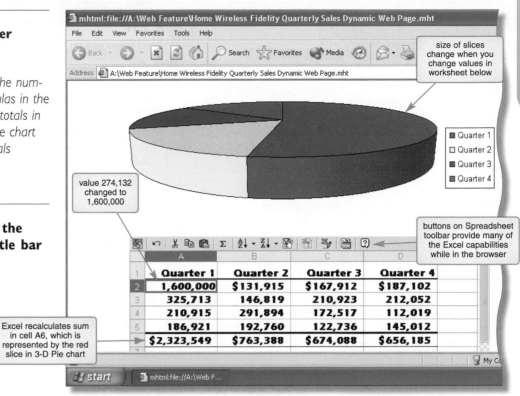

mhtml:file://A:\Web Feature\Home Wireless Fidelity Quarterly Sales Dynamic Web Page.mht

File   Edit   View   Favorites   Tools   Help

Back   Search   Favorites   Media

Address: A:\Web Feature\Home Wireless Fidelity Quarterly Sales Dynamic Web Page.mht

size of slices change when you change values in worksheet below

■ Quarter 1
□ Quarter 2
■ Quarter 3
■ Quarter 4

value 274,132 changed to 1,600,000

buttons on Spreadsheet toolbar provide many of the Excel capabilities while in the browser

	A	B	C	D
1	**Quarter 1**	**Quarter 2**	**Quarter 3**	**Quarter 4**
2	**1,600,000**	**$131,915**	**$167,912**	**$187,102**
3	325,713	146,819	210,923	212,052
4	210,915	291,894	172,517	112,019
5	186,921	192,760	122,736	145,012
6	**$2,323,549**	**$763,388**	**$674,088**	**$656,185**

Excel recalculates sum in cell A6, which is represented by the red slice in 3-D Pie chart

start   mhtml:file://A:\Web F...

My C

FIGURE 15

Figure 14 shows the result of saving the 3-D Pie chart as a dynamic Web page. Excel displays a slightly rounded version of the 3-D Pie chart and automatically adds the columns and rows from the worksheet that affect the chart directly below the chart. As shown in Figure 15, when a number in the worksheet that determines the size of the slices in the 3-D Pie chart is changed, the Web page instantaneously recalculates all formulas and redraws the 3-D Pie chart. For example, when cell A2 is changed from 274,132 to 1,600,000, the Web page recalculates the totals in row 6. The slice representing Quarter 1 is based on the number in cell A6. Thus, when the number in cell A6 changes from 997,681 to 2,323,549 because of the change made in cell A2, the slice representing Quarter 1 changes to a much larger slice in relation to the others. The interactivity and functionality allow you to share a workbook's formulas and charts with others who may not have access to Excel, but do have access to a browser.

Modifying the Worksheet on a Dynamic Web Page

As shown in Figure 15, the Web page displays a toolbar immediately above the rows and columns in the worksheet. This toolbar, called the Spreadsheet toolbar, allows you to invoke the most commonly used worksheet commands. For example, you can select a cell immediately below a column of numbers and click the AutoSum button to sum the numbers in the column. Cut, copy, and paste capabilities also are available. Table 1 on the next page summarizes the functions of the buttons on the Spreadsheet toolbar shown in Figure 15.

More About

Creating Links

You can add hyperlinks to an Excel workbook before you save it as a Web page. The hyperlinks in the Excel workbook can link to a Web page, a location in a Web page, or an e-mail address that automatically starts the viewer's e-mail program.

More About

The Quick Reference

For a table that lists how to complete the tasks covered in this book using the mouse, menu, shortcut menu, and keyboard, see the Quick Reference Summary at the back of this book or visit the Excel 2003 Quick Reference Web page (scsite.com/ex2003/qr).

Table 1 Spreadsheet Toolbar Options

BUTTON	NAME OF BUTTON	FUNCTION	BUTTON	NAME OF BUTTON	FUNCTION
	Office Logo	Displays information about the Microsoft Office Web component, including the version number installed		Sort Ascending	Sorts the selected items in ascending sequence
	Undo	Reverses the last command or action, or deletes the last entry typed		Sort Descending	Sorts the selected items in descending sequence
	Cut	Removes the selection and places it on the Office Clipboard		AutoFilter	Selects specific items you want to display in a list
	Copy	Copy the selection to the Office Clipboard		Refresh All	Refreshes data when connected to the Web
	Paste	Inserts the most recent item placed on the Office Clipboard		Export to Excel	Opens the Web page as a workbook in Excel
	AutoSum	Inserts the SUM function in a cell and selects a range to sum		Commands and Options	Displays the Commands and Options dialog box
				Help	Displays Microsoft Office 2003 Spreadsheet Components Help

---

More About

Microsoft Certification

The Microsoft Office Specialist Certification program provides an opportunity for you to obtain a valuable industry credential — proof that you have the Excel 2003 skills required by employers. For more information, see Appendix E or visit the Excel 2003 Certification Web page (scsite.com/ex2003/cert).

In general, the Spreadsheet toolbar allows you to add formulas, format, sort, and export the Web page to Excel. Many additional Excel capabilities are available through the Commands and Options dialog box. You display the Commands and Options dialog box by clicking the Commands and Options button on the Spreadsheet toolbar. When Excel displays the Command and Options dialog box, click the Format tab. The Format sheet makes formatting options, such as bold, italic, underline, font color, font style, and font size, available through your browser for the purpose of formatting cells in the worksheet below the 3-D Pie chart on the Web page.

Modifying the dynamic Web page does not change the makeup of the original workbook or the Web page stored on disk, even if you use the Save As command on the browser's File menu. If you do use the Save As command in your browser, it will save the original mht file without any changes you might have made. You can, however, use the Export to Excel button on the Spreadsheet toolbar to create a workbook that will include any changes you made in your browser. The Export to Excel button only saves the worksheet and not the chart.

Web Feature Summary

This Web feature introduced you to previewing a workbook as a Web page, creating a new folder on disk, and publishing and viewing two types of Web pages: static and dynamic. Whereas the static Web page is a snapshot of the workbook, a dynamic Web page adds functionality and interactivity to the Web page. Besides changing the data and generating new results with a dynamic Web page, you also learned how to use your browser to add formulas and change the formats to improve the appearance of the Web page.

 If you have a SAM user profile, you may have access to hands-on instruction, practice, and assessment of the skills covered in this project. Log in to your SAM account and go to your assignments page to see what your instructor has assigned.

What You Should Know

Having completed this Web feature, you should be able to perform the tasks listed below. The tasks are listed in the same order they were presented in this Web feature. For a list of the buttons, menus, toolbars, and commands introduced in this Web feature, see the Quick Reference Summary at the back of this book and refer to the Page Number column.

1. Preview the Workbook as a Web Page   (EX 228)
2. Save an Excel Workbook as a Static Web Page in a Newly Created Folder   (EX 230)
3. View and Manipulate the Static Web Page Using a Browser   (EX 233)
4. Save an Excel Chart as a Dynamic Web Page   (EX 234)
5. View and Manipulate the Dynamic Web Page Using a Browser   (EX 236)

1 Creating Static and Dynamic Web Pages I

Problem: You are a student employed part-time as a spreadsheet specialist by Awesome Intranets. Your supervisor has asked you to create a static Web page and dynamic Web page from the company's annual sales workbook.

Instructions Part 1:   Start Excel and open the Lab WF-1 Awesome Intranets Annual Sales workbook from the Data Disk. Perform the following tasks:

1. Review the worksheet and chart so you have an idea of what the workbook contains. Preview the workbook as a Web page. Close the browser.
2. Save the workbook as a single file Web page in a new folder titled Web Feature Exercises on the Data Disk in drive A using the file name, Lab WF-1 Awesome Intranets Annual Sales Static Web Page. Make sure you select Entire Workbook in the Save area before you click the Save button. Quit Excel.
3. Start your browser. Type a:\web feature exercises\lab wf-1 awesome intranets annual sales static web page.mht in the Address box. When the browser displays the Web page, click the tabs at the bottom of the window to view the sheets. As you view each sheet, print it in landscape orientation. Close the browser.

Instructions Part 2:   Start Excel and open the Lab WF-1 Awesome Intranets Annual Sales workbook from the Data Disk. Perform the following tasks:

1. Click File on the menu bar and then click Save as Web Page. Use the Publish button to save the workbook as a single file Web page in the Web Feature Exercises folder on the Data Disk in drive A using the file name, Lab WF-1 Awesome Intranets Annual Sales Dynamic Web Page. In the Publish as Web Page dialog box, select Items on Bar Chart in the Choose list and click the Add Interactivity with check box to add chart functionality. Click the Publish button. Quit Excel.
2. Start your browser. Type a:\web feature exercises\lab wf-1 awesome intranets annual sales dynamic web page.mht in the Address box. When the browser displays the Web page, click cell B6 and then click the AutoSum button on the Spreadsheet toolbar twice. Cell B6 should equal $8,948,686. Print the Web page.
3. Update the range B1:B5 by entering the following gross sales: East = 1,545,000; North = 1,111,250; South = 1,500,300; West = 1,400,000; and International = 1,250,000. Cell B6 should equal $6,806,550. Print the Web page. Close the browser.

In the Lab

2 Creating Static and Dynamic Web Pages II

Problem: You are the spreadsheet analyst for Hard Disk Storage Plus. You have been asked to create a static Web page and dynamic Web page from the workbook that the company uses to project sales and payroll expenses.

Instructions Part 1: Start Excel and open the Lab WF-2 Hard Disk Storage Plus Projections workbook from the Data Disk. Perform the following tasks:

1. Display the 3-D Pie Chart sheet. Redisplay the Projected Expenses sheet. Preview the workbook as a Web page. Close the browser.

2. Save the workbook as a Web page (select Web Page in the Save as type box) in the Web Feature Exercises folder on the Data Disk in drive A using the file name, Lab WF-2 Hard Disk Storage Plus Projections Static Web Page. Make sure you select Entire Workbook in the Save area before you click the Save button. Quit Excel. Saving the workbook as a Web page, rather than a single file Web page, will result in an additional folder being added to the Web Feature Exercises folder.

3. Start your browser. Type a:\web feature exercises\lab wf-2 hard disk storage plus projections static web page.htm in the Address box. When the browser displays the Web page, click the tabs at the bottom of the window to view the sheets. Print each sheet in landscape orientation. Close the browser.

Instructions Part 2: Start Excel and open the Lab WF-2 Hard Disk Storage Plus Projections workbook from the Data Disk. Perform the following tasks:

1. Click File on the menu bar and then click Save as Web Page. Use the Publish button to save the workbook as a single file Web page in the Web Feature Exercises folder on the Data Disk in drive A using the file name, Lab WF-2 Hard Disk Storage Plus Projections Dynamic Web Page. In the Publish as Web Page dialog box, select Items on 3-D Pie Chart in the Choose list and click the Add Interactivity with check box to add chart functionality. Click the Publish button. Quit Excel.

2. Start your browser. Type a:\web feature exercises\lab wf-2 hard disk storage plus projections dynamic web page.mht in the Address box. When the browser displays the Web page, print it in landscape orientation.

3. Scroll down and change the values of the following cells: cell B15 = 28%; cell B16 = 4.5%; cell B17 = 25,000; cell B19 = 20.25%; and cell B20 = 7.75%. Cell H12 should equal $3,555,899.49. The 3-D Pie chart should change to show the new contributions to the projected payroll expenses. Close the browser.

3 File Management within Excel

Problem: Your manager at Hard Disk Storage Plus as asked you to teach him to complete basic file management tasks from within Excel.

Instructions: Start Excel and click the Open button on the Standard toolbar. When Excel displays the Open dialog box, create a new folder called In the Lab 3 on the Data Disk in drive A. Click the Up One Level button to reselect 3½ Floppy (A:) in the Look in box. Use the shortcut menu to complete the following tasks: (1) rename the In the Lab 3 folder to In the Lab 4; (2) show the properties of the In the Lab 4 folder; and (3) delete the In the Lab 4 folder.

Appendix A

Microsoft Excel Help System

Using the Excel Help System

This appendix shows you how to use the Excel Help system. At anytime while you are using Excel, you can interact with its Help system and display information on any Excel topic. It is a complete reference manual at your fingertips.

As shown in Figure A-1, five methods for accessing the Excel Help system are available:

1. Microsoft Excel Help button on the Standard toolbar
2. Microsoft Excel Help command on the Help menu
3. Function key F1 on the keyboard
4. Type a question for help box on the menu bar
5. Office Assistant

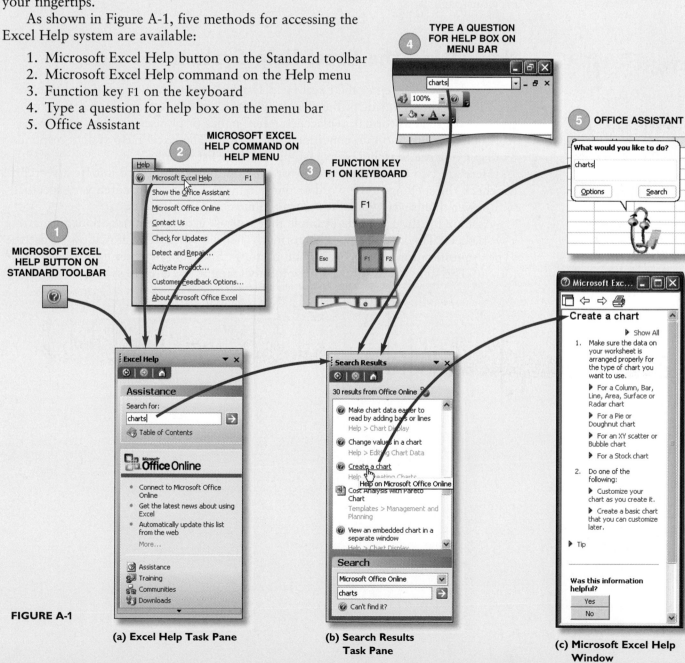

FIGURE A-1

(a) Excel Help Task Pane

(b) Search Results Task Pane

(c) Microsoft Excel Help Window

All five methods result in the Excel Help system displaying a task pane on the right side of the Excel window. The first three methods cause the **Excel Help task pane** to appear (Figure A-1a on the previous page). This task pane includes a Search text box in which you can enter a word or phrase on which you want help. Once you enter the word or phrase, the Excel Help system displays the Search Results task pane (Figure A-1b on the previous page). With the Search Results task pane displayed, you can select specific Help topics.

As shown in Figure A-1, methods 4 and 5 bypass the Excel Help task pane and immediately display the **Search Results task pane** (Figure A-1b) with a list of links that pertain to the selected topic. Thus, the result of any of the five methods for accessing the Excel Help system is the Search Results task pane. Once the Excel Help system displays this task pane, you can choose links that relate to the word or phrase on which you searched. In Figure A-1, for example, charts was the searched topic (Create a chart), which resulted in the Excel Help system displaying the Microsoft Excel Help window with information about creating charts (Figure A-1c on the previous page).

Navigating the Excel Help System

The quickest way to enter the Excel Help system is through the Type a question for help box on the right side of the menu bar at the top of the screen. Here you can type words, such as format, replace, or freeze panes or phrases, such as preview a workbook, or how do I do conditional formatting. The Excel Help system responds by displaying the Search Results task pane with a list of links.

Here are two tips regarding the words or phrases you enter to initiate a search: (1) check the spelling of the word or phrase; and (2) keep your search very specific, with fewer than seven words, to return the most accurate results.

Assume for the following example that you want to learn more about formatting a worksheet. The likely keyword is format. The following steps show how to use the Type a question for help box to obtain useful information by entering the keyword format. The steps also show you how to navigate the Excel Help system.

To Obtain Help Using the Type a Question for Help Box

1

• **Click the Type a question for help box on the right side of the menu bar, type** format **and then press the ENTER key.**

The Excel Help system displays the Search Results task pane on the right side of the window. The Search Results task pane includes 30 resulting links (Figure A-2). If you do not find what you are looking for, you can modify or refine the search in the Search area at the bottom of the Search Results task pane. The results returned in your Search Results task pane may be different.

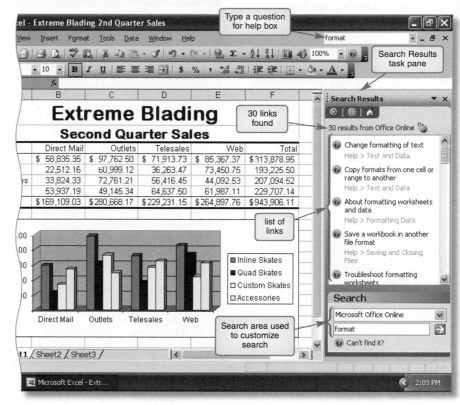

FIGURE A-2

2

• **Click the About formatting worksheets and data link in the Search Results task pane.**

• **When Excel displays the Microsoft Excel Help window, if necessary, click its Auto Tile button in the upper-right corner of the window (Figure A-4 on the next page) to tile the windows.**

Excel displays the Microsoft Excel Help window with the desired information (Figure A-3). With the Microsoft Excel Help window and Microsoft Excel window tiled, you can read the information in one window and complete the task in the other window.

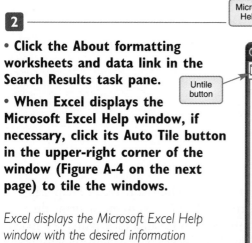

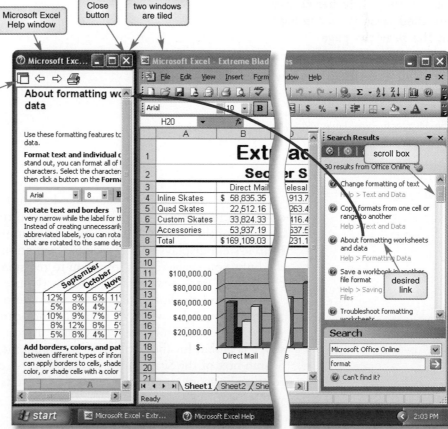

FIGURE A-3

3

• **Double-click the Microsoft Excel Help window title bar.**

• **Click the Show All link in the upper-right corner of the window.**

• **After reviewing the information, click the Hide All link that replaced the Show All link.**

The Microsoft Excel Help window is maximized so it fills the entire screen (Figure A-4). If you are connected to the Internet, you can give Microsoft your opinion as to whether the information was helpful by clicking the Yes or No button at the bottom of the page. The Show All link expands the coverage of information and the Hide All link condenses the information displayed on the topic in the Microsoft Excel Help window.

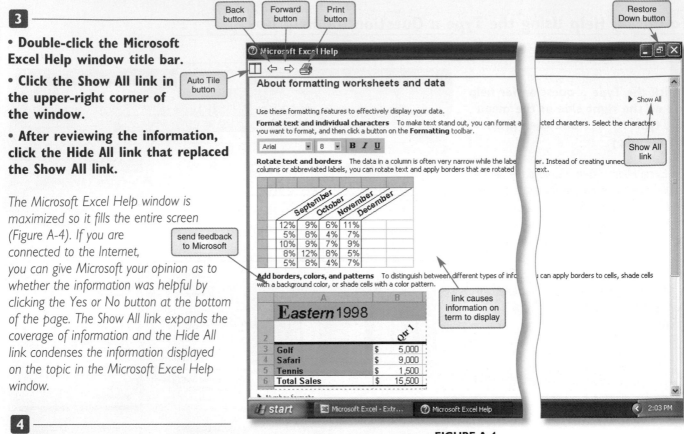

FIGURE A-4

4

• **Click the Restore Down button on the right side of the Microsoft Excel Help window title bar to return to the tiled state shown in Figure A-3 on the previous page.**

• **Click the Close button on the Microsoft Excel Help window title bar.**

The Microsoft Excel Help window is closed and the worksheet is active.

Use the four buttons in the upper-left corner of the Microsoft Excel Help window (Figure A-4) to tile or untile, navigate through the Help system, or print the contents of the window. As you click links in the Search Results task pane, the Excel Help system displays new pages of information. The Excel Help system remembers the links you visited and allows you to redisplay the pages visited during a session by clicking the Back and Forward buttons (Figure A-4).

If none of the links presents the information you want, you can refine the search by entering another word or phrase in the Search text box in the Search Results task pane (Figure A-2 on the previous page). If you have access to the Web, then the scope is global for the initial search. **Global** means all the categories listed in the Search box of the Search area in Figure A-5 are searched. For example, you can, restrict the scope to **Offline Help**, which results in a search of related links only on your hard disk.

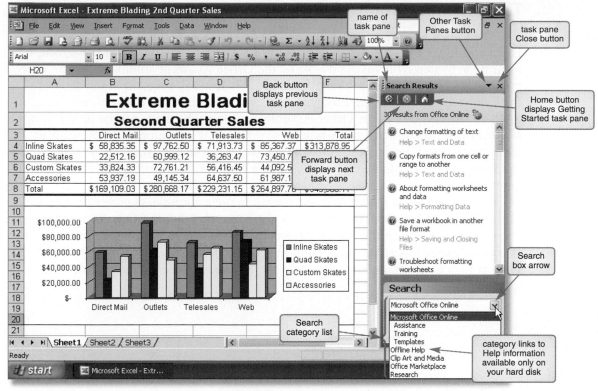

FIGURE A-5

Figure A-5 shows several additional features of the Search Results task pane with which you should be familiar. The buttons immediately below the name of the task pane allow you to navigate between task panes. The Other Task Panes button and the Close button on the Search Results task pane title bar let you change task panes and close the active task pane.

As you enter questions and terms in the Type a question for help box, the Excel Help system adds them to its list. Thus, if you click the Type a question for help box arrow, a list of previously used words and phrases are displayed (Figure A-6).

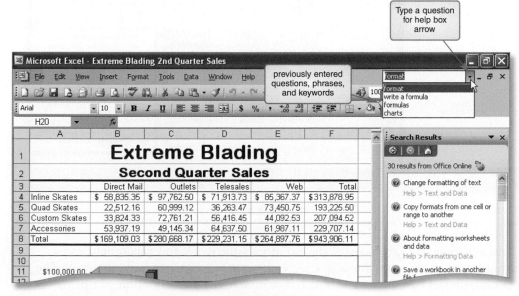

FIGURE A-6

The Office Assistant

The **Office Assistant** is an icon (middle of Figure A-7) that Excel displays in the Excel window while you work. For the Office Assistant to appear on the screen, it must be activated by invoking the Show the Office Assistant command on the Help menu. This Help tool has multiple functions. First, it will respond in the same way as the Type a question for help box with a list of topics that relate to the entry you make in the text box in the Office Assistant balloon. The entry can be in the form of a word or phrase as if you were talking to a person. For example, if you want to learn more about writing a formula, in the balloon text box, you can type any of the following words or phrases: formula, write a formula, how do I write a formula, or anything similar.

In the example in Figure A-7, the phrase, write a formula, is entered into the Office Assistant balloon. After you click the Search button, the Office Assistant responds by displaying the Search Results task pane with a list of links from which you can choose. Once you click a link in the Search Results task pane, the Excel Help system displays the information in the Microsoft Excel Help window (Figure A-7).

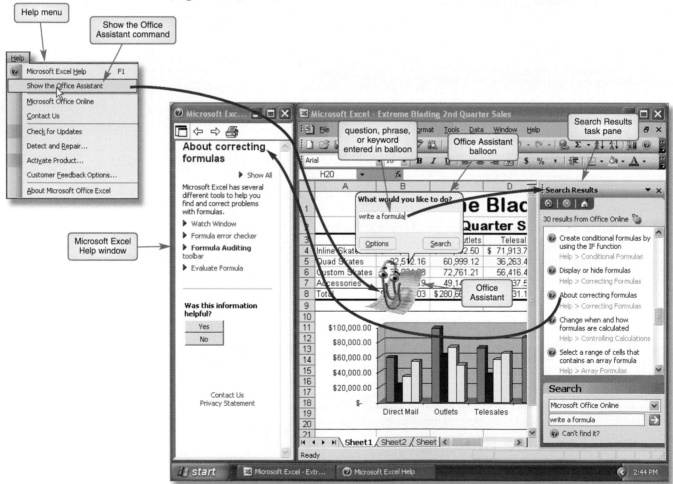

FIGURE A-7

In addition, the Office Assistant monitors your work and accumulates tips during a session on how you might increase your productivity and efficiency. The accumulation of tips must be enabled. You enable the accumulation of tips by right-clicking the Office Assistant, clicking Options on the shortcut menu, and then selecting the types of tips you want accumulated. You can view the tips at anytime. The accumulated tips appear when you activate the Office Assistant balloon. Also, if at anytime you see a light bulb above the Office Assistant, click it to display the most recent tip. If the Office Assistant is hidden, then the light bulb shows on the Microsoft Excel Help button on the Standard toolbar.

You hide the Office Assistant by invoking the Hide the Office Assistant command on the Help menu or by right-clicking the Office Assistant and then clicking Hide on the shortcut menu. The Hide the Office Assistant command shows on the Help menu only when the Office Assistant is active in the Excel window. If the Office Assistant begins showing up on your screen without you instructing it to show, then right-click the Office Assistant, click Options on the shortcut menu, click the Use the Office Assistant check box to remove the check mark, and then click the OK button.

If the Office Assistant is active in the Excel window, then Excel displays all program and system messages in the Office Assistant balloon.

You may or may not want the Office Assistant to display on the screen at all times. As indicated earlier, you can hide it and then show it later through the Help menu. For more information about the Office Assistant, type office assistant in the Type a question for help box and then click the links in the Search Results task pane.

Help Buttons in Dialog Boxes and Subsystem Windows

As you invoke commands that display dialog boxes or other windows, such as the Print Preview window, you will see buttons and links that offer helpful information. Figure A-8 shows the types of Help buttons and links you will see as you work with Excel.

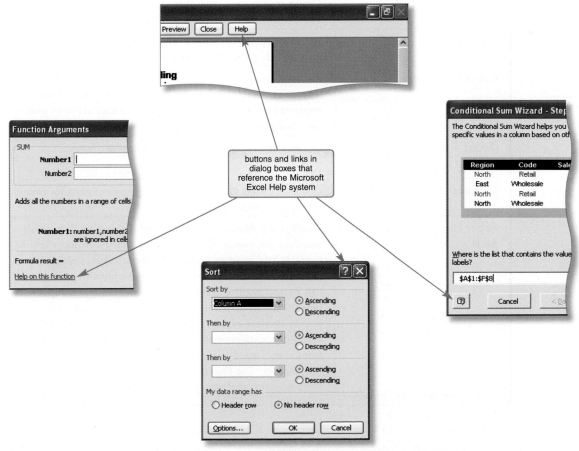

FIGURE A-8

Other Help Commands on the Help Menu

Thus far, this appendix has discussed the first two commands on the Help menu: (1) the Microsoft Excel Help command (Figure A-1 on page APP 1) and (2) the Show the Office Assistant command (Figure A-7 on page APP 6). Several additional commands are available on the Help menu as shown in Figure A-9. Table A-1 summarizes these commands.

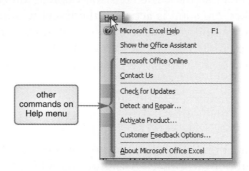

FIGURE A-9

Table A-1	Summary of Other Help Commands on the Help Menu
COMMAND ON HELP MENU	**FUNCTION**
Microsoft Office Online	Activates your browser, which displays the Microsoft Office Online Home page. The Microsoft Office Online Home page contains links that can improve your Office productivity.
Contact Us	Activates your browser, which displays Microsoft contact information and a list of useful links.
Check for Updates	Activates your browser, which displays a list of updates to Office. These updates can be downloaded and installed to improve the efficiency of Office or to fix an error in one or more of the Office applications.
Detect and Repair	Detects and repairs errors in the Excel program.
Activate Product	Activates Excel if it has not already been activated.
Customer Feedback Options	Gives or denies Microsoft permission to collect anonymous information about your hardware.
About Microsoft Office Excel	Displays the About Microsoft Excel dialog box. The dialog box lists the owner of the software and the product identification. You need to know the product identification if you call Microsoft for assistance. The three buttons below the OK button are the System Info button, the Tech Support button, and the Disabled Items button. The System Info button displays system information, including hardware resources, components, software environment, and applications. The Tech Support button displays technical assistance information. The Disabled Items button displays a list of disabled items that prevents Excel from functioning properly.

Use Help

1 Using the Type a Question for Help Box

Instructions: Perform the following tasks using the Excel Help system.

1. Use the Type a question for help box on the menu bar to get help on entering formulas.
2. Click Create a formula in the list of links in the Search Results task pane. Tile the windows. Double-click the Microsoft Excel Help window title bar to maximize it. Click the Show All button. Read and print the information. At the top of the printout, write down the number of links the Excel Help system found.
3. One at a time, click two additional links in the Search Results task pane and print the information. Hand in the printouts to your instructor. Use the Back and Forward buttons to return to the original page.
4. Use the Type a question for help box to search for information on IF functions. Click the IF link in the Search Results task pane. When the Microsoft Excel Help window is displayed, maximize the window. Read and print the information. One at a time, click the links on the page and print the information for any new page that is displayed. Close the Microsoft Excel Help window.
5. For each of the following words and phrases, click one link in the Search Results task pane, click the Show All link, and then print the page: text; date; statistical functions; logical functions; autoformat; conditional formatting; and what-if analysis.

2 Expanding on the Excel Help System Basics

Instructions: Use the Excel Help system to understand the topics better and answer the questions listed below. Answer the questions on your own paper, or hand in the printed Help information to your instructor.

1. Show the Office Assistant. Right-click the Office Assistant and then click Animate! on the shortcut menu. Repeat invoking the Animate command to see various animations. Right-click the Office Assistant, click Options on the shortcut menu, click the Reset my tips button, and then click the OK button. Click the light bulb above the Office Assistant if it appears. When you see the light bulb, it indicates that the Office Assistant has a tip to share with you.
2. Use the Office Assistant to find help on undoing tasks. Print the Help information for three links in the Search Results task pane. Close the Microsoft Excel Help window. Hand in the printouts to your instructor. Hide the Office Assistant.
3. Press the F1 key. Search for information on Help. Click the first two links in the Search Results task pane. Read and print the information for both.
4. One at a time, invoke the first three commands in Table A-1. Print each page. Click two links on one of the pages and print the information. Hand in the printouts to your instructor.
5. Click About Microsoft Office Excel on the Help menu. Click the Tech Support button and print the resulting page. Click the System Info button. Below the Components category, print the CD-ROM and Display information. Hand in the printouts to your instructor.

Appendix B

Speech and Handwriting Recognition and Speech Playback

Introduction

This appendix discusses the Office capability that allows users to create and modify worksheets using its alternative input technologies available through **text services**. Office provides a variety of text services, which enable you to speak commands and enter text in an application. The most common text service is the keyboard. Other text services include speech recognition and handwriting recognition.

The Language Bar

The **Language bar** allows you to use text services in the Office applications. You can utilize the Language bar in one of three states: (1) in a restored state as a floating toolbar in the Excel window (Figure B-1a or Figure B-1b if Text Labels are enabled); (2) in a minimized state docked next to the notification area on the Windows taskbar (Figure B-1c); or (3) hidden (temporarily closed and out of the way). If the Language bar is hidden, you can activate it by right-clicking the Windows taskbar, pointing to Toolbars on the shortcut menu (Figure B-1d), and clicking Language bar on the Toolbars submenu. If you want to close the Language bar, right-click the Language bar and then click Close the Language bar on the shortcut menu (Figure B-1e).

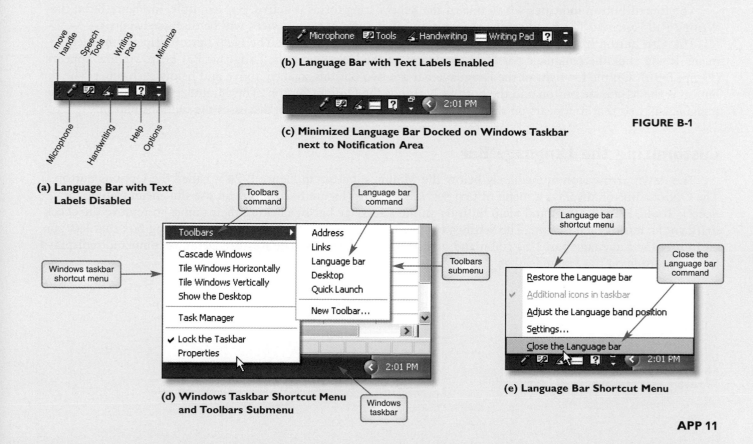

(b) **Language Bar with Text Labels Enabled**

(c) **Minimized Language Bar Docked on Windows Taskbar next to Notification Area**

FIGURE B-1

(a) **Language Bar with Text Labels Disabled**

(d) **Windows Taskbar Shortcut Menu and Toolbars Submenu**

(e) **Language Bar Shortcut Menu**

When Windows was installed on your computer, the installer specified a default language. For example, most users in the United States select English (United States) as the default language. You can add more than 90 additional languages and varying dialects such as Basque, English (Zimbabwe), French (France), French (Canada), German (Germany), German (Austria), and Swahili. With multiple languages available, you can switch from one language to another while working in Excel. If you change the language or dialect, then text services may change the functions of the keys on the keyboard, adjust speech recognition, and alter handwriting recognition. If a second language is activated, then a Language icon appears immediately to the right of the move handle on the Language bar. This appendix assumes that English (United States) is the only language installed. Thus, the Language icon does not appear in the examples in Figure B-1 on the previous page.

Buttons on the Language Bar

The Language bar shown in Figure B-2a contains seven buttons. The number of buttons on your Language bar may be different. These buttons are used to select the language, customize the Language bar, control the microphone, control handwriting, and obtain help.

The first button on the left is the Microphone button, which enables and disables the microphone. When the microphone is enabled, text services adds two buttons and a balloon to the Language bar (Figure B-2b). These additional buttons and the balloon will be discussed shortly.

The second button from the left is the Speech Tools button. The Speech Tools button displays a menu of commands (Figure B-2c) that allow you to hide or show the balloon on the Language bar; train the Speech Recognition service so that it can interpret your voice better; add and delete words from its dictionary, such as names and other words not understood easily; and change the user profile so more than one person can use the microphone on the same computer.

The third button from the left on the Language bar is the Handwriting button. The Handwriting button displays the Handwriting menu (Figure B-2d), which lets you choose the Writing Pad (Figure B-2e), Write Anywhere (Figure B-2f), or the on-screen keyboard (Figure B-2g). The On-Screen Symbol Keyboard command on the Handwriting menu displays an on-screen keyboard that allows you to enter special symbols that are not available on a standard keyboard. You can choose only one form of handwriting at a time.

The fourth button indicates which one of the handwriting forms is active. For example, in Figure B-2a, the Writing Pad is active. The handwriting recognition capabilities of text services will be discussed shortly.

The fifth button from the left on the Language bar is the Help button. The Help button displays the Help menu. If you click the Language Bar Help command on the Help menu, the Language Bar Help window appears (Figure B-2h). On the far right of the Language bar are two buttons stacked above and below each other. The top button is the Minimize button and the bottom button is the Options button. The Minimize button minimizes the Language bar so that it appears on the Windows taskbar. The next section discusses the Options button.

Customizing the Language Bar

The down arrow icon immediately below the Minimize button in Figure B-2a is called the Options button. The Options button displays a menu of text services options (Figure B-2i). You can use this menu to hide the Speech Tools, Handwriting, and Help buttons on the Language bar by clicking their names to remove the check mark to the left of each button. The Settings command on the Options menu displays a dialog box that lets you customize the Language bar. This command will be discussed shortly. The Restore Defaults command redisplays hidden buttons on the Language bar.

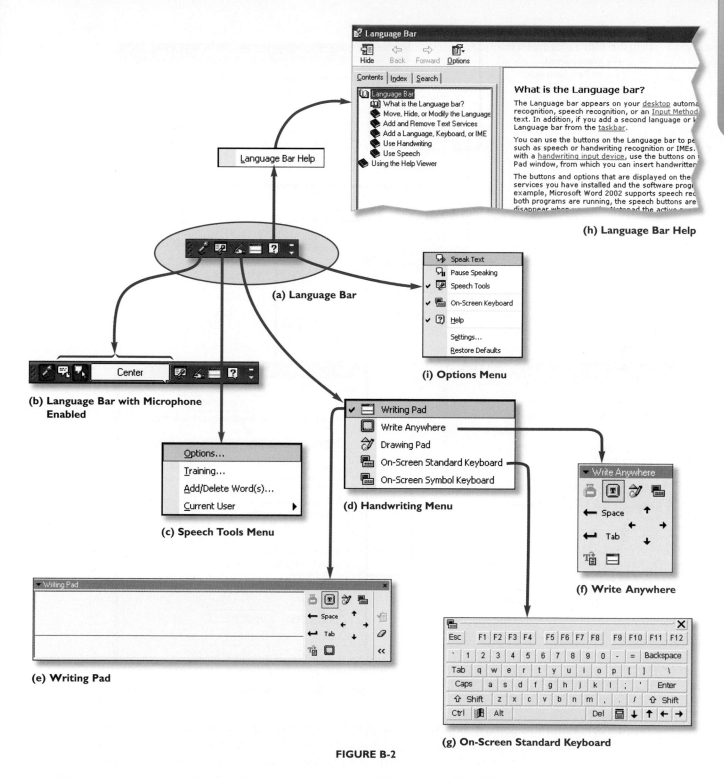

(a) Language Bar

(b) Language Bar with Microphone Enabled

(c) Speech Tools Menu

(d) Handwriting Menu

(e) Writing Pad

(f) Write Anywhere

(g) On-Screen Standard Keyboard

(h) Language Bar Help

(i) Options Menu

FIGURE B-2

If you right-click the Language bar, a shortcut menu appears (Figure B-3a on the next page). This shortcut menu lets you further customize the Language bar. The Minimize command on the shortcut menu docks the Language bar on the Windows taskbar. The Transparency command in Figure B-3a toggles the Language bar between being solid and transparent. You can see through a transparent Language bar (Figure B-3b). The Text Labels command toggles on text labels on the Language bar (Figure B-3c) and off (Figure B-3b).

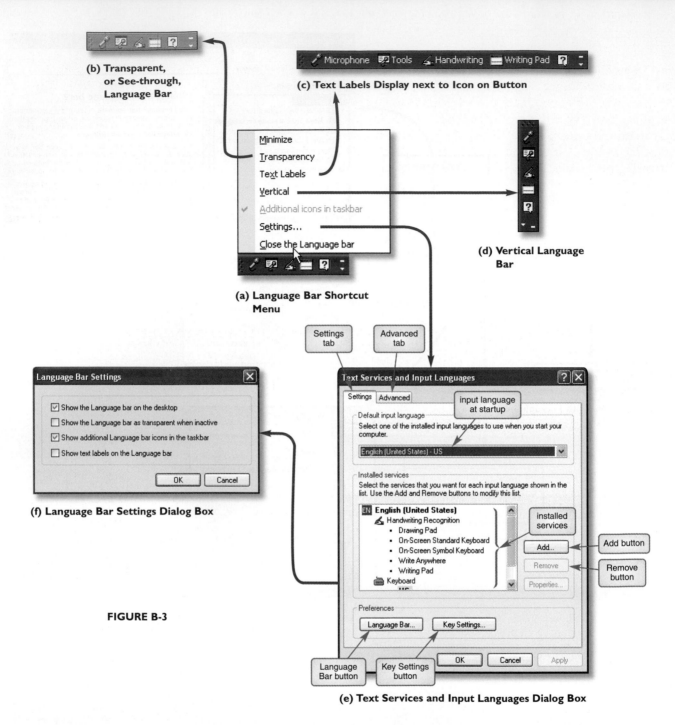

FIGURE B-3

The Settings command in Figure B-3a displays the Text Services and Input Languages dialog box (Figure B-3e). The Text Services and Input Languages dialog box allows you to add additonal languages, add and remove text services, modify keys on the keyboard, modify the Language bar, and extend support of advanced text services to all programs, including Notepad and other programs that normally do not support text services (through the Advanced tab). If you want to remove any one of the services in the Installed services list, select the service, and then click the Remove button. If you want to add a service, click the Add button. The Key Settings button allows you to modify the keyboard. If you click the Language Bar button in the Text Services and Input Languages dialog box, the Language Bar Settings dialog box appears (Figure B-3f). This dialog box contains Language bar options, some of which are the same as the commands on the Language bar shortcut menu shown in Figure B-3a.

The Close the Language bar command on the shortcut menu shown in Figure B-3a closes or hides the Language bar. If you close the Language bar and want to redisplay it, see Figure B-1d on page APP 11.

Speech Recognition

The **Speech Recognition service** available with Office enables your computer to recognize human speech through a microphone. The microphone has two modes: Dictation and Voice Command (Figure B-4). You switch between the two modes by clicking the Dictation button and the Voice Command button on the Language bar. These buttons appear only when you turn on Speech Recognition by clicking the Microphone button on the Language bar (Figure B-5a on the next page). If you are using the Microphone button for the very first time in Excel, it will require that you check your microphone settings and step through voice training before activating the Speech Recognition service.

The Dictation button places the microphone in Dictation mode. In **Dictation mode**, whatever you speak is entered as text in the active cell. The Voice Command button places the microphone in Voice Command mode. In **Voice Command mode**, whatever you speak is interpreted as a command. If you want to turn off the microphone, click the Microphone button on the Language bar or in Voice Command mode, say "Mic off" (pronounced mike off). It is important to remember that minimizing the Language bar does not turn off the microphone.

(a) Enter Text in the Active Cell (A1) in Dictation Mode

(b) Enter Commands in Voice Command Mode

FIGURE B-4

The Language bar speech message balloon shown in Figure B-5b displays messages that may offer help or hints. In Voice Command mode, the name of the last recognized command you said appears. If you use the mouse or keyboard instead of the microphone, a message will appear in the Language bar speech message balloon indicating the word you could say. In Dictation mode, the message, Dictating, usually appears. The Speech Recognition service, however, will display messages to inform you that you are talking too soft, too loud, too fast, or to ask you to repeat what you said by displaying, What was that?

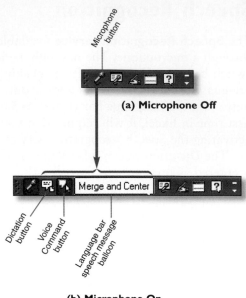

(a) Microphone Off

(b) Microphone On

FIGURE B-5

Getting Started with Speech Recognition

For the microphone to function properly, you should follow these steps:

1. Make sure your computer meets the minimum requirements.
2. Start Excel. Activate Speech Recognition by clicking Tools on the menu bar, pointing to Speech, and then clicking Speech Recognition on the Speech submenu.
3. Set up and position your microphone, preferably a close-talk headset with gain adjustment support.
4. Train Speech Recognition.

The following sections describe these steps in more detail.

SPEECH RECOGNITION SYSTEM REQUIREMENTS   For Speech Recognition to work on your computer, it needs the following:

1. Microsoft Windows 98 or later or Microsoft Windows NT 4.0 or later
2. At least 128 MB RAM
3. 400 MHz or faster processor
4. Microphone and sound card

SETUP AND POSITION YOUR MICROPHONE   Set up your microphone as follows:

1. Connect your microphone to the sound card in the back of the computer.
2. Position the microphone approximately one inch out from and to the side of your mouth. Position it so you are not breathing into it.
3. On the Language bar, click the Speech Tools button, and then click Options on the Speech Tools menu (Figure B-6a).
4. When text services displays the Speech input settings dialog box (Figure B-6b), click the Advanced Speech button. When text services displays the Speech Properties dialog box (Figure B-6c), click the Speech Recognition tab.
5. Click the Configure Microphone button. Follow the Microphone Wizard directions as shown in Figures B-6d, B-6e, and B-6f. The Next button will remain dimmed in Figure B-6e until the volume meter consistently stays in the green area.
6. If someone else installed Speech Recognition, click the New button in the Speech Properties dialog box and enter your name. Click the Train Profile button and step through the Voice Training dialog boxes. The Voice Training dialog boxes will require that you enter your gender and age group. It then will step you through voice training.

You can adjust the microphone further by clicking the Settings button in the Speech Properties dialog box (Figure B-6c). The Settings button displays the Recognition Profile Settings dialog box that allows you to adjust the pronunciation sensitivity and accuracy versus recognition response time.

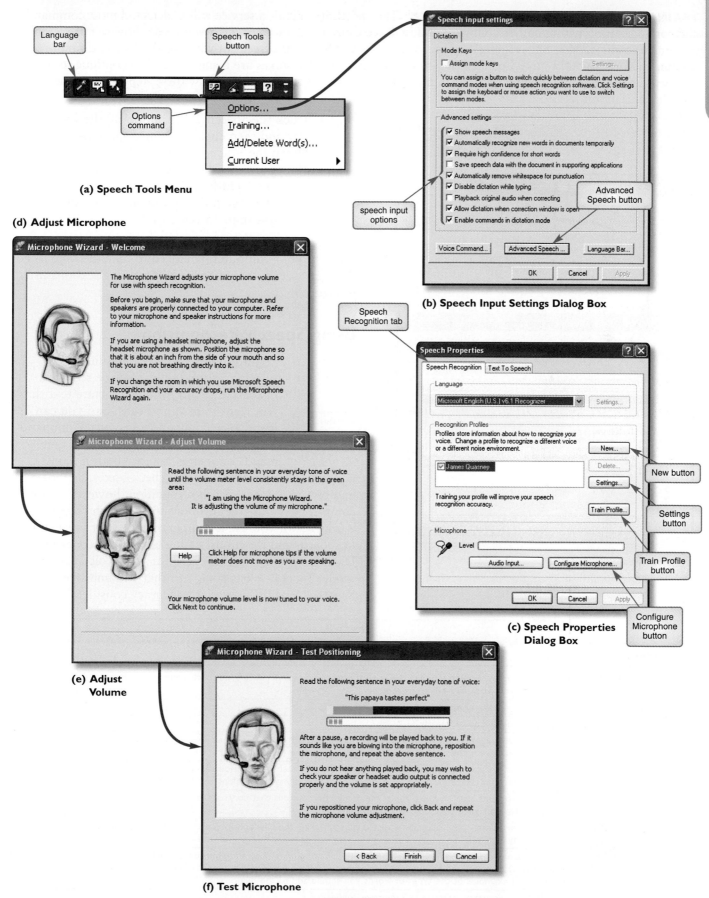

(a) **Speech Tools Menu**

(b) **Speech Input Settings Dialog Box**

(c) **Speech Properties Dialog Box**

(d) **Adjust Microphone**

(e) **Adjust Volume**

(f) **Test Microphone**

FIGURE B-6

TRAIN THE SPEECH RECOGNITION SERVICE The Speech Recognition service will understand most commands and some dictation without any training at all. It will recognize much more of what you speak, however, if you take the time to train it. After one training session, it will recognize 85 to 90 percent of your words. As you do more training, accuracy will rise to 95 percent. If you feel that too many mistakes are being made, then continue to train the service. The more training you do, the more accurately it will work for you. Follow these steps to train the Speech Recognition service:

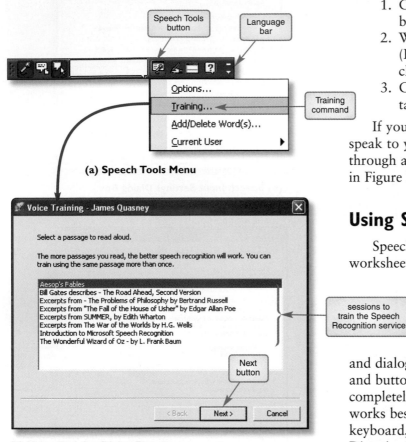

(a) Speech Tools Menu

(b) Voice Training Dialog Box

FIGURE B-7

1. Click the Speech Tools button on the Language bar and then click Training (Figure B-7a).
2. When the Voice Training dialog box appears (Figure B-7b), click one of the sessions and then click the Next button.
3. Complete the training session, which should take less than 15 minutes.

If you are serious about using a microphone to speak to your computer, you need to take the time to go through at least three of the eight training sessions listed in Figure B-7b.

Using Speech Recognition

Speech recognition lets you enter text into a worksheet similarly to speaking into a tape recorder. Instead of typing, you can dictate text that you want to assign to cells, and you can issue voice commands. In Voice Command mode, you can speak menu names, commands on menus, toolbar button names, and dialog box option buttons, check boxes, list boxes, and button names. Speech recognition, however, is not a completely hands-free form of input. Speech recognition works best if you use a combination of your voice, the keyboard, and the mouse. You soon will discover that Dictation mode is far less accurate than Voice Command mode. Table B-1 lists some tips that will improve the Speech Recognition service's accuracy considerably.

Table B-1	Tips to Improve Speech Recognition
NUMBER	**TIP**
1	The microphone hears everything. Though the Speech Recognition service filters out background noise, it is recommended that you work in a quiet environment.
2	Try not to move the microphone around once it is adjusted.
3	Speak in a steady tone and speak clearly.
4	In Dictation mode, do not pause between words. A phrase is easier to interpret than a word. Sounding out syllables in a word will make it more difficult for the Speech Recognition service to interpret what you are saying.
5	If you speak too loudly or too softly, it makes it difficult for the Speech Recognition service to interpret what you said. Check the Language bar speech message balloon for an indication that you may be speaking too loudly or too softly.
6	If you experience problems after training, adjust the recognition options that control accuracy and rejection by clicking the Settings button shown in Figure B-6c on the previous page.
7	When you are finished using the microphone, turn it off by clicking the Microphone button on the Language bar or in Voice Command mode, say "Mic off." Leaving the microphone on is the same as leaning on the keyboard.
8	If the Speech Recognition service is having difficulty with unusual words, then add the words to its dictionary by using the Add/Delete Word(s) command on the Speech Tools menu (Figure B-8a). The last names of individuals and the names of companies are good examples of the types of words you should add to the dictionary.
9	Training will improve accuracy; practice will improve confidence.

The last command on the Speech Tools menu is the Current User command (Figure B-8a). The Current User command is useful for multiple users who share a computer. It allows them to configure their own individual profiles, and then switch between users as they use the computer.

For additional information on the Speech Recognition service, enter speech recognition in the Type a question for help box on the menu bar.

Handwriting Recognition

Using the Office **Handwriting Recognition service**, you can enter text and numbers into Excel by writing instead of typing. You can write using a special handwriting device that connects to your computer or you can write on the screen using your mouse. Four basic methods of handwriting are available by clicking the Handwriting button on the Language bar: Writing Pad; Write Anywhere; Drawing Pad; and On-Screen Keyboard. The Drawing Pad button is not available in Excel. Although the on-screen keyboard does not involve handwriting recognition, it is part of the Handwriting menu and, therefore, will be discussed in this section.

If your Language bar does not include the Handwriting button, then for installation instructions, enter install handwriting recognition in the Type a question for help box on the menu bar.

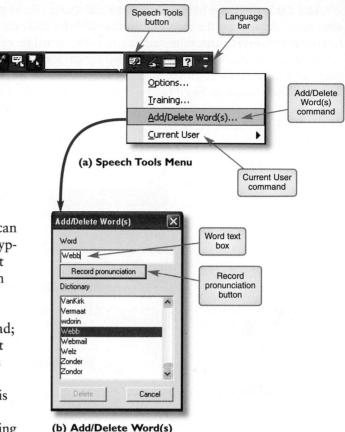

(a) Speech Tools Menu

(b) Add/Delete Word(s) Dialog Box

FIGURE B-8

Writing Pad

To display the Writing Pad, click the Handwriting button on the Language bar and then click Writing Pad (Figure B-9). The **Writing Pad** resembles a notepad with one or more lines on which you can use freehand to print or write in cursive. With the Text button enabled, you can form letters on the line by moving the mouse while holding down the mouse button. To the right of the notepad is a rectangular toolbar. Use the buttons on this toolbar to adjust the Writing Pad, select cells, and activate other handwriting applications.

FIGURE B-9

Consider the example in Figure B-9 on the previous page. With cell A1 selected, the word, Computers, is written in cursive on the **Pen line** in the Writing Pad. As soon as the word is complete, the Handwriting Recognition service automatically assigns the word to cell A1.

You can customize the Writing Pad by clicking the Options button on the left side of the title bar and then clicking the Options command (Figure B-10a). Invoking the Options command causes the Handwriting Options dialog box to display. The Handwriting Options dialog box contains two sheets: Common and Writing Pad. The Common sheet lets you change the pen color and pen width, adjust recognition, and customize the toolbar area of the Writing Pad. The Writing Pad sheet allows you to change the background color and the number of lines that are displayed in the Writing Pad. Both sheets contain a Restore Default button to restore the settings to what they were when the software was installed initially.

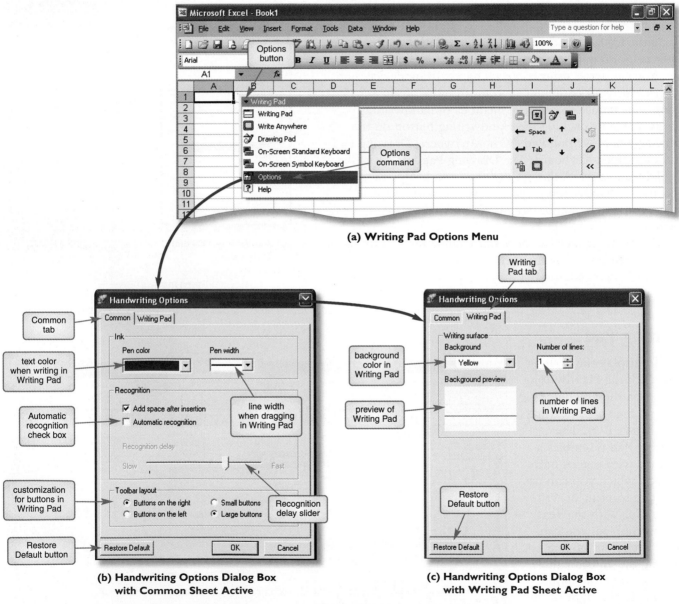

(a) **Writing Pad Options Menu**

(b) **Handwriting Options Dialog Box with Common Sheet Active**

(c) **Handwriting Options Dialog Box with Writing Pad Sheet Active**

FIGURE B-10

When you first start using the Writing Pad, you may want to remove the check mark from the Automatic recognition check box in the Common sheet in the Handwriting Options dialog box (Figure B-10b). With the check mark removed, the Handwriting Recognition service will not interpret what you write in the Writing Pad until you click the Recognize Now button on the toolbar (Figure B-9 on the previous page). This allows you to pause and adjust your writing.

The best way to learn how to use the Writing Pad is to practice with it. Also, for more information, enter handwriting recognition in the Type a question for help box on the menu bar.

Write Anywhere

Rather than use Writing Pad, you can write anywhere on the screen by invoking the Write Anywhere command on the Handwriting menu (Figure B-11) that appears when you click the Handwriting button on the Language bar. In this case, the entire window is your writing pad.

In Figure B-11, the word, Budget, is written in cursive using the mouse button. Shortly after the word is written, the Handwriting Recognition service interprets it, assigns it to the active cell, and erases what was written.

It is recommended that when you first start using the Writing Anywhere service that you remove the check mark from the Automatic recognition check box in the Common sheet in the Handwriting Options dialog box (Figure B-10b). With the check mark removed, the Handwriting Recognition service will not interpret what you write on the screen until you click the Recognize Now button on the toolbar (Figure B-11).

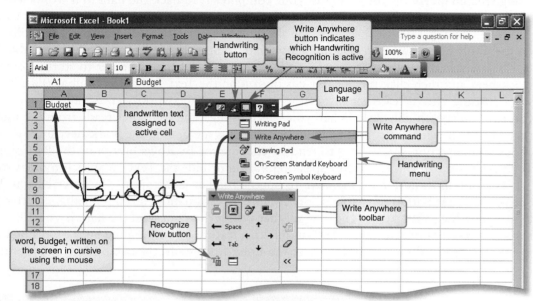

FIGURE B-11

Write Anywhere is more difficult to use than the Writing Pad, because when you click the mouse button, Excel may interpret the action as selecting a cell rather than starting to write. For this reason, it is recommended that you use the Writing Pad.

On-Screen Keyboard

The On-Screen Standard Keyboard command on the Handwriting menu (Figure B-12) displays an on-screen keyboard. The **on-screen keyboard** lets you enter data into a cell by using your mouse to click the keys. The on-screen keyboard is similar to the type found on handheld computers.

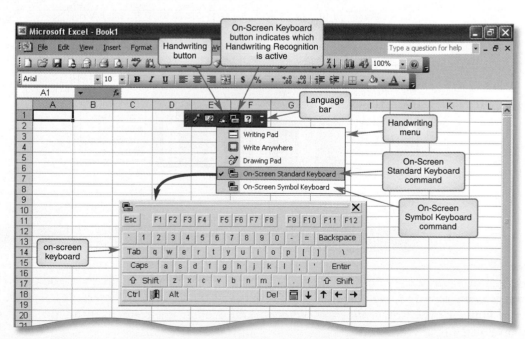

FIGURE B-12

The On-Screen Symbol Keyboard command on the Handwriting menu (Figure B-12 on the previous page) displays a special on-screen keyboard that allows you to enter symbols that are not on your keyboard, as well as Unicode characters. **Unicode characters** use a coding scheme capable of representing all the world's current languages.

Speech Playback

Using **speech playback**, you can have your computer read back the data in a worksheet. To enable speech playback, you use the Text To Speech toolbar (Figure B-13). You display the toolbar by right-clicking a toolbar and then clicking Text To Speech on the shortcut menu. You also can display the toolbar by pointing to Speech on the Tools menu and then clicking Show Text To Speech Toolbar on the Speech submenu.

To use speech playback, select the cell where you want the computer to start reading back the data in the worksheet and then click the Speak Cells button on the Text To Speech toolbar (Figure B-13). The computer stops reading after it reads the last cell with an entry in the worksheet. An alternative is to select a range before you turn on speech playback. When you select a range, the computer reads from the upper-left corner of the range to the lower-right corner of the range. It reads the data in the worksheet by rows or by columns. You choose the direction you want it to read by clicking the By Rows button or the By Columns button on the Text To Speech toolbar. Click the Stop Speaking button or hide the Text To Speech toolbar to stop speech playback.

The rightmost button on the Text To Speech toolbar is the Speak On Enter button. When you click the Speak On Enter button to enable it, the computer reads data in a cell immediately after you complete the entry by pressing the ENTER key or clicking another cell. It does not read the data if you click the Enter box on the formula bar to complete the entry. You disable this feature by clicking the Speak On Enter button while the feature is enabled. If you do not turn the Speak On Enter feature off, the computer will continue to read new cell entries even if the toolbar is hidden.

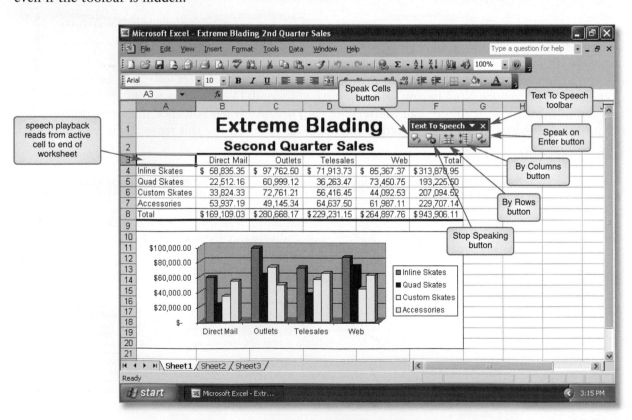

FIGURE B-13

Customizing Speech Playback

You can customize speech playback by clicking the Text To Speech tab in the Speech Properties dialog box (Figure B-6c on page APP 17) or by double-clicking the Speech icon in the Control Panel window in Classic View (Figure B-14a). To display the Control Panel, click Control Panel on the Start menu. When you double-click the Speech icon, the Speech Properties dialog box appears. Click the Text To Speech tab (Figure B-14b). The Text To Speech sheet has two areas: Voice selection and Voice speed. The Voice selection area lets you choose between two male voices and one female voice. You can click the Preview Voice button to preview the voice. The Voice speed area contains a slider. Drag the slider to slow down or speed up the voice.

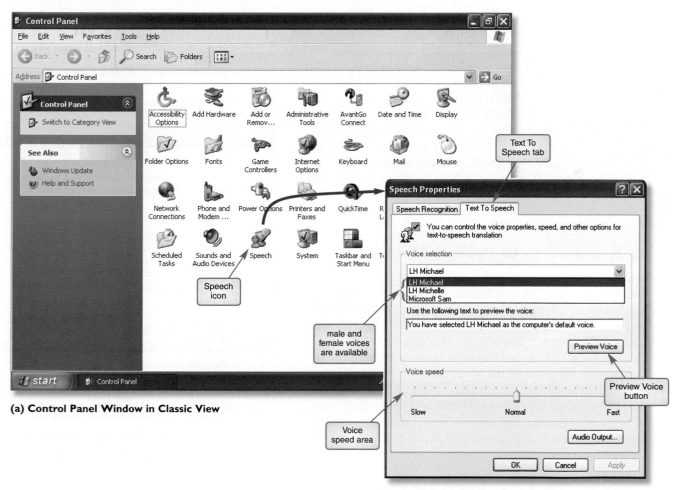

(a) Control Panel Window in Classic View

(b) Speech Properties Dialog Box

FIGURE B-14

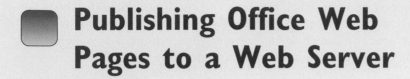

Appendix C

Publishing Office Web Pages to a Web Server

With the Office applications, you use the Save as Web Page command on the File menu to save the Web page to a Web server using one of two techniques: Web folders or File Transfer Protocol. A **Web folder** is an Office shortcut to a Web server. **File Transfer Protocol** (**FTP**) is an Internet standard that allows computers to exchange files with other computers on the Internet.

You should contact your network system administrator or technical support staff at your ISP to determine if their Web server supports Web folders, FTP, or both, and to obtain necessary permissions to access the Web server. If you decide to publish Web pages using a Web folder, you must have the Office Server Extensions (OSE) installed on your computer.

Using Web Folders to Publish Office Web Pages

When publishing to a Web folder, someone first must create the Web folder before you can save to it. If you are granted permission to create a Web folder, you must obtain the URL of the Web server, a user name, and possibly a password that allows you to access the Web server. You also must decide on a name for the Web folder. Table C-1 explains how to create a Web folder.

Office adds the name of the Web folder to the list of current Web folders. You can save to this folder, open files in the folder, rename the folder, or perform any operations you would to a folder on your hard disk. You can use your Office program or Windows Explorer to access this folder. Table C-2 explains how to save to a Web folder.

Using FTP to Publish Office Web Pages

When publishing a Web page using FTP, you first must add the FTP location to your computer before you can save to it. An FTP location, also called an **FTP site**, is a collection of files that reside on an FTP server. In this case, the FTP server is the Web server.

To add an FTP location, you must obtain the name of the FTP site, which usually is the address (URL) of the FTP server, and a user name and a password that allows you to access the FTP server. You save and open the Web pages on the FTP server using the name of the FTP site. Table C-3 explains how to add an FTP site.

Office adds the name of the FTP site to the FTP locations list in the Save As and Open dialog boxes. You can open and save files using this list. Table C-4 explains how to save to an FTP location.

Table C-1   Creating a Web Folder

1. Click File on the menu bar and then click Save As (or Open).
2. When the Save As dialog box (or Open dialog box) appears, click My Network Places on the My Places bar, and then click the Create New Folder button on the toolbar
3. When the Add Network Place Wizard dialog box appears, click the Next button. If necessary, click Choose another network location. Click the Next button. Click the View some examples link, type the Internet or network address, and then click the Next button. Click Log on anonymously to deselect the check box, type your user name in the User name text box, and then click the Next button. Enter the name you want to call this network place and then click the Next button. Click the Finish button.

Table C-2   Saving to a Web Folder

1. Click File on the menu bar and then click Save As.
2. When the Save As dialog box appears, type the Web page file name in the File name text box. Do not press the ENTER key.
3. Click My Network Places on the My Places bar.
4. Double-click the Web folder name in the Save in list.
5. If the Enter Network Password dialog box appears, type the user name and password in the respective text boxes and then click the OK button.
6. Click the Save button in the Save As dialog box.

Table C-3   Adding an FTP Location

1. Click File on the menu bar and then click Save As (or Open).
2. In the Save As dialog box, click the Save in box arrow and then click Add/Modify FTP Locations in the Save in list; or in the Open dialog box, click the Look in box arrow and then click Add/Modify FTP Locations in the Look in list.
3. When the Add/Modify FTP Locations dialog box appears, type the name of the FTP site in the Name of FTP site text box. If the site allows anonymous logon, click Anonymous in the Log on as area; if you have a user name for the site, click User in the Log on as area and then enter the user name. Enter the password in the Password text box. Click the OK button.
4. Close the Save As or the Open dialog box.

Table C-4   Saving to an FTP Location

1. Click File on the menu bar and then click Save As.
2. When the Save As dialog box appears, type the Web page file name in the File name text box. Do not press the ENTER key.
3. Click the Save in box arrow and then click FTP Locations.
4. Double-click the name of the FTP site to which you wish to save.
5. When the FTP Log On dialog box appears, enter your user name and password and then click the OK button.
6. Click the Save button in the Save As dialog box.

Appendix D

Changing Screen Resolution and Resetting the Excel Toolbars and Menus

This appendix explains how to change your screen resolution in Windows to the resolution used in this book. It also describes how to reset the Excel toolbars and menus to their installation settings.

Changing Screen Resolution

The **screen resolution** indicates the number of pixels (dots) that your system uses to display the letters, numbers, graphics, and background you see on your screen. The screen resolution usually is stated as the product of two numbers, such as 800 × 600. An 800 × 600 screen resolution results in a display of 800 distinct pixels on each of 600 lines, or about 480,000 pixels. The figures in this book were created using a screen resolution of 800 × 600.

The screen resolutions most commonly used today are 800 × 600 and 1024 × 768, although some Office specialists operate their computers at a much higher screen resolution, such as 2048 × 1536. The following steps show how to change the screen resolution from 1024 × 768 to 800 × 600.

To Change the Screen Resolution

1

- **If necessary, minimize all applications so that the Windows desktop appears.**
- **Right-click the Windows desktop.**

Windows displays the Windows desktop shortcut menu (Figure D-1).

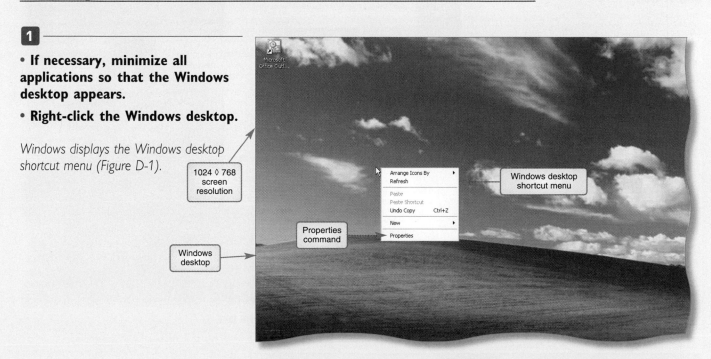

FIGURE D-1

2

• **Click Properties on the shortcut menu.**

• **When Windows displays the Display Properties dialog box, click the Settings tab.**

Windows displays the Settings sheet in the Display Properties dialog box (Figure D-2). The Settings sheet shows a preview of the Windows desktop using the current screen resolution (1024 × 768). The Settings sheet also shows the screen resolution and the color quality settings.

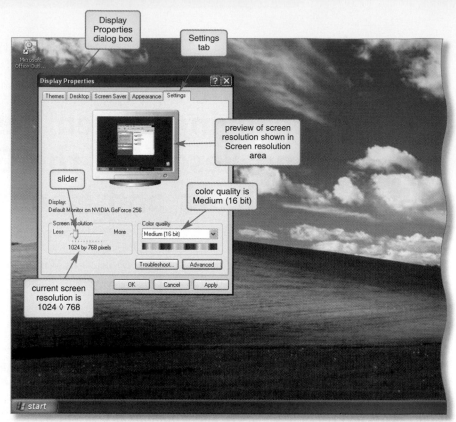

FIGURE D-2

3

• **Drag the slider in the Screen resolution area to the left so that the screen resolution changes to 800 × 600.**

The screen resolution in the Screen resolution area changes to 800 × 600 (Figure D-3). The Settings sheet shows a preview of the Windows desktop using the new screen resolution (800 × 600).

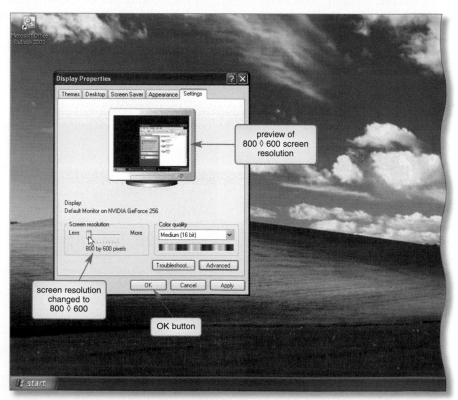

FIGURE D-3

4

• **Click the OK button.**

• **If Windows displays the Monitor Settings dialog box, click the Yes button.**

Windows changes the screen resolution from 1024 × 768 to 800 × 600 (Figure D-4).

800 ◊ 600
screen resolution

FIGURE D-4

As shown in the previous steps, as you decrease the screen resolution, Windows displays less information on your screen, but the information increases in size. The reverse also is true: as you increase the screen resolution, Windows displays more information on your screen, but the information decreases in size.

Resetting the Excel Toolbars and Menus

Excel customization capabilities allow you to create custom toolbars by adding and deleting buttons and personalize menus based on their usage. Each time you start Excel, the toolbars and menus are displayed using the same settings as the last time you used Excel. The figures in this book were created with the Excel toolbars and menus set to the original, or installation, settings.

Resetting the Standard and Formatting Toolbars

The steps on the next page show how to reset the Standard and Formatting toolbars.

To Reset the Standard and Formatting Toolbars

1

• **Start Excel following the steps outlined at the beginning of Project 1 on page EX 7.**

• **Click the Toolbar Options button on the Standard toolbar and then point to Add or Remove Buttons on the Toolbar Options menu.**

Excel displays the Toolbar Options menu and the Add or Remove Buttons submenu (Figure D-5).

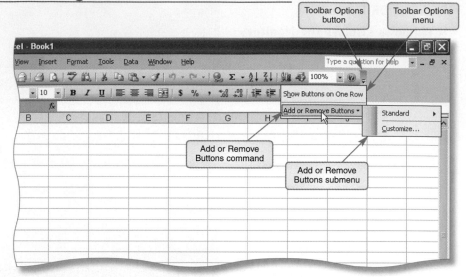

FIGURE D-5

2

• **Point to Standard on the Add or Remove Buttons submenu.**

• **Scroll down and then point to Reset Toolbar on the Standard submenu.**

Excel displays the Standard submenu indicating the buttons and boxes that appear on the Standard toolbar (Figure D-6). To remove a button from the Standard toolbar, click a button name with a check mark to the left of the name to remove the check mark.

3

• **Click Reset Toolbar.**

• **If Excel displays the Microsoft Excel dialog box, click the Yes button.**

Excel resets the Standard toolbar to its original settings.

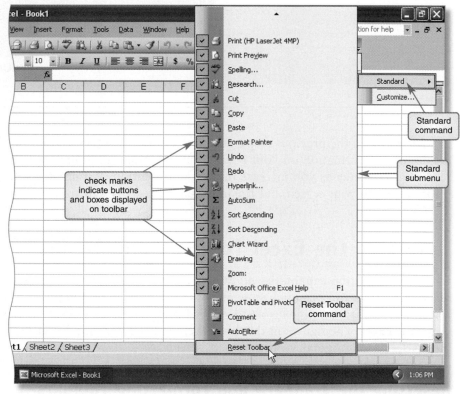

FIGURE D-6

4

• **Reset the Formatting toolbar by following Steps 1 through 3 and replacing any reference to the Standard toolbar with the Formatting toolbar.**

Not only can you use the Standard submenu shown in Figure D-6 to reset the Standard toolbar to its original settings, but you also can use it to customize the Standard toolbar by adding and deleting buttons. To add or delete buttons, click the button name on the Standard submenu to add or remove the check mark. Buttons with a check mark to the left currently are displayed on the Standard toolbar; buttons without a check mark are not displayed on the Standard toolbar. You can complete the same tasks for the Formatting toolbar, using the Formatting submenu to add to and delete buttons from the Formatting toolbar.

Resetting the Excel Menus

The following steps show how to reset the Excel menus to their original settings.

To Reset the Excel Menus

Other Ways

1. On View menu point to Toolbars, click Customize on Toolbars submenu, click Toolbars tab, click toolbar name, click Reset button, click OK button, click Close button
2. Right-click toolbar, click Customize on shortcut menu, click Toolbars tab, click toolbar name, click Reset button, click OK button, click Close button
3. In Voice Command mode, say "View, Toolbars, Customize, Toolbars, [desired toolbar name], Reset, OK, Close"

1

• **Click the Toolbar Options button on the Standard toolbar and then point to Add or Remove Buttons on the Toolbar Options menu.**

Excel displays the Toolbar Options menu and the Add or Remove Buttons submenu (Figure D-7).

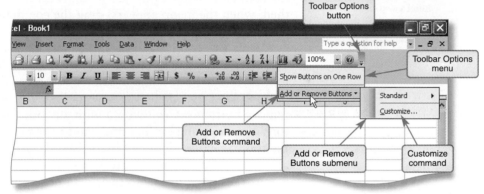

FIGURE D-7

2

• **Click Customize on the Add or Remove Buttons submenu.**

• **When Excel displays the Customize dialog box, click the Options tab.**

Excel displays the Customize dialog box (Figure D-8). The Customize dialog box contains three sheets used for customizing the Excel toolbars and menus.

3

• **Click the Reset menu and toolbar usage data button. When Excel displays the Microsoft Excel dialog box, click the Yes button. Click the Close button in the Customize dialog box.**

Excel resets the menus to the original settings.

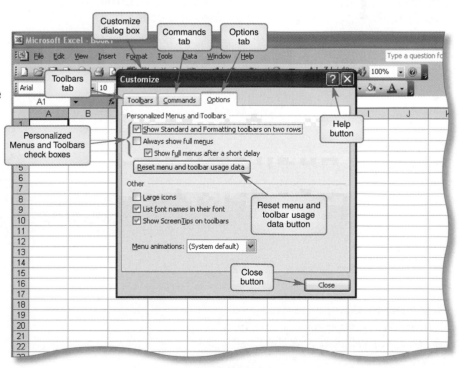

FIGURE D-8

Other Ways

1. On View menu point to Toolbars, click Customize on Toolbars submenu, click Options tab, click Reset menu and toolbar usage data button, click Yes button, click Close button
2. Right-click toolbar, click Customize on shortcut menu, click Options tab, click Reset menu and toolbar usage data button, click Yes button, click Close button
3. In Voice Command mode, say "View, Toolbars, Customize, Options, Reset menu and toolbar usage data, Yes, Close"

Using the Options sheet in the Customize dialog box, as shown in Figure D-8 on the previous page, you can select options to personalize menus and toolbars. For example, you can select or deselect a check mark that instructs Excel to display the Standard and Formatting toolbars on two rows. You also can select whether Excel always displays full menus or displays short menus followed by full menus, after a short delay. Other options available in the Options sheet include settings to instruct Excel to display toolbars with large icons; to use the appropriate font to display font names in the Font list; and to display a ScreenTip when a user points to a toolbar button. Clicking the Help button immediately to the left of the Close button on the Customize dialog box's title bar (Figure D-8) instructs Excel to display topics that will assist you in customizing toolbars and menus.

Using the Commands sheet in the Customize dialog box, you can add buttons to toolbars and commands to menus. Recall that the menu bar at the top of the Excel window is a special toolbar. To add buttons to a toolbar, click a category name in the Categories list and then drag the command name in the Commands list to a toolbar. To add commands to a menu, click a category name in the Categories list, drag the command name in the Commands list to a menu name on the menu bar, and then, when the menu appears, drag the command to the desired location in the list of menu commands.

Using the Toolbars sheet in the Customize dialog box, you can add new toolbars and reset existing toolbars and the menu. To add a new toolbar, click the New button, enter a toolbar name in the New Toolbar dialog box, and then click the OK button. After you create the new toolbar, you can use the Commands sheet to add or remove buttons, as you would with any other toolbar. If you add one or more buttons to an existing toolbar and want to reset the toolbar to its original settings, click the toolbar name in the Toolbars list so a check mark displays to the left of the name and then click the Reset button. If you add commands to one or more menus and want to reset the menus to their default settings, click Worksheet Menu Bar in the Toolbars list on the Toolbars sheet so a check mark displays to the left of the name and then click the Reset button. When you have finished, click the Close button to close the Customize dialog box.

Appendix E

Microsoft Office Specialist Certification

What Is Microsoft Office Specialist Certification?

Microsoft Office Specialist certification provides a framework for measuring your proficiency with the Microsoft Office 2003 applications, such as Microsoft Office Word 2003, Microsoft Office Excel 2003, Microsoft Office Access 2003, Microsoft Office PowerPoint 2003, and Microsoft Office Outlook 2003. The levels of certification are described in Table E-1.

Table E-1 Levels of Microsoft Office Specialist Certification

LEVEL	DESCRIPTION	REQUIREMENTS	CREDENTIAL AWARDED

Microsoft Office Specialist	Indicates that you have an understanding of the basic features in a specific Microsoft Office 2003 application	Pass any ONE of the following:
		  Microsoft Office Word 2003
		  Microsoft Office Excel 2003
		  Microsoft Office Access 2003
		  Microsoft Office PowerPoint 2003
		  Microsoft Office Outlook 2003
			Candidates will be awarded one certificate for each of the Specialist-level exams they have passed:
			  Microsoft Office Word 2003
			  Microsoft Office Excel 2003
			  Microsoft Office Access 2003
			  Microsoft Office PowerPoint 2003
			  Microsoft Office Outlook 2003

Microsoft Office Expert	Indicates that you have an understanding of the advanced features in a specific Microsoft Office 2003 application	Pass any ONE of the following:
		  Microsoft Office Word 2003 Expert
		  Microsoft Office Excel 2003 Expert
			Candidates will be awarded one certificate for each of the Expert-level exams they have passed:
			  Microsoft Office Word 2003 Expert
			  Microsoft Office Excel 2003 Expert

Microsoft Office Master	Indicates that you have a comprehensive understanding of the features of four of the five primary Microsoft Office 2003 applications	Pass the following:
		  Microsoft Office Word 2003 Expert
		  Microsoft Office Excel 2003 Expert
		  Microsoft Office PowerPoint 2003
		And pass ONE of the following:
		  Microsoft Office Access 2003 or
		  Microsoft Office Outlook 2003
			Candidates will be awarded the Microsoft Office Master certificate for fulfilling the requirements.

Why Should You Be Certified?

Being Microsoft Office certified provides a valuable industry credential — proof that you have the Office 2003 applications skills required by employers. By passing one or more Microsoft Office Specialist certification exams, you demonstrate your proficiency in a given Office 2003 application to employers. With more than 400 million people in 175 nations and 70 languages using Office applications, Microsoft is targeting Office 2003 certification to a wide variety of companies. These companies include temporary employment agencies that want to prove the expertise of their workers, large corporations looking for a way to measure the skill set of employees, and training companies and educational institutions seeking Microsoft Office 2003 teachers with appropriate credentials.

The Microsoft Office Specialist Certification Exams

You pay $50 to $100 each time you take an exam, whether you pass or fail. The fee varies among testing centers. The **Microsoft Office Expert** exams, which you can take up to 60 minutes to complete, consist of between 40 and 60 tasks that you perform on a personal computer in a simulated environment. The tasks require you to use the application just as you would in doing your job. The **Microsoft Office Specialist** exams contain fewer tasks, and you will have slightly less time to complete them. The tasks you will perform differ on the two types of exams. After passing designated Expert and Specialist exams, candidates are awarded the **Microsoft Office Master** certificate (see the requirements in Table E-1 on the previous page).

How to Prepare for the Microsoft Office Specialist Certification Exams

The Shelly Cashman Series offers several Microsoft-approved textbooks that cover the required objectives of the Microsoft Office Specialist certification exams. For a listing of the textbooks, visit the Shelly Cashman Series Microsoft Office Specialist Center at scsite.com/winoff2003/cert. Click the link Shelly Cashman Series Microsoft Office 2003-Approved Microsoft Office Textbooks (Figure E-1). After using any of the books listed in an instructor-led course, you should be prepared to take the indicated Microsoft Office Specialist certification exam.

How to Find an Authorized Testing Center

To locate a testing center, call 1-800-933-4493 in North America, or visit the Shelly Cashman Series Microsoft Office Specialist Center at scsite.com/winoff2003/cert. Click the link Locate an Authorized Testing Center Near You (Figure E-1). At this Web site, you can look for testing centers around the world.

Shelly Cashman Series Microsoft Office Specialist Center

The Shelly Cashman Series Microsoft Office Specialist Center (Figure E-1) lists more than 15 Web sites you can visit to obtain additional information about certification. The Web page (scsite.com/winoff2003/cert) includes links to general information about certification, choosing an application for certification, preparing for the certification exam, and taking and passing the certification exam.

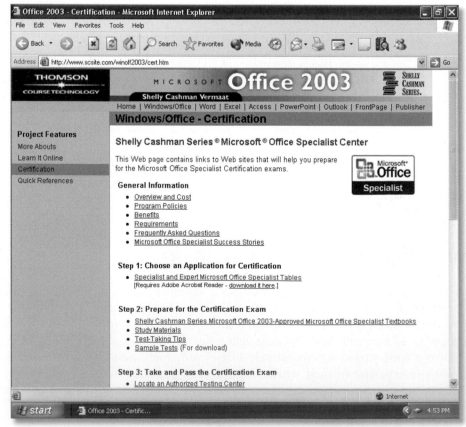

FIGURE E-1

Index

Absolute addressing, relative
  addressing versus, EX 168-170
Absolute cell reference, **EX 168**
  copying formula with, EX 174-175
Active cell, **EX 11**, EX 16, EX 20
  bold, EX 30
  worksheet title in, EX 17
Active cell reference, in Name box,
  EX 16
Align Left button (Formatting toolbar),
  EX 96
Align Right button (Formatting
  toolbar), EX 96
Alignment
  cell contents, EX 96
  centering, see Centering
  date, EX 167
  horizontal, EX 92, EX 96
  rotating text, EX 151
  shrink to fit, EX 157
  text in cell, EX 18
  vertical, EX 92, EX 96
  worksheet title using Format Cells
    dialog box, EX 92-93
  See also Indentation
All Programs submenu (Start menu),
  Microsoft Office, Microsoft Office
  Excel 2003 command, EX 7
Aquatics Wear worksheet, EX 145-208
Arguments, **EX 81**
  IF function, EX 171
Arithmetic operators, EX 74
Arrow keys
  completing entry using, EX 20
  selecting cell using, EX 16
Assumptions, **EX 146**
Asterisk (*), multiplication and, **EX 74**
Attachment, workbook as,
  EX 125-126
Auditing command (Tools menu),
  EX 148
Auto Fill Options button, EX 26
  month name series, EX 153
Auto Fill Options menu, options
  available on, EX 153
AutoCalculate area (status bar),
  EX 14, **EX 48**
  determining average using, EX 49
AutoCalculate shortcut menu, EX 48
AutoCorrect feature, **EX 18**
  smart tags and, EX 78
  spell checking using, EX 18, EX 113
AutoCorrect Options command (Tools
  menu), smart tags, EX 78
Autoformat, **EX 34-36**
AutoFormat command (Format menu),
  EX 34-35
AutoSum button (Standard toolbar),
  EX 165
  determining totals using, EX 23-24,
    EX 27, EX 79-80
  functions and, EX 84, EX 85
Average
  determining using AutoCalculate
    area, EX 49
  determining using AVERAGE
    function, EX 81-82
Average command (shortcut menu),
  EX 49
AVERAGE function, **EX 81-82**

Background, Blue Chip Stock Club
  worksheet, EX 94-95
BACKSPACE key, deleting characters
  using, EX 18, EX 50
Backup copy, **EX 44**
Bar charts, EX 187
Best fit (column width), **EX 107**
Black and white, printing in, EX 116,
  EX 200
Blank cell, **EX 80**
  statistical functions and, EX 81
Blank characters, EX 52
Blue Chip Stock Club Investment
  Analysis worksheet, EX 65-128

Bold, EX 29, **EX 30**
  alternatives to, EX 150
Blue Chip Stock Club worksheet,
  EX 92, EX 93, EX 96
  column titles using Formatting
    toolbar, EX 96
  entire worksheet, EX 150
  row titles, EX 100
Bold button (Formatting toolbar),
  EX 30
Border
  bottom, see Bottom border
  worksheet title, EX 95
Borders palette, EX 95
Bottom border
  column titles, EX 96
  row, EX 100
Browser
  dynamic Web page in, EX 226,
    EX 236-237
  static Web page in, EX 226, EX 232,
    EX 233
  Web page preview and, EX 228-229

Cancel box (formula bar) , EX 17,
  EX 18, **EX 20**
Case-sensitive, **EX 44**
Category axis, see X-axis
Category names, **EX 187**
Cell, **EX 10**
  active, see Active cell
  aligning contents of, EX 96
  blank, EX 80
  clearing, EX 52
  color, EX 105
  copying format using Format Painter
    button, EX 154-156
  copying to adjacent cells, using fill
    handle, EX 24-26
  deleting versus clearing, EX 161
  editing using formula bar, EX 51
  editing using in-cell editing, EX 50
  formatting, EX 28-34
  formatting nonadjacent, EX 184-185
  formatting using Format Painter
    button, EX 154-156
  hiding, EX 109
  inserting, EX 159-161
  merging, see Merging cells
  rotating entries, EX 98, EX 151-152
  selecting, EX 16
  selecting for formula, EX 75
  selecting using keyboard, EX 80
  selecting using Name box, EX 36-37
  selecting using Select All button,
    EX 53, EX 150
  selection methods, EX 37
  shrinking entries, EX 98, EX 157
  undoing last entry, EX 51-52
  wrapping text in, EX 71
Cell reference, **EX 11**, EX 16
  absolute, **EX 168**
  copying formulas and, EX 78
  deleted cells and, EX 162
  errors, EX 162
  formulas, EX 74
  inserting rows and, EX 161
  mixed, EX 168
  Range Finder verifying, EX 89
  relative, EX 25, EX 78, EX 168
  selecting cell by typing in Name box,
    EX 36
Cells command (Format menu),
  EX 161
  alignment, EX 33
  font color, EX 32
  font size, EX 31
  font style, EX 30
  font type, EX 29
  formatting, EX 93, EX 29-33
  numbers, EX 163
  shrink to fit, EX 157
Center button (Formatting toolbar),
  EX 96

Centering
  cell entry across columns by merging
    cells, EX 32-33
  column titles using Formatting
    toolbar, EX 96
  horizontal, EX 92, EX 96
  vertical, EX 92, EX 96
  worksheet title using Format Cells
    dialog box, EX 92-93
Character, **EX 107**
  blank, EX 52
  deleting, EX 18, EX 50
  inserting, EX 50
  shrink to fit, EX 157
  Unicode, APP 22
Chart location, **EX 38**, EX 191
Chart menu, 3-D View command,
  EX 195
Chart sheet, **EX 187**
Chart Wizard button (Standard
  toolbar)
  3-D clustered column chart, EX 39
  3-D Pie chart, EX 188-192
Charts, **EX 4**
  bar, EX 187
  default type, EX 41
  deleting, EX 52-53
  embedded, EX 38-41
  formatting, EX 41
  location, EX 38, EX 191
  moving, EX 40-41
  rotating, EX 194-196
  saving as dynamic Web page,
    EX 234-236
  selected, EX 40
  3-D clustered column, EX 39
  3-D Pie, EX 187-197
  tilting, EX 194-196
  title, EX 189, EX 192
Clear command (Edit menu), EX 52
Clearing
  entire worksheet, EX 52-53
  range, EX 52
Clearing cells, EX 52
  deleting versus, EX 161
Clipboard, Office, EX 157
Close button (title bar), EX 46
Closed (Language bar), EX 9, **EX 15**,
  APP 11
Closing
  task pane, EX 9
  window, EX 46
Color
  cells, EX 105
  choosing for worksheet, EX 91
  sheet tab, EX 198
  slices in pie chart, EX 193
Column command (Format menu),
  width, EX 109
Column heading, **EX 10**
  active cell, EX 16
Column titles
  Blue Chip Stock Club worksheet,
    EX 70-71, EX 96
  bottom border, EX 96
  centering using Formatting toolbar,
    EX 96
  entering, EX 19-20
  freezing, EX 163-164
Column width
  Aquatics Wear worksheet,
    EX 155-156
  best fit, EX 107
  Blue Chip Stock Club worksheet,
    EX 107-109
  increasing after entering values,
    EX 107-109
  increasing before entering values,
    EX 155-156
  text and, EX 18
Column Width command (shortcut
  menu), EX 109
Columns
  deleting, EX 161
  hidden, EX 109, EX 110

inserting, EX 161
number of, EX 10
summing, EX 23-24, EX 27
titles, see Column titles
width, see Column width
Columns command (Insert menu),
  EX 161
Comma Style button (Formatting
  toolbar), EX 98
Comma style format, **EX 98**
Command-line switch, starting Excel
  using, EX 70
Commands
  dimmed, EX 12
  hidden, EX 12-13
  menu, EX 11
  toggle, EX 175
Comparing workbooks, EX 4
Comparison operator, EX 171
Condition, **EX 104**
Conditional formatting, EX 103-106
Conditional Formatting command
  (Format menu), EX 104
Constant, replacing formula with,
  EX 173
Copy area, see Source area
Copy button (Standard toolbar)
  formats, EX 155
  Office Clipboard, EX 157-158
Copy command (Edit menu)
  cell, EX 26
  functions, EX 88
  Office Clipboard, EX 157, EX 158
Copying
  cell format using Format Painter
    button, EX 154-156
  cell to adjacent cells using fill handle,
    EX 24-26
  cells between workbooks, EX 157
  copy and paste used in, EX 157-158
  cut and paste used in, EX 159
  drag and drop used in, EX 159
  formulas using fill handle, EX 77-78
  formulas with absolute cell
    references, EX 174-175
  functions using fill handle, EX 87-88
  moving versus, EX 159
  range, EX 26
  range to nonadjacent destination
    area, EX 157-158
Correcting errors, EX 18
  debugging, EX 119
  formulas, EX 77, EX 90, EX 113,
    EX 148
  Trace Error, EX 79
  worksheet, EX 50-53
CTRL key, selecting nonadjacent ranges
  using, EX 177
Currency Style button (Formatting
  toolbar), EX 98
Currency Style format
  Format Cells command, EX 100-101
  Formatting toolbar, **EX 98**
  with floating dollar sign, EX 177
Cut button (Standard toolbar), EX 50,
  EX 52, EX 159

Data
  importing using Web query,
    EX 120-123
  refreshing external, EX 123
Data labels
  formatting, EX 192, EX 197
  leader lines with, EX 197
  3-D Pie chart, EX 190, EX 197
Data menu, Import External Data
  command, EX 121
Data series, **EX 187**
Date
  formatting, EX 96-97
  system, EX 165-167
Date stamp, **EX 165**
Debugging, EX 118

Decimal places
  date, EX 167
  decreasing, EX 100
  increasing, EX 99-100, EX 102-103
Decision making, EX 170
Decrease Decimal button (Formatting toolbar), EX 100
Decrease Indent button (Formatting toolbar), EX 156
Default chart type, **EX 41**
Delete command (Edit menu), EX 161-162
DELETE key
  clearing cell entries using, EX 52
  deleting characters using, EX 50
Deleting
  cells, *see* Deleting cells
  characters, EX 18, EX 50
  chart, EX 52-53
  columns, EX 161
  drop shadow, EX 186
  formatting, EX 52
  range, EX 162
  rows, EX 161-162
  toolbar button, EX 91
Deleting cells
  clearing cells versus, EX 161
  formulas and, EX 162
Destination area, **EX 25**
  copying functions, EX 88
  copying range to nonadjacent, EX 157-158
Dialog boxes, Help buttons in, APP 7
Dictation mode, **APP 15**
Dictionary, custom, EX 111
Dimmed command, **EX 12**
Displaying
  Drawing toolbar, EX 181-182
  hidden columns, EX 109
  hidden rows, EX 111
  Language bar, EX 15
  system date, EX 165-167
Docking toolbar, EX 182
Dollar sign
  fixed, EX 98, EX 102
  floating, EX 98, EX 100-102, EX 177
Drag, EX 159
  averaging range of numbers using, EX 81
  column width changed using, EX 107-109
  ranges, EX 161
  row height changed using, EX 110
Drag and drop, **EX 159**
Drawing button (Standard toolbar), EX 181-182
Drawing toolbar, **EX 181**
  displaying, EX 181-182
  docking, EX 182-183
  hiding, EX 187
Drop shadow, EX 183-184
  deleting, EX 186
Dynamic Web page, **EX 226,** EX 234-238
  modifying worksheet on, EX 237-238
  saving chart as, EX 234-236
  viewing and manipulating, EX 236-237

Edit menu
  Clear command, EX 52
  Copy command, cell, EX 26
  Copy command, functions, EX 88
  Copy command, Office Clipboard, EX 157, EX 158
  Delete command, EX 161-162
  Paste command, cell, EX 26
  Paste command, functions, EX 88
  Paste command, Office Clipboard, EX 157, EX 158
  Paste Special command, formats, EX 155
  Redo command, EX 52
  Undo command, EX 51
  Undo Paste command, EX 158
Edit mode, **EX 50-51**
Editing
  in-cell, EX 50-51
  using formula bar, EX 51

E-mail (electronic mail), **EX 125**
  workbook attachment, EX 125-126
E-mail button (Standard toolbar), EX 126
Embedded chart, **EX 38-41**
Enter box, EX 17, **EX 18**, EX 20
ENTER key
  completing entry by pressing, EX 18, EX 20
  paste operation and, EX 159
Enter mode, **EX 14**
Equal sign (=), **EX 74**
Error Checking command (Tools menu), formulas, EX 90, EX 113, EX 148
Error messages, formulas and, EX 175
Errors, *see* Correcting errors
Excel 2003, **EX 4**
  Help system, EX 9, EX 53-54, APP 1-8
  new features, EX 4, EX 6
  quitting, EX 46, EX 54-55
  starting using Start menu, EX 47, EX 6-8
  starting using command-line switch, EX 70
  tips and tricks, EX 53
Excel Help task pane, **APP 2**
Excel window, *see* Window
Exit command (File menu), EX 46
Exploded Pie chart, **EX 187,** EX 194
External Data toolbar, EX 123
Extreme Blading Second Quarter Sales worksheet, EX 3-55

F1 key (Help), APP 1
F4 (absolute cell reference), EX 169
File, **EX 42**
  attachment to e-mail, *see* Attachment
  name, *see* File name
  File formats, EX 44, EX 89
  File management tools, EX 232
File menu
  Exit command, EX 46
  Page Setup command, black and white printing, EX 116
  Page Setup command, print scaling, EX 120
  Print Area command, EX 117
  Print command, EX 45
  Print Preview command, EX 115
  Save As command, EX 43
  Save as Web Page command, EX 231, EX 234-235
  Send To command, e-mail, EX 125-126
  Web Page Preview command, EX 228-229
File name
  saving workbook using same, EX 88-90
  saving workbook with new, EX 42, EX 43
File Transfer Protocol, *see* FTP
Fill color
  font, EX 94-95, EX 180
  slices in pie chart, EX 193
Fill Color button (Formatting toolbar), font, EX 94-95, EX 180
Fill handle, **EX 25**
  clearing cell entries using, EX 52
  copying cell to adjacent cells using, EX 24-26
  copying formulas using, EX 77-78
  copying formulas with absolute cell references using, EX 174
  copying functions using, EX 87-88
  creating series of month names, EX 152-153
Fixed dollar sign, **EX 98**, EX 102
Floating dollar sign, **EX 98,** EX 100-102, EX 177
Floating toolbar, **EX 182**
Folder, Web, EX 228, APP 24
Font, Blue Chip Stock Club worksheet, EX 91-94
Font box arrow (Formatting toolbar), EX 29

Font color, **EX 28**
  Blue Chip Stock Club worksheet, EX 94-95
  Extreme Blading Second Quarter Sales worksheet, EX 31-32
Font Color button (Formatting toolbar), EX 95, EX 180
Font size, **EX 28**
  Blue Chip Stock Club worksheet, EX 92, EX 93
  Extreme Blading Second Quarter Sales worksheet, EX 30-31
Font Size box arrow (Formatting toolbar), EX 31
Font style, **EX 28**
Font type, **EX 28**
  Extreme Blading Second Quarter Sales worksheet, EX 29-30
Format, **EX 28**. *See also* Formatting
Format Cells command (shortcut menu)
  font, EX 29, EX 30, EX 31, EX 32
  date, EX 97, EX 167
  numbers, EX 100-102
Format Cells dialog box
  centering worksheet title using, EX 92-93
  date, EX 97, EX 167
  numbers, EX 100-102
  rotating text, EX 151-152
Format menu
  AutoFormat command, EX 34-35
  Cells command, alignment, EX 33
  Cells command, font color, EX 32
  Cells command, font size, EX 31
  Cells command, font style, EX 30
  Cells command, font type, EX 29
  Cells command, formatting, EX 93
  Cells command, numbers, EX 163
  Cells command, shrink to fit, EX 157
  Column command, width, EX 109
  Conditional Formatting command, EX 104
Format Painter button (Standard toolbar), copying cell format using, EX 107, EX 154-156
Format symbol, **EX 162-**163
Formatting, **EX 28**
  Aquatics Wear worksheet, EX 177-187
  autoformat used in, EX 34-36
  Blue Chip Stock Club worksheet, EX 72, EX 90-11
  chart, EX 41
  chart title, EX 192
  column titles, EX 96
  conditional, EX 103-106
  currency style, *see* Currency Style format
  data labels, EX 192, EX 197
  date, EX 96-97, EX 165, EX 167
  deleting, EX 52
  Formatting toolbar used in, EX 28-34
  inserted row and, EX 161
  negative numbers, EX 180
  numbers as they are entered, EX 100
  numbers in nonadjacent ranges, EX 177
  numbers using Format Cells command, EX 100-102
  numbers using Formatting toolbar, EX 98-100
  painting, EX 107, EX 154-156
  worksheet subtitle, EX 33-34
Formatting toolbar, EX 13-14
  formatting cells using, EX 28-34
  formatting numbers using, EX 98-100
  resetting, APP 27-28
Formula, **EX 73**
  absolute cell reference, EX 168-170
  Blue Chip Stock Club worksheet, EX 72-80
  changing to number, EX 77
  checking, EX 90
  copying, with absolute cell references, EX 174-175
  copying using fill handle, EX 77-78
  correcting errors, EX 77, EX 113
  deleted cells and, EX 162

entering using keyboard, EX 73-74
entering using Point mode, EX 75-77
equal sign (=) and, EX 74
error checking, EX 90, EX 113, EX 148
error messages, EX 175
inserting rows and, EX 161
order of operations, EX 74-75
replacing with constant, EX 173
values versus, EX 118
verifying using Range Finder, EX 89-90
Formula Auditing toolbar, EX 118
Formula bar, **EX 14**
  editing cell using, EX 51
Formula Palette, EX 82
Formulas version, **EX 118**
  displaying, EX 118
  printing, EX 119
Freeze Panes command (Window menu), EX 163-164
Freeze the titles, **EX 163**
Freezing worksheet titles, EX 163-164
FTP (File Transfer Protocol), **APP 24**
FTP locations, EX 228, EX 232
Full menu, **EX 12**
Full Screen command (View menu), viewing area, EX 11
Function, **EX 81**
  arguments, EX 81
  AVERAGE, EX 81-82
  blank cell and, EX 81
  copying using fill handle, EX 87-88
  IF, EX 170-172
  MAX, EX 82-84
  MIN, EX 84-87
  NOW, EX 165-167
  ROUND, EX 100
  statistical, EX 4, EX 81
Function command (Insert menu), EX 24, EX 84, EX 86, EX 167

General format, date, EX 167
Getting Started task pane, EX 8
Global (search), **APP 3**
Goal Seek command (Tools menu), EX 206-207
Goal seeking, **EX 206-**208
Gridlines, **EX 11**

Handwriting menu, Write Anywhere command, APP 21
Handwriting Recognition service, **APP 19-22**
Hard copy, **EX 44**
Height, row, *see* Row height
Help menu
  commands on, APP 8
  Microsoft Excel Help command, APP 1
Help system, EX 9, EX 53, APP 1-8
  accessing, APP 1
  navigating, APP 2-5
Hidden (Language bar), **EX 15,** APP 11
Hidden columns, EX 109, EX 110
Hidden commands, **EX 12-13**
Hidden rows, EX 111
Hiding
  cells, EX 109
  Drawing toolbar, EX 187
  Office Assistant, APP 7
Hiding cells, **EX 109**
Horizontal alignment, EX 92, EX 96
Horizontal split bar, **EX 204**
HTML (Hypertext Markup Language) format, EX 232
Hyperlink, EX 237

IF function, EX 170, **EX 171-**172
  nested, EX 176
Import External Data command (Data menu), EX 121
Importing data, using Web query, EX 120-123
In-cell editing, EX 50-51
Increase Decimal button (Formatting toolbar), EX 99-100, EX 102-103
Increase Indent button (Formatting toolbar), row titles, EX 156

Indentation, of row titles, EX 156
Information rights management, EX 4
Insert command (shortcut menu)
  cells, EX 161
  columns, EX 161
  rows, EX 159, EX 160
Insert Function box (formula bar),
  EX 84, EX 86
Insert Function button (Formula bar),
  EX 24
Insert menu
  Cells command, EX 161
  Columns command, EX 161
  Function command, EX 24, EX 84,
    EX 86, EX 167
  Rows command, EX 159, EX 160
Insert mode, **EX 51**
Insert Options button, EX 161
Inserting
  cells, EX 159-161
  characters, EX 50
  columns, EX 161
  function, EX 24, EX 84, EX 86,
    EX 167
  range, EX 161
  rows, EX 159-161
Insertion point, **EX 18**
  Edit mode, EX 50, EX 51
Interactive Web page, *see* Dynamic
  Web page
Italic, **EX 187**

Keyboard
  entering formulas using, EX 73-74
  on-screen, APP 21-22
  selecting range using, EX 80
Keyboard indicators, **EX 15**

Labels, chart, *see* Data labels
Landscape orientation, **EX 113,**
  EX 114, EX 118
Language bar, **EX 8, APP 11-14**
  buttons on, APP 12
  closing, EX 9
  customizing, APP 12-14
  displaying, EX 15
  states, EX 15, APP 11
Leader lines, with data labels, EX 197
Left-aligned, text in cell, **EX 18**
Legend, **EX 41**
  3-D clustered column chart, EX 41
  3-D Pie chart, EX 190
Lists, **EX 4**
Logical operators, in IF functions,
  EX 171

Marquee, EX 157
MAX function, **EX 82-84**
Memory, EX 42, EX 43, EX 157
Menu, **EX 11**
  full, EX 12
  resetting, APP 29-30
  short, EX 12
  shortcut, EX 49
  sub-, EX 11
Menu bar, **EX 11**
Menu name, **EX 11-12**
Merge and Center button (Formatting
  toolbar), EX 33, EX 93
Merged cells
  centering text using, EX 32-33,
    EX 92-93
  splitting, EX 33
Merging cells, **EX 32,** EX 92
Merging table formats, EX 36
Microphone
  active, EX 8
  setting up, APP 16
Microphone button (Language bar),
  EX 8, APP 15
Microsoft Excel Help button (Standard
  toolbar), APP 1
Microsoft Excel Help command (Help
  menu), APP 1
Microsoft Office Excel 2003, *see* Excel
  2003
Microsoft Office Excel 2003 command
  (Microsoft Office submenu), EX 7
Microsoft Office Expert exams,
  APP 32

Microsoft Office Specialist
  certification, EX 53, EX 126,
  EX 209, EX 238, **APP 31-32**
Microsoft Office Specialist exams,
  APP 32
Microsoft Office submenu, Microsoft
  Office Excel 2003 command, EX 7
MIN function, **EX 84-87**
Minimized (Language bar), **EX 15,**
  APP 11
Mixed cell reference, **EX 168**
Mode indicator, **EX 14**
Month names, creating series of, using
  fill handle, EX 152-153
Mouse pointer, EX 11
Move handle, **EX 13**
Moving
  chart, EX 40-41
  copy and paste used in, EX 157-158
  copying versus, EX 159
  cut and paste used in, EX 159
  drag and drop used in, EX 159
  sheet, EX 199
  toolbar, EX 13, EX 182
MSN MoneyCentral Investor Stock
  Quotes, EX 122
Multiplication (*), EX 74

Name
  file, EX 42, EX 43
  menu, EX 11-12
  sheet, EX 10, EX 197
  sheet tabs, EX 124
  workbook, EX 43, EX 44
Name box, EX 16
  selecting cell using, EX 36-37
Negative numbers, formatting, EX 180
Nested IF function, **EX 176**
Noninteractive Web page, *see* Static
  Web page
Normal style, EX 52
NOW function, **EX 165-167**
Number, **EX 21**
  average of, EX 49, EX 81-82
  changing formula to, EX 77
  entering, EX 21-23
  entering as text, EX 21
  entering in range, EX 72
  highest, EX 82-84
  lowest, EX 84-87
  format symbols, EX 162-163
  formatting as they are entered,
    EX 100
  formatting negative, EX 180
  formatting in nonadjacent ranges,
    EX 177
  formatting using Format Cells
    command, EX 100-102
  formatting using Formatting toolbar,
    EX 98-100
  negative, EX 180
  series of, creating using fill handle,
    EX 153
  zeros, EX 23, EX 177

Office Assistant, APP 1, **APP 6-7**
Office Clipboard, **EX 157**
Office Speech Recognition software,
  EX 8, EX 15-16, APP 15-19
Office Web pages, publishing to Web
  server, APP 24
Offline Help, **APP 3**
Offsetting, **EX 194**
On-screen keyboard, APP 21-22
Opening
  existing workbook, EX 47-48
  task pane, EX 9
Options buttons, EX 78-79
Options command (Tools menu),
  formulas version, EX 119
Order of operations, **EX 74-75**
Other Task Panes button (task pane
  title bar), EX 9

Page Setup command (File menu)
  black and white printing, EX 116
  print scaling, EX 120
Page Setup dialog box
  orientation, EX 118
  print orientation, EX 114

print scaling, EX 120
print settings, EX 114, EX 116
Painting formats, EX 107
Panes
  splitting window into, EX 202-204
Parentheses
  arguments in, EX 82
  order of operations and, EX 75
Password, EX 44
Paste, undoing, EX 158
Paste area, *see* Destination area
Paste button (Standard toolbar)
  advanced options, EX 159
  copy operations and, EX 157-158
  cut operations and, EX 159
  Office Clipboard, EX 157-158
Paste command (Edit menu)
  cell, EX 26
  functions, EX 88
  Office Clipboard, EX 157, EX 158
Paste Options menu, items on, EX 158
Paste Special command (Edit menu),
  formats, EX 155
Pen line (Writing Pad), **APP 20**
Percent, worksheet view in, EX 201
Percent Style button (Formatting
  toolbar), EX 103
Pie chart, **EX 187**
  color in slices, EX 193
  exploded, EX 187, EX 194
  3-D, EX 187-197
Pixel, APP 25, **EX 107**
Point mode, entering formulas using,
  EX 75-77
Point size, **EX 28**
Portrait orientation, **EX 113,** EX 116
Position, of chart, EX 194
Power to computer, lost, EX 42
Previewing the worksheet, **EX 113**-115
Previewing Web page, EX 228-229
Print area, EX 45, EX 116-117
Print Area command (File menu),
  EX 117
Print button (Standard toolbar), EX 45
Print command (File menu),
  worksheet, EX 45
Print dialog box, Print what area,
  EX 116-117
Print Preview button (Standard
  toolbar), EX 47, EX 114
Print Preview command (File menu),
  EX 115
Print Scaling option, EX 120
Printing, EX 44
  black and white, EX 116, EX 200
  Blue Chip Stock Club worksheet,
    EX 115-120
  Extreme Blading Second Quarter
    Sales worksheet, EX 44-45
  formulas version, EX 119
  orientation, EX 113, EX 114,
    EX 116, EX 118
  previewing, EX 47, EX 114-115
  range, EX 45, EX 116-117
  section of worksheet, EX 116-117
Printout, **EX 44**
Publish workbooks, EX 228, EX 235
Publishing Web pages, EX 228,
  EX 230, APP 24

Query, Web, EX 120-123
Quitting Excel, EX 46, EX 54-55

Range, **EX 23**
  AutoCalculate, EX 48
  AutoSum, EX 165
  average of, EX 81-82
  charting, EX 189
  clearing, EX 52
  copying to adjacent destination area,
    EX 26
  copying to nonadjacent destination
    area, EX 157-158
  deleting, EX 162
  dragging, EX 161
  entering numbers in, EX 72
  highest number in, EX 82-84
  inserting, EX 161
  lowest number in, EX 84-87
  printing, EX 45, EX 116-117

selecting nonadjacent, EX 177
selecting using keyboard, EX 80
selecting using mouse, EX 26
summing, EX 23-24
Range Finder, verifying formulas using,
  EX 89-90, EX 148
Ready mode, **EX 14,** EX 44
Recalculation, automatic, EX 74
Redo button (Standard toolbar),
  EX 52
Redo command (Edit menu), EX 52
#REF!, **EX 162**
Refresh All button (External Data
  toolbar), EX 123
Relational operator, EX 104
  conditional formatting, EX 106
Relative addressing, absolute address
  versus, EX 168-170
Relative cell reference, **EX 168**
Relative reference, **EX 25, EX 78**
Requirements document, **EX 5-6**
  Aquatics Wear worksheet, EX 148
  Blue Chip Stock Club Investment
    Analysis worksheet, EX 67-68
Resolution, screen, EX 6, EX 10,
  EX 11, EX 13, APP 25-27
Restored (Language bar), **EX 15,**
  APP 11
Rotating
  cell entries, EX 98
  text, EX 151-152
  3-D Pie chart, EX 194-196
ROUND function, EX 100
Round tripping, **EX 232**
Row heading, **EX 10**
  active cell, EX 16
  best fit, EX 111
  Blue Chip Stock Club worksheet,
    EX 107, EX 110
  white space and, EX 72
Row titles
  Aquatics Wear worksheet, EX 156
  Blue Chip Stock Club worksheet,
    EX 70-71
  bold, EX 100
  copying to nonadjacent destination
    area, EX 157-158
  entering, EX 20-21
  freezing, EX 163-164
  indenting, EX 156
Row totals, for nonadjacent cells,
  EX 175
Rows
  bottom border, EX 100
  deleting, EX 161-162
  hidden, EX 111
  inserting, EX 159-161
  inserting multiple, EX 159, EX 161
  number of, EX 10
  summing, EX 27
  titles, *see* Row titles
Rows command (Insert menu),
  EX 159, EX 160

Save As command (File menu), EX 43
Save As dialog box, EX 43-44
Save as Web Page command (Excel File
  menu), EX 231, EX 234-235
Save button (Standard toolbar), EX 42
Saving
  backup, EX 44
  chart as dynamic Web page,
    EX 234-236
  workbook as static Web page,
    EX 230-232
  workbook using same file name,
    EX 88-89
  workbook with new file name,
    EX 42-44
Saving mode, EX 44
Screen
  resolution, EX 6, EX 10, EX 11,
    EX 13, APP 25-27
  viewing area, EX 11
Screen resolution, EX 6, EX 10, EX 11,
  EX 11, EX 13, **APP 25-27**
ScreenTip, **EX 13**
Scroll arrows, **EX 11**
Scroll bars, **EX 11**
Scroll boxes, **EX 11**

Search Results task pane, **APP 2-3**
Searching, EX 4
  Help system, EX 53, EX 54, APP 2
See-through view, **EX 26**
Select a cell, **EX 16**
  for formula, EX 75
  methods, EX 37
  using keyboard, EX 80
  using Name box, EX 36-37
  using Select All button, EX 53, EX 150
Select All button
  bolding entire worksheet, EX 150
  clearing worksheet, EX 53
Selected chart, EX 40
Selecting
  cell, *see* Select a cell
  clearing, EX 52
  entire worksheet, EX 53, EX 150
  methods, EX 37
  nonadjacent ranges, EX 177
  range using keyboard, EX 80
  range using mouse, EX 26
Send To command (File menu), e-mail, EX 125-126
Sensitivity analysis, **EX 204**
Series of month names, creating using fill handle, EX 152-153
Series of numbers, creating using fill handle, EX 153
Shadow, drop, EX 183-184
Shadow Style button (Drawing toolbar), EX 184
Sheet
  chart, EX 187, EX 188-192
  moving, EX 199
  name, *see* Sheet name
  reordering, EX 197-198
  See also Worksheet
Sheet name, EX 10
  changing, EX 197
Sheet tab, **EX 10**
  color, EX 198
  renaming, EX 124, EX 197
Shelly Cashman Series Microsoft Office Specialist Center, APP 32
Short menu, **EX 12**
Shortcut menu, EX 49
  clearing cell entries using, EX 52
Show Buttons on Two Rows command (Toolbar Options list), EX 9, EX 14
Shrink to fit, EX 157
Shrinking cell entries, EX 98
  copying between workbooks and, EX 157
Single File Web Page format, **EX 230**
Size
  font, *see* Font size
  toolbar buttons, EX 14
  worksheet, EX 10
  worksheet window, EX 11
Sizing handles, chart, EX 40
Smart documents, EX 4
Smart tag indicator, **EX 78**
Smart tags, **EX 78**
Snaps, **EX 41**
Source area, **EX 25**, EX 88, EX 157
SPACEBAR, entering blank characters using, EX 52
Speech command (Tools menu), APP 16
Speech playback, **EX 16, APP 22-23**
Speech recognition, EX 15-16, APP 15-19
  using, APP 18-19
Speech Recognition service, **APP 15-19**
Spell checker, **EX 111**
Spell checking
  multiple sheets, EX 199
  using AutoCorrect feature, EX 18, EX 113
  using Spelling button, EX 111-112
Spelling button (Standard toolbar), EX 112
Spelling command (Tools menu), EX 112
Split command (Window menu), EX 203
Splitting a merged cell, **EX 33**

Spreadsheet program, *see* Excel 2003
Standard toolbar, EX 13-14
  resetting, APP 27-28
Start button (Windows taskbar), All Programs, Microsoft Office, Microsoft Office Excel 2003 command, EX 7, EX 47
Start menu (Windows), All Programs, Microsoft Office, Microsoft Office Excel 2003 command, EX 7, EX 47
Starting
  Excel using command-line switch, EX 70
  Excel using Windows Start menu, EX 6-8, EX 47
Startup submenu, adding Excel to, EX 150
Static Web page, **EX 226**, EX 228-233
  saving workbook as, EX 230-232
  viewing in browser, EX 226, EX 232, EX 233
Statistical functions, EX 4
  blank cell and, EX 81
Status bar, **EX 14**-15
Submenu, EX 11
Subtitle, Blue Chip Stock Club worksheet, EX 91
SUM function, **EX 23**
  copying using fill handle, EX 25
  entering using AutoSum button, EX 23-24, EX 27
  entering using Function command, EX 24
  entering using Insert Function button, EX 24
Sum
  calculating using SUM function, EX 23-25, EX 27
  See also Totals
Symbols, format, EX 162-163
System date, EX 165-167

Tab split box, **EX 11**
Table formats, merging, EX 36
Task pane, **EX 8**
  closing, EX 9
  opening, EX 9
Task Pane command (View menu), EX 9
Text, **EX 16**
  Blue Chip Stock Club worksheet, EX 70-72
  entering in worksheet, EX 16-21
  entering numbers as, EX 21
  formatting worksheet, EX 28-32
  rotating, EX 151-152
  wrapping, EX 71
3-D clustered column chart, EX 39
3-D Pie chart, EX 187-197
3-D View command (Chart menu), EX 195
Tilting 3-D Pie chart, EX 194-196
Time, system, EX 165
Titles
  Blue Chip Stock Club worksheet, EX 70-72
  chart, EX 189, EX 192
  column, *see* Column titles
  freezing, EX 163-164
  row, *see* Row titles
  worksheet, *see* Worksheet title
Toggle commands, EX 175
Toolbar, **EX 8**
  customizing, EX 181, EX 183
  docking, EX 182-183
  floating, EX 182
  Formatting, *see* Formatting toolbar
  moving, EX 13, EX 182
  removing button from, EX 91
  resetting, EX 13, APP 27-29
  showing buttons on two rows, EX 9, EX 14
  Standard, *see* Standard toolbar
Toolbar buttons
  hidden, EX 13
  size of, EX 14
Toolbar dock, **EX 182**
Toolbar Options list, showing toolbar buttons on two rows, EX 9, EX 14

Toolbars command (shortcut menu), Language bar command, EX 15
Toolbars command (View menu), APP 29
Tools menu (menu bar)
  Auditing command, EX 148
  AutoCorrect Options command, smart tags, EX 78
  Error Checking command, EX 90, EX 113, EX 148
  Goal Seek command, EX 206-207
  Options command, formulas version, EX 119
  Speech command, APP 16
  Spelling command, EX 112
Tools menu (Save As dialog box), EX 44
Totals
  AutoCalculate, EX 48
  AutoSum button and, EX 79-80
  determining multiple, EX 26-27
  nonadjacent cells, EX 175
  summing, *see* SUM function
Trace Error button, EX 79
Type a question for help box, EX 9, EX 53-54, APP 1, APP 2-5

Underline, **EX 187**
Undo
  deletions, EX 162
  entries, EX 51
  paste operation, EX 158
  what-if questions, EX 206
Undo button (Standard toolbar), EX 51-52
Undo command (Edit menu), EX 51
Undo Paste command (Edit menu), EX 158
Unfreeze Panes command (Window menu), EX 176
Unfreezing worksheet titles, EX 175-176
Unicode characters, **APP 22**

Value axis, *see* Y-axis
Values
  assumptions, EX 146
  formulas versus, EX 118
Values version, **EX 118**
Vertical alignment, EX 92, EX 96
Vertical split bar, **EX 204**
View, worksheet, EX 201-204
View menu
  Full Screen command, viewing area, EX 11
  Task Pane command, EX 9
  Toolbars command, APP 29
  Zoom command, EX 202
View-only Web page, *see* Static Web page
Voice Command mode, **APP 15**

Web folder, EX 228, **APP 24**
Web page
  dynamic, EX 226, EX 234-238
  formats, EX 230
  noninteractive, *see* Static Web page
  previewing, EX 228-229
  publishing, EX 228, EX 230, APP 24
  static, EX 226, EX 228-233
  view-only, *see* Static Web page
Web Page format, **EX 230**
Web Page Preview command (Excel File menu), EX 228-229
Web query, importing data using, **EX 120-123**
Web server, publishing Office pages to, APP 24
Web source, importing external data from, using Web query, EX 120-123
Web support, EX 4
What-if analysis, EX 148, **EX 204**-208
White space, EX 72
Window
  customizing, EX 8-9
  freezing panes, EX 163-164
  Help buttons in, APP 7
  splitting into panes, EX 202-204
  unfreezing panes, EX 176

Window menu
  Freeze Panes command, EX 163-164
  Split command, EX 203
  Unfreeze Panes command, EX 176
Workbook, **EX 9**
  blank, EX 7
  comparing, EX 4
  copying cells from one to another, EX 157
  e-mailing, EX 125-126
  hyperlinks in, EX 237
  name, EX 43, EX 44
  opening existing, EX 47-48
  publishing, EX 228, EX 235
  saving as static Web page, EX 230-232
  saving new, EX 42-44
  saving using same file name, EX 88-89
Worksheet, **EX 4, EX 9**
  Aquatics Wear, EX 145-208
  Blue Chip Stock Club Investment Analysis, EX 65-128
  clearing entire, EX 52-53
  color in, EX 91
  design, EX 68
  development cycle, EX 5
  errors in, *see* Correcting errors
  Extreme Blading Second Quarter Sales, EX 3-55
  formatting, *see* Formatting
  formulas version, EX 118
  moving between, EX 124
  name, EX 124
  numbers entered in, EX 21-23
  organization of, EX 10-11
  previewing, EX 113-115
  printing, *see* Printing
  requirements document, *see* Requirements document
  selecting, *see* Selecting
  sheet name, EX 10
  size of, EX 10
  sketch of, EX 68-69
  text entered in, EX 16-21
  values version, EX 118
  view of, EX 201-204
Worksheet name, changing, EX 124
Worksheet subtitle, formatting, EX 33-34
Worksheet title
  Aquatics Wear, EX 150
  Blue Chip Stock Club worksheet, EX 91-94
  border, EX 95
  centering, EX 32-33
  entering, EX 17-18
  formatting, EX 28-33, EX 180-181
  freezing, EX 163-164
  unfreezing, EX 175-176
Worksheet window, **EX 11**
  elements of, EX 11-15
  size, EX 11
  See also Window
Wrapping text, EX 71
Write Anywhere command (Handwriting menu), APP 21
Writing Pad, **APP 19-21**

X-axis (category axis), **EX 41**
.xls extension, **EX 43**
XML support, EX 4

Y-axis (value axis), **EX 38**
  chart scale and, EX 41
Years, two-digit, EX 72

Zero
  displaying value of, EX 177
  trailing, EX 23
Zoom box (Standard toolbar), EX 201
Zoom command (View menu), EX 202

Quick Reference Summary

In Microsoft Excel 2003, you can accomplish a task in a number of ways. The following table provides a quick reference to each task presented in this textbook. The first column identifies the task. The second column indicates the page number on which the task is discussed in the book. The subsequent four columns list the different ways the task in column one can be carried out. You can invoke the commands listed in the MOUSE, MENU BAR, and SHORTCUT MENU columns using Voice commands.

Microsoft Excel 2003 Quick Reference Summary

TASK	PAGE NUMBER	MOUSE	MENU BAR	SHORTCUT MENU	KEYBOARD SHORTCUT
AutoFormat	EX 34		Format | AutoFormat		ALT+O | A
AutoSum	EX 23	AutoSum button on Standard toolbar	Insert | Function		ALT+=
Bold	EX 30	Bold button on Formatting toolbar	Format | Cells | Font tab	Format Cells | Font tab	CTRL+B
Borders	EX 96	Borders button on Formatting toolbar	Format | Cells | Border tab	Format Cells | Border tab	CTRL+1 | B
Center	EX 97	Center button on Formatting toolbar	Format | Cells | Alignment tab	Format Cells | Alignment tab	CTRL+1 | A
Center Across Columns	EX 33	Merge and Center button on Formatting toolbar	Format | Cells | Alignment tab	Format Cells | Alignment tab	CTRL+1 | A
Chart	EX 39	Chart Wizard button on Standard toolbar	Insert | Chart		F11
Clear Cell	EX 52	Drag fill handle back	Edit | Clear | All	Clear Contents	DELETE
Close Workbook	EX 46	Close button on menu bar or workbook Control-menu icon	File | Close		CTRL+W
Color Background	EX 94	Fill Color button on Formatting toolbar	Format | Cells | Patterns tab	Format Cells | Patterns tab	CTRL+1 | P
Color Tab	EX 198			Tab Color	
Column Width	EX 107	Drag column heading boundary	Format | Column | Width	Column Width	ALT+O | C | W
Comma Style Format	EX 108	Comma Style button on Formatting toolbar	Format | Cells | Number tab | Accounting	Format Cells | Number tab | Accounting	CTRL+1 | N
Conditional Formatting	EX 104		Format | Conditional Formatting		ALT+O | D
Copy and Paste	EX 157	Copy button and Paste button on Standard toolbar	Edit | Copy; Edit | Paste	Copy to copy; Paste to paste	CTRL+C; CTRL+V
Currency Style Format	EX 98	Currency Style button on Formatting toolbar	Format | Cells | Number | Currency	Format Cells | Number | Currency	CTRL+1 | N
Cut	EX 159	Cut button on Standard toolbar	Edit | Cut	Cut	CTRL+X
Date	EX 166	Insert Function box in formula bar	Insert | Function		CTRL+SEMICOLON
Decimal Place, Decrease	EX 100	Decrease Decimal button on Formatting toolbar	Format | Cells | Number tab | Currency	Format Cells | Number tab | Currency	CTRL+1 | N
Decimal Place, Increase	EX 99	Increase Decimal button on Formatting toolbar	Format | Cells | Number tab | Currency	Format Cells | Number tab | Currency	CTRL+1 | N

Microsoft Excel 2003 Quick Reference Summary *(continued)*

TASK	PAGE NUMBER	MOUSE	MENU BAR	SHORTCUT MENU	KEYBOARD SHORTCUT
Delete Rows or Columns	EX 161		Edit | Delete	Delete	
Drop Shadow	EX 184	Shadow Style button on Drawing toolbar			
E-Mail from Excel	EX 125	E-mail button on Standard toolbar	File | Send To | Mail Recipient		ALT+F | D | A
File Management	EX 232		File | Save As, right-click file name		ALT+F | A, right-click file name
Fit to Print	EX 118		File | Page Setup | Page tab		ALT+F | U | P
Folder, New	EX 230		File | Save As		ALT+F | A
Font Color	EX 32	Font Color button on Formatting toolbar	Format | Cells | Font tab	Format Cells | Font tab	CTRL+1 | F
Font Size	EX 31	Font Size box arrow on Formatting toolbar	Format | Cells | Font tab	Format Cells | Font tab	CTRL+1 | F
Font Type	EX 29	Font box arrow on Formatting toolbar	Format | Cells | Font tab	Format Cells | Font tab	CTRL+1 | F
Formula Assistance	EX 83	Insert Function box in formula bar	Insert | Function		CTRL+A after you type function name
Formulas Version	EX 118		Tools | Options | View tab | Formulas		CTRL+ACCENT MARK
Freeze Worksheet Titles	EX 163		Window | Freeze Panes		ALT+W | F
Full Screen	EX 11		View | Full Screen		ALT+V | U
Function	EX 81	Insert Function box in formula bar	Insert | Function		SHIFT+F3
Go To	EX 37	Click cell	Edit | Go To		F5
Goal Seek	EX 206		Tools | Goal Seek		ALT+T | G
Help	EX 53 and Appendix A	Microsoft Excel Help button on Standard toolbar	Help | Microsoft Excel Help		F1
Hide Column	EX 109	Drag column heading boundary	Format | Column | Hide	Hide	CTRL+0 (zero) to hide CTRL+SHIFT+) to display
Hide Row	EX 111	Drag row heading boundary	Format | Row | Hide	Hide	CTRL+9 to hide CTRL+SHIFT+(to display
In-Cell Editing	EX 50	Double-click cell			F2
Insert Rows or Columns	EX 160		Insert | Rows or Insert | Columns	Insert	ALT+I | R or C
Italicize	EX 186	Italic button on Formatting toolbar	Format | Cells | Font tab	Format Cells | Font tab	CTRL+I
Language Bar	EX 15 and Appendix B		Tools | Speech | Speech Recognition	Toolbars | Language bar	ALT+T | H | H
Merge Cells	EX 33	Merge and Center button on Formatting toolbar	Format | Cells | Alignment tab	Format Cells | Font tab | Alignment tab	ALT+O | E | A
Move Cells	EX 159	Point to border and drag	Edit | Cut; Edit | Paste	Cut; Paste	CTRL+X; CTRL+V
Name Cells	EX 37	Click Name box in formula bar, type name	Insert | Name | Define		ALT+I | N | D
New Workbook	EX 53	New button on Standard toolbar	File | New		CTRL+N
Open Workbook	EX 47	Open button on Standard toolbar	File | Open		CTRL+O
Percent Style Format	EX 103	Percent Style button on Formatting toolbar	Format | Cells | Number tab | Percentage	Format Cells | Number tab | Percentage	CTRL+1 | N

Microsoft Excel 2003 Quick Reference Summary

TASK	PAGE NUMBER	MOUSE	MENU BAR	SHORTCUT MENU	KEYBOARD SHORTCUT
Preview Worksheet	EX 114	Print Preview button on Standard toolbar	File | Print Preview		ALT+F | V
Print Worksheet	EX 113	Print button on Standard toolbar	File | Print		CTRL+P
Quit Excel	EX 46	Close button on title bar	File | Exit		ALT+F4
Range Finder	EX 89	Double-click cell			
Redo	EX 52	Redo button on Standard toolbar	Edit | Redo		ALT+E | R
Remove Splits	EX 204	Double-click split bar	Window | Split		ALT+W | S
Rename Sheet Tab	EX 198	Double-click sheet tab		Rename	
Rotate Text	EX 151		Format | Cells | Alignment tab	Format Cells | Alignment tab	ALT+O | E | A
Row Height	EX 110	Drag row heading boundary	Format | Row | Height	Row Height	ALT+O | R | E
Save as Web Page	EX 230		File | Save as Web Page		ALT+F | G
Save Workbook, New Name	EX 42		File | Save As		ALT+F | A
Save Workbook, Same Name	EX 89	Save button on Standard toolbar	File | Save		CTRL+S
Select All of Worksheet	EX 53	Select All button on worksheet			CTRL+A
Select Cell	EX 16	Click cell			Use arrow keys
Select Multiple Sheets	EX 200	CTRL+click tab or SHIFT+click tab		Select All Sheets	
Series	EX 151	Drag fill handle	Edit | Fill | Series		ALT+E | I | S
Shortcut Menu	EX 92	Right-click object			SHIFT+F10
Spell Check	EX 112	Spelling button on Standard toolbar	Tools | Spelling		F7
Split Cell	EX 33	Merge and Center button on Formatting toolbar	Format | Cells | Alignment tab	Format Cells | Alignment tab	ALT+O | E | A
Split Window into Panes	EX 203	Drag vertical or horizontal split box	Window | Split		ALT+W | S
Stock Quotes	EX 121		Data | Import External Data | Import Data		ALT+D | D | D
Task Pane	EX 8		View | Task Pane		ALT+V | K
Toolbar, Dock	EX 182	Drag toolbar to dock			
Toolbar, Reset	Appendix D	Toolbar Options button on toolbar, Add or Remove Buttons, Customize, Toolbars tab		Customize | Toolbars	ALT+V | T | C | B
Toolbar, Show Entire	EX 13	Double-click move handle			
Toolbar, Show or Hide	EX 182	Right-click toolbar, click toolbar name	View | Toolbars		ALT+V | T
Underline	EX 187	Underline button on Formatting toolbar	Format | Cells | Font tab	Format Cells | Font tab	CTRL+U
Undo	EX 51	Undo button on Standard toolbar	Edit | Undo		CTRL+Z
Unfreeze Worksheet Titles	EX 176		Windows | Unfreeze Panes		ALT+W | F
Unhide Column	EX 109	Drag hidden column heading boundary to right	Format | Column | Unhide	Unhide	ALT+O | C | U
Unhide Row	EX 111	Drag hidden row heading boundary down	Format | Row | Unhide	Unhide	ALT+O | R | U
Web Page Preview	EX 228		File | Web Page Preview		ALT+F | B
Zoom	EX 201	Zoom box on Standard toolbar	View | Zoom		ALT+V | Z